The Pearson
Custom Program for

University of Cincinnati Blue Ash
IS 2080C
Digital Technologies for Business

PEARSON

ISBN 10: 1-269-13016-1
ISBN 13: 978-1-269-13016-5

Table of Contents

Excel

Introduction to Excel

What Is a Spreadsheet?

Yuri Arcurs/Shutterstock

OBJECTIVES AFTER YOU READ THIS CHAPTER, YOU WILL BE ABLE TO:

1. Explore the Excel window
2. Enter and edit cell data
3. Create formulas
4. Use Auto Fill
5. Display cell formulas
6. Manage worksheets

7. Manage columns and rows
8. Select, move, copy, and paste data
9. Apply alignment and font options
10. Apply number formats
11. Select page setup options
12. Preview and print a worksheet

CASE STUDY | OK Office Systems

You are an assistant manager at OK Office Systems (OKOS) in Oklahoma City. OKOS sells a wide range of computer systems, peripherals, and furniture for small- and medium-sized organizations in the metropolitan area. To compete against large, global, big-box office supply stores, OKOS provides competitive pricing by ordering directly from local manufacturers rather than dealing with distributors.

Alesha Bennett, the general manager, asked you to calculate the retail price, sale price, and profit analysis for selected items on sale this month. Using markup rates provided by Alesha, you need to calculate the retail price, the amount OKOS charges its customers for the products. For the sale, Alesha wants to give customers between a 10% and 30% discount on select items. You need to use those discount rates to calculate the sale prices. Finally, you will calculate the profit margin to determine the percentage of the final sale price over the cost.

After you create the initial pricing spreadsheet, you will be able to change values and see that the formulas update the results automatically. In addition, you will be able to insert data for additional sale items or delete an item based on the manager's decision.

Although your experience with Microsoft Office Excel 2013 may be limited, you are excited to apply your knowledge and skills to your newly assigned responsibility. In the Hands-On Exercises for this chapter, you will create and format the analytical spreadsheet to practice the skills you learn.

From Excel Chapter 1 of *Microsoft® Excel 2013 Comprehensive*, First edition. Mary Anne Poatsy, Keith Mulbery, Jason Davidson, Robert T. Grauer. Copyright © 2014 by Pearson Education, Inc. Published by Pearson Prentice Hall. All Rights Reserved. Download student resources at http://www.pearsonhighered.com/exploring.

Introduction to Spreadsheets

Organizing, calculating, and evaluating quantitative data are important skills needed today for personal and managerial decision making. You track expenses for your household budget, maintain a savings plan, and determine what amount you can afford for a house or car payment. Retail managers create and analyze their organizations' annual budgets, sales projections, and inventory records. Charitable organizations track the donations they receive, the distribution of those donations, and overhead expenditures.

You can use a spreadsheet to maintain data and perform calculations. A *spreadsheet* is an electronic file that contains a grid of columns and rows used to organize related data and to display results of calculations, enabling interpretation of quantitative data for decision making.

Performing calculations using a calculator and entering the results into a ledger can lead to inaccurate values. If an input value is incorrect or needs to be updated, you have to recalculate the results manually, which is time-consuming and can lead to inaccuracies. A spreadsheet makes data entry changes easy. If the formulas are correctly constructed, the results recalculate automatically and accurately, saving time and reducing room for error.

In this section, you will learn how to design spreadsheets. In addition, you will explore the Excel window and learn the name of each window element. Then, you will enter text, values, and dates in a spreadsheet.

Exploring the Excel Window

In Excel, a *worksheet* is a single spreadsheet that typically contains descriptive labels, numeric values, formulas, functions, and graphical representations of data. A *workbook* is a collection of one or more related worksheets contained within a single file. By default, new workbooks contain one worksheet. Storing multiple worksheets within one workbook helps organize related data together in one file and enables you to perform calculations among the worksheets within the workbook. For example, you can create a budget workbook of 13 worksheets, one for each month to store your personal income and expenses and a final worksheet to calculate totals across the entire year.

Excel contains the standard interface of Microsoft Office applications:

- **Quick Access Toolbar:** Save, Undo, and Redo/Repeat commands
- **Title bar:** File name (such as Book1) and software name (such as Excel)
- **Control buttons:** Microsoft Excel Help, Full Screen Mode, Minimize, Restore Down, and Close
- **Ribbon:** Commands (such as Align Left) organized within groups (such as Alignment) on various tabs (such as Home)
- **Scroll bars:** Tools to scroll vertically and horizontally through a worksheet

Identify Excel Window Elements

Figure 1 identifies elements specific to the Excel window, and Table 1 lists and describes the Excel window elements.

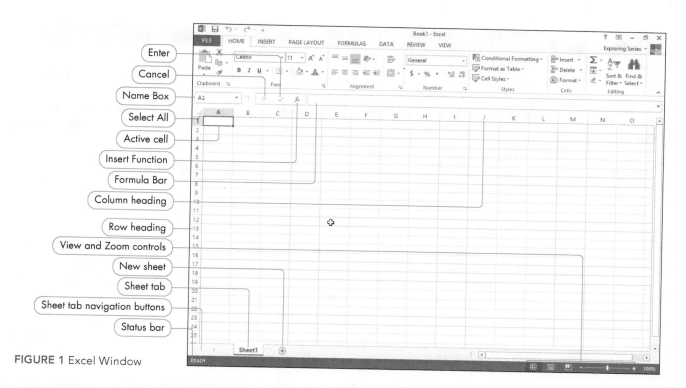

FIGURE 1 Excel Window

TABLE 1	Excel Elements
Element	**Description**
Name Box	The **Name Box** is an identifier that displays the address of the current cell in the worksheet. Use the Name Box to go to a cell, assign a name to one or more cells, or select a function.
Cancel ☒	When you enter or edit data, click Cancel to cancel the data entry or edit and revert back to the previous data in the cell, if any. The Cancel icon changes from gray to red when you position the mouse pointer over it.
Enter ☑	When you enter or edit data, click Enter to accept data typed in the active cell and keep the current cell active. The Enter icon changes from gray to blue when you position the mouse pointer over it.
Insert Function *fx*	Click to display the Insert Function dialog box to search for and select a function to insert into the active cell. The Insert Function icon changes from gray to green when you position the mouse pointer over it.
Formula Bar	The **Formula Bar** shows the contents of the active cell. You can enter or edit cell contents here or directly in the active cell. Drag the bottom border of the Formula Bar down to increase the height of the Formula Bar to display large amounts of data or a long formula contained in the active cell.
Select All ◰	The triangle at the intersection of the row and column headings in the top-left corner of the worksheet. Click it to select everything contained in the active worksheet.
Column headings	The letters above the columns, such as A, B, C, and so on.
Row headings	The numbers to the left of the rows, such as 1, 2, 3, and so on.
Active cell	The active cell is the current cell, which is indicated by a dark green border.
Sheet tab	A **sheet tab** shows the name of a worksheet contained in the workbook. When you create a new Excel workbook, the default worksheet is named Sheet1.
New sheet ⊕	Inserts a new worksheet to the right of the current worksheet.
Sheet tab navigation buttons	If your workbook contains several worksheets, Excel may not show all the sheet tabs at the same time. Use the buttons to display the first, previous, next, or last worksheet.

TABLE 1 Excel Elements *(continued)*

Element	Description
Status bar	Displays information about a selected command or operation in progress. For example, it displays *Select destination and press ENTER or choose Paste* after you use the Copy command.
View controls	Click a view control to display the worksheet in Normal, Page Layout, or Page Break Preview. Normal view displays the worksheet without showing margins, headers, footers, and page breaks. Page Layout view shows the margins, header and footer area, and a ruler. Page Break Preview indicates where the worksheet will be divided into pages.
Zoom control	Drag the zoom control to increase the size of the worksheet onscreen to see more or less of the worksheet data.

Identify Columns, Rows, and Cells

A worksheet contains columns and rows, with each column and row assigned a heading. Columns are assigned alphabetical headings from columns A to Z, continuing from AA to AZ, and then from BA to BZ until XFD, which is the last of the possible 16,384 columns. Rows have numeric headings ranging from 1 to 1,048,576.

The intersection of a column and row is a *cell*; a total of more than 17 billion cells are available in a worksheet. Each cell has a unique *cell address*, identified by first its column letter and then its row number. For example, the cell at the intersection of column A and row 9 is cell A9. Cell references are useful when referencing data in formulas, or in navigation.

Navigate In and Among Worksheets

The *active cell* is the current cell. Excel displays a dark green border around the active cell in the worksheet, and the cell address of the active cell appears in the Name Box. The contents of the active cell, or the formula used to calculate the results of the active cell, appear in the Formula Bar. You can change the active cell by using the mouse to click in a different cell. If you work in a large worksheet, use the vertical and horizontal scroll bars to display another area of the worksheet and click in the desired cell to make it the active cell.

To navigate to a new cell, click it or use the arrow keys on the keyboard. When you press Enter, the next cell down in the same column becomes the active cell. Table 2 lists the keyboard navigation methods. The Go To command is helpful for navigating to a cell that is not visible onscreen.

TABLE 2 Keystrokes and Actions

Keystroke	Used to
↑	Move up one cell in the same column.
↓	Move down one cell in the same column.
←	Move left one cell in the same row.
→	Move right one cell in the same row.
Tab	Move right one cell in the same row.
Page Up	Move the active cell up one screen.
Page Down	Move the active cell down one screen.
Home	Move the active cell to column A of the current row.
Ctrl+Home	Make cell A1 the active cell.
Ctrl+End	Make the rightmost, lowermost active corner of the worksheet—the intersection of the last column and row that contains data—the active cell. Does not move to cell XFD1048576 unless that cell contains data.
F5 or Ctrl+G	Display the Go To dialog box to enter any cell address.

Introduction to Excel

To display the contents of another worksheet within the workbook, click the sheet tab at the bottom-left corner of the workbook window. The active sheet tab has a white background color. After you click a sheet tab, you can then navigate within that worksheet.

Entering and Editing Cell Data

You should plan the structure before you start entering data into a worksheet. Using the OKOS case presented at the beginning of the chapter as an example, use the following steps to plan the worksheet design, enter and format data, and complete the workbook:

Plan the Worksheet Design

1. **State the purpose of the worksheet.** The purpose of the OKOS worksheet is to store data about products on sale and to calculate important details, such as the retail price based on markup, the sales price based on a discount rate, and the profit margin.

2. **Decide what input values are needed.** Input values are the initial values, such as variables and assumptions. You may change these values to see what type of effects different values have on the end results. For the OKOS worksheet, the input values include the costs OKOS pays the manufacturers, the markup rates, and the proposed discount rates for the sale. In some worksheets, you can create an *input area*, a specific region in the worksheet to store and change the variables used in calculations. For example, if you applied the same Markup Rate and same Percent Off for all products, it would be easier to create an input area at the top of the worksheet to change the values in one location rather than in several locations.

3. **Decide what outputs are needed to achieve the purpose of the worksheet.** Outputs are the results you need to calculate. For the OKOS worksheet, the outputs include columns to calculate the retail price (i.e., the selling price to your customers), the sale price, and the profit margin. In some worksheets, you can create an *output area*, the region in the worksheet to contain formulas dependent on the values in the input area.

Enter and Format the Data

4. **Enter the labels, values, and formulas in Excel.** Use the design plan (steps 2–3) as you enter labels, input values, and formulas to calculate the output. In the OKOS worksheet, descriptive labels (the product names) appear in the first column to indicate that the values on a specific row pertain to a specific product. Descriptive labels appear at the top of each column, such as Cost and Retail Price, to describe the values in the respective column. Change the input values to test that your formulas produce correct results. If necessary, correct any errors in the formulas to produce correct results. For the OKOS worksheet, change some of the original costs and markup rates to ensure the calculated retail price, selling price, and profit margin percentage results update correctly.

5. **Format the numerical values in the worksheet.** Align decimal points in columns of numbers and add number formats and styles. In the OKOS worksheet, use Accounting Number Format and the Percent Style to format the numerical data. Adjust the number of decimal places as needed.

6. **Format the descriptive titles and labels so that they stand out.** Add bold and color to headings so that they stand out and are attractive. Apply other formatting to headings and descriptive labels. In the OKOS worksheet, you will center the main title over all the columns, bold and center column labels over the columns, and apply other formatting to the headings. Figure 2 shows the completed OKOS worksheet.

Complete the Workbook

7. **Document the workbook as thoroughly as possible.** Include the current date, your name as the workbook author, assumptions, and purpose of the workbook. You can provide this documentation in a separate worksheet within the workbook. You can also add some documentation in the *Properties* section when you click the File tab.

8. **Save and share the completed workbook.** Preview and prepare printouts for distribution in meetings, send an electronic copy of the workbook to those who need it, or upload the workbook on a shared network drive or in the cloud.

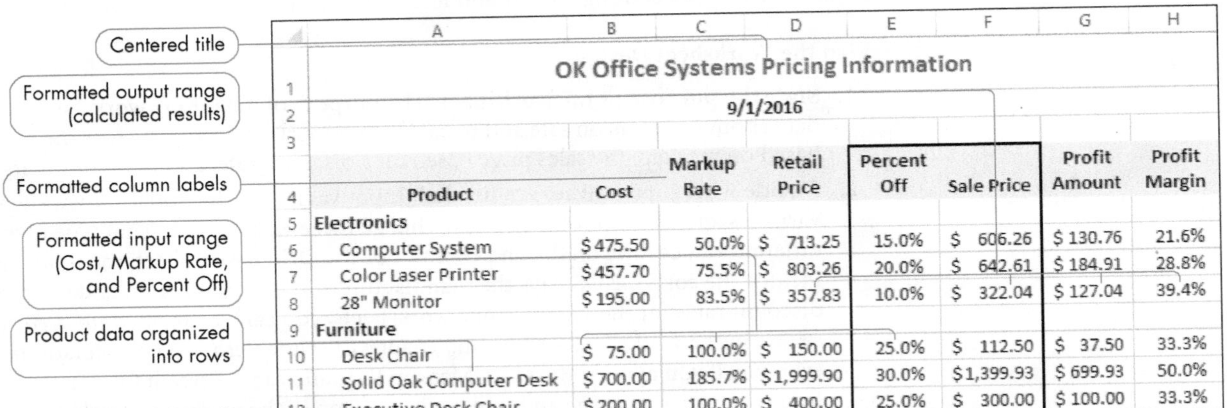

	Product	Cost	Markup Rate	Retail Price	Percent Off	Sale Price	Profit Amount	Profit Margin
1				OK Office Systems Pricing Information				
2				9/1/2016				
3								
4	Product	Cost	Markup Rate	Retail Price	Percent Off	Sale Price	Profit Amount	Profit Margin
5	Electronics							
6	Computer System	$ 475.50	50.0%	$ 713.25	15.0%	$ 606.26	$ 130.76	21.6%
7	Color Laser Printer	$ 457.70	75.5%	$ 803.26	20.0%	$ 642.61	$ 184.91	28.8%
8	28" Monitor	$ 195.00	83.5%	$ 357.83	10.0%	$ 322.04	$ 127.04	39.4%
9	Furniture							
10	Desk Chair	$ 75.00	100.0%	$ 150.00	25.0%	$ 112.50	$ 37.50	33.3%
11	Solid Oak Computer Desk	$ 700.00	185.7%	$1,999.90	30.0%	$1,399.93	$ 699.93	50.0%
12	Executive Desk Chair	$ 200.00	100.0%	$ 400.00	25.0%	$ 300.00	$ 100.00	33.3%
13								

Labels (pointing to table): Centered title; Formatted output range (calculated results); Formatted column labels; Formatted input range (Cost, Markup Rate, and Percent Off); Product data organized into rows

FIGURE 2 Completed OKOS Worksheet

Enter Text

Text is any combination of letters, numbers, symbols, and spaces not used in calculations. Excel treats phone numbers, such as 555-1234, and Social Security numbers, such as 123-45-6789, as text entries. You enter text for a worksheet title to describe the contents of the worksheet, as row and column labels to describe data, and as cell data. In Figure 2, the cells in column A, row 1, and row 4 contain text, such as *Product.* Text aligns at the left cell margin by default. To enter text in a cell, do the following:

STEP 1 ≫

1. Make sure the cell is active where you want to enter text.
2. Type the text.
3. Do one of the following to make another cell the active cell after entering data:
   - Press Enter on the keyboard.
   - Press an arrow key on the keyboard.
   - Press Tab on the keyboard.

   Do one of the following to keep the current cell the active cell after entering data:
   - Press Ctrl+Enter.
   - Click Enter (the check mark between the Name Box and the Formula Bar).

As soon as you begin typing a label into a cell, the *AutoComplete* feature searches for and automatically displays any other label in that column that matches the letters you typed. For example, *Computer System* is typed in cell A6 in Figure 2. When you start to type *Co* in cell A7, AutoComplete displays *Computer System* because a text entry previously typed starts with *Co*. Press Enter to accept the repeated label, or continue typing to enter a different label, such as *Color Laser Printer*.

Enter Values

STEP 2>> **Values** are numbers that represent a quantity or a measurable amount. Excel usually distinguishes between text and value data based on what you enter. The primary difference between text and value entries is that value entries can be the basis of calculations, whereas text cannot. In Figure 2, the data below the *Cost*, *Markup Rates*, and *Percent Off* labels are values. Values align at the right cell margin by default. After entering values, you can align decimal places and apply formatting by adding characters, such as $ or %.

Enter Dates

STEP 3>> You can enter dates and times in a variety of formats in cells, such as 9/1/2016; 9/1/16; September 1, 2016; or 1-Sep-16. You can also enter times, such as 1:30 PM or 13:30. You should enter a static date to document when you create or modify a workbook or to document the specific point in time when the data were accurate, such as on a balance sheet or income statement. Later, you will learn how to use formulas to enter dates that update to the current date. In Figure 2, cell A2 contains a date. Dates are values, so they align at the right cell margin. However, the date in Figure 2 has been centered by the user.

Excel displays dates differently from the way it stores dates. For example, the displayed date 9/1/2016 represents the first day in September in the year 2016. Excel stores dates as serial numbers starting at 1 with January 1, 1900, so 9/1/2016 is stored as 42614 so that you can create formulas, such as to calculate how many days exist between two dates.

Enter Formulas

Formulas combine cell references, arithmetic operations, values, and/or functions used in a calculation. You must start the formula with an equal sign (=). In Figure 3, the data below the *Retail Price*, *Sale Price*, *Profit Amount*, and *Profit Margin* labels contain formulas. When a cell containing a formula is the active cell, the formula displays in the Formula Bar, and the result of the formula displays in the cell.

Edit and Clear Cell Contents

You can edit a cell's contents by doing one of the following:

- Click the cell, click in the Formula Bar, make the changes, and then click Enter (the check mark between the Name Box and the Formula Bar) to keep the cell the active cell.
- Double-click the cell, make changes in the cell, and then press Enter.
- Click the cell, press F2, make changes in the cell, and then press Enter.

You can clear a cell's contents by doing one of the following:

- Click the cell and press Delete.
- Click the cell, click Clear in the Editing group on the HOME tab, and then select Clear Contents.

Quick Concepts

1. What are two major advantages of using an electronic spreadsheet instead of a paper-based ledger?

2. What visual indicators let you know which cell is the active cell?

3. What steps should you perform before entering data into a worksheet?

4. What are four major things you can enter into a cell? Give an example (different from those in the text) for each type.

Hands-On Exercises

Watch the Video
for this Hands-
On Exercise!

MyITLab®
HOE1 Training

1 Introduction to Spreadsheets

As the assistant manager of OKOS, you need to create a worksheet that shows the cost (the amount OKOS pays its suppliers), the markup percentage (the amount by which the cost is increased), and the retail selling price. You also need to list the discount percentage (such as 25% off) for each product, the sale price, and the profit margin percentage.

Skills covered: Enter Text • Enter Values • Enter a Date and Clear Cell Contents

STEP 1 ≫ ENTER TEXT

Now that you have planned the OKOS worksheet, you are ready to enter labels for the title, column labels, and row labels. You will type a title in cell A1, product labels in the first column, and row labels in the fourth row. Refer to Figure 3 as you complete Step 1.

FIGURE 3 Text Entered in Cells

a. Start Excel and open a new blank workbook. Save the new workbook as **e01h1Markup_LastFirst**.

When you save files, use your last and first names. For example, as the Excel author, I would save my workbook as *e01h1Markup_MulberyKeith*.

b. Type **OK Office Systems Pricing Information** in **cell A1** and press **Enter**.

When you press Enter, the next cell down—cell A2 in this case—becomes the active cell. The text does not completely fit in cell A1, and some of the text appears in cells B1, C1, D1, and possibly E1. If you make cell B1, C1, D1, or E1 the active cell, the Formula Bar is empty, indicating that nothing is stored in those cells.

c. Click **cell A4**, type **Product**, and then press **Enter**.

d. Continue typing the rest of the text in **cells A5** through **A10** as shown in Figure 4. Text in column A appears to flow into column B.

When you start typing *Co* in cell A6, AutoComplete displays a ScreenTip suggesting a previous text entry starting with *Co—Computer System*—but keep typing to enter *Color Laser Printer* instead. You just entered the product labels to describe the data in each row.

e. Click **cell B4** to make it the active cell. Type **Cost** and press **Tab**.

Instead of pressing Enter to move down column B, you pressed Tab to make the cell to the right the active cell.

f. Type the following text in the respective cells, pressing **Tab** after typing each of the first four column labels and pressing **Enter** after the last column label:

- **Markup Rate** in **cell C4**
- **Retail Price** in **cell D4**
- **Percent Off** in **cell E4**
- **Sale Price** in **cell F4**
- **Profit Margin** in **cell G4**

The text looks cut off when you enter data in the cell to the right. Do not worry about this now. You will adjust column widths and formatting later in this chapter.

> **TROUBLESHOOTING:** If you notice a typographical error, click in the cell containing the error and retype the label. Or press F2 to edit the cell contents, move the insertion point using the arrow keys, press Backspace or Delete to delete the incorrect characters, type the correct characters, and then press Enter. If you type a label in an incorrect cell, click the cell and press Delete.

g. Save the changes you made to the workbook.

You should develop a habit of saving periodically. That way if your system unexpectedly shuts down, you will not lose everything you worked on.

STEP 2 ≫ ENTER VALUES

Now that you have entered the descriptive labels, you need to enter the cost, markup rate, and percent off for each product. Refer to Figure 4 as you complete Step 2.

	A	B	C	D	E	F	G	H
1	OK Office Systems Pricing Information							
2								
3								
4	Product	Cost	Markup Ra	Retail Pric	Percent O	Sale Price	Profit Margin	
5	Computer	400	0.5		0.15			
6	Color Lase	457.7	0.75		0.2			
7	Filing Cab	68.75	0.905		0.1			
8	Desk Chai	75	1		0.25			
9	Solid Oak	700	1.857		0.3			
10	28" Monit	195	0.835		0.1			
11								
12								

Steps e–f: Percent Off values

Steps c–d: Markup Rate values

Steps a–b: Cost values

FIGURE 4 Values Entered in Cells

a. Click **cell B5**, type **400**, and then press **Enter**.

b. Type the remaining costs in **cells B6** through **B10** shown in Figure 4.

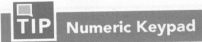

TIP | Numeric Keypad

To improve your productivity, use the number keypad (if available) on the right side of your keyboard. It is much faster to type values and press Enter on the number keypad rather than using the numbers on the keyboard. Make sure Num Lock is active before using the number keypad to enter values.

Hands-On Exercise 1

c. Click **cell C5**, type **0.5**, and then press **Enter**.

You entered the markup rate as a decimal instead of a percentage. You will apply Percent Style later, but now you can concentrate on data entry. When you enter decimal values less than zero, you can type the period and value without typing the zero first, such as .5. Excel will automatically add the zero. You can also enter percentages as 50%, but the approach this text takes is to enter raw data without typing formatting such as % and to use number formatting options through Excel to display formatting symbols.

d. Type the remaining markup rates in **cells C6** through **C10** as shown in Figure 4.

e. Click **cell E5**, type **0.15**, and then press **Enter**.

You entered the Percent Off or markdown sale value as a decimal.

f. Type the remaining Percent Off values in **cells E6** through **E10** as shown in Figure 4 and save the workbook.

STEP 3 ≫ ENTER A DATE AND CLEAR CELL CONTENTS

As you review the worksheet, you realize you need to provide a date to indicate when the sale starts. Refer to Figure 5 as you complete Step 3.

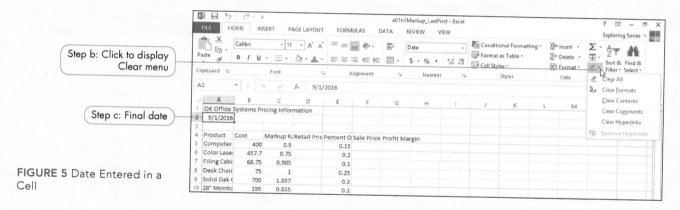

FIGURE 5 Date Entered in a Cell

a. Click **cell A2**, type **9/1**, and then press **Enter**.

The date aligns on the right cell margin by default. Excel displays *1-Sep* instead of *9/1*.

b. Click **cell A2**, click **Clear** in the Editing group on the HOME tab, and then select **Clear All**.

The Clear All command clears both cell contents and formatting in the selected cell(s).

c. Type **9/1/2016** in **cell A2** and press **Enter**.

> **TROUBLESHOOTING:** If you did not use Clear All and typed 9/1/2016 in cell A2, Excel would have retained the previous date format and displayed 1-Sep again.

d. Save the workbook. Keep the workbook open if you plan to continue with the next Hands-On Exercise. If not, close the workbook and exit Excel.

Hands-On Exercise 1

Mathematics and Formulas

Formulas transform static numbers into meaningful results that can update as values change. For example, a payroll manager can build formulas to calculate the gross pay, deductions, and net pay for an organization's employees, or a doctoral student can create formulas to perform various statistical calculations to interpret his or her research data.

You can use formulas to help you analyze how results will change as the input data change. You can change the value of your assumptions or inputs and explore the results quickly and accurately. For example, if the interest rate changes from 4% to 5%, how would that affect your monthly payment? Analyzing different input values in Excel is easy after you build formulas. Simply change an input value and observe the change in the formula results.

In this section, you will learn how to use mathematical operations in Excel formulas. You will refresh your memory of mathematical order of precedence and how to construct formulas using cell addresses so that when the value of an input cell changes, the result of the formula changes without you having to modify the formula.

Creating Formulas

Start a formula by typing the equal sign (=), followed by the arithmetic expression. Do not include a space before or after the arithmetic operator. Figure 6 shows a worksheet containing data and results of formulas. The figure also displays the actual formulas used to generate the calculated results. For example, cell B6 contains the formula =B2+B3. Excel uses the value stored in cell B2 (10) and adds it to the value stored in cell B3 (2). The result—12—appears in cell B6 instead of the actual formula. The Formula Bar displays the formula entered into the active cell.

	A	B	C	D	E	F
1	Description	Values		Description	Results	Formulas in Column E
2	First input value	10		Sum of 10 and 2	12	=B2+B3
3	Second input value	2		Difference between 10 and 2	8	=B2-B3
4				Product of 10 and 2	20	=B2*B3
5				Results of dividing 10 by 2	5	=B2/B3
6				Results of 10 to the 2nd power	100	=B2^B3

FIGURE 6 Formula Results

> **TROUBLESHOOTING:** If you type B2+B3 without the equal sign, Excel does not recognize that you entered a formula and stores the data as text.

Use Cell References in Formulas

STEP 1 >>
STEP 2 >>
STEP 3 >>

You should use cell references instead of values in formulas where possible. You may include values in an input area—such as dates, salary, or costs—that you will need to reference in formulas. Referencing these cells in your formulas, instead of typing the value of the cell to which you are referring, keeps your formulas accurate if the values change.

When you create a formula, you can type the cell references in uppercase, such as =B2+B3, or lowercase, such as =b2+b3. Excel changes cell references to uppercase.

In Figure 6, cell B2 contains 10, and cell B3 contains 2. Cell E2 contains =B2+B3 but shows the result, 12. If you change the value of cell B3 to 5, cell E2 displays the new result, which is 15. However, if you had typed actual values in the formula, =10+2, you would have to edit the formula each time an input value changes. This would be problematic, as you might forget to edit the formula or you might have a typographical error if you edit the formula. Always design worksheets in such a way as to be able to change input values without having to modify your formulas if an input value changes later.

Apply the Order of Precedence

The *order of precedence* (also called order of operations) is a rule that controls the sequence in which arithmetic operations are performed, which affects the results of the calculation. Excel performs mathematical calculations left to right in this order: **Percent, Exponentiation, Multiplication or Division,** and finally **Addition or Subtraction.** Some people remember the order of precedence with the phrase *Please Excuse My Dear Aunt Sally*.

Table 3 lists the complete order of precedence. This chapter focuses on orders 4, 5, and 6.

TABLE 3	Order of Precedence	
Order	Description	Symbols
1	Reference Operators	colon (:), space, and comma (,)
2	Negation	-
3	Percent	%
4	Exponentiation	∧
5	Multiplication and Division	* and / (respectively)
6	Addition and Subtraction	+ and – (respectively)
7	Concatenation	ampersand symbol (&) to connect two text strings
8	Comparison	Equal sign (=), greater than (>), and less than (<)

Figure 7 shows formulas, the sequence in which calculations occur, calculations, the description, and the results of each order of precedence. The highlighted results are the final formula results. This figure illustrates the importance of symbols and use of parentheses.

	A	B	C	D	E	F
1	Input		Formula	Sequence	Description	Result
2	2		=A2+A3*A4+A5	1	3 (cell A3) * 4 (cell A4)	12
3	3			2	2 (cell A2) + 12 (order 1)	14
4	4			3	14 (order 2) + 5 (cell A5)	19
5	5					
6			=(A2+A3)*(A4+A5)	1	2 (cell A2) + 3 (cell A3)	5
7				2	4 (cell A4) + 5 (cell A5)	9
8				3	5 (order 1) * 9 (order 2)	45
9						
10			=A2/A3+A4*A5	1	2 (cell A2) / 3 (cell A3)	0.666667
11				2	4 (cell A4) * 5 (cell A5)	20
12				3	0.666667 (order 1) + 20 (order 2)	20.66667
13						
14			=A2/(A3+A4)*A5	1	3 (cell A3) + 4 (cell A4)	7
15				2	2 (cell A2) / 7 (order 1)	0.285714
16				3	0.285714 (order 2) * 5 (cell A5)	1.428571
17						
18			=A2^2+A3*A4%	1	4 (cell A4) is converted to percentage	0.04
19				2	2 (cell A2) to the power of 2	4
20				3	3 (cell A3) * 0.04 (order 1)	0.12
21				4	4 (order 2) + 0.12 (order 3)	4.12

FIGURE 7 Formula Results Based on Order of Precedence

Use Semi-Selection to Create a Formula

To decrease typing time and ensure accuracy, you can use *semi-selection*, a process of selecting a cell or range of cells for entering cell references as you create formulas. Semi-selection is often called *pointing* because you use the mouse pointer to select cells as you build the formula. To use the semi-selection technique to create a formula, do the following:

1. Click the cell where you want to create the formula.
2. Type an equal sign (=) to start a formula.
3. Click the cell or drag to select the cell range that contains the value(s) to use in the formula. A moving marquee appears around the cell or range you select, and Excel displays the cell or range reference in the formula.
4. Type a mathematical operator.
5. Continue clicking cells, selecting ranges, and typing operators to finish the formula. Use the scroll bars if the cell is in a remote location in the worksheet, or click a worksheet tab to see a cell in another worksheet.
6. Press Enter to complete the formula.

Using Auto Fill

Auto Fill enables you to copy the contents of a cell or a range of cells by dragging the *fill handle* (a small green square appearing in the bottom-right corner of the active cell) over an adjacent cell or range of cells. To use Auto Fill, do the following:

1. Click the cell with the content you want to copy to make it the active cell.
2. Point to the fill handle in the bottom-right corner of the cell until the mouse pointer changes to the fill pointer (a thin black plus sign).
3. Drag the fill handle to repeat the content in other cells.

Copy Formulas with Auto Fill

STEP 4 ≫

After you enter a formula in a cell, you can duplicate the formula without retyping it by using the fill handle to copy the formula in the active cell down a column or across a row, depending on how the data are organized. Excel adapts each copied formula based on the type of cell references in the original formula.

Complete Sequences with Auto Fill

You can also use Auto Fill to complete a sequence. For example, if you enter January in a cell, you can use Auto Fill to enter the rest of the months in adjacent cells. Other sequences you can complete are quarters (Qtr 1, etc.), weekdays, and weekday abbreviations, by typing the first item and using Auto Fill to complete the other entries. For numeric sequences, however, you must specify the first two values in sequence. For example, if you want to fill in 5, 10, 15, and so on, you must enter 5 and 10 in two adjacent cells, select the two cells, and then use Auto Fill so that Excel knows to increment by 5. Figure 8 shows the results of filling in months, abbreviated months, quarters, weekdays, abbreviated weekdays, and increments of 5.

Incremented values filled in

Click to see Auto Fill Options

	A	B	C	D	E	F	G	H	I
1	January	Jan	Qtr 1	Monday	Mon	5			
2	February	Feb	Qtr 2	Tuesday	Tue	10			
3	March	Mar	Qtr 3	Wednesday	Wed	15			
4	April	Apr	Qtr 4	Thursday	Thu	20			
5	May	May		Friday	Fri	25			
6	June	Jun		Saturday	Sat	30			
7	July	Jul		Sunday	Sun	35			
8	August	Aug							
9	September	Sep							
10	October	Oct							
11	November	Nov							
12	December	Dec							
13									
14									
15									

○ Copy Cells
◉ Fill Series
○ Fill Formatting Only
○ Fill Without Formatting
○ Flash Fill

FIGURE 8 Auto Fill Examples

Immediately after you use Auto Fill, Excel displays the Auto Fill Options button in the bottom-right corner of the filled data (see Figure 8). Click Auto Fill Options to display five fill options: Copy Cells, Fill Series, Fill Formatting Only, Fill Without Formatting, or Flash Fill.

TIP **Double-Clicking the Fill Handle**

You can double-click the fill handle to quickly copy a formula down a column. Excel will copy the formula in the active cell for each row of data to calculate in your worksheet.

Displaying Cell Formulas

Excel shows the result of the formula in the cell (see the top half of Figure 9); however, you might want to display the formulas instead of the calculated results in the cells (see the bottom half of Figure 9). To display cell formulas, do one of the following:

STEP 5 ⟩⟩

- Press Ctrl and the grave accent (`) key, sometimes referred to as the tilde key, in the top-left corner of the keyboard, below the Esc key.
- Click Show Formulas in the Formula Auditing group on the FORMULAS tab.

To hide the formulas and display the formula results again, repeat the preceding process.

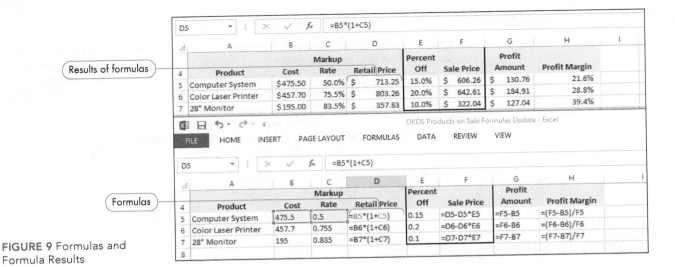

Results of formulas

Formulas

FIGURE 9 Formulas and Formula Results

Quick
Concepts ✓

1. What is the order of precedence? Provide and explain two examples that use four different operators, one with parentheses and one without.

2. What is the purpose of Auto Fill? Provide an example of data you can complete using Auto Fill.

3. Why would it be useful to display formulas instead of formula results in a worksheet?

Hands-On Exercises

2 Mathematics and Formulas

In Hands-On Exercise 1, you created the basic worksheet for OKOS by entering text, values, and a date for items on sale. Now you need to insert formulas to calculate the missing results—specifically, the retail (before sale) value, sale price, and profit margin. You will use cell addresses in your formulas, so when you change a referenced value, the formula results will update automatically.

Skills covered: Use Cell References in a Formula and Apply the Order of Precedence • Use the Semi-Selection Method to Enter a Formula • Use Cell References in a Formula and Apply the Order of Precedence • Copy Formulas with Auto Fill • Change Values and Display Cell Formulas

STEP 1 ≫ USE CELL REFERENCES IN A FORMULA AND APPLY THE ORDER OF PRECEDENCE

The first formula you need to create will calculate the retail price. The retail price is the price you originally charge. It is based on a percentage of the original cost so that you earn a profit. Refer to Figure 10 as you complete Step 1.

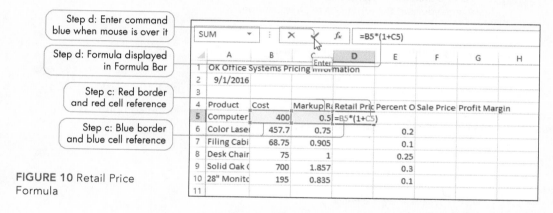

FIGURE 10 Retail Price Formula

a. Open *e01h1Markup_LastFirst* if you closed it at the end of Hands-On Exercise 1 and save it as **e01h2Markup_LastFirst**, changing *h1* to *h2*.

> **TROUBLESHOOTING:** If you make any major mistakes in this exercise, you can close the file, open *e01h1Markup_LastFirst* again, and then start this exercise over.

b. Click **cell D5**, the cell where you will enter the formula to calculate the retail selling price of the first item.

c. Type **=B5*(1+C5)** and view the formula and the colored cells and borders on the screen.

As you type or edit a formula, each cell address in the formula displays in a specific color, and while you type or edit the formula, the cells referenced in the formula have a temporarily colored border. For example, in the formula =B5*(1+C5), B5 appears in blue, and C5 appears in red. Cell B5 has a temporarily blue border and cell C5 has a temporarily red border to help you identify cells as you construct your formulas (see Figure 10).

TIP | Alternative Formula

An alternative formula also calculates the correct retail price: =B5*C5+B5 or =B5+B5*C5. In this formula, 400 (cell B5) is multiplied by 0.5 (cell C5); that result (200) represents the dollar value of the markup. Excel adds the value 200 to the original cost of 400 to obtain 600, the retail price. You were instructed to enter =B5*(1+C5) to demonstrate the order of precedence.

d. Click **Enter** (the check mark ☑ between the Name Box and the Formula Bar) and view the formula in the Formula Bar to check it for accuracy.

The result of the formula, 600, appears in cell D5, and the formula displays in the Formula Bar. This formula first adds 1 (the decimal equivalent of 100%) to 0.5 (the value stored in cell C5). Excel multiplies that sum of 1.5 by 400 (the value stored in cell B5). The theory behind this formula is that the retail price is 150% of the original cost.

> **TROUBLESHOOTING:** If the result is not correct, click the cell and look at the formula in the Formula Bar. Click in the Formula Bar, edit the formula to match the formula shown in Step c, and then click Enter (the check mark between the Name Box and the Formula Bar). Make sure you start the formula with an equal sign.

e. Save the workbook with the new formula.

STEP 2 » USE THE SEMI-SELECTION METHOD TO ENTER A FORMULA

Now that you have calculated the retail price, you need to calculate a sale price. This week, the computer is on sale for 15% off the retail price. Refer to Figure 11 as you complete Step 2.

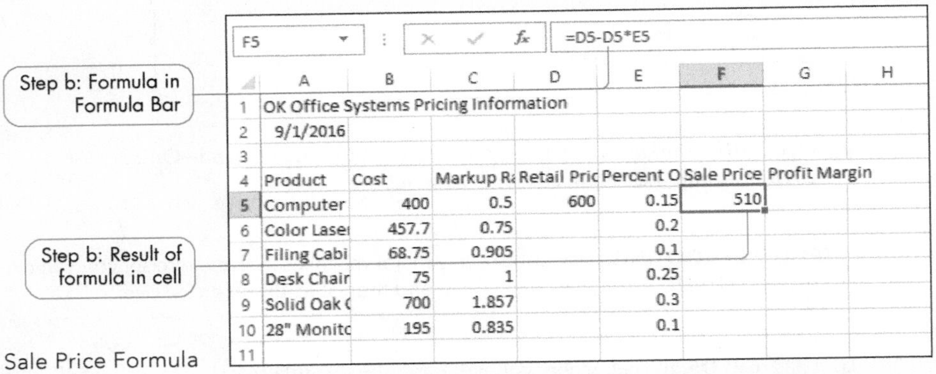

FIGURE 11 Sale Price Formula

a. Click **cell F5**, the cell where you will enter the formula to calculate the sale price.

b. Type =, click **cell D5**, type -, click **cell D5**, type *, and then click **cell E5**. Notice the color-coding in the cell addresses. Press **Ctrl+Enter** to keep the current cell the active cell.

You used the semi-selection method to enter a formula. The result is 510. Looking at the formula, you might think D5–D5 equals zero; remember that because of the order of precedence rules, multiplication is calculated before subtraction. The product of 600 (cell D5) and 0.15 (cell E5) equals 90, which is then subtracted from 600 (cell D5), so the sale price is 510. If it helps to understand the formula better, add parentheses: =D5-(D5*E5).

c. Save the workbook with the new formula.

TIP Spot-Check Your Work

You should check the result for logic. Use a calculator to spot-check the accuracy of formulas. If you mark down merchandise by 15% of its regular price, you are charging 85% of the regular price. You can spot-check your formula to ensure that 85% of 600 is 510 by multiplying 600 by 0.85.

STEP 3 » USE CELL REFERENCES IN A FORMULA AND APPLY THE ORDER OF PRECEDENCE

After calculating the sale price, you want to know the profit margin OKOS will earn. OKOS paid $400 for the computer and will sell it for $510. The profit of $110 is then divided by the $400 cost, which gives OKOS a profit margin of 21.57%. Refer to Figure 12 as you complete Step 3.

Step b: Formula in Formula Bar

Step b: Result of formula in cell

FIGURE 12 Profit Margin Formula

G5			fx	=(F5-B5)/F5			
	A	B	C	D	E	F	G	H
1	OK Office Systems Pricing Information							
2	9/1/2016							
3								
4	Product	Cost	Markup R;	Retail Pric	Percent O	Sale Price	Profit Margin	
5	Computer	400	0.5	600	0.15	510	0.215686	
6	Color Lase	457.7	0.75		0.2			
7	Filing Cabi	68.75	0.905		0.1			
8	Desk Chair	75	1		0.25			
9	Solid Oak (	700	1.857		0.3			
10	28" Monitc	195	0.835		0.1			
11								

a. Click **cell G5**, the cell where you will enter the formula to calculate the profit margin.

The profit margin is the profit (difference in sales price and cost) percentage of the sale price.

b. Type **=(F5-B5)/F5** and notice the color-coding in the cell addresses. Press **Ctrl+Enter**.

The formula must first calculate the profit, which is the difference between the sale price (510) and the original cost (400). The difference (110) is then divided by the sale price (510) to determine the profit margin of 0.215686, or 21.6%.

> **TROUBLESHOOTING:** If you type a backslash (\) instead of a forward slash (/), Excel will display an error message box. Make sure you type / as the division operator.

c. Look at the Formula Bar and save the workbook with the new formula.

STEP 4 » COPY FORMULAS WITH AUTO FILL

After double-checking the accuracy of your calculations for the first product, you are ready to copy the formulas down the columns to calculate the retail price, sale price, and profit margin for the other products. Refer to Figure 13 as you complete Step 4.

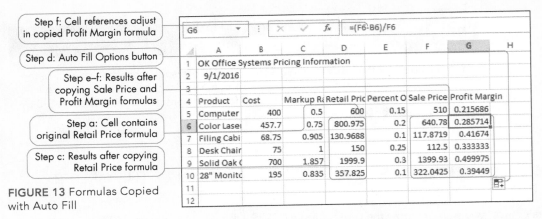

Step f: Cell references adjust in copied Profit Margin formula

Step d: Auto Fill Options button

Step e–f: Results after copying Sale Price and Profit Margin formulas

Step a: Cell contains original Retail Price formula

Step c: Results after copying Retail Price formula

FIGURE 13 Formulas Copied with Auto Fill

a. Click **cell D5**, the cell containing the formula to calculate the retail price for the first item.

b. Position the mouse pointer on the **cell D5 fill handle**. When the pointer changes from a white plus sign to a thin black plus sign, double-click the **fill handle**.

Excel's Auto Fill feature copies the retail price formula for the remaining products in your worksheet. Excel detects when to stop copying the formula when it encounters a blank row, such as in row 11.

c. Click **cell D6**, the cell containing the first copied retail price formula, and look at the Formula Bar.

The formula in cell D5 is =B5*(1+C5). The copied formula in cell D6 is =B6*(1+C6). Excel adjusts the cell addresses in the formula as it copies the formula down a column so that the results are based on each row's data rather than using the original formula's cell addresses for other products.

> **TROUBLESHOOTING:** The result in cell D7 may show more decimal places than shown in Figure 13. This may be due to different screen resolutions. Do not worry about this slight difference.

d. Select the **range F5:G5**. Double-click the **fill handle** in the bottom-right corner of **cell G5**.

Auto Fill copies the selected formulas down their respective columns. Auto Fill Options are available down and to the right of the cell G10 fill handle, indicating you could select different fill options if you want.

> **TROUBLESHOOTING:** If Excel displays pound symbols, such as ####, instead of results, that means the column is not wide enough to show results. You will learn how to adjust column widths in the third section.

e. Click **cell F6**, the cell containing the first copied sale price formula, and view the Formula Bar.

The original formula was =D5-D5*E5. The copied formula in cell F6 is adjusted to =D6-D6*E6 so that it calculates the sales price based on the data in row 6.

f. Click **cell G6**, the cell containing the first copied profit margin formula, and look at the Formula Bar. Save the workbook.

The original formula was =(F5-B5)/F5, and the copied formula in cell G6 is =(F6-B6)/F6.

STEP 5 >> CHANGE VALUES AND DISPLAY CELL FORMULAS

You want to see how the prices and profit margins are affected when you change some of the original cost values. For example, the supplier might notify you that the cost to you will increase. In addition, you want to see the formulas displayed in the cells temporarily. Refer to Figures 14 and 15 as you complete Step 5.

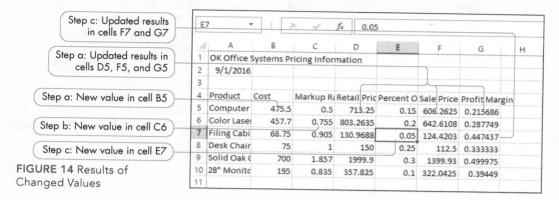

Step c: Updated results in cells F7 and G7

Step a: Updated results in cells D5, F5, and G5

Step a: New value in cell B5

Step b: New value in cell C6

Step c: New value in cell E7

FIGURE 14 Results of Changed Values

a. Click **cell B5**, type **475.5**, and then press **Enter**.

The results of the retail price, sale price, and profit margin formulas change based on the new cost.

b. Click **cell C6**, type **0.755**, and then press **Enter**.

The results of the retail price, sale price, and profit margin formulas change based on the new markup rate.

c. Click **cell E7**, type **0.05**, and then press **Ctrl+Enter**.

The results of the sale price and profit margin formulas change based on the new markdown rate. Note that the retail price did not change, since that formula is not based on the markdown rate.

d. Press **Ctrl+`** (the grave accent mark).

The workbook now displays the formulas rather than the formula results (see Figure 15). This is helpful when you want to review several formulas at one time.

Step d: Formulas displayed instead of results

Step d: Date displays as serial number

Step d: Values appear left aligned

FIGURE 15 Formulas in Cells

e. Press **Ctrl+`** (the grave accent mark).

The workbook now displays the formula results in the cells again.

f. Save the workbook. Keep the workbook open if you plan to continue with the next Hands-On Exercise. If not, close the workbook and exit Excel.

Hands-On Exercise 2

21

Workbook and Worksheet Management

When you start a new blank workbook in Excel, the workbook contains one worksheet named Sheet1. However, you can add additional worksheets. The text, values, dates, and formulas you enter into the individual sheets are saved under one workbook file name. Having multiple worksheets in one workbook is helpful to keep related items together. For example, you might want one worksheet for each month to track your monthly income and expenses for one year. When tax time comes around, you have all your data stored in one workbook file.

Although you should plan the worksheet and workbook before you start entering data, you might need to add, delete, or rename worksheets. Furthermore, within a worksheet you may want to insert a new row to accommodate new data, delete a column that you no longer need, or adjust the size of columns and rows.

In this section, you will learn how to manage workbooks by renaming, inserting, and deleting worksheets. You will also learn how to make changes to worksheet columns and rows, such as inserting, deleting, and adjusting sizes.

Managing Worksheets

Creating a multiple-worksheet workbook takes some planning and maintenance. Worksheet tab names should reflect the contents of the respective worksheets. In addition, you can insert, copy, move, and delete worksheets within the workbook. You can even apply background color to the worksheet tabs so that they stand out onscreen. Figure 16 shows a workbook in which the sheet tabs have been renamed, colors have been applied to worksheet tabs, and a worksheet tab has been right-clicked so that the shortcut menu appears.

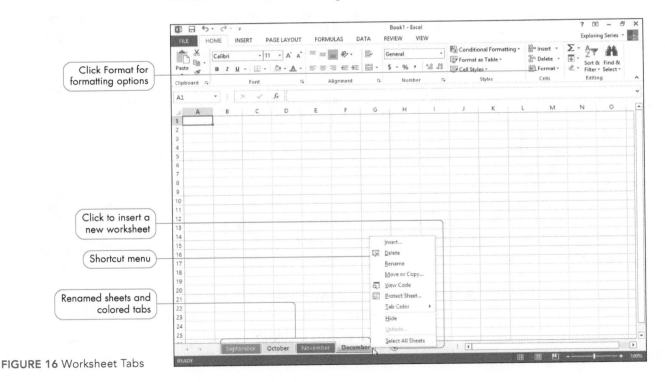

FIGURE 16 Worksheet Tabs

Rename a Worksheet

STEP 1 » The default worksheet name Sheet1 does not describe the contents of the worksheet. You should rename worksheet tabs to reflect the sheet contents. For example, if your budget workbook contains monthly worksheets, name the worksheets September, October, etc. Although you can have spaces in worksheet names, keep worksheet names relatively short. The longer the worksheet names, the fewer sheet tabs you will see at the bottom of the workbook window without scrolling.

To rename a worksheet, do one of the following:

- Double-click a sheet tab, type the new name, and then press Enter.
- Click the sheet tab for the sheet you want to rename, click Format in the Cells group on the HOME tab (refer to Figure 16), select Rename Sheet (see Figure 17), type the new sheet name, and then press Enter.
- Right-click the sheet tab, select Rename from the shortcut menu (see Figure 16), type the new sheet name, and then press Enter.

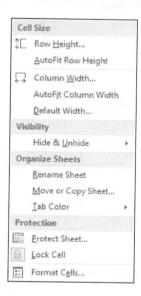

FIGURE 17 Format Menu

Change Worksheet Tab Color

STEP 1 » The active worksheet tab is white with a green bottom border. When you use multiple worksheets, you might want to apply a different color to each worksheet tab to make the tab stand out or to emphasize the difference between sheets. For example, you might apply red to the September tab, green to the October tab, dark blue to the November tab, and purple to the December tab.

To change the color of a worksheet tab, do one of the following:

- Click the sheet tab for the sheet you want to rename, click Format in the Cells group on the HOME tab (refer to Figure 16), point to Tab Color (refer to Figure 17), and then click a color on the Tab Color palette.
- Right-click the sheet tab, point to Tab Color on the shortcut menu (refer to Figure 16), and then click a color on the Tab Color palette.

Insert and Delete a Worksheet

STEP 2 » Sometimes you need more than one worksheet in the workbook. For example, you might create a workbook that contains 12 worksheets—a worksheet for each month of the year. To insert a new worksheet, do one of the following:

- Click *New sheet* to the right of the last worksheet tab.
- Click the Insert arrow—either to the right or below Insert—in the Cells group on the HOME tab and select Insert Sheet.
- Right-click any sheet tab, select Insert from the shortcut menu (refer to Figure 16), click Worksheet in the Insert dialog box, and then click OK.
- Press Shift+F11.

TIP   Ribbon Commands with Arrows

Some commands, such as Insert in the Cells group, contain two parts: the main command and an arrow. The arrow may be below or to the right of the command, depending on the command, window size, or screen resolution. Instructions in the Exploring Series use the command name to instruct you to click the main command to perform the default action, such as *Click Insert in the Cells group* or *Click Delete in the Cells group*. Instructions include the word arrow when you need to select an additional option, such as *Click the Insert arrow in the Cells group* or *Click the Delete arrow in the Cells group*.

If you no longer need the data in a worksheet, delete the worksheet. Doing so will eliminate extra data in a file and reduce file size. To delete a worksheet in a workbook, do one of the following:

- Click the Delete arrow—either to the right or below Delete—in the Cells group on the HOME tab and select Delete Sheet.
- Right-click any sheet tab and select Delete from the shortcut menu (refer to Figure 16).

If the sheet you are trying to delete contains data, Excel will display a warning: *You can't undo deleting sheets, and you might be removing some data. If you don't need it, click Delete.* If you try to delete a blank worksheet, Excel will not display a warning; it will immediately delete the sheet.

Move or Copy a Worksheet

After inserting and deleting worksheets, you can arrange the worksheet tabs in a different sequence, especially if the newly inserted worksheets do not fall within a logical sequence. To move a worksheet, do one of the following:

- Drag a worksheet tab to the desired location. As you drag a sheet tab, the pointer resembles a piece of paper. A down-pointing triangle appears between sheet tabs to indicate where the sheet will be placed when you release the mouse button.
- Click Format in the Cells group on the HOME tab (refer to Figure 16) and select *Move or Copy Sheet*, or right-click the sheet tab you want to move and select *Move or Copy* to display the *Move or Copy* dialog box (see Figure 18). You can move the worksheet within the current workbook, or you can move the worksheet to a different workbook. In the *Before sheet* list, select the worksheet you want to come after the moved worksheet and click OK. For example, you have just created a new worksheet named August and you want it to come before the September worksheet. You would select September in the *Before sheet* list.

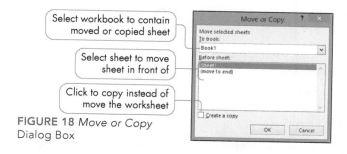

Select workbook to contain moved or copied sheet

Select sheet to move sheet in front of

Click to copy instead of move the worksheet

FIGURE 18 *Move or Copy* Dialog Box

After creating a worksheet, you may want to copy it to use as a template or starting point for similar data. For example, if you create a worksheet for your September budget, you can copy the worksheet and then easily edit the data on the copied worksheet to enter data for your October budget. Copying the entire worksheet would save you a lot of valuable time in entering and formatting the new worksheet. The process for copying a worksheet is similar to moving a sheet. To copy a worksheet, press and hold Ctrl as you drag the worksheet tab. Alternatively, display the *Move or Copy* dialog box, select the *To book* and *Before sheet* options (refer to Figure 18), click the *Create a copy* check box, and then click OK.

Managing Columns and Rows

As you enter and edit worksheet data, you can adjust the row and column structure. You can add rows and columns to add new data, or you can delete data you no longer need. Adjusting the height and width of rows and columns, respectively, can present the data better.

Insert Cells, Columns, and Rows

STEP 3 After you construct a worksheet, you might need to insert cells, columns, or rows to accommodate new data. For example, you might need to insert a new column to perform calculations or a new row to list a new product. When you insert cells, rows, and columns, cell addresses in formulas adjust automatically.

To insert a new column or row, do one of the following:

- Click in the column or row for which you want to insert a new column to the left or a new row above, respectively. Click the Insert arrow in the Cells group on the HOME tab and select Insert Sheet Columns or Insert Sheet Rows.

- Right-click the column (letter) or row (number) heading for which you want to insert a new column to the left or a new row above, respectively, and select Insert from the shortcut menu.

Excel inserts new columns to the left of the current column and new rows above the active row. If the current column is column C and you insert a new column, the new column becomes column C, and the original column C data are now in column D. Likewise, if the current row is 5 and you insert a new row, the new row is row 5, and the original row 5 data are now in row 6.

Inserting a cell is helpful when you realize that you left out an entry in one column after you have entered columns of data. Instead of inserting a new row for all columns, you just want to move the existing content down in one column to enter the missing value. You can insert a single cell in a particular row or column. To insert a cell, click in the cell where you want the new cell, click the Insert arrow in the Cells group on the Home tab, and then select Insert Cells. Select an option from the Insert dialog box (see Figure 19) to position the new cell and click OK. Alternatively, click Insert in the Cells group. The default action of clicking Insert is to insert a cell at the current location, which moves existing data down in that column only.

FIGURE 19 Insert Dialog Box

Delete Cells, Columns, and Rows

STEP 4》 If you no longer need a cell, column, or row, you can delete it. In these situations, you are deleting the entire cell, column, or row, not just the contents of the cell to leave empty cells. As with inserting new cells, any affected formulas adjust the cell references automatically. To delete a column or row, do one of the following:

- Click the column or row heading for the column or row you want to delete. Click Delete in the Cells group on the HOME tab.
- Click in any cell within the column or row you want to delete. Click the Delete arrow in the Cells group on the HOME tab and select Delete Sheet Columns or Delete Sheet Rows, respectively.
- Right-click the column letter or row number for the column or row you want to delete and select Delete from the shortcut menu.

To delete a cell or cells, select the cell(s), click the Delete arrow in the Cells group, and then select Delete Cells to display the Delete dialog box (see Figure 20). Click the appropriate option to shift cells left or up and click OK. Alternatively, click Delete in the Cells group. The default action of clicking Delete is to delete the active cell, which moves existing data up in that column only.

FIGURE 20 Delete Dialog Box

Adjust Column Width

STEP 5》 After you enter data in a column, you often need to adjust the *column width*—the number of characters that can fit horizontally using the default font or the number of horizontal pixels—to show the contents of cells. For example, in the worksheet you created in Hands-On Exercises 1 and 2, the labels in column A displayed into column B when those adjacent cells were empty. However, after you typed values in column B, the labels in column A appeared cut off. You will need to widen column A to show the full name of all of your products.

TIP **Pound Signs Displayed**

Numbers appear as a series of pound signs (######) when the cell is too narrow to display the complete value, and text appears to be truncated.

To widen a column to accommodate the longest label or value in a column, do one of the following:

- Position the pointer on the vertical border between the current column heading and the next column heading. When the pointer displays as a two-headed arrow, double-click the border. For example, if column B is too narrow to display the content in that column, double-click the border between the column B and C headings.
- Click Format in the Cells group on the HOME tab (refer to Figure 16) and select AutoFit Column Width (refer to Figure 17).

To widen a column to an exact width, do one of the following:

- Drag the vertical border to the left to decrease the column width or to the right to increase the column width. As you drag the vertical border, Excel displays a ScreenTip specifying the width (see Figure 21) from 0 to 255 characters and in pixels.
- Click Format in the Cells group on the HOME tab (refer to Figure 16), select Column Width (refer to Figure 17), type a value in the Column width box in the Column Width dialog box, and then click OK.

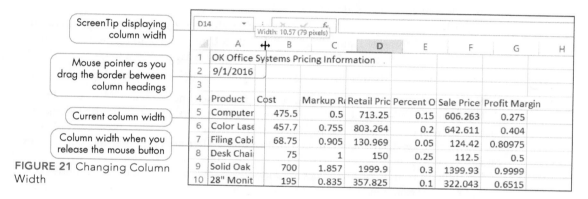

FIGURE 21 Changing Column Width

Adjust Row Height

When you increase the font size of cell contents, Excel automatically increases the *row height*—the vertical measurement of the row. However, if you insert a line break or wrap text to create multiple lines of text in a cell, Excel might not increase the row height. You can adjust the row height in a way similar to how you change column width by double-clicking the border between row numbers or by selecting Row Height or AutoFit Row Height from the Format menu (refer to Figure 17). In Excel, row height is a value between 0 and 409 based on point size (abbreviated as pt) and pixels. Whether you are measuring font sizes or row heights, one point size is equal to 1/72 of an inch. Your row height should be taller than your font size. For example, with an 11-pt font size, the default row height is 15.

TIP Multiple Column Widths and Row Heights

You can set the size for more than one column or row at a time to make the selected columns or rows the same size. Drag across the column or row headings for the area you want to format, and then set the size using any method.

Hide and Unhide Columns and Rows

STEP 6 » If your worksheet contains confidential information, you might need to hide some columns and/or rows before you print a copy for public distribution. However, the column or row is not deleted. If you hide column B, you will see columns A and C side by side. If you hide row 3, you will see rows 2 and 4 together. Figure 22 shows that column B and row 3 are hidden. Excel displays a double line between *column headings* (such as between A and C), indicating one or more columns are hidden, and a double line between row headings (such as between 2 and 4), indicating one or more rows are hidden.

Double vertical line indicates hidden column

Double horizontal line indicates hidden row

FIGURE 22 Hidden Column and Row

To hide a column or row, do one of the following:

- Click in the column or row you want to hide, click Format in the Cells group on the HOME tab (refer to Figure 16), point to Hide & Unhide (refer to Figure 17), and then select Hide Columns or Hide Rows, depending on what you want to hide.
- Right-click the column or row heading(s) you want to hide and select Hide.

You can hide multiple columns and rows at the same time. To select adjacent columns (such as columns B through E) or adjacent rows (such as rows 2 through 4), drag across the adjacent column or row headings. To hide nonadjacent columns or rows, press and hold Ctrl while you click the desired column or row headings. After selecting multiple columns or rows, use any acceptable method to hide the selected columns or rows.

To unhide a column or row, select the columns or rows on both sides of the hidden column or row. For example, if column B is hidden, drag across column letters A and C. Then do one of the following:

- Click Format in the Cells group on the HOME tab (refer to Figure 16), point to Hide & Unhide (refer to Figure 17), and then select Unhide Columns or Unhide Rows, depending on what you want to display again.
- Right-click the column(s) or row(s) you want to hide and select Unhide.

TIP Unhiding Column A, Row 1, and All Hidden Rows/ Columns

Unhiding column A or row 1 is different because you cannot select the row or column on either side. To unhide column A or row 1, type A1 in the Name Box and press Enter. Click Format in the Cells group on the Home tab, point to Hide & Unhide, and then select Unhide Columns or Unhide Rows to display column A or row 1, respectively. If you want to unhide all columns and rows, click Select All and use the Hide & Unhide submenu.

Quick Concepts ✓

1. What is the benefit of renaming a worksheet?

2. What are two ways to insert a new row in a worksheet?

3. How can you delete cell B5 without deleting the entire row or column?

4. When should you adjust column widths instead of using the default width?

Hands-On Exercises

Watch the Video for this Hands-On Exercise!

MyITLab®
HOE3 Training

3 Workbook and Worksheet Management

After reviewing the OKOS worksheet, you decide to rename the worksheet, change the worksheet tab color, insert a worksheet, and delete an empty worksheet. In addition, you need to insert a column to calculate the amount of markup and delete a row containing data you no longer need. You also need to adjust column widths to display the labels in the columns.

Skills covered: Rename a Worksheet and Select a Tab Color • Insert, Move, and Delete a Worksheet • Insert a Column and Rows • Delete a Row • Adjust Column Width and Row Height • Hide and Unhide Columns

STEP 1 ≫ RENAME A WORKSHEET AND SELECT A TAB COLOR

You want to rename Sheet1 to describe the worksheet contents and add a color to the sheet tab. Refer to Figure 23 as you complete Step 1.

FIGURE 23 Renamed Worksheet with Tab Color

a. Open *e01h2Markup_LastFirst* if you closed it at the end of Hands-On Exercise 2 and save it as **e01h3Markup_LastFirst**, changing *h2* to *h3*.

b. Double-click the **Sheet1 sheet tab**, type **September**, and then press **Enter**.

   You renamed Sheet1 September.

c. Right-click the **September sheet tab**, point to *Tab Color*, and then click **Red** in the *Standard Colors* section.

   The worksheet tab color is red.

d. Save the workbook.

STEP 2 ≫ INSERT, MOVE, AND DELETE A WORKSHEET

Your supervisor asks you to add another worksheet to the workbook. She wants you to place it before the September worksheet so that she can add August data. After you do this, she calls you on the phone and tells you that she won't be adding the August data after all. Therefore, you will delete that worksheet. Refer to Figure 24 as you complete Step 2.

Step a: Click to insert new sheet

Step b: New sheet moved to the left

FIGURE 24 New Sheet Inserted

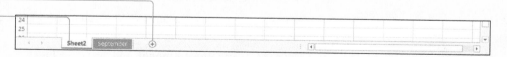

a. Click **New sheet**, the plus icon to the right of the September sheet tab.

   Excel adds a new worksheet named either Sheet1 or Sheet2 to the right of the previously active sheet.

b. Drag the **Sheet tab** to the left of the September sheet tab.

c. Click the **Sheet tab**, click the **Delete arrow** in the Cells group on the HOME tab, and then select **Delete Sheet**.

   You deleted the blank worksheet from the workbook.

> **TROUBLESHOOTING:** Delete in the Cells group, like some other commands in Excel, contains two parts: the main command icon and an arrow. Click the main command icon when instructed to click Delete to perform the default action. Click the arrow when instructed to click the Delete arrow for additional command options.

> **TROUBLESHOOTING:** Notice that Undo is unavailable on the Quick Access Toolbar. You cannot undo deleting a worksheet. It is deleted!

    d. Save the workbook.

STEP 3 >> INSERT A COLUMN AND ROWS

You decide that you need a column to display the amount of profit. Because profit is a dollar amount, you want to keep the profit column close to another column of dollar amounts. Therefore, you will insert the profit column before the profit margin (percentage) column. You also want to insert new rows for product information and category names. Refer to Figure 25 as you complete Step 3.

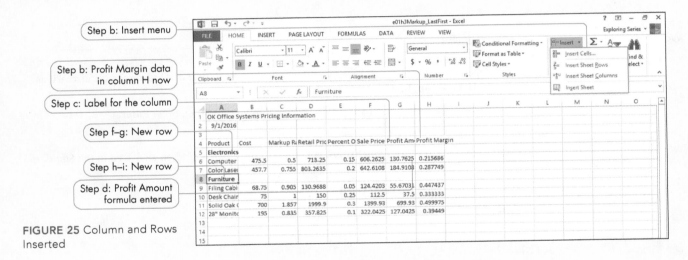

FIGURE 25 Column and Rows Inserted

    a. Click **cell G5** (or any cell in column G), the column containing the Profit Margin.

        You want to insert a column between the Sale Price and Profit Margin columns so that you can calculate the profit amount in dollars.

    b. Click the **Insert arrow** in the Cells group and select **Insert Sheet Columns**.

        You inserted a new, blank column G. The data in the original column G are now in column H.

    c. Click **cell G4**, type **Profit Amount**, and then press **Enter**.

    d. Make sure the active cell is **cell G5**. Type **=F5-B5** and click **Enter** (the check mark between the Name Box and the Formula Bar). Double-click the **cell G5 fill handle** to copy the formula down the column.

        You calculated the profit amount by subtracting the original cost from the sale price. Although steps e and f below illustrate one way to insert a row, you can use other methods presented in this chapter.

    e. Right-click the **row 5 heading**, the row containing the Computer System data.

        Excel displays a shortcut menu consisting of commands you can perform.

f. Select **Insert** from the shortcut menu.

You inserted a new blank row 5, which is selected. The original rows of data move down a row each.

g. Click **cell A5**. Type **Electronics** and press **Ctrl+Enter**. Click **Bold** in the Font group on the HOME tab.

You typed and bolded the category name *Electronics* above the list of electronic products.

h. Right-click the **row 8 heading**, the row containing the Filing Cabinet data, and select **Insert** from the shortcut menu.

i. Click **cell A8**. Type **Furniture** and press **Ctrl+Enter**. Click **Bold** in the Font group on the HOME tab.

You typed and bolded the category name *Furniture* above the list of furniture products.

j. Save the workbook.

STEP 4 ≫ DELETE A ROW

You just realized that you do not have enough filing cabinets in stock to offer on sale, so you need to delete the Filing Cabinet row. Refer to Figure 26 as you complete Step 4.

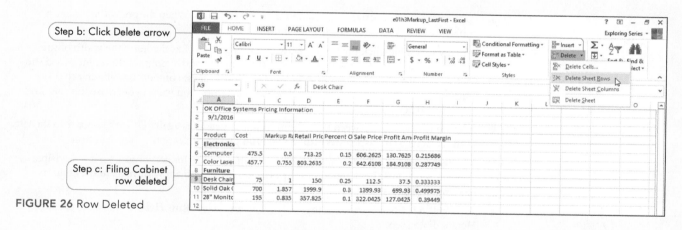

FIGURE 26 Row Deleted

a. Click **cell A9** (or any cell on row 9), the row that contains the Filing Cabinet data.

b. Click the **Delete arrow** in the Cells group.

c. Select **Delete Sheet Rows** and save the workbook.

The Filing Cabinet row is deleted and the remaining rows move up one row.

> **TROUBLESHOOTING:** If you accidentally delete the wrong row or accidentally select Delete Sheet Columns instead of Delete Sheet Rows, click Undo on the Quick Access Toolbar to restore the deleted row or column.

STEP 5 >> ADJUST COLUMN WIDTH AND ROW HEIGHT

As you review your worksheet, you notice that the labels in column A appear cut off. You need to increase the width of that column to display the entire product names. In addition, you want to make row 1 taller. Refer to Figure 27 as you complete Step 5.

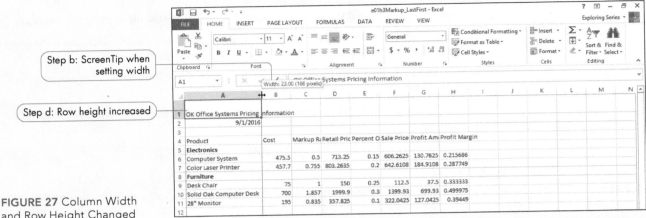

FIGURE 27 Column Width and Row Height Changed

a. Position the pointer between the column A and B headings. When the pointer looks like a double-headed arrow, double-click the border.

When you double-click the border between two columns, Excel adjusts the width of the column on the left side of the border to fit the contents of that column. Excel increased the width of column A based on the cell containing the longest content (the title in cell A1, which will eventually span over all columns). Therefore, you want to decrease the column to avoid so much empty space in column A.

b. Position the pointer between the column A and B headings again. Drag the border to the left until the ScreenTip displays **Width: 23.00 (166 pixels)**. Release the mouse button.

You decreased the column width to 23 for column A. The longest product name is visible. You will not adjust the other column widths until after you apply formats to the column headings in Hands-On Exercise 5.

c. Click **cell A1**. Click **Format** in the Cells group and select **Row Height** to display the Row Height dialog box.

d. Type **30** in the **Row height box** and click **OK**. Save the workbook.

You increased the height of the row that contains the worksheet title so that it is more prominent.

STEP 6 » HIDE AND UNHIDE COLUMNS

To focus on the dollar amounts, you decide to hide the markup rate, discount rate, and profit margin columns. Refer to Figure 28 as you complete Step 6.

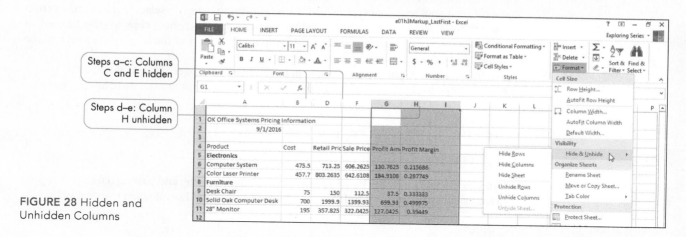

FIGURE 28 Hidden and Unhidden Columns

a. Click the **column C heading**, the column containing the Markup Rate values.

b. Press and hold **Ctrl** as you click the **column E heading** and the **column H heading**. Release Ctrl after selecting the headings.

Holding down Ctrl enables you to select nonadjacent ranges. You want to hide the rate columns temporarily.

c. Click **Format** in the Cells group, point to *Hide & Unhide*, and then select **Hide Columns**.

Excel hides the selected columns. You see a gap in column heading letters, indicating columns are hidden (refer to Figure 28).

d. Drag to select the **column G and I headings**.

You want to unhide column H, so you must select the columns on both sides of the hidden column.

e. Click **Format** in the Cells group, point to *Hide & Unhide*, and then select **Unhide Columns**.

Column H, which contains the Profit Margin values, is no longer hidden. You will keep the other columns hidden and save the workbook as evidence that you know how to hide columns. You will unhide the remaining columns in the next Hands-On Exercise.

f. Save the workbook. Keep the workbook open if you plan to continue with the next Hands-On Exercise. If not, close the workbook and exit Excel.

Clipboard Tasks

Although you plan worksheets before entering data, you might decide to move data to a different location in the same worksheet or even in a different worksheet. Instead of deleting the original data and then typing it in the new location, you can select and move data from one cell to another. In some instances, you might want to create a copy of data entered so that you can explore different values and compare the results of the original data set and the copied and edited data set.

In this section, you will learn how to select different ranges. Then you will learn how to move a range to another location, make a copy of a range, and use the Paste Special feature.

Selecting, Moving, Copying, and Pasting Data

You may already know the basics of selecting, cutting, copying, and pasting data in other programs, such as Microsoft Word. These tasks are somewhat different when working in Excel.

Select a Range

STEP 1 ≫ A *range* refers to a group of adjacent or contiguous cells. A range may be as small as a single cell or as large as the entire worksheet. It may consist of a row or part of a row, a column or part of a column, or multiple rows or columns, but will always be a rectangular shape, as you must select the same number of cells in each row or column for the entire range. A range is specified by indicating the top-left and bottom-right cells in the selection. For example, in Figure 29, the date is a single-cell range in cell A2, the Color Laser Printer data are stored in the range A6:G6, the cost values are stored in the range B5:B10, and the sales prices and profit margins are stored in range F5:G10. A *nonadjacent range* contains multiple ranges, such as C5:C10 and E5:E10. At times, you need to select nonadjacent ranges so that you can apply the same formatting at the same time, such as formatting the nonadjacent range C5:C10 and E5:E10 with Percent Style.

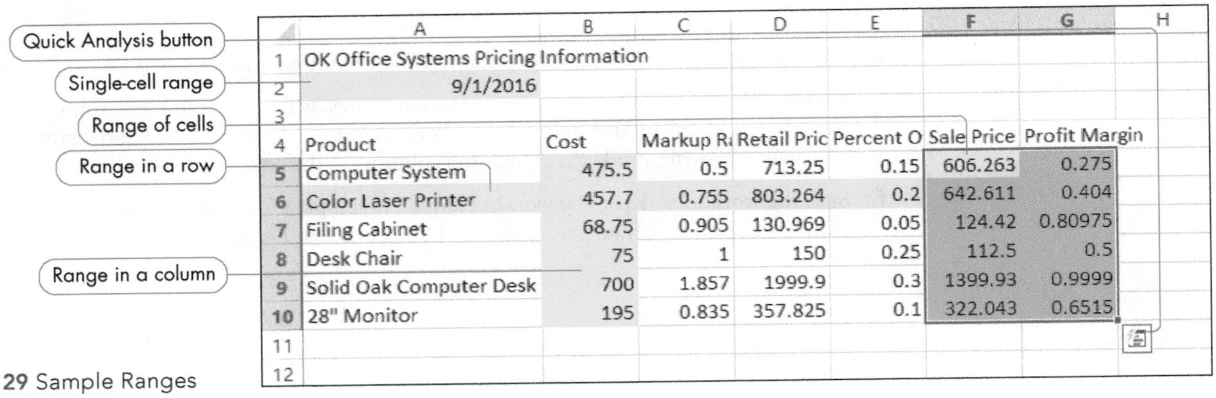

	A	B	C	D	E	F	G	H
1	OK Office Systems Pricing Information							
2	9/1/2016							
3								
4	Product	Cost	Markup R₂	Retail Pric	Percent O	Sale Price	Profit Margin	
5	Computer System	475.5	0.5	713.25	0.15	606.263	0.275	
6	Color Laser Printer	457.7	0.755	803.264	0.2	642.611	0.404	
7	Filing Cabinet	68.75	0.905	130.969	0.05	124.42	0.80975	
8	Desk Chair	75	1	150	0.25	112.5	0.5	
9	Solid Oak Computer Desk	700	1.857	1999.9	0.3	1399.93	0.9999	
10	28" Monitor	195	0.835	357.825	0.1	322.043	0.6515	
11								
12								

Labels: Quick Analysis button, Single-cell range, Range of cells, Range in a row, Range in a column

FIGURE 29 Sample Ranges

Table 4 lists methods you can use to select ranges, including nonadjacent ranges.

TABLE 4	Selecting Ranges
To Select:	**Do This:**
A range	Drag until you select the entire range. Alternatively, click the first cell in the range, press and hold Shift, and then click the last cell in the range.
An entire column	Click the column heading.
An entire row	Click the row heading.
Current range containing data	Click in the range of data and press Ctrl+A.
All cells in a worksheet	Click Select All or press Ctrl+A twice.
Nonadjacent range	Select the first range, press and hold Ctrl, and then select additional range(s).

A green border appears around a selected range, and the Quick Analysis button displays in the bottom-right corner of the selected range. Any command you execute will affect the entire range. The range remains selected until you select another range or click in any cell in the worksheet.

 TIP Name Box

You can use the Name Box to select a range by clicking in the Name Box, typing a range address such as B15:D25, and then pressing Enter.

Move a Range to Another Location

STEP 1 » You can move cell contents from one range to another. For example, you might need to move an input area from the right side of the worksheet to above the output range. When you move a range containing text and values, the text and values do not change. However, any formulas that refer to cells in that range will update to reflect the new cell addresses. To move a range, do the following:

1. Select the range.
2. Use the Cut command to copy the range to the Clipboard. Unlike cutting data in other Microsoft Office applications, the data you cut in Excel remain in their locations until you paste them elsewhere. After you click Cut, a moving dashed green border surrounds the selected range and the status bar displays *Select destination and press ENTER or choose Paste*.
3. Make sure the destination range—the range where you want to move the data—is the same size or greater than the size of the cut range. If any cells within the destination range contain data, Excel overwrites that data when you use the Paste command.
4. Click in the top-left corner of the destination range, and then use the Paste command to insert the data contained in the selected range and remove that data from the original range.

Copy and Paste a Range

STEP 2 » You may need to copy cell contents from one range to another. For example, you might copy your January budget to another worksheet to use as a model for creating your February budget. When you copy a range, the original data remain in their original locations. Cell references in copied formulas adjust based on their relative locations to the original data. To copy a range, do the following:

1. Select the range.
2. Use the Copy command to copy the contents of the selected range to the Clipboard. After you click Copy, a moving dashed green border surrounds the selected range and the status bar displays *Select destination and press ENTER or choose Paste*.
3. Make sure the destination range—the range where you want to copy the data—is the same size or greater than the size of the copied range. If any cells within the destination range contain data, Excel overwrites that data when you use the Paste command.
4. Click in the top-left corner of the destination range where you want the duplicate data, and then use the Paste command. The original range still has the moving dashed green border, and the pasted copied range is selected with a solid green border. Figure 30 shows a selected range and a copy of the range.
5. Press Esc to turn off the moving dashed border around the originally selected range.

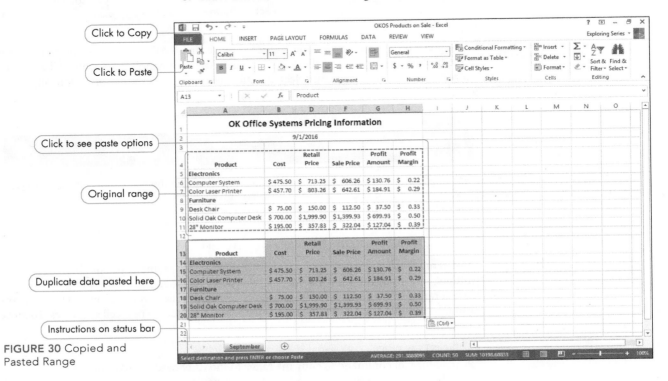

FIGURE 30 Copied and Pasted Range

Instead of clicking Copy, if you click the Copy arrow in the Clipboard group, you can select Copy (the default option) or Copy as Picture. When you select Copy as Picture, you copy an image of the selected data. You can then paste the image elsewhere in the workbook or in a Word document or PowerPoint presentation. However, when you copy the data as an image, you cannot edit individual cell data after you paste the image.

Use Paste Options and Paste Special

STEP 3 ❯❯ Sometimes you might want to paste data in a different format than they are in the Clipboard. For example, you might want to copy a range containing formulas and cell references, and paste the range as values in another workbook that does not have the referenced cells. If you want to copy data from Excel and paste them into a Word document, you can paste the Excel data as a worksheet object, as unformatted text, or in another format. To paste data from the Clipboard into a different format, click the Paste arrow in the Clipboard group, and hover over

Introduction to Excel

a command to see a ScreenTip and a preview of how the pasted data will look. In Figure 31, the preview shows that a particular paste option will maintain formulas and number formatting; however, it will not maintain the text formatting, such as font color and centered text. After previewing different paste options, click the one you want in order to apply it.

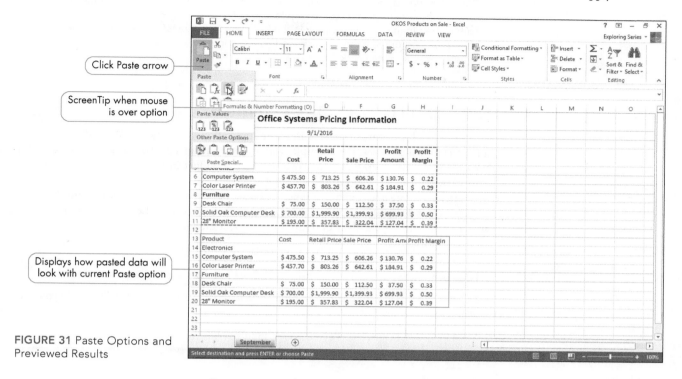

FIGURE 31 Paste Options and Previewed Results

For more specific paste options, click the Paste arrow, and then select Paste Special to display the Paste Special dialog box (see Figure 32). This dialog box contains more options than the Paste menu. Click the desired option and click OK.

FIGURE 32 Paste Special Dialog Box

TIP **Paste Options Button**

When you copy or paste data, Excel displays the *Paste Options button* in the bottom-right corner of the pasted data (refer to Figure 30). Click Paste Options to see different results for the pasted data.

Copy Excel Data to Other Programs

You can copy Excel data and use it in other applications, such as in a Word document or in a PowerPoint slide show. For example, you might perform statistical analyses in Excel, copy the data into a research paper in Word or create a budget in Excel, and then copy the data into a PowerPoint slide show for a meeting.

After selecting and copying a range in Excel, you must decide how you want the data to appear in the destination application. Click the Paste arrow in the destination application, such as Word, to see a gallery of options or to select the Paste Special option.

Quick Concepts

1. When you move or copy a worksheet, what are some of the decisions you must make?

2. How can you select nonadjacent ranges, such as B5:B10 and F5:F10? Why would you select nonadjacent ranges?

3. Why would you use the Paste Special options in Excel?

Hands-On Exercises

Watch the Video
for this Hands-
On Exercise!

MyITLab®
HOE4 Training

4 Clipboard Tasks

You realize the 28" Monitor data is in the Furniture category instead of the Electronics category. You need to move the product to its appropriate location. In addition, your supervisor will ask you to enter data for a new product. Because it is almost identical to an existing product, you can copy the original data and edit the copied data to save time. You also want to experiment with the Paste Special option to see the results of using it in the OKOS workbook.

Skills covered: Select a Range and Move a Row to a New Location • Copy and Paste a Range • Use Paste Special

STEP 1 ≫ SELECT A RANGE AND MOVE A ROW TO A NEW LOCATION

You want to move the 28" Monitor product to be immediately after the Color Laser Printer product. Before moving the 28" Monitor row, you need to insert a blank row between the Color Laser Printer and Furniture rows. Refer to Figure 33 as you complete Step 1.

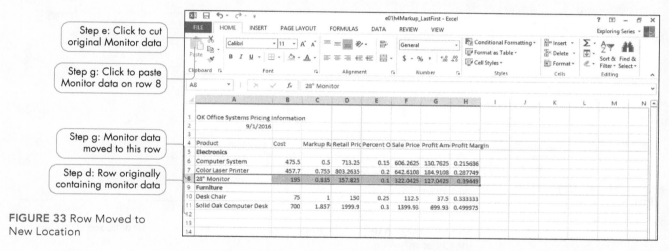

FIGURE 33 Row Moved to New Location

a. Open *e01h3Markup_LastFirst* if you closed it at the end of Hands-On Exercise 3 and save it as **e01h4Markup_LastFirst**, changing *h3* to *h4*.

b. Select the **column B, D, and F headings**. Unhide columns C and E as you learned in Hands-On Exercise 3.

   You kept those columns hidden when you saved the *e01h3Markup_LastFirst* workbook to preserve evidence that you know how to hide columns. Now you need the columns visible to continue.

c. Right-click the **row 8 heading** and select **Insert** from the menu.

   You need to insert a blank row so that you can move the *28" Computer Monitor* data to be between the *Color Laser Printer* and *Furniture* rows.

d. Select the **range A12:H12**.

   You selected the range of cells containing the 28" Monitor data.

e. Click **Cut** in the Clipboard group.

   A moving dashed green border outlines the selected range. The status bar displays the message *Select destination and press ENTER or choose Paste.*

f. Click **cell A8**, the new blank row you inserted in step c.

This is the first cell in the destination range.

g. Click **Paste** in the Clipboard group and save the workbook.

The 28" Monitor data are now located on row 8.

> **TROUBLESHOOTING:** If you cut and paste a row without inserting a new row first, Excel will overwrite the original row of data, which is why you inserted a new row in step c. If you forgot to do step c, click Undo until the 28" Monitor data is back in its original location and start with step c again.

STEP 2 ›› COPY AND PASTE A RANGE

Alesha told you that a new chair is on its way. She asked you to enter the data for the Executive Desk Chair. Because most of the data is the same as the Desk Chair data, you will copy the original Desk Chair data, edit the product name, and then change the cost to reflect the cost of the second chair. Refer to Figure 34 as you complete Step 2.

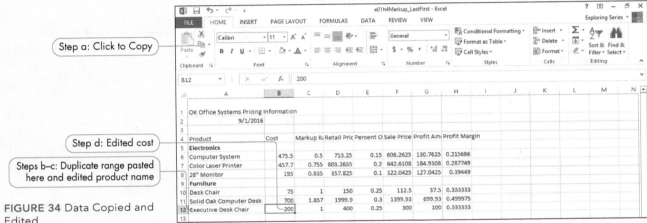

FIGURE 34 Data Copied and Edited

a. Select the **range A10:H10**, the row containing the Desk Chair product data, and click **Copy** in the Clipboard group.

b. Click **cell A12**, the location for the duplicate data, and click **Paste** in the Clipboard group. Press **Esc**.

The pasted range is selected in row 12.

c. Click **cell A12**, press F2 to activate Edit Mode, press **Home**, type **Executive**, press **Spacebar**, and then press **Enter**.

You edited the product name.

d. Change the value in **cell B12** to **200**. Save the workbook.

The formulas calculate the results based on the new cost of 200 for the Executive Desk Chair.

STEP 3 ≫ USE PASTE SPECIAL

During your lunch break, you want to experiment with some of the Paste Special options. Particularly, you are interested in pasting Formulas and Value & Source Formatting. First, you will bold the title and apply a font color to help you test these Paste Special options. Refer to Figure 35 as you complete Step 3.

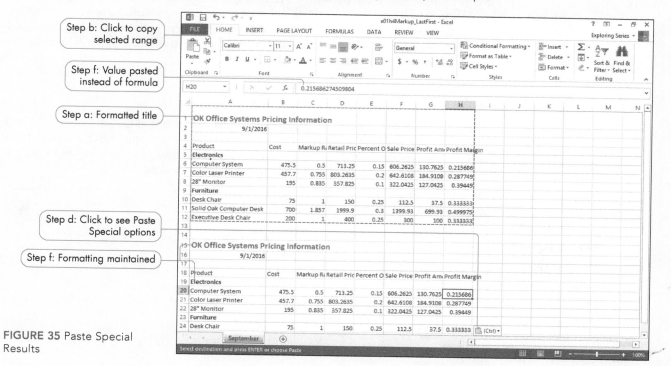

FIGURE 35 Paste Special Results

a. Click **cell A1**. Apply these font formats to the title: **14 pt**, **Bold**, and **Gold, Accent 4, Darker 50% font color** in the Font group on the HOME tab.

You need to format text to see the effects of using different Paste Special options.

b. Select the **range A1:H12** and click **Copy** in the Clipboard group.

c. Click **cell A15**, the top-left corner of the destination range.

d. Click the **Paste arrow** in the Clipboard group and position the mouse pointer over *Formulas*.

Without clicking the command, Excel shows you a preview of what that option would do. The pasted copy would not contain the font formatting you applied to the title or the bold on the two category names. In addition, the pasted date would appear as a serial number. The formulas would be maintained.

e. Position the mouse pointer over *Values & Source Formatting*.

This option would preserve the formatting, but it would convert the formulas into the current value results.

f. Click **Values & Source Formatting**, click **cell H6** to see a formula, and then click **cell H20**. Press **Esc** to turn off the border.

Cell H6 contains a formula, but in the pasted version, the equivalent cell H20 has converted the formula result into an actual value. If you were to change the original cost on row 20, the contents of cell H20 would not change. In a working environment, this is useful only if you want to capture the exact value in a point in time before making changes to the original data.

g. Save the workbook. Keep the workbook open if you plan to continue with the next Hands-On Exercise. If not, close the workbook and exit Excel.

Hands-On Exercise 4

41

Formatting

After entering data and formulas, you should format the worksheet. A professionally formatted worksheet—through adding appropriate symbols, aligning decimals, and using fonts and colors to make data stand out—makes finding and analyzing data easy. You apply different formats to accentuate meaningful details or to draw attention to specific ranges in a worksheet.

In this section, you will learn to apply different alignment options, including horizontal and vertical alignment, text wrapping, and indent options. In addition, you will learn how to format different types of values.

Applying Alignment and Font Options

Alignment refers to how data are positioned in cells. Text aligns at the left cell margin, and dates and values align at the right cell margin. You can change the alignment of cell contents to improve the appearance of data within the cells. The Alignment group (see Figure 36) on the Home tab contains several features to help you align and format data.

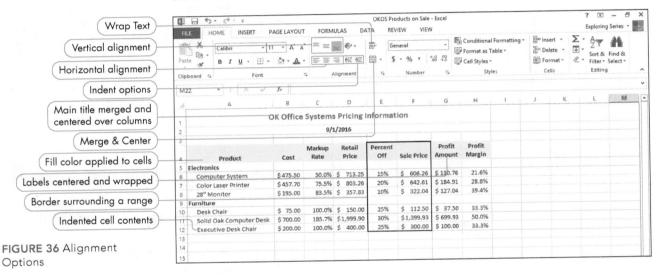

FIGURE 36 Alignment Options

 Alignment Options

The Format Cells dialog box contains additional alignment options. To open the Format Cells dialog box, click the Dialog Box Launcher in the Alignment group on the Home tab. The Alignment tab in the dialog box contains the options for aligning data.

Merge and Center Labels

STEP 1 >> You may want to place a title at the top of a worksheet and center it over the columns of data in the worksheet. You can center main titles over all columns in the worksheet, and you can center category titles over groups of related columns. To create a title, enter the text in the far left cell of the range. Select the range of cells across which you want to center the title and click Merge & Center in the Alignment group on the Home tab. Only data in the far left cell (or top right cell) are merged. Any other data in the merged cells are deleted. Excel merges the selected cells together into one cell, and the merged cell address is that of the original cell on the left. The data are centered between the left and right sides of the merged cell.

If you merge too many cells and want to split the merged cell back into its original multiple cells, click the merged cell and click Merge & Center. Unmerging places the data in the top-left cell.

For additional options, click the Merge & Center arrow. Table 5 lists the four merge options.

TABLE 5	Merge Options
Option	**Results**
Merge & Center	Merges selected cells and centers data into one cell.
Merge Across	Merges the selected cells but keeps text left aligned or values right aligned.
Merge Cells	Enables you to merge a range of cells on multiple rows as well as in multiple columns.
Unmerge Cells	Separates a merged cell into multiple cells again.

Change Horizontal and Vertical Cell Alignment

STEP 2 ▶ *Horizontal alignment* specifies the position of data between the left and right cell margins, and *vertical alignment* specifies the position of data between the top and bottom cell margins. Bottom Align is the default vertical alignment (as indicated by the light green background), and Align Left is the default horizontal alignment for text. In Figure 36, the labels on row 4 have Center horizontal alignment and the title in row 1 has Middle Align vertical alignment.

If you increase row height, you might need to change the vertical alignment to position data better in conjunction with data in adjacent cells. To change alignments, click the desired alignment setting(s) in the Alignment group on the Home tab.

TIP Rotate Cell Data

People sometimes rotate headings in cells. You can rotate data in a cell by clicking Orientation in the Alignment group and selecting an option, such as Angle Clockwise.

Wrap Text

STEP 2 ▶ Sometimes you have to maintain specific column widths, but the data do not fit entirely. You can use *wrap text* to make data appear on multiple lines by adjusting the row height to fit the cell contents within the column width. When you click Wrap Text in the Alignment group, Excel wraps the text on two or more lines within the cell. This alignment option is helpful when the column headings are wider than the values contained in the column. In Figure 36, the *Markup Rate* and *Percent Off* labels on row 4 are examples of wrapped text.

Increase and Decrease Indent

STEP 3 ▶ To offset labels, you can indent text within a cell. *Indenting* helps others see the hierarchical structure of data. Accountants often indent the word *Totals* in financial statements so that it stands out from a list of items above the total row. To indent the contents of a cell, click Increase Indent in the Alignment group on the Home tab. The more you click Increase Indent, the more text is indented in the cell. To decrease the indent, click Decrease Indent in the Alignment group. In Figure 36, *Computer System* and *Desk Chair* are indented.

Apply Borders and Fill Color

STEP 4 ≫

You can apply a border or fill color to accentuate data in a worksheet. A *border* is a line that surrounds a cell or a range of cells. You can use borders to offset some data from the rest of the worksheet data. To apply a border, select the cell or range that you want to have a border, click the Borders arrow in the Font group, and then select the desired border type. In Figure 36, a border surrounds the range E4:F12. To remove a border, select No Border from the Borders menu.

To add some color to your worksheet to add emphasis to data or headers, you can apply a fill color. *Fill color* is a background color that displays behind the data. You should choose a fill color that contrasts with the font color. For example, if the font color is Black, you might want to choose Yellow fill color. If the font color is White, you might want to apply Blue or Dark Blue fill color. To apply a fill color, select the cell or range that you want to have a fill color, click the Fill Color arrow on the Home tab, and then select the color choice from the Fill Color palette. In Figure 36, the column labels in row 4 contain the Gold, Accent 4, Lighter 80% fill color. If you want to remove a fill color, select No Fill from the bottom of the palette.

For additional border and fill color options, click the Dialog Box Launcher in the Font group to display the Format Cells dialog box. Click the Border tab to select border options, including the border line style and color. Click the Fill tab to set the background color, fill effects, and patterns.

Applying Number Formats

Values have no special formatting when you enter data. You should apply *number formats* based on the type of values in a cell, such as applying either the Accounting or Currency number format to monetary values. Changing the number format changes the way the number displays in a cell, but the format does not change the number's value. If, for example, you enter 123.456 into a cell and format the cell with the Currency number type, the value shows as $123.46 onscreen, but the actual value 123.456 is used for calculations. When you apply a number format, you can specify the number of decimal places to display onscreen.

Apply a Number Format

STEP 5 ≫

The default number format is General, which displays values as you originally enter them. General does not align decimal points in a column or include symbols, such as dollar signs, percent signs, or commas. Table 6 lists and describes the primary number formats in Excel.

TABLE 6 Number Formats

Format Style	Display
General	A number as it was originally entered. Numbers are shown as integers (e.g., 12345), decimal fractions (e.g., 1234.5), or in scientific notation (e.g., 1.23E+10) if the number exceeds 11 digits.
Number	A number with or without the 1,000 separator (e.g., a comma) and with any number of decimal places. Negative numbers can be displayed with parentheses and/or red.
Currency	A number with the 1,000 separator and an optional dollar sign (which is placed immediately to the left of the number). Negative values are preceded by a minus sign or are displayed with parentheses or in red. Two decimal places display by default.
Accounting Number Format	A number with the 1,000 separator, an optional dollar sign (at the left border of the cell, vertically aligned within a column), negative values in parentheses, and zero values as hyphens. Two decimal places display by default. Changes alignment slightly within the cell.
Comma	A number with the 1,000 separator. Used in conjunction with Accounting Number Style to align commas and decimal places.
Date	The date in different ways, such as Long Date (March 14, 2016) or Short Date (3/14/16 or 14-Mar-16).
Time	The time in different formats, such as 10:50 PM or 22:50.
Percent Style	The value as it would be multiplied by 100 (for display purpose), with the percent sign. The default number of decimal places is zero if you click Percent Style in the Number group or two decimal places if you use the Format Cells dialog box. However, you should typically increase the number of decimal points to show greater accuracy.
Fraction	A number as a fraction; use when no exact decimal equivalent exists. A fraction is entered into a cell as a formula such as =1/3. If the cell is not formatted as a fraction, the formula results display.
Scientific	A number as a decimal fraction followed by a whole number exponent of 10; for example, the number 12345 would appear as 1.23E+04. The exponent, +04 in the example, is the number of places the decimal point is moved to the left (or right if the exponent is negative). Very small numbers have negative exponents.
Text	The data left aligned; is useful for numerical values that have leading zeros and should be treated as text, such as postal codes or phone numbers. Apply Text format before typing a leading zero so that the zero displays in the cell.
Special	A number with editing characters, such as hyphens in a Social Security number.
Custom	Predefined customized number formats or special symbols to create your own customized number format.

The Number group on the Home tab contains commands for applying **Accounting Number Format**, **Percent Style**, and **Comma Style** numbering formats. You can click the Accounting Number Format arrow and select other denominations, such as English pounds or euros. For other number formats, click the Number Format arrow and select the numbering format you want to use. For more specific numbering formats than those provided, select More Number Formats from the Number Format menu or click the Number Dialog Box Launcher to open the Format Cells dialog box with the Number tab options readily available. Figure 37 shows different number formats applied to values.

	A	B
1	General	1234.567
2	Number	1234.57
3	Currency	$1,234.57
4	Accounting	$ 1,234.57
5	Comma	1,234.57
6	Percent	12%
7	Short Date	3/1/2016
8	Long Date	Tuesday, March 1, 2016

FIGURE 37 Number Formats

Increase and Decrease Decimal Places

STEP 5 >> After applying a number format, you may need to adjust the number of decimal places that display. For example, if you have an entire column of monetary values formatted in Accounting Number Format, Excel displays two decimal places by default. If the entire column of values contains whole dollar values and no cents, displaying *.00* down the column looks cluttered. You can decrease the number of decimal places to show whole numbers only.

To change the number of decimal places displayed, click Increase Decimal in the Number group on the Home tab to display more decimal places for greater precision or Decrease Decimal to display fewer or no decimal places.

Quick Concepts

1. What is the importance of formatting a worksheet?

2. Describe five alignment and font formatting techniques used to format labels that are discussed in this section.

3. What are the main differences between Accounting Number Format and Currency format? Which format has its own command on the Ribbon?

Hands-On Exercises

Watch the Video
for this Hands-
On Exercise!

MyITLab®
HOE5 Training

5 Formatting

In the first four Hands-On Exercises, you entered data about products on sale, created formulas to calculate markup and profit, and inserted new rows and columns to accommodate the labels *Electronics* and *Furniture* to identify the specific products. You are ready to format the worksheet. Specifically, you need to center the title, align text, format values, and then apply other formatting to enhance the readability of the worksheet.

Skills covered: Merge and Center the Title • Align Text Horizontally and Vertically and Wrap Text • Increase Indent • Apply Borders and Fill Color • Apply Number Formats and Increase and Decrease Decimal Places

STEP 1 ≫ MERGE AND CENTER THE TITLE

To make the title stand out, you want to center it over all the data columns. You will use the Merge & Center command to merge cells and center the title at the same time. Refer to Figure 38 as you complete Step 1.

Step e: Date merged, centered, and bold A2:H2

	A	B	C	D	E	F	G	H	I
1	OK Office Systems Pricing Information								
2	9/1/2016								
3									
4	Product	Cost	Markup Ra	Retail Pric	Percent O	Sale Price	Profit Am	Profit Margin	
5	Electronics								
6	Computer System	475.5	0.5	713.25	0.15	606.2625	130.7625	0.215686	
7	Color Laser Printer	457.7	0.755	803.2635	0.2	642.6108	184.9108	0.287749	
8	28" Monitor	195	0.835	357.825	0.1	322.0425	127.0425	0.39449	
9	Furniture								
10	Desk Chair	75	1	150	0.25	112.5	37.5	0.333333	
11	Solid Oak Computer Desk	700	1.857	1999.9	0.3	1399.93	699.93	0.499975	
12	Executive Desk Chair	200	1	400	0.25	300	100	0.333333	
13									

FIGURE 38 Title and Date Merged and Centered

a. Open *e01h4Markup_LastFirst* if you closed it at the end of Hands-On Exercise 4 and save it as **e01h5Markup_LastFirst**, changing *h4* to *h5*.

b. Select the **range A15:H26** and press **Delete**.

You maintained a copy of your Paste Special results in the *e01h4Markup_LastFirst* workbook, but you do not need it to continue.

c. Select the **range A1:H1**.

You want to center the title over all columns of data.

d. Click **Merge & Center** in the Alignment group.

Excel merges cells in the range A1:H1 into one cell and centers the title horizontally within the merged cell, which is cell A1.

TROUBLESHOOTING: If you merge too many or not enough cells, you can unmerge the cells and start again. To unmerge cells, click in the merged cell. The Merge & Center command is shaded in green when the active cell is merged. Click Merge & Center to unmerge the cell. Then select the correct range to merge and use Merge & Center again.

Hands-On Exercise 5

47

e. Select the **range A2:H2**. Merge and center the date and bold it.

> **TROUBLESHOOTING:** If you try to merge and center data in the range A1:H2, Excel will keep the top-left data only and delete the date. To merge separate data on separate rows, you must merge and center data separately.

f. Save the workbook.

STEP 2 ≫ ALIGN TEXT HORIZONTALLY AND VERTICALLY AND WRAP TEXT

You will wrap the text in the column headings to avoid columns that are too wide for the data, but which will display the entire text of the column labels. In addition, you will horizontally center column labels between the left and right cell margins. Refer to Figure 39 as you complete Step 2.

Step d: Title with Middle (vertical) Align

Steps b–c: Column labels wrapped, centered, and bold

	A	B	C	D	E	F	G	H
1	OK Office Systems Pricing Information							
2	9/1/2016							
3								
4	Product	Cost	Markup Rate	Retail Price	Percent Off	Sale Price	Profit Amount	Profit Margin
5	Electronics							
6	Computer System	475.5	0.5	713.25	0.15	606.2625	130.7625	0.215686
7	Color Laser Printer	457.7	0.755	803.2635	0.2	642.6108	184.9108	0.287749
8	28" Monitor	195	0.835	357.825	0.1	322.0425	127.0425	0.39449
9	Furniture							
10	Desk Chair	75	1	150	0.25	112.5	37.5	0.333333
11	Solid Oak Computer Desk	700	1.857	1999.9	0.3	1399.93	699.93	0.499975
12	Executive Desk Chair	200	1	400	0.25	300	100	0.333333
13								

FIGURE 39 Formatted Column Labels

a. Select the **range A4:H4** to select the column labels.

b. Click **Wrap Text** in the Alignment group.

The multiple-word column headings are now visible on two lines within each cell.

c. Click **Center** in the Alignment group. Bold the selected column headings.

The column headings are centered horizontally between the left and right edges of each cell.

d. Click **cell A1**, which contains the title, click **Middle Align** in the Alignment group, and then save the workbook.

Middle Align vertically centers data between the top and bottom edges of the cell.

STEP 3 ≫ INCREASE INDENT

As you review the first column, you notice that the category names, Electronics and Furniture, do not stand out. You decide to indent the labels within each category to better display which products are in each category. Refer to Figure 40 as you complete Step 3.

Hands-On Exercise 5

	A	B	C	D	E	F	G	H	I
1	OK Office Systems Pricing Information								
2	9/1/2016								
3									
4	Product	Cost	Markup Rate	Retail Price	Percent Off	Sale Price	Profit Amount	Profit Margin	
5	Electronics								
6	Computer System	475.5	0.5	713.25	0.15	606.2625	130.7625	0.215686	
7	Color Laser Printer	457.7	0.755	803.2635	0.2	642.6108	184.9108	0.287749	
8	28" Monitor	195	0.835	357.825	0.1	322.0425	127.0425	0.39449	
9	Furniture								
10	Desk Chair	75	1	150	0.25	112.5	37.5	0.333333	
11	Solid Oak Computer Desk	700	1.857	1999.9	0.3	1399.93	699.93	0.499975	
12	Executive Desk Chair	200	1	400	0.25	300	100	0.333333	
13									

Step b: Electronics product labels indented twice

Step c: Furniture product labels indented twice

FIGURE 40 Indented Cell Contents

a. Select the **range A6:A8**, the cells containing electronic products labels.

b. Click **Increase Indent** in the Alignment group twice.

The three selected product names are indented below the *Electronics* heading.

c. Select the **range A10:A12**, the cells containing furniture products, and click **Increase Indent** twice.

The three selected product names are indented below the *Furniture* heading. Notice that the one product name appears cut off.

d. Increase the column A width to **26.00**. Save the workbook.

STEP 4 » APPLY BORDERS AND FILL COLOR

You want to apply a light gold fill color to highlight the column headings. In addition, you want to emphasize the percent off and sale prices. You will do this by applying a border around that range. Refer to Figure 41 as you complete Step 4.

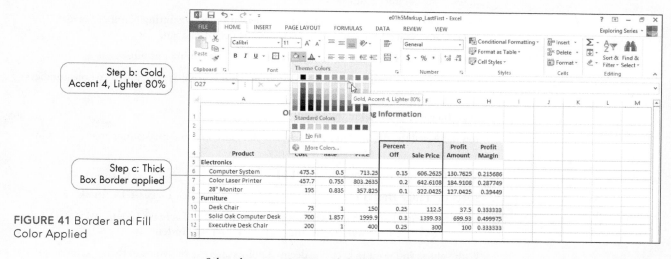

Step b: Gold, Accent 4, Lighter 80%

Step c: Thick Box Border applied

FIGURE 41 Border and Fill Color Applied

a. Select the **range A4:H4** and click the **Fill Color arrow** in the Font group.

b. Click **Gold, Accent 4, Lighter 80%** in the *Theme Colors* section. It is the second color down in the third column from the right.

You applied a fill color to the selected cells to draw attention to these cells.

Hands-On Exercise 5

c. Select the **range E4:F12**, click the **Border arrow** in the Font group, and then select **Thick Box Border**.

You applied a border around the selected cells.

d. Click in an empty cell below the columns of data to deselect the cells. Save the workbook.

STEP 5 » APPLY NUMBER FORMATS AND INCREASE AND DECREASE DECIMAL PLACES

You need to format the values to increase readability and look more professional. You will apply number formats and adjust the number of decimal points displayed. Refer to Figure 42 as you complete Step 5.

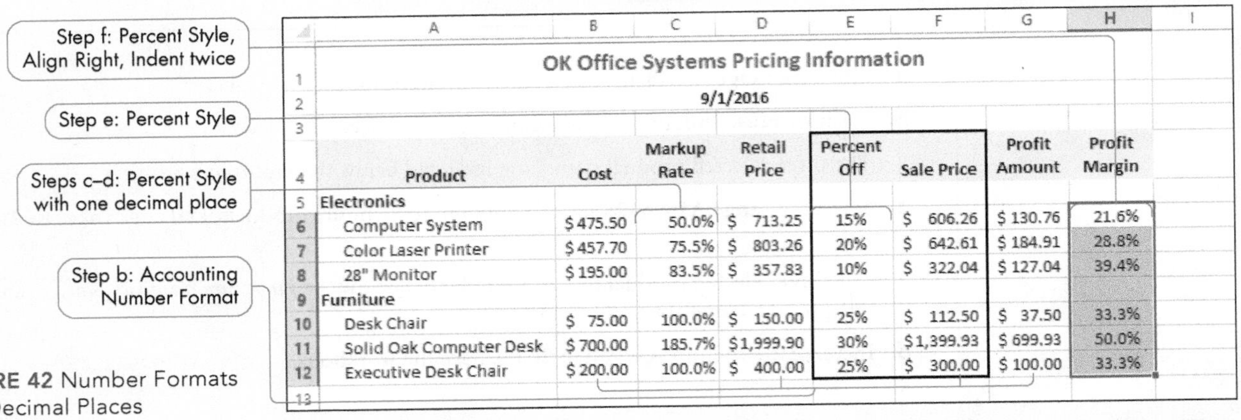

FIGURE 42 Number Formats and Decimal Places

a. Select the **range B6:B12.** Press and hold **Ctrl** as you select the **ranges D6:D12** and **F6:G12**.

Because you want to format nonadjacent ranges with the same formats, you hold down Ctrl.

b. Click **Accounting Number Format** in the Number group. If some cells contain pound signs, increase the column widths as needed.

You formatted the selected nonadjacent ranges with the Accounting Number Format. The dollar signs align on the left cell margins and the decimals align.

c. Select the **range C6:C12** and click **Percent Style** in the Number group.

You formatted the values in the selected ranges with Percent Style, showing whole numbers only.

d. Click **Increase Decimal** in the Number group.

You increased the decimal to show one decimal place to avoid misleading your readers by displaying the values as whole percentages.

e. Apply **Percent Style** to the **range E6:E12**.

f. Select the **range H6:H12**, apply **Percent Style**, and then click **Increase Decimal**.

g. Select the **range E6:E12**, click **Align Right**, and then click **Increase Indent** twice. Select the **range H6:H12**, click **Align Right**, and then click **Increase Indent**.

With values, you want to keep the decimal points aligned, but you can then use Increase Indent to adjust the indent so that the values appear more centered below the column labels.

h. Save the workbook. Keep the workbook open if you plan to continue with the next Hands-On Exercise. If not, close the workbook and exit Excel.

Hands-On Exercise 5

Page Setup and Printing

Although you might distribute workbooks electronically as e-mail attachments or you might upload workbooks to a corporate server, you should prepare the worksheets in the workbook for printing. You should prepare worksheets in case you need to print them or in case others who receive an electronic copy of your workbook need to print the worksheets. The Page Layout tab provides options for controlling the printed worksheet (see Figure 43).

FIGURE 43 Page Layout Tab

In this section, you will select options on the Page Layout tab. Specifically, you will use the Page Setup, Scale to Fit, and Sheet Options groups. After selecting page setup options, you are ready to print your worksheet.

Selecting Page Setup Options

The Page Setup group on the Page Layout tab contains options to set the margins, select orientation, specify page size, select the print area, and apply other options. The *Scale to Fit* group contains options for adjusting the scaling of the spreadsheet on the printed page. When possible, use the commands in these groups to apply page settings. Table 7 lists and describes the commands in the Page Setup group.

TABLE 7 Page Setup Commands	
Command	**Description**
Margins	Displays a menu to select predefined margin settings. The default margins are 0.75" top and bottom and 0.7" left and right. You will often change these margin settings to balance the worksheet data better on the printed page. If you need different margins, select Custom Margins.
Orientation	Displays orientation options. The default page orientation is portrait, which is appropriate for worksheets that contain more rows than columns. Select landscape orientation when worksheets contain more columns than can fit in portrait orientation. For example, the OKOS worksheet might appear better balanced in landscape orientation because it has eight columns.
Size	Displays a list of standard paper sizes. The default size is 8 1/2" by 11". If you have a different paper size, such as legal paper, select it from the list.
Print Area	Displays a list to set or clear the print area. When you have very large worksheets, you might want to print only a portion of that worksheet. To do so, select the range you want to print, click Print Area in the Page Setup group, and then select Set Print Area. When you use the Print commands, only the range you specified will be printed. To clear the print area, click Print Area and select Clear Print Area.
Breaks	Displays a list to insert or remove page breaks.
Background	Enables you to select an image to appear as the background behind the worksheet data when viewed onscreen (backgrounds do not appear when the worksheet is printed).
Print Titles	Enables you to select column headings and row labels to repeat on multiple-page printouts.

Specify Page Options

STEP 1 ≫   To apply several page setup options at once or to access options not found on the Ribbon, click the Page Setup Dialog Box Launcher. The Page Setup dialog box organizes options into four tabs: Page, Margins, Header/Footer, and Sheet. All tabs contain Print and Print Preview buttons. Figure 44 shows the Page tab.

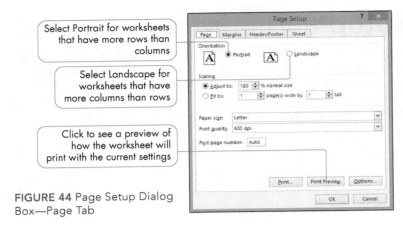

Select Portrait for worksheets that have more rows than columns

Select Landscape for worksheets that have more columns than rows

Click to see a preview of how the worksheet will print with the current settings

FIGURE 44 Page Setup Dialog Box—Page Tab

The Page tab contains options to select the orientation and paper size. In addition, it contains scaling options that are similar to the options in the *Scale to Fit* group on the Page Layout tab. You use scaling options to increase or decrease the size of characters on a printed page, similar to using a zoom setting on a photocopy machine. You can also use the *Fit to* option to force the data to print on a specified number of pages.

Set Margins Options

STEP 2 ›› The Margins tab (see Figure 45) contains options for setting the specific margins. In addition, it contains options to center the worksheet data horizontally or vertically on the page. To balance worksheet data equally between the left and right margins, Excel users often center the page horizontally.

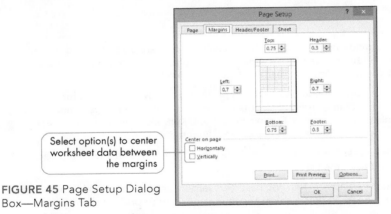

Select option(s) to center worksheet data between the margins

FIGURE 45 Page Setup Dialog Box—Margins Tab

Create Headers and Footers

STEP 3 ›› The Header/Footer tab (see Figure 46) lets you create a header and/or footer that appears at the top and/or bottom of every printed page. Click the arrows to choose from several preformatted entries, or alternatively, you can click Custom Header or Custom Footer, insert text and other objects, and then click the appropriate formatting button to customize your headers and footers. You can use headers and footers to provide additional information about the worksheet. You can include your name, the date the worksheet was prepared, and page numbers, for example.

You can create different headers or footers on different pages, such as one header with the file name on odd-numbered pages and a header containing the date on even-numbered pages. Click the *Different odd and even pages* check box in the Page Setup dialog box (see Figure 46).

Introduction to Excel

You might want the first page to have a different header or footer from the rest of the printed pages, or you might not want a header or footer to show up on the first page but want the header or footer to display on the remaining pages. Click the *Different first page* check box in the Page Setup dialog box to specify a different first page header or footer (see Figure 46).

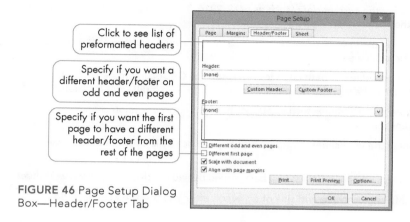

Click to see list of preformatted headers

Specify if you want a different header/footer on odd and even pages

Specify if you want the first page to have a different header/footer from the rest of the pages

FIGURE 46 Page Setup Dialog Box—Header/Footer Tab

Instead of creating headers and footers using the Page Setup dialog box, you can click the Insert tab and click Header & Footer in the Text group. Excel displays the worksheet in ***Page Layout view*** with the insertion point in the center area of the header. You can click inside the left, center, or right section of a header or footer. When you do, Excel displays the Header & Footer Tools Design contextual tab (see Figure 47). You can enter text or insert data from the Header & Footer Elements group on the tab. Table 8 lists and describes the options in the Header & Footer Elements group. To get back to ***Normal view***, click any cell in the worksheet and click Normal in the Workbook Views group on the View tab.

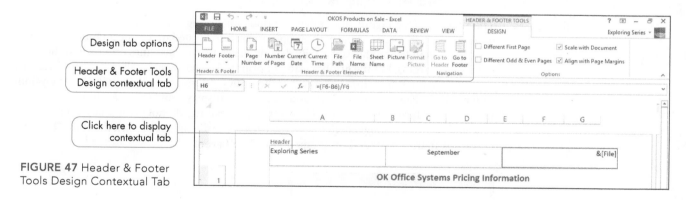

Design tab options

Header & Footer Tools Design contextual tab

Click here to display contextual tab

FIGURE 47 Header & Footer Tools Design Contextual Tab

TABLE 8 Header & Footer Elements Options

Option Name	Result
Page Number	Inserts the code &[Page] to display the current page number.
Number of Pages	Inserts the code &[Pages] to display the total number of pages that will print.
Current Date	Inserts the code &[Date] to display the current date, such as 5/19/2016. The date updates to the current date when you open or print the worksheet.
Current Time	Inserts the code &[Time] to display the current time, such as 5:15 PM. The time updates to the current time when you open or print the worksheet.
File Path	Inserts the code &[Path]&[File] to display the path and file name, such as C:\Documents\e01h4Markup. This information changes if you save the workbook with a different name or in a different location.
File Name	Inserts the code &[File] to display the file name, such as e01h4Markup. This information changes if you save the workbook with a different name.
Sheet Name	Inserts the code &[Tab] to display the worksheet name, such as September. This information changes if you rename the worksheet.
Picture	Inserts the code &[Picture] to display and print an image as a background behind the data, not just the worksheet.
Format Picture	Enables you to adjust the brightness, contrast, and size of an image after you use the Picture option.

TIP View Tab

If you click the View tab and click Page Layout, Excel displays an area *Click to add header* at the top of the worksheet.

Select Sheet Options

STEP 5 ›› The Sheet tab (see Figure 48) contains options for setting the print area, print titles, print options, and page order. Some of these options are also located in the Sheet Options group on the Page Layout tab on the Ribbon. By default, Excel displays gridlines onscreen to show you each cell's margins, but the gridlines do not print unless you specifically select the Gridlines check box in the Page Setup dialog box or the Print Gridlines check box in the Sheet Options group on the Page Layout tab. In addition, Excel displays row (1, 2, 3, etc.) and column (A, B, C, etc.) headings onscreen. However, these headings do not print unless you click the *Row and column headings* check box in the Page Setup dialog box or click the Print Headings check box in the Sheet Options group on the Page Layout tab.

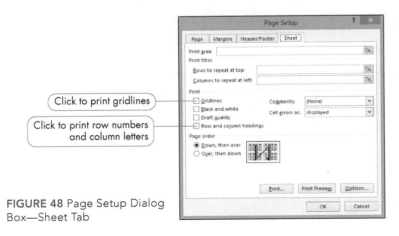

FIGURE 48 Page Setup Dialog Box—Sheet Tab

Click to print gridlines

Click to print row numbers and column letters

TIP | Printing Gridlines and Headings

For most worksheets, you do not need to print gridlines and row/column headings. However, when you want to display and print cell formulas instead of formula results, you might want to print the gridlines and row/column headings. Doing so will help you analyze your formulas. The gridlines help you see the cell boundaries, and the headings help you identify what data are in each cell. At times, you might want to display gridlines to separate data on a regular printout to increase readability.

Previewing and Printing a Worksheet

STEP 4 Before printing a worksheet, you should click the File tab and select Print. The Microsoft Office Backstage view displays print options and displays the worksheet in print preview mode. This mode helps you see in advance if the data are balanced on the page or if data will print on multiple pages.

You can specify the number of copies to print and which printer to use to print the worksheet. The first option in the Settings area enables you to specify what to print. The default option is Print Active Sheets. You can choose other options, such as Print Entire Workbook or Print Selection. You can also specify which pages to print. If you are connected to a printer capable of duplex printing, you can print on only one side or print on both sides. You can also collate, change the orientation, specify the paper size, adjust the margins, and adjust the scaling.

The bottom of the Print window indicates how many pages will print. If you do not like how the worksheet will print, click the Page Layout tab so that you can adjust margins, scaling, column widths, and so on until the worksheet data appear the way you want them to print.

TIP | Printing Multiple Worksheets

To print more than one worksheet at a time, select the sheets you want to print. To select adjacent sheets, click the first sheet tab, press and hold Shift, and then click the last sheet tab. To select nonadjacent sheets, press and hold Ctrl as you click each sheet tab. When you display the Print options in the Microsoft Office Backstage view, Print Active Sheets is one of the default settings. If you want to print all of the worksheets within the workbook, change the setting to Print Entire Workbook.

Quick
Concepts

1. What helps determine whether you use portrait or landscape orientation for a worksheet?

2. Why would you select a *Center on page* option if you have already set the margins?

3. List at least five elements you can insert in a header or footer.

4. Why would you want to print gridlines and row and column headings?

6 Page Setup and Printing

You are ready to complete the OKOS worksheet. Before printing the worksheet for your supervisor, you want to make sure the data will appear professional when printed. You will adjust some page setup options to put the finishing touches on the worksheet.

Skills covered: Set Page Orientation • Set Margin Options • Create a Header • View in Print Preview and Print • Adjust Scaling and Set Sheet Options

STEP 1 » SET PAGE ORIENTATION

Because the worksheet has several columns, you decide to print it in landscape orientation.

    a. Open *e01h5Markup_LastFirst* if you closed it at the end of Hands-On Exercise 5 and save it as **e01h6Markup_LastFirst**, changing *h5* to *h6*.

    b. Click the **PAGE LAYOUT tab**.

    c. Click **Orientation** in the Page Setup group.

    d. Select **Landscape** from the list. Save the workbook.

    If you print the worksheet, the data will print in landscape orientation.

STEP 2 » SET MARGIN OPTIONS

You want to set a 1" top margin and center the data between the left and right margins.

    a. Click **Margins** in the Page Setup group on the PAGE LAYOUT tab.

    As you review the list of options, you notice the list does not contain an option to center the worksheet data horizontally.

    b. Select **Custom Margins**.

    The Page Setup dialog box opens with the Margins tab options displayed.

    c. Click the **Top spin arrow** to display **1**.

    You set a 1" top margin. For the OKOS worksheet, you do not need to change the left and right margins because you will center the worksheet data horizontally between the original margins.

    d. Click the **Horizontally check box** in the *Center on page* section and click **OK**. Save the workbook.

    The worksheet data are centered between the left and right margins.

 TIP **Page Setup Dialog Box**

You can click the Page Setup Dialog Box Launcher in the Page Setup group to quickly display the Page Setup dialog box. From there, you can click the Margins tab and set the desired margins.

Hands-On Exercise 6

STEP 3 ≫ CREATE A HEADER

To document the worksheet, you want to include your name, the current date, and the worksheet tab name in a header. Refer to Figure 49 as you complete Step 3.

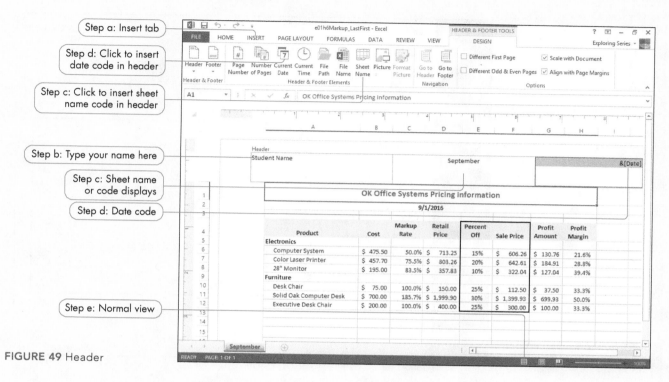

FIGURE 49 Header

Step a: Insert tab

Step d: Click to insert date code in header

Step c: Click to insert sheet name code in header

Step b: Type your name here

Step c: Sheet name or code displays

Step d: Date code

Step e: Normal view

a. Click the **INSERT tab** and click **Header & Footer** in the Text group.

Excel displays the DESIGN tab and the worksheet displays in Page Layout view, which displays the header area, margin space, and ruler. The insertion point blinks inside the center section of the header.

b. Click in the left section of the header and type your name.

c. Click in the center section of the header and click **Sheet Name** in the Header & Footer Elements group on the DESIGN tab.

Excel inserts the code &[Tab]. This code displays the name of the worksheet. If you change the worksheet tab name, the header will reflect the new sheet name.

d. Click in the right section of the header and click **Current Date** in the Header & Footer Elements group on the DESIGN tab.

Excel inserts the code &[Date]. This code displays the current date based on the computer clock when you print the worksheet. If you want a specific date to appear regardless of the date you open or print the worksheet, you would have to type that date manually. When you click in a different header section, the codes, such as &[Tab], display the actual tab name instead of the code.

e. Click in any cell in the worksheet, click **Normal** on the status bar, and then save the workbook.

Normal view displays the worksheet, but does not display the header or margins.

Hands-On Exercise 6

57

STEP 4 ›› VIEW IN PRINT PREVIEW AND PRINT

Before printing the worksheet, you should preview it. Doing so helps you detect margin problems and other issues, such as a single row or column of data flowing onto a new page. Refer to Figure 50 as you complete Step 4.

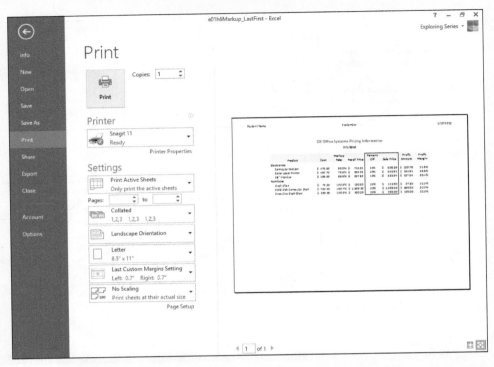

FIGURE 50 Worksheet in Print Preview

a. Click the **FILE tab** and click **Print**.

The Microsoft Office Backstage view displays print options and a preview of the worksheet.

b. Verify the Printer box displays the printer that you want to use to print your worksheet.

c. Click **Print** to print the worksheet and save the workbook.

Check your printed worksheet to make sure the data are formatted correctly. After you click Print, the HOME tab displays. If you decide not to print at this time, click the **Back arrow** to display the Ribbon again.

STEP 5 ›› ADJUST SCALING AND SET SHEET OPTIONS

You want to print a copy of the worksheet formulas to check the logic of the formulas. You need to display the formulas, select options to print gridlines and headings, and then decrease the scaling so that the data print on one page. Refer to Figure 51 as you complete Step 5.

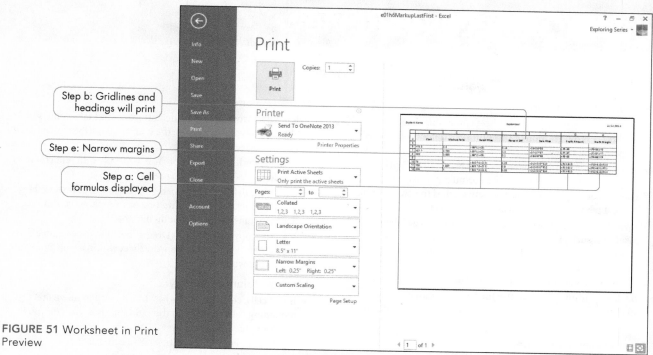

Step b: Gridlines and headings will print

Step e: Narrow margins

Step a: Cell formulas displayed

FIGURE 51 Worksheet in Print Preview

a. Press **Ctrl+`** to display cell formulas.

b. Click the **PAGE LAYOUT tab**. Click the **Print Gridlines check box** in the Sheet Options group and click the **Print Headings check box** in the Sheet Options group.

   Because you want to print cell formulas, it is helpful to display the gridlines and row and column headings on that printout.

c. Click the **FILE tab** and click **Print**.

   The bottom of the Print Preview displays 1 of 2, indicating the worksheet no longer prints on one page.

d. Click **Next Page** (the right triangle at the bottom of the Microsoft Office Backstage view) to view the contents of the second page and click the **Back arrow** to display the Ribbon again.

e. Click **Margins** in the Page Setup group and select **Narrow**.

f. Select the **range B4:H12**, click **Print Area** in the Page Setup group, and then select **Set Print Area**.

g. Click the **Scale spin arrow** in the *Scale to Fit* group on the PAGE LAYOUT tab until it displays **90%**.

   If you want to verify that the worksheet will print on one page, display it in print preview.

h. Save and close the workbook, and submit based on your instructor's directions.

   Check your printed worksheet to make sure the data are formatted correctly.

Chapter Objectives Review

After reading this chapter, you have accomplished the following objectives:

1. Explore the Excel window.
- A worksheet is a single spreadsheet containing data. A workbook is a collection of one or more related worksheets contained in a single file.
- Identify Excel window elements: The Name Box displays the name of the current cell. The Formula Bar displays the contents of the current cell. The active cell is the current cell. A sheet tab shows the name of the worksheet.
- Identify columns, rows, and cells: Columns have alphabetical headings, such as A, B, C. Rows have numbers, such as 1, 2, 3. A cell is the intersection of a column and row and is indicated like A5.
- Navigate in and among worksheets: Use the arrow keys to navigate within a sheet, or use the Go To command to go to a specific cell. Click a sheet tab to display the contents on another worksheet.

2. Enter and edit cell data.
- You should plan the worksheet design by stating the purpose, deciding what input values are needed, and then deciding what outputs are needed. Next, you enter and format data in a worksheet. Finally, you document, save, and then share a workbook.
- Enter text: Text may contain letters, numbers, symbols, and spaces. Text aligns at the left side of a cell.
- Enter values: Values are numbers that represent a quantity. Values align at the right side of a cell by default.
- Enter dates: Excel stores dates as serial numbers so that you can calculate the number of days between dates.
- Enter formulas: A formula is used to perform calculations. The formula results display in the cells.
- Edit and clear contents: You can clear the cell contents and/or formats.

3. Create formulas.
- Use cell references in formulas: Use references, such as =B5+B6, instead of values within formulas.
- Apply the order of precedence: The most commonly used operators are performed in this sequence: Exponentiation, Multiplication, Division, Addition, and Subtraction. Use parentheses to perform a lower operation first.
- Use semi-selection to create a formula: When building a formula, you can click a cell containing a value to enter that cell reference in the formula.

4. Use Auto Fill.
- Copy formulas with Auto Fill: To copy a formula down a column or across a row, double-click or drag the fill handle.
- Complete sequences with Auto Fill: Use Auto Fill to copy formulas, number patterns, month names, etc.

5. Display cell formulas.
- By default, the results of formulas appear in cells.
- You can display formulas by pressing Ctrl+`.

6. Manage worksheets.
- Rename a worksheet: The default worksheet tab name is Sheet1, but you can change the name to describe the contents of a worksheet.
- Change worksheet tab color: You can apply different colors to the sheet tabs so they stand out.
- Insert and delete a worksheet: You can insert new worksheets to include related data within one workbook, or you can delete extra worksheets you do not need.
- Move or copy a worksheet: Drag a sheet tab to rearrange the worksheets. You can copy a worksheet within a workbook or to another workbook.

7. Manage columns and rows.
- Insert cells, columns, and rows: Insert a cell to move the remaining cells down or to the right. Insert a new column or row for data.
- Delete cells, columns, and rows: You can delete cells, columns, and rows you no longer need.
- Adjust column width: Double-click between the column headings to widen a column based on the longest item in that column, or drag the border between column headings to increase or decrease a column width.
- Adjust row height: Drag the border between row headings to increase or decrease the height of a row.
- Hide and unhide columns and rows: Hiding rows and columns protects confidential data from being displayed.

8. Select, move, copy, and paste data.
- Select a range: A range may be a single cell or a rectangular block of cells.
- Move a range to another location: After selecting a range, cut it from its location. Then make the top-left corner of the destination range the active cell and paste the range there.
- Copy and paste a range: After selecting a range, click Copy, click the top-left corner of the destination range, and then click Paste to make a copy of the original range.
- Use Paste Options and Paste Special: The Paste Special option enables you to specify how the data are pasted into the worksheet.
- Copy Excel data to other programs: You can copy Excel data and paste it in other programs, such as in Word or PowerPoint.

9. Apply alignment and font options.
- Merge and center labels: Type a label in the left cell, select a range including the data you typed, and then click Merge & Center to merge cells and center the label within the newly merged cell.
- Change horizontal and vertical cell alignment: The default horizontal alignment depends on the data entered, and the default vertical alignment is Bottom Align.

- Wrap text: Use the Wrap Text option to present text on multiple lines in order to avoid having extra-wide columns.
- Increase and decrease indent: To indicate hierarchy of data or to offset a label you can increase or decrease how much the data are indented in a cell.
- Apply borders and fill colors: Borders and fill colors help improve readability of worksheets.

10. Apply number formats.

- The default number format is General, which does not apply any particular format to values. Apply appropriate formats to values to present the data with the correct symbols and decimal alignment. For example, Accounting Number Format is a common number format for monetary values.
- Increase and decrease decimal places: After applying a number format, you can increase or decrease the number of decimal places displayed.

11. Select page setup options.

- The Page Layout tab on the Ribbon contains options for setting margins, selecting orientation, specifying page size, selecting the print area, and applying other settings.

- Specify page options: Page options include orientation, paper size, and scaling.
- Set margin options: You can set the left, right, top, and bottom margins. In addition, you can center worksheet data horizontally and vertically on a page.
- Create headers and footers: You can insert a header or footer to display documentation, such as your name, date, time, and worksheet tab name.
- Select sheet options: Sheet options control the print area, print titles, print options, and page order.

12. Preview and print a worksheet.

- Before printing a worksheet, you should display a preview to ensure the data will print correctly. The Print Preview helps you see if margins are correct or if isolated rows or columns will print on separate pages.
- After making appropriate adjustments, you can print the worksheet.

Key Terms Matching

Match the key terms with their definitions. Write the key term letter by the appropriate numbered definition.

a. Alignment
b. Auto Fill
c. Cell
d. Column width
e. Fill color
f. Fill handle
g. Formula
h. Formula Bar
i. Input area
j. Name Box

k. Order of precedence
l. Output area
m. Range
n. Row height
o. Sheet tab
p. Text
q. Value
r. Workbook
s. Worksheet
t. Wrap text

1. _____ A spreadsheet that contains formulas, functions, values, text, and visual aids.

2. _____ A file containing related worksheets.

3. _____ A range of cells containing values for variables used in formulas.

4. _____ A range of cells containing results based on manipulating the variables.

5. _____ Identifies the address of the current cell.

6. _____ Displays the content (text, value, date, or formula) in the active cell.

7. _____ Displays the name of a worksheet within a workbook.

8. _____ The intersection of a column and row.

9. _____ Includes letters, numbers, symbols, and spaces.

10. _____ A number that represents a quantity or an amount.

11. _____ Rules that control the sequence in which Excel performs arithmetic operations.

12. _____ Enables you to copy the contents of a cell or cell range or to continue a sequence by dragging the fill handle over an adjacent cell or range of cells.

13. _____ A small green square at the bottom-right corner of a cell.

14. _____ The horizontal measurement of a column.

15. _____ The vertical measurement of a row.

16. _____ A rectangular group of cells.

17. _____ The position of data between the cell margins.

18. _____ Formatting that enables a label to appear on multiple lines within the current cell.

19. _____ The background color appearing behind data in a cell.

20. _____ A combination of cell references, operators, values, and/or functions used to perform a calculation.

Multiple Choice

1. What is the first step in planning an effective worksheet?

   (a) Enter labels, values, and formulas.

   (b) State the purpose of the worksheet.

   (c) Identify the input and output areas.

   (d) Decide how to format the worksheet data.

2. What Excel interface item displays the address of the current cell?

   (a) Quick Access Toolbar

   (b) Formula Bar

   (c) Status bar

   (d) Name Box

3. Given the formula =B1*B2+B3/B4^2 where B1 contains 3, B2 contains 4, B3 contains 32, and B4 contains 4, what is the result?

   (a) 14

   (b) 121

   (c) 76

   (d) 9216

4. Why would you press Ctrl+` in Excel?

   (a) To display the print options

   (b) To undo a mistake you made

   (c) To display cell formulas

   (d) To enable the AutoComplete feature

5. Which of the following is a nonadjacent range?

   (a) C15:D30

   (b) L15:L65

   (c) A1:Z99

   (d) A1:A10, D1:D10

6. If you want to balance a title over several columns, what do you do?

   (a) Enter the data in the cell that is about midway across the spreadsheet.

   (b) Merge and center the data over all columns.

   (c) Use the Increase Indent command until the title looks balanced.

   (d) Click Center to center the title horizontally over several columns.

7. Which of the following characteristics is not applicable to the Accounting Number Format?

   (a) Dollar sign immediately on the left side of the value

   (b) Commas to separate thousands

   (c) Two decimal places

   (d) Zero values displayed as hyphens

8. You selected and copied worksheet data containing formulas. However, you want the pasted copy to contain the current formula results rather than formulas. What do you do?

   (a) Click Paste in the Clipboard group on the Home tab.

   (b) Click the Paste arrow in the Clipboard group and select Formulas.

   (c) Click the Paste arrow in the Clipboard group and select Values & Source Formatting.

   (d) Display the Paste Special dialog box and select *Formulas and number formats*.

9. Assume that the data on a worksheet consume a whole printed page and a couple of columns on a second page. You can do all of the following except what to force the data to print all on one page?

   (a) Decrease the Scale value.

   (b) Increase the left and right margins.

   (c) Decrease column widths if possible.

   (d) Select a smaller range as the print area.

10. What should you do if you see a column of pound signs (###) instead of values or results of formulas?

    (a) Increase the zoom percentage.

    (b) Delete the column.

    (c) Adjust the row height.

    (d) Increase the column width.

Practice Exercises

1 Mathematics Review

You want to brush up on your math skills to test your logic by creating formulas in Excel. You realize that you should avoid values in formulas most of the time. Therefore, you created an input area that contains values you will use in your formulas. To test your knowledge of formulas, you will create an output area that will contain a variety of formulas using cell references from the input area. You also need to include a formatted title, the date prepared, and your name. After creating and verifying formula results, you will change input values and observe changes in the formula results. You want to display cell formulas, so you will create a picture copy of the formulas view. This exercise follows the same set of skills as used in Hands-On Exercises 1–4 and 6 in the chapter. Refer to Figure 52 as you complete this exercise.

	A	B	C	D	E
1				Excel Formulas and Order of Precedence	
2	Date Created:	42614		Student Name	
3					
4	Input Area:			Output Area:	
5	First Value	2		Sum of 1st and 2nd values	=B5+B6
6	Second Value	4		Difference between 4th and 1st values	=B8-B5
7	Third Value	6		Product of 2nd and 3rd values	=B6*B7
8	Fourth Value	8		Quotient of 3rd and 1st values	=B7/B5
9				2nd value to the power of 3rd value	=B6^B7
10				1st value added to product of 2nd and 4th values and difference between sum and 3rd value	=B5+B6*B8-B7
11				Product of sum of 1st and 2nd and difference between 4th and 3rd values	=(B5+B6)*(B8-B7)
12				Product of 1st and 2nd added to product of 3rd and 4th values	=(B5*B6)+(B7*B8)

FIGURE 52 Formula Practice

a. Open *e01p1Math* and save it as **e01p1Math_LastFirst**.

b. Type the current date in **cell B2** in this format: 9/1/2016. Type your first and last names in **cell D2**.

c. Adjust the column widths by doing the following:
   - Click in any cell in column A and click **Format** in the Cells group.
   - Select **Column Width**, type **12.57** in the **Column width box**, and then click **OK**.
   - Click in any cell in column B and set the width to **11**.
   - Click in any cell in column D and set the width to **35.57**.

d. Select the **range A1:E1**, click **Merge & Center** in the Alignment group, click **Bold**, and then apply **14 pt font size**.

e. Select the **range B5:B8** and click **Center** in the Alignment group.

f. Select the **range D10:D12** and click **Wrap Text** in the Alignment group.

g. Enter the following formulas in column E:
   - Click **cell E5**. Type **=B5+B6** and press **Enter**. Excel adds the value stored in cell B5 (1) to the value stored in cell B6 (2). The result (3) appears in cell E5, as described in cell D5.
   - Enter appropriate formulas in **cells E6:E8**, pressing **Enter** after entering each formula. Subtract to calculate a difference, multiply to calculate a product, and divide to calculate a quotient.
   - Type **=B6^B7** in **cell E9** and press **Enter**. Calculate the answer: 2*2*2 = 8.
   - Enter **=B5+B6*B8-B7** in **cell E10** and press **Enter**. Calculate the answer: 2*4 = 8; 1+8 = 9; 9−3 = 6. Multiplication occurs first, followed by addition, and finally subtraction.
   - Enter **=(B5+B6)*(B8-B7)** in **cell E11** and press **Enter**. Calculate the answer: 1+2 = 3; 4−3 = 1; 3*1 = 3. This formula is almost identical to the previous formula; however, calculations in parentheses occur before the multiplication.
   - Enter **=B5*B6+B7*B8** in **cell E12** and press **Enter**. Calculate the answer: 1*2 = 2; 3*4 = 12; 2+12 = 14.

h. Edit a formula and the input values:

- Click **cell E12** and click in the Formula Bar to edit the formula. Add parentheses as shown: **=(B5*B6)+(B7*B8)** and click **Enter** to the left side of the Formula Bar. The answer is still 14. The parentheses do not affect order of precedence because multiplication occurred before the addition. The parentheses help improve the readability of the formula.
- Type **2** in **cell B5**, **4** in **cell B6**, **6** in **cell B7**, and **8** in **cell B8**.
- Double-check the results of the formulas using a calculator or your head. The new results in cells E5:E12 should be 6, 6, 24, 3, 4096, 28, 12, and 56, respectively.

i. Double-click the **Sheet1 tab**, type **Results**, and then press **Enter**. Right-click the **Results tab**, select **Move or Copy**, click **(move to end)** in the *Before sheet* section, click the **Create a copy check box**, and then click **OK**. Double-click the **Results (2) tab**, type **Formulas**, and then press **Enter**.

j. Click the **FORMULAS tab** and click **Show Formulas** in the Formula Auditing group. Double-click between the column A and column B headings to adjust the column A width. Double-click between the column B and column C headings to adjust the column B width. Set **24.0 width** for column D.

k. Select the **range A1:E12**, click the **HOME tab**, click the **Copy arrow** in the Clipboard group, and then select **Copy as Picture**. In the Copy Picture dialog box, click **As shown on screen** and click **OK**.

l. Press **Delete** to delete the selected worksheet data and click **Paste**.

> **TROUBLESHOOTING:** If you do not delete the worksheet data, the pasted picture image will display over the data, creating a double effect.

m. Make sure the Formulas worksheet is active, click the **PAGE LAYOUT tab**, and then do the following:

- Click **Orientation** in the Page Setup group and select **Landscape**.
- Click the **View Gridlines check box** in the Sheet Options group to deselect it. The worksheet gridlines are hidden, but the gridlines in the picture still display.

n. Click the **FILE tab** and click **Print**. Verify that the worksheet will print on one page. Press **Esc** to close the Print Preview.

o. Save and close the file, and submit based on your instructor's directions.

2 Calendar Formatting

 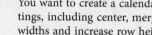

You want to create a calendar for May 2016. The calendar will enable you to practice alignment settings, including center, merge and center, and indents. In addition, you will need to adjust column widths and increase row height to create cells large enough to enter important information, such as birthdays, in your calendar. You will create a formula and use Auto Fill to complete the days of the week and the days within each week. To improve the appearance of the calendar, you will add fill colors, font colors, borders, and clip art. This exercise follows the same set of skills as used in Hands-On Exercises 1–6 in the chapter. Refer to Figure 53 as you complete this exercise.

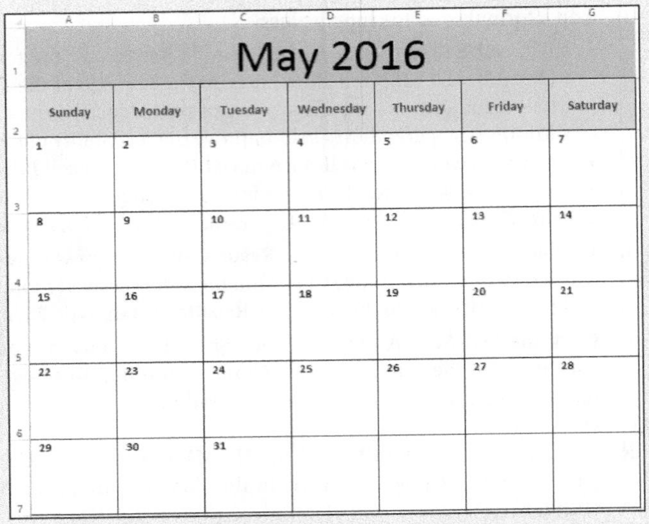

FIGURE 53 May 2016 Calendar

a. Click the **FILE tab**, select **New**, and then click **Blank workbook**. Save the workbook as **e01p2May2016_LastFirst**.

b. Type '**May 2016** in **cell A1** and click **Enter** on the left side of the Formula Bar.

> **TROUBLESHOOTING:** If you do not type the apostrophe before *May 2016*, the cell will display *May-16* instead of *May 2016*.

c. Format the title:
   - Select the **range A1:G1** and click **Merge & Center** in the Alignment group.
   - Apply **48 pt font size**.
   - Click the **Fill Color arrow** and click **Green, Accent 6, Lighter 40%** in the *Theme Colors* section of the color palette.

d. Complete the days of the week:
   - Type **Sunday** in **cell A2** and click **Enter** on the left side of the Formula Bar.
   - Drag the **cell A2 fill handle** across the row through **cell G2** to use Auto Fill to complete the rest of the weekdays.
   - Click the **Fill Color arrow** and select **Green, Accent 6, Lighter 60%**. Click the **Font Color arrow** and click **Green, Accent 6, Darker 50%**. Apply bold and **14 pt font size**. Click **Middle Align** and click **Center** in the Alignment group.

e. Complete the days of the month:
   - Type **1** in **cell A3** and press **Ctrl+Enter**. Drag the **cell A3 fill handle** across the row through **cell G3**. Click **Auto Fill Options** in the bottom-right corner of the filled data and select **Fill Series**.
   - Type **=A3+7** in **cell A4** and press **Ctrl+Enter**. Usually you avoid numbers in formulas, but the number of days in a week is always 7. Drag the **cell A4 fill handle** down through **cell A7** to get the date for each Sunday in May.
   - Keep the **range A4:A7** selected and drag the fill handle across through **cell G7**. Select the **range D7:G7** and press **Delete** to delete the extra days.

f. Format the columns and rows:
   - Select **columns A:G**. Click **Format** in the Cells group, select **Column Width**, type **16** in the **Column width box**, and then click **OK**.
   - Select **row 2**. Click **Format** in the Cells group, select **Row Height**, type **54**, and then click **OK**.

- Select **rows 3:7**. Set an **80 row height**.
- Select the **range A2:G7**. Click the **Borders arrow** in the Font group and select **All Borders**.
- Select the **range A3:G7**. Click **Top Align** and **Align Left** in the Alignment group. Click **Increase Indent**. Bold the numbers and apply **12 pt font size**.

g. Double-click the **Sheet1 tab**, type **May**, and then press **Enter**.

h. Deselect the range and click the **PAGE LAYOUT tab**. Click **Orientation** in the Page Setup group and select **Landscape**.

i. Click the **INSERT tab** and click **Header & Footer** in the Text group. Click in the left side of the header and type your name. Click in the center of the header and click **Sheet Name** in the Header & Footer Elements group on the DESIGN tab. Click in the right side of the header and click **File Name** in the Header & Footer Elements group on the DESIGN tab. Click in any cell in the workbook and click **Normal** on the status bar.

j. Save and close the file, and submit based on your instructor's directions.

3 Downtown Theatre

You are the assistant manager at Downtown Theatre, where touring Broadway plays and musicals are performed. You need to complete a spreadsheet to help you analyze ticket sales by seating chart for each performance. The spreadsheet will identify the seating sections, total seats in each section, and the number of seats sold for a performance. You will then calculate the percentage of seats sold and unsold. This exercise follows the same set of skills as used in Hands-On Exercises 1–6 in the chapter. Refer to Figure 54 as you complete this exercise.

	A	B	C	D	E
1	Downtown Theatre				
2	Ticket Sales by Seating Section				
3	3/31/2016				
4					
5	Section	Available Seats	Seats Sold	Percentage Sold	Percentage Unsold
6	Box Seats	25	12	48.0%	52.0%
7	Front Floor	120	114	95.0%	5.0%
8	Back Floor	132	108	81.8%	18.2%
9	Tier 1	40	40	100.0%	0.0%
10	Mezzanine	144	138	95.8%	4.2%
11	Balcony	106	84	79.2%	20.8%

FIGURE 54 Theatre Seating Data

a. Open *e01p3TicketSales* and save it as **e01p3TicketSales_LastFirst**.

b. Double-click the **Sheet1 tab**, type **Seating**, and then press **Enter**.

c. Type **3/31/2016** in **cell A3** and press **Enter**.

d. Adjust alignments and font attributes by doing the following from the Alignment and Font groups on the HOME tab:
- Select the **range A1:E1**, click **Merge & Center**, click **Bold**, click the **Font Size arrow**, and then select **16**.
- Use the Merge & Center command to merge the **range A2:E2** and center the subtitle.
- Use the Merge & Center command to merge the **range A3:E3** and center the date.
- Select the **range A5:E5**, click **Wrap Text**, click **Center**, and then click **Bold** to format the column labels.

e. Right-click the **row 9 heading** and select **Insert** from the shortcut menu to insert a new row. Type the following data in the new row: **Back Floor, 132, 108**.

f. Move the Balcony row to be the last row by doing the following:

- Click the **row 6 heading** and click **Cut** in the Clipboard group on the HOME tab.
- Right-click the **row 12 heading** and select **Insert Cut Cells** from the menu.

g. Adjust column widths by doing the following:

- Double-click between the column A and column B headings.
- Select **columns B** and **C headings** to select the columns, click **Format** in the Cells group, select **Column Width**, type **9** in the **Column width box**, and then click **OK**. Because columns B and C contain similar data, you set the same width for these columns.
- Set the width of columns D and E to **12**.

h. Select the **range B6:C11**, click **Align Right** in the Alignment group on the HOME tab, and then click **Increase Indent** twice in the Alignment group.

i. Calculate and format the percentage of sold and unsold seats by doing the following:

- Click **cell D6**. Type **=C6/B6** and press **Tab** to enter the formula and make cell E6 the active cell. This formula divides the number of seats sold by the total number of Box Seats.
- Type **=(B6-C6)/B6** and click **Enter** on the left side of the Formula Bar to enter the formula and keep cell E6 the active cell. This formula must first subtract the number of sold seats from the available seats to calculate the number of unsold seats. The difference is divided by the total number of available seats to determine the percentage of unsold seats.
- Select the **range D6:E6**, click **Percent Style** in the Number group on the HOME tab, and then click **Increase Decimal** in the Number group. Keep the range selected.
- Double-click the **cell E6 fill handle** to copy the selected formulas down their respective columns. Keep the range selected.
- Click **Align Right** in the Alignment group and click **Increase Indent** twice in the Alignment group. These actions will help center the data below the column labels. Do not click Center; doing so will center each value and cause the decimal points not to align. Deselect the range.

j. Display and preserve a screenshot of the formulas by doing the following:

- Click **New sheet**, double-click the **Sheet1 tab**, type **Formulas**, and then press **Enter**.
- Click **Select All** in the top-left corner above the row headings and to the left of the column headings, click the **Fill Color arrow** in the Font group, and then click **White, Background 1**. Applying this fill color will prevent the cell gridlines from bleeding through the screenshot you are about to embed.
- Click the **Seating sheet tab**, click the **FORMULAS tab**, and then click **Show Formulas** in the Formula Auditing group to display cell formulas.
- Click **cell A1** and drag down to **cell E11** to select the range of data. Click the **HOME tab**, click **Copy arrow** in the Clipboard group, select **Copy as Picture**, and then click **OK**.
- Click the **Formulas sheet tab**, click **cell A1**, and then click **Paste**.
- Click the **PAGE LAYOUT tab**, click **Orientation** in the Page Setup group, and then select **Landscape**.
- Click the **Seating sheet tab**, click the **FORMULAS tab**, and then click **Show Formulas** in the Formula Auditing group to hide the cell formulas.

k. Click **cell A1**. Click the **PAGE LAYOUT tab**, click **Margins** in the Page Setup group, and then select **Custom Margins**. Click the **Horizontally check box** and click **Print Preview**. Excel centers the data horizontally based on the widest item. Press **Esc** to leave the Print Preview mode.

l. Click the **Page Setup Dialog Box Launcher**, click the **Header/Footer tab** in the Page Setup dialog box, click **Custom Footer**, type your name in the **Left section box**, click in the **Center section box**, click **Insert File Name**, click in the **Right section box**, click **Insert Sheet Name**, and then click **OK**. Click **OK**.

m. Save and close the file, and submit based on your instructor's directions.

1 Restaurant Receipt

FROM SCRATCH

Matt, the owner of Matt's Sports Grill in Toledo, Ohio, asked you to help him create a receipt spreadsheet that he can use until his new system arrives. He wants an input area for the total food and beverage purchases, the sales tax rate, and the tip rate. The formatted receipt should include the subtotal, tax, tip, and total amount for a customer. Refer to Figure 55 as you complete this exercise.

	A	B	C	D	E
1	**Input Area**			**Matt's Sports Grill**	
2	Food & Beverages	$ 9.39		Toledo, Ohio	
3	Sales Tax Rate	6.5%			
4	Tip Rate	18.0%		Food & Beverages	$ 9.39
5				Sales Tax Amount	0.61
6				Subtotal	$ 10.00
7				Tip Amount	1.69
8				**Total Bill**	$ 11.69
9					
10				*Thank you for dining with us.*	

FIGURE 55 Matt's Sports Grill Receipt

a. Open a new Excel workbook, save it as **e01m1Receipt_LastFirst**, and then rename *Sheet1* as **Receipt**.

b. Enter the four labels in the **range A1:A4** in the Input Area as shown in Figure 56. Type **9.39**, **0.065**, and **.18** in the **range B2:B4**. Apply these formats to the Input Area:
   - Merge and center the *Input Area* title over both columns. Apply bold and **Blue, Accent 1, Lighter 40% fill color** to the title. Adjust the width of the first column.
   - Apply the **Accounting Number Format** and **Percent Style** format with the respective decimal places as shown in the **range B2:B4**.

c. Enter the labels in the receipt area in column D. Use Format Painter to copy the formats of the title in **cells A1** and **D1**. Merge and center the city and state in the **range D2:E2**. Change the width of column D to **17**. Indent the *Subtotal* and *Tip Amount* labels twice each. Apply bold to *Total Bill* and apply italic to *Thank you for dining with us*.

d. Enter the following formulas for the receipt:
   - **Food & Beverages:** Enter a formula that reads the value in the Input Area; do not retype the value in cell E4.
   - **Sales Tax Amount:** Calculate the product of the food & beverages and the sales tax rate.
   - **Subtotal:** Determine the formula needed.
   - **Tip Amount:** Calculate the tip based on the pretax amount and the tip rate.
   - **Total Bill:** Determine the formula needed.

e. Apply **Accounting Number Format** to the *Food & Beverages*, *Subtotal*, and *Total Bill* values, if necessary. Apply **Comma Style** and underline to the *Sales Tax Amount* and *Tip Amount* values. Apply the **Double Underline style** to the *Total Bill* value.

f. Set **1.5"** top margin and center the data horizontally on the page.

g. Insert a footer with your name on the left side, the sheet name code in the center, and the file name code on the right side.

h. Create a copy of the Receipt worksheet, move the new sheet to the end, and then rename the copied sheet **Formulas**. Display cell formulas on the Formulas worksheet, select **Landscape orientation**, and then select the options to print gridlines and headings. Adjust column widths so that the data will fit on one page.

DISCOVER

i. Open the Excel Options dialog box while displaying the Formulas worksheet. In the Advanced category, under *Display options for this worksheet:*, select the **Show formulas in cells instead of their calculated results check box**. This option will make sure the active worksheet will display the formulas when you open the workbook again. The Receipt worksheet will continue showing the results.

j. Save and close the file, and submit based on your instructor's directions.

2 | Guest House Rental Rates

ANALYSIS CASE

You manage a beach guest house in Ft. Lauderdale containing three types of rental units. Prices are based on peak and off-peak times of the year. You need to calculate the maximum daily revenue for each rental type, assuming all units are rented. In addition, you need to calculate the discount rate for off-peak rental times. Finally, you will improve the appearance of the worksheet by applying font, alignment, and number formats.

a. Open **e01m2Rentals** and save it as **e01m2Rentals_LastFirst**.

b. Merge and center *Peak Rentals* in the **range C4:D4**, over the two columns of peak rental data. Apply **Dark Red fill color** and **White, Background 1 font color**.

c. Merge and center *Off-Peak Rentals* in the **range E4:G4** over the three columns of off-peak rental data. Apply **Blue fill color** and **White, Background 1 font color**.

d. Center and wrap the headings on row 5. Adjust the width of columns D and F, if needed. Center the data in the **range B6:B8**.

e. Create and copy the following formulas:
   - Calculate the Peak Rentals Maximum Revenue by multiplying the number of units by the peak rental price per day.
   - Calculate the Off-Peak Rentals Maximum Revenue by multiplying the number of units by the off-peak rental price per day.
   - Calculate the Discount rate for the Off-Peak rental price per day. For example, using the peak and off-peak per day values, the studio apartment rents for 75% of its peak rental rate. However, you need to calculate and display the off-peak discount rate, which is .24975.

f. Format the monetary values with **Accounting Number Format**. Format the Discount Rate formula results in **Percent Style** with one decimal place.

DISCOVER

g. Apply **Blue, Accent 1, Lighter 80% fill color** to the **range E5:G8**.

h. Select the **range C5:D8** and apply a custom color with **Red 242**, **Green 220**, and **Blue 219**.

i. Answer the four questions below the worksheet data. If you change any values to answer the questions, change the values back to the original values.

j. Set **1"** top, bottom, left, and right margins. Center the data horizontally on the page.

k. Insert a footer with your name on the left side, the sheet name code in the center, and the file name code on the right side.

l. Create a copy of the Rental Rates worksheet, place the new sheet to the right side of the original worksheet, and rename the new sheet **Formulas**. On the Formulas worksheet, select **Landscape orientation** and the options to print gridlines and headings. Delete the question and answer section on the Formulas sheet.

DISCOVER

m. Open the Excel Options dialog box while displaying the Formulas worksheet. In the Advanced category, under *Display options for this worksheet:*, select the **Show formulas in cells instead of their calculated results check box**. This option will make sure the active worksheet will display the formulas when you open the workbook again. The Rental Rates worksheet will continue showing the results. Adjust column widths so that the data will fit on one page.

n. Save and close the file, and submit based on your instructor's directions.

3 | Real Estate Sales Report

You own a small real estate company in Indianapolis. You want to analyze sales for selected properties. Your assistant has prepared a spreadsheet with sales data. You need to calculate the number of days that the houses were on the market and their sales percentage of the list price. In one situation, the house was involved in a bidding war between two families that really wanted the house. Therefore, the sale price exceeded the list price.

a. Open *e01m3Sales* and save it as **e01m3Sales_LastFirst**.

b. Delete the row that has incomplete sales data. The owners took their house off the market.

c. Calculate the number of days each house was on the market. Copy the formula down that column.

d. Format prices with **Accounting Number Format** with zero decimal places.

e. Calculate the sales price percentage of the list price. The second house was listed for $500,250, but it sold for only $400,125. Therefore, the sale percentage of the list price is 79.99%. Format the percentages with two decimal places.

f. Wrap the headings on row 4.

g. Insert a new column between the *Date Sold* and *List Price* columns. Move the *Days on Market* column to the new location. Apply **Align Right** and increase the indent on the days on market formula results. Then delete the empty column B.

h. Edit the list date of the 41 Chestnut Circle house to be **4/22/2016**. Edit the list price of the house on Amsterdam Drive to be **$355,000**.

i. Select the property rows and set a **20 row height**. Adjust column widths as necessary.

j. Select **Landscape orientation** and set the scaling to **130%**. Center the data horizontally and vertically on the page.

k. Insert a header with your name, the current date code, and the current time code.

l. Save and close the file, and submit based on your instructor's directions.

4 Problem-Solving with Classmates

COLLABORATION CASE

Your instructor wants all students in the class to practice their problem-solving skills. Pair up with a classmate so that you can create errors in a workbook and then see how many errors your classmate can find in your worksheet and how many errors you can find in your classmate's worksheet.

a. Create a folder named **Exploring** on your SkyDrive and give access to that drive to a classmate and your instructor.

b. Open *e01h6Markup_LastFirst*, which you created in the Hands-On Exercises, and save it as **e01m4Markup_LastFirst**.

c. Edit each main formula to have a deliberate error (such as a value or incorrect cell reference) in it and then copy the formulas down the columns.

d. Save the workbook to your shared folder on your SkyDrive.

e. Open the workbook your classmate saved on his or her SkyDrive and save the workbook with your name after theirs, such as *e01m4Markup_MulberyKeith_KrebsCynthia*.

f. Find the errors in your classmate's workbook, insert comments to describe the errors, and then correct the errors.

g. Save the workbook back to your classmate's SkyDrive and submit based on your instructor's directions.

Beyond the Classroom

Credit Card Rebate

RESEARCH CASE

FROM SCRATCH

You recently found out the Costco TrueEarnings® American Express credit card earns annual rebates on all purchases. You want to see how much rebate you would have received had you used this credit card for purchases in the past year. Use the Internet to research the percentage rebates for different categories. Plan the design of the spreadsheet. Enter the categories, rebate percentages, amount of money you spent in each category, and a formula to calculate the amount of rebate. Use the Excel Help feature to learn how to add several cells using a function instead of adding cells individually and how to apply a Double Accounting underline. Insert the appropriate function to total your categorical purchases and rebate amounts. Apply appropriate formatting and page setup options for readability. Underline the last monetary values for the last data row and apply the **Double Accounting underline style** to the totals. Insert a header. Save the workbook as **e01b2Rebate_LastFirst**. Close the workbook and submit based on your instructor's directions.

Net Proceeds from House Sale

DISASTER RECOVERY

Garrett Frazier is a real estate agent. He wants his clients to have a realistic expectation of how much money they will receive when they sell their houses. Sellers know they have to pay a commission to the agent and pay off their existing mortgages; however, many sellers forget to consider they might have to pay some of the buyer's closing costs, title insurance, and prorated property taxes. The realtor commission and estimated closing costs are based on the selling price and the respective rates. The estimated property taxes are prorated based on the annual property taxes and percentage of the year. For example, if a house sells three months into the year, the seller pays 25% of the property taxes. Garrett created a worksheet to enter values in an input area to calculate the estimated deductions at closing and calculate the estimated net proceeds the seller will receive. However, the worksheet contains errors. Open *e01b3Proceeds* and save it as **e01b3Proceeds_LastFirst**.

Use Help to learn how to insert comments into cells. As you identify the errors, insert comments in the respective cells to explain the errors. Correct the errors, including formatting errors. Apply **Landscape orientation**, **115% scaling**, **1.5" top margin**, and center horizontally. Insert your name on the left side of the header, the sheet name code in the center, and the file name code on the right side. Save and close the workbook, and submit based on your instructor's directions.

Goal Setting

SOFT SKILLS CASE

FROM SCRATCH

After watching the Goal Setting video, start a new Excel workbook and save it as **e01b4Goals_LastFirst**. List three descriptive goals in column A relating to your schoolwork and degree completion. For example, maybe you usually study three hours a week for your algebra class, and you want to increase your study time by 20%. Enter *Algebra homework & study time (hours)* in column A, *3* in column B, the percentage change in column C, and create a formula that calculates the total goal in column D. Adjust column widths as needed.

Insert column labels above each column. Format the labels and values using information you learned earlier in the chapter. Merge and center a title at the top of the worksheet. Use the Page Setup dialog box to center the worksheet horizontally. Rename Sheet1 using the term, such as *Fall 2016*. Create a footer with your name on the left side, sheet name code in the center, and file name code on the right side. Save and close the workbook, and submit based on your instructor's directions.

Capstone Exercise

You manage a publishing company that publishes and sells books to bookstores in Austin. Your assistant prepared a standard six-month royalty statement for one author. You need to insert formulas, format the worksheets, and then prepare royalty statements for other authors.

Enter Data into the Worksheet

You need to format a title, enter the date indicating the end of the statement period, and delete a blank column. You also need to insert a row for the standard discount rate, a percentage that you discount the books from the retail price to sell to the bookstores.

a. Open *e01c1Royalty* and save it as **e01c1Royalty_LastFirst**.

b. Merge and center the title over the **range A1:D1**.

c. Type **6/30/2016** in **cell B3** and left align the date.

d. Delete the blank column between the Hardback and Paperback columns.

e. Insert a new row between Retail Price and Price to Bookstore. Enter **Standard Discount Rate**, **0.55**, and **0.5**. Format the two values as **Percent Style**.

Calculate Values

You need to insert formulas to perform necessary calculations.

a. Enter the Percent Returned formula in **cell B10**. The percent returned indicates the percentage of books sold but returned to the publisher.

b. Enter the Price to Bookstore formula in **cell B15**. This is the price at which you sell the books to the bookstore. It is based on the retail price and the standard discount. For example, if a text has a $10 retail price and a 55% discount, you sell the text for $4.50.

c. Enter the Net Retail Sales formula in **cell B16**. The net retail sales is the revenue from the net units sold at the retail price. Gross units sold minus the returned units equals net units sold.

d. Enter the Royalty to Author formula in **cell B20**. Royalties are based on net retail sales and the applicable royalty rate.

e. Enter the Royalty per text formula in **cell B21**. This amount is the author's earnings on every text sold but not returned.

f. Copy the formulas to the Paperback column.

Format the Values

You are ready to format the values to improve readability.

a. Apply **Comma Style** with zero decimal places to the **range B8:C9**.

b. Apply **Percent Style** with one decimal place to the **range B10:C10** and **Percent Style** with two decimal places to the **range B19:C19**.

c. Apply **Accounting Number Format** to all monetary values.

Format the Worksheet

You want to improve the appearance of the rest of the worksheet.

a. Select the **range B6:C6**. Apply bold, right alignment, and **Purple font color**.

b. Click **cell A7**, apply **Purple font color**, and then apply **Gray-25%, Background 2, Darker 10% fill color**. Select the **range A7:C7** and select **Merge Across**.

c. Use Format Painter to apply the formats from **cell A7** to **cells A12** and **A18**.

d. Select the **ranges A8:A10, A13:A16**, and **A19:A21**. Indent the labels twice. Widen column A as needed.

e. Select the **range A7:C10** (the *Units Sold* section) and apply the **Outside Borders** border style. Apply the same border style to the *Pricing* and *Royalty Information* sections.

Manage the Workbook

You will apply page setup options insert a footer, and, then duplicate the royalty statement worksheet to use as a model to prepare a royalty statement for another author.

a. Select the margin setting to center the data horizontally on the page. Insert a footer with your name on the left side, the sheet name code in the center, and the file name code on the right side.

b. Copy the Jacobs worksheet, move the new worksheet to the end, and then rename it **Lopez**.

c. Change the Jacobs sheet tab to **Red**. Change the Lopez sheet tab to **Dark Blue**.

d. Make these changes on the Lopez worksheet: **Lopez** (author), **5000** (hardback gross units), **14000** (paperback gross units), **400** (hardback returns), **1925** (paperback returns), **19.95** (hardback retail price), and **6.95** (paperback retail price).

Display Formulas and Print the Workbook

You want to print the formatted Jacobs worksheet to display the calculated results. To provide evidence of the formulas, you want to display and print cell formulas in the Lopez worksheet.

a. Display the cell formulas for the Lopez worksheet.

b. Select options to print the gridlines and headings.

c. Change the Options setting to make sure the formulas display instead of cell results on this worksheet when you open it again.

d. Adjust the column widths so that the formula printout will print on one page.

e. Save and close the workbook, and submit based on your instructor's directions.

Glossary

Accounting Number Format A number format that displays $ on the left side of a cell and formats values with commas for the thousands separator and two decimal places.

Active cell The current cell in a worksheet. It is indicated by a dark green border onscreen.

Alignment Placement of data within cell boundaries.

AutoComplete A feature that searches for and automatically displays any other label in that column that matches the letters you typed.

Auto Fill A feature that enables you to copy the contents of a cell or a range of cells or to continue a sequence by dragging the fill handle over an adjacent cell or range of cells.

Border A line that surrounds a cell or a range of cells to offset particular data from the rest of the data in a worksheet.

Cell The intersection of a column and row in a worksheet.

Cell address The unique identifier of a cell, starting with the column letter and then the row number, such as A9.

Column heading The alphabetical letters above the columns in a worksheet.

Column width The horizontal measurement of a column in a table or a worksheet. In Excel, it is measured by the number of characters or pixels.

Comma Style A number format that formats values with commas for the thousands separator and two decimal places.

Fill color The background color that displays behind the data in a cell.

Fill handle A small square at the bottom-right corner of a cell used to copy cell contents or text or number patterns to adjacent cells.

Formula A combination of cell references, operators, values, and/or functions used to perform a calculation. A formula starts with an equal sign (=).

Formula Bar An element in Excel that appears below the Ribbon and to the right of the Insert Function command. It shows the contents of the active cell.

Horizontal alignment The placement of cell data between the left and right cell margins in a worksheet.

Indent A format that positions cell contents to the right of the left cell margin to offset the data.

Input area A range of cells in a worksheet used to store and change the variables used in calculations.

Name Box An identifier that displays the address or the range name of the current cell in an Excel worksheet.

Nonadjacent range A collection of multiple ranges that are not positioned in a contiguous cluster in an Excel worksheet.

Normal view The default view of a worksheet that shows worksheet data but not margins, headers, footers, or page breaks.

Number formats Predefined settings that control how values appear in cells.

Order of operations (order of precedence) A set of rules that determines the sequence by which operations are calculated in an expression.

Output area The range of cells in an Excel worksheet that contain formulas dependent on the values in the input area.

Page Break Preview The display that shows the worksheet data and page breaks within the worksheet.

Page Layout view The display that shows the worksheet data, margins, headers, and footers.

Paste Options button An icon that displays in the bottom-right corner immediately after using the Paste command. It enables the user to apply different paste options.

Percent Style A number format that displays values as if they were multiplied by 100 and with the % symbol.

Pointing The process of using the mouse pointer to select cells while building a formula. Also known as *semi-selection*.

Range A group of adjacent or contiguous cells in an Excel worksheet.

Row heading The numbers to the left side of rows in a worksheet.

Row height The vertical measurement of the row in a worksheet.

Semi-selection The process of using the mouse pointer to select cells while building a formula. Also known as *pointing*.

Sheet tab A visual element that shows the name of a worksheet contained in the workbook.

Sheet tab navigation Visual elements that help you navigate to the first, previous, next, or last sheet within a workbook.

Spreadsheet An electronic file that contains a grid of columns and rows used to organize related data and to display results of calculations, enabling interpretation of quantitative data for decision making.

Status bar The row at the bottom of the Excel window that displays instructions and other details about the status of a worksheet.

Text Any combination of letters, numbers, symbols, and spaces not used in Excel calculations.

Value A number that represents a quantity or a measurable amount.

Vertical alignment The position of data between the top and bottom cell margins.

View controls Icons on the right side of the status bar that enable to change to Normal, Page Layout, or Page Break view to display the worksheet.

Workbook A collection of one or more related worksheets contained within a single file.

Worksheet A single spreadsheet that typically contains descriptive labels, numeric values, formulas, functions, and graphical representations of data.

Wrap text An Excel feature that makes data appear on multiple lines within a cell.

Zoom control A control that enables you to increase or decrease the size of the worksheet data onscreen.

Excel

Formulas and Functions

Performing Quantitative Analysis

Yuri Arcurs/Shutterstock

OBJECTIVES AFTER YOU READ THIS CHAPTER, YOU WILL BE ABLE TO:

1. Use relative, absolute, and mixed cell references in formulas
2. Correct circular references
3. Insert a function
4. Insert basic math and statistics functions
5. Use date functions
6. Determine results with the IF function
7. Use lookup functions
8. Calculate payments with the PMT function
9. Create and maintain range names
10. Use range names in formulas

CASE STUDY | Townsend Mortgage Company

You are an assistant to Erica Matheson, a mortgage broker at the Townsend Mortgage Company. Erica spends her days reviewing mortgage rates and trends, meeting with clients, and preparing paperwork. She relies on your expertise in using Excel to help analyze mortgage data.

Today, Erica provided you with sample mortgage data: loan number, house cost, down payment, mortgage rate, and the length of the loan in years. She asked you to perform some basic calculations so that she can check the output provided by her system to verify if it is calculating results correctly. She needs you to calculate the amount financed, the periodic interest rate, the total number of payment periods, the percent of the house cost that is financed, and the payoff year for each loan. In addition, you will calculate totals, averages, and other basic statistics.

Furthermore, you need to complete another worksheet that uses functions to look up interest rates from another table, calculate the monthly payments, and determine how much (if any) the borrower will have to pay for private mortgage insurance (PMI).

From Excel Chapter 2 of *Microsoft® Excel 2013 Comprehensive*, First edition. Mary Anne Poatsy, Keith Mulbery, Jason Davidson, Robert T. Grauer. Copyright © 2014 by Pearson Education, Inc. Published by Pearson Prentice Hall. All Rights Reserved. Download student resources at http://www.pearsonhighered.com/exploring.

Formula Basics

When you increase your understanding of formulas, you can build robust workbooks that perform a variety of calculations for quantitative analysis. Your ability to build sophisticated workbooks and to interpret the results increases your value to any organization. By now, you should be able to build simple formulas using cell references and mathematical operators and using the order of precedence to control the sequence of calculations in formulas.

In this section, you will create formulas in which cell addresses change or remain fixed when you copy them. Finally, you will learn how to identify and prevent circular references in formulas.

Using Relative, Absolute, and Mixed Cell References in Formulas

When you copy a formula, Excel either adjusts or preserves the cell references in the copied formulas based on how the cell references appear in the original formula. Excel uses three different ways to reference a cell in a formula: relative, absolute, and mixed. When you create a formula that you will copy to other cells, ask yourself the following question:

> Do the cell references need to adjust for the copied formulas, or should the cell references always refer to the same cell location, regardless of where the copied formula is located?

Use a Relative Cell Reference

STEP 1 A *relative cell reference* indicates a cell's relative location, such as five rows up and one column to the left, from the cell containing the formula. When you copy a formula containing a relative cell reference, the cell references in the copied formula change relative to the position of the copied formula. Regardless of where you copy the formula, the cell references in the copied formula maintain the same relative distance from the cell containing the copied formula, as the cell references the relative location to the original formula cell.

In Figure 1, the formulas in column F contain relative cell references. When you copy the original formula =D2-E2 from cell F2 down to cell F3, the copied formula changes to =D3-E3. Because you copy the formula *down* the column to cell F3, the column letters in the formula stay the same, but the row numbers change to reflect the row to which you copied the formula. Using relative cell addresses to calculate the amount financed ensures that each borrower's down payment is subtracted from his or her respective house cost.

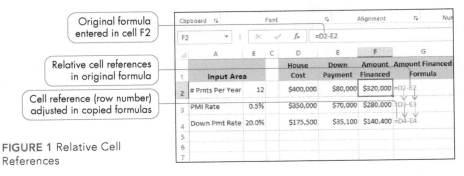

FIGURE 1 Relative Cell References

Use an Absolute Cell Reference

STEP 2 An *absolute cell reference* provides a permanent reference to a specific cell. When you copy a formula containing an absolute cell reference, the cell reference in the copied formula does not change, regardless of where you copy the formula. An absolute cell reference appears with a dollar sign before both the column letter and row number, such as $B$4.

In Figure 2, each down payment is calculated by multiplying the respective house cost by the down payment rate (20%). Cell E2 contains =D2*$B$4 ($400,000*20.0%) to calculate the first borrower's down payment ($80,000). When you copy the formula down to the next row, the copied formula in cell E3 is =D3*$B$4. The relative cell reference D2 changes to D3 (for the next house cost) and the absolute cell reference $B$4 remains the same to refer to the 20.0% down payment rate. This formula ensures that the cell reference to the house cost changes for each row but that the house cost is always multiplied by the rate in cell B4.

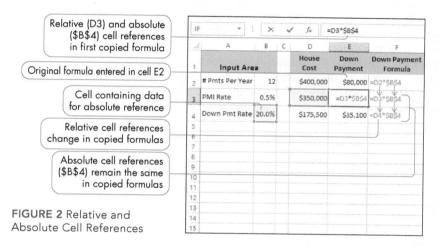

FIGURE 2 Relative and Absolute Cell References

TIP Input Area and Absolute Cell References

Figure 2 illustrates an input area, a range in a worksheet that contains values that you can change. You build formulas using absolute references to the cells in the input area. By using cell references from an input area, you can change the value in the input area and the formulas that refer to those cells will update automatically. If an input value changes (e.g., the down payment rate changes from 20% to 25%), enter the new input value in only one cell (e.g., B4), and Excel recalculates the amount of down payment for all the formulas.

Figure 3 shows what happens if the down payment formula used a relative reference to cell B4. If the original formula in cell E2 is =D2*B4, the copied formula becomes =D3*B5 in cell E3. The relative cell reference to B4 changes to B5 when you copy the formula down. Because cell B5 is empty, the $350,000 house cost in cell D3 is multiplied by 0, giving a $0 down payment, which is not a valid down payment amount.

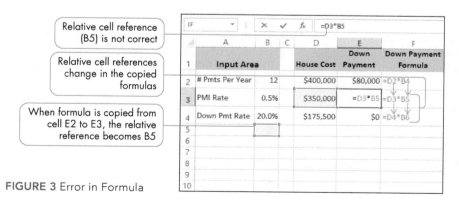

FIGURE 3 Error in Formula

Use a Mixed Cell Reference

STEP 3》

A **mixed cell reference** combines an absolute cell reference with a relative cell reference. When you copy a formula containing a mixed cell reference, either the column letter or the row number that has the absolute reference remains fixed while the other part of the cell reference that is relative changes in the copied formula. $B4 and B$4 are examples of mixed cell references. In the reference $B4, the column B is absolute, and the row number is relative; when you copy the formula, the column letter, B, does not change, but the row number will change. In the reference B$4, the column letter, B, changes, but the row number, 4, does not change. To create a mixed reference, type the dollar sign to the left of the part of the cell reference you want to be absolute.

In the down payment formula, you can change the formula in cell E2 to be =D2*B$4. Because you are copying down the same column, only the row reference 4 must be absolute; the column letter stays the same. Figure 4 shows the copied formula =D3*B$4 in cell E3. In situations where you can use either absolute or mixed references, consider using mixed references to shorten the length of the formula.

Mixed cell references in original formula

Row numbers stay the same for copied mixed cell references

Copied formulas still point to cell B4 with mixed cell reference

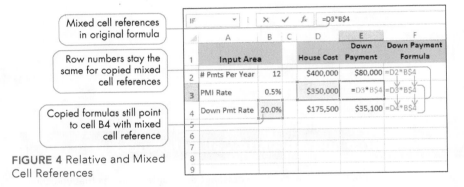

FIGURE 4 Relative and Mixed Cell References

TIP The F4 Key

The F4 key toggles through relative, absolute, and mixed references. Click a cell reference within a formula on the Formula Bar and press F4 to change it. For example, click in B4 in the formula =D2*B4. Press F4 and the relative cell reference (B4) changes to an absolute cell reference ($B$4). Press F4 again and $B$4 becomes a mixed reference (B$4); press F4 again and it becomes another mixed reference ($B4). Press F4 a fourth time and the cell reference returns to the original relative reference (B4).

Correcting Circular References

If a formula contains a direct or an indirect reference to the cell containing the formula, a **circular reference** exists. Figure 5 shows an example of a circular reference in a formula. The formula in cell E2 is =E2*$B$4. Because the formula is in cell E2, using the cell address E2 within the formula creates a circular reference.

Active cell

Formula contains reference to active cell

Error message

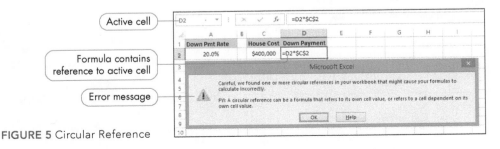

FIGURE 5 Circular Reference

Formulas and Functions

STEP 4 »   Circular references usually cause inaccurate results. Excel displays a warning message when you enter a formula containing a circular reference or when you open an Excel workbook that contains an existing circular reference. Click Help to display the *Find and fix a circular reference* Help topic or click OK to accept the circular reference. Until you resolve a circular reference, the status bar indicates the location of a circular reference, such as CIRCULAR REFERENCES: E2.

> ### TIP Green Triangles
>
> Excel displays a green triangle in the top-left corner of a cell if it detects a potential error in a formula. Click the cell to see the Trace Error button (yellow diamond with exclamation mark). When you click Trace Error, Excel displays information about the potential error and how to correct it. In some cases, Excel may anticipate an inconsistent formula or the omission of adjacent cells in a formula. For example, if a column contains values for the year 2016, the error message indicates that you did not include the year itself. However, the year 2016 is merely a label and should not be included; therefore, you would ignore that error message.

Quick Concepts ✓

1. What happens when you copy a formula containing a relative cell reference one column to the right?

2. Why would you use an absolute reference in a formula?

3. What is a circular reference? Provide an example.

Hands-On Exercises

 Watch the Video for this Hands-On Exercise!

 MyITLab® HOE1 Training

1 Formula Basics

Erica prepared a workbook containing data for five mortgages financed with the Townsend Mortgage Company. The data include house cost, down payment, mortgage rate, number of years to pay off the mortgage, and the financing date for each mortgage.

Skills covered: Use a Relative Cell Reference in a Formula • Use an Absolute Cell Reference in a Formula • Use a Mixed Cell Reference in a Formula • Correct a Circular Reference

STEP 1 ≫ USE A RELATIVE CELL REFERENCE IN A FORMULA

You need to calculate the amount financed by each borrower by creating a formula with relative cell references that calculates the difference between the house cost and the down payment. After verifying the results of the amount financed by the first borrower, you will copy the formula down the Amount Financed column to calculate the other borrowers' amounts financed. Refer to Figure 6 as you complete Step 1.

Step d: Click after typing formula

Steps b–c: Enter formula =B8-C8

Step e: AutoFill Options button displays after copying formula

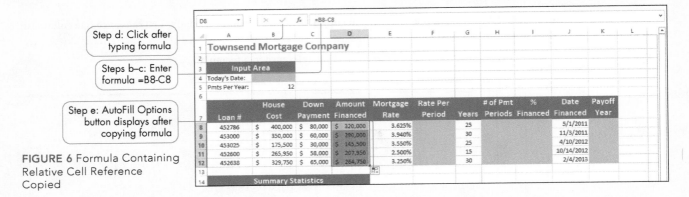

FIGURE 6 Formula Containing Relative Cell Reference Copied

a. Open *e02h1Loans* and save it as **e02h1Loans_LastFirst**.

> **TROUBLESHOOTING:** If you make any major mistakes in this exercise, you can close the file, open *e02h1Loans* again, and then start this exercise over.

The workbook contains two worksheets: Details (for Hands-On Exercises 1 and 2) and Payment Info (for Hands-On Exercises 3 and 4). You will enter formulas in the shaded cells.

b. Click **cell D8** in the Details sheet. Type = and click **cell B8**, the cell containing the first borrower's house cost.

c. Type - and click **cell C8**, the cell containing the down payment by the first borrower.

d. Click **Enter** (the check mark between the Name Box and Formula Bar) to complete the formula.

The first borrower financed (i.e., borrowed) $320,000, the difference between the cost ($400,000) and the down payment ($80,000).

e. Double-click the **cell D8 fill handle**.

You copied the formula down the Amount Financed column for each mortgage row.

The Auto Fill Options button appears in the bottom-right corner of the copied formulas. If you click it, you can see that the default is Copy Cells. If you want to copy only formatting, click Fill Formatting Only. If you want to copy data only, click Fill Without Formatting.

f. Click **cell D9** and view the formula in the Formula Bar.

The formula in cell D8 is =B8-C8. The formula pasted in cell D9 is =B9-C9. Because the original formula contained relative cell references, when you copy the formula down to the next row, the row numbers for the cell references change. Each result represents the amount financed for that particular borrower.

g. Press [↓] and look at the cell references in the Formula Bar to see how the references change for each formula you copied. Save the workbook with the new formula you created.

STEP 2 » USE AN ABSOLUTE CELL REFERENCE IN A FORMULA

Column E contains the annual percentage rate (APR) for each mortgage. Because the borrowers will make monthly payments, you need to calculate the monthly interest rate by dividing the APR by 12 (the number of payments in one year) for each borrower. Refer to Figure 7 as you complete Step 2.

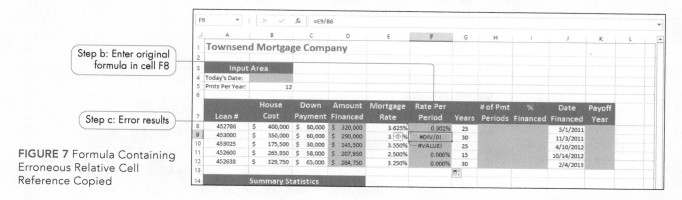

FIGURE 7 Formula Containing Erroneous Relative Cell Reference Copied

a. Click **cell F8**.

You need to create a formula to calculate the monthly interest rate for the first borrower.

b. Type **=E8/B5** and click **Enter** (the checkmark between the Name Box and the Formula Bar).

Typically, you should avoid typing values directly in formulas. Although the number of months in one year is always 12, use a reference to cell B5, where the number of payments per year is placed in the input area, so that the company can change the payment period to bimonthly (24 payments per year) or quarterly (four payments per year) without adjusting the formula.

c. Double-click the **cell F8 fill handle**, click **cell F9**, and then view the results (see Figure 7).

An error icon displays to the left of cell F9, cell F9 displays #DIV/0!, and cell F10 displays #VALUE!. The original formula was =E8/B5. Because you copied the formula =E8/B5 down the column, the first copied formula is =E9/B6, and the second copied formula is =E10/B7. Although you want the mortgage rate cell reference (E8) to change (E9, E10, etc.) from row to row, you do not want the divisor (cell B5) to change. You need all formulas to divide by the value stored in cell B5, so you will edit the formula to make B5 an absolute reference.

TIP | Error Icons

You can position the mouse pointer over the error icon to see a tip indicating what is wrong, such as *The formula or function used is dividing by zero or empty cells.* You can click the icon to see a menu of options to learn more about the error and how to correct it.

d. Click **Undo** in the Quick Access Toolbar to undo the Auto Fill process. Click within or to the right of **B5** in the Formula Bar.

e. Press **F4** and click **Enter** (the checkmark between the Name Box and the Formula Bar).

Excel changes the cell reference from B5 to $B$5, making it an absolute cell reference.

f. Copy the formula down the Rate Per Period column. Click **cell F9** and view the formula in the Formula Bar. Save the workbook.

The formula in cell F9 is =E9/$B$5. The reference to E9 is relative and the reference to B5 is absolute.

STEP 3 >> USE A MIXED CELL REFERENCE IN A FORMULA

The next formula you create will calculate the total number of payment periods for each loan. Refer to Figure 8 as you complete Step 3.

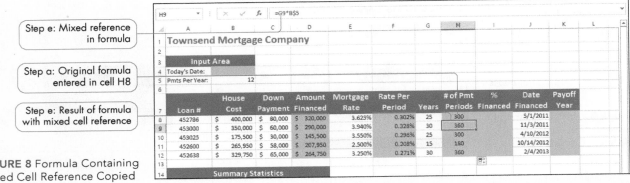

FIGURE 8 Formula Containing Mixed Cell Reference Copied

a. Click **cell H8** and type **=G8*B5**.

You need to multiply the number of years (25) by the number of payment periods in one year (12) using cell references.

b. Press **F4** to make the B5 cell reference absolute and click **Enter** (the checkmark between the Name Box and Formula Bar).

You want B5 to be absolute so that the cell reference remains B5 when you copy the formula. The product of 25 years and 12 months is 300 months or payment periods.

c. Copy the formula down the # of Pmt Periods column.

The first copied formula is =G9*$B$5, and the result is 360. You want to see what happens if you change the absolute reference to a mixed reference and copy the formula again. Because you are copying down a column, the column letter B can be relative because it will not change either way, but the row number 5 must be absolute.

d. Click **Undo** on the Quick Access Toolbar to undo the copied formulas.

Cell H8 is the active cell.

Hands-On Exercise 1

82

e. Click within the **$B$5 cell reference** in the Formula Bar. Press **F4** to change the cell reference to a mixed cell reference: B$5. Press **Ctrl+Enter** and copy the formula down the # of Pmt Periods column. Click **cell H9**. Save the workbook.

The first copied formula is =G9*B$5 and the result is still 360. In this situation, using either an absolute reference or a mixed reference provides the same results.

STEP 4 ≫ CORRECT A CIRCULAR REFERENCE

Erica wants to know what percentage of the house cost each borrower will finance. As you create the formula, you enter a circular reference. After studying the results, you correct the circular error and plan future formulas that avoid this problem. Refer to Figure 9 as you complete Step 4.

Step d: Corrected formula in cell I8

Step d: Results of copied formulas

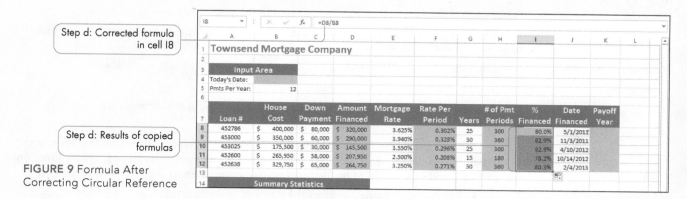

FIGURE 9 Formula After Correcting Circular Reference

a. Click **cell I8**, type **=I8/B8**, and then press **Enter**.

The Circular Reference Warning message box displays.

> **TROUBLESHOOTING:** If the message box does not display, close the workbook and exit Excel. Start Excel, open the workbook again, and then repeat Step 4a. Sometimes the message box appears only once while Excel is running. If you had previously experimented with a circular reference during a work session, the message box might not display. However, exiting Excel and opening it again will enable the message box to display.

b. Read the description of the error and click **Help**.

The Excel Help window opens, displaying information about circular references.

c. Read the circular reference information, close the Excel Help window, and then click **OK** in the message box.

The left side of the status bar displays *CIRCULAR REFERENCES: I8*.

Because the formula is stored in cell I8, the formula cannot refer to the cell itself. You need to divide the value in the Amount Financed column by the value in the House Cost column.

d. Click **cell I8** and edit the formula to be **=D8/B8**. Copy the formula down the % Financed column.

The first borrower financed 80% of the cost of the house: $320,000 financed divided by $400,000 cost.

e. Save the workbook. Keep the workbook open if you plan to continue with the next Hands-On Exercise. If not, close the workbook and exit Excel.

Function Basics

An Excel *function* is a predefined computation that simplifies creating a formula that performs a complex calculation. Excel contains more than 400 functions, which are organized into 14 categories. Table 1 lists and describes the primary function categories used in this chapter.

TABLE 1	Function Categories and Descriptions
Category	**Description**
Date & Time	Provides methods for manipulating date and time values.
Financial	Performs financial calculations, such as payments, rates, present value, and future value.
Logical	Performs logical tests and returns the value of the tests. Includes logical operators for combined tests, such as AND, OR, and NOT.
Lookup & Reference	Looks up values, creates links to cells, or provides references to cells in a worksheet.
Math & Trig	Performs standard math and trigonometry calculations.
Statistical	Performs common statistical calculations, such as averages and standard deviations.

When using functions, you must adhere to correct *syntax*, the rules that dictate the structure and components required to perform the necessary calculations. Start a function with an equal sign, followed by the function name, and then its arguments in parentheses.

- The function name describes the purpose of the function. For example, the function name SUM indicates that the function sums, or adds, values.

- A function's *arguments* specify the inputs—such as cells, values, or arithmetic expressions—that are required to complete the operation. In some cases, a function requires multiple arguments separated by commas.

In this section, you will learn how to insert common functions using the keyboard and the Insert Function and Function Arguments dialog boxes.

Inserting a Function

To insert a function by typing, first type an equal sign, and then begin typing the function name. *Formula AutoComplete* displays a list of functions and defined names that match letters as you type a formula. For example, if you type =SU, Formula AutoComplete displays a list of functions and names that start with *SU* (see Figure 10). You can double-click the function name from the list or continue typing the function name. You can even scroll through the list to see the ScreenTip describing the function.

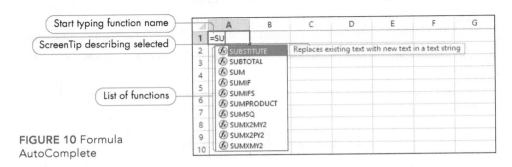

FIGURE 10 Formula AutoComplete

After you type the function name and opening parenthesis, Excel displays the *function ScreenTip*, a small pop-up description that displays the function's arguments. The argument you are currently entering is bold in the function ScreenTip (see Figure 11). Square brackets indicate optional arguments. For example, the SUM function requires the number1 argument, but the number2 argument is optional. Click the argument name in the function ScreenTip to select the actual argument in the formula you are creating if you want to make changes to the argument.

FIGURE 11 Function ScreenTip

You can also use the Insert Function dialog box to search for a function, select a function category, and select a function from the list (see Figure 12). The dialog box is helpful if you want to browse a list of functions, especially if you are not sure of the function you need and want to see descriptions.

To display the Insert Function dialog box, click Insert Function f_x (located between the Name Box and the Formula Bar) or click Insert Function in the Function Library group on the Formulas tab. From within the dialog box, select a function category, such as Most Recently Used, and select a function to display the syntax and a brief description of that function. Click *Help on this function* to display details about the selected function.

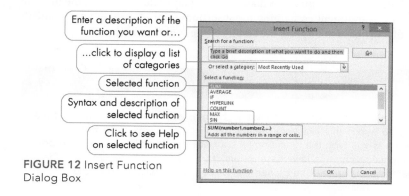

Enter a description of the function you want or...

...click to display a list of categories

Selected function

Syntax and description of selected function

Click to see Help on selected function

FIGURE 12 Insert Function Dialog Box

When you find the function you want, click OK. The Function Arguments dialog box opens so that you can enter the arguments for that specific function (see Figure 13). The following list explains the arguments in the Function Arguments dialog box:

- Argument names in **bold** (such as Number1 in the SUM function) are required.

- Argument names that are not bold (such as Number2 in the SUM function) are optional. The function can operate without the optional argument, which is used when you need additional specifications to calculate a result.

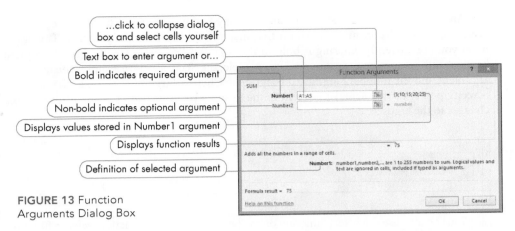

...click to collapse dialog box and select cells yourself

Text box to enter argument or...

Bold indicates required argument

Non-bold indicates optional argument

Displays values stored in Number1 argument

Displays function results

Definition of selected argument

FIGURE 13 Function Arguments Dialog Box

Type the cell references in the argument boxes or click a collapse button to the right side of an argument box to collapse the dialog box and select the cell or range of cells in the worksheet to designate as that argument. If you click the collapse button to select a range, you need to click the expand button to expand the dialog box again. The value, or results, of a formula contained in the argument cell displays on the right side of the argument box (such as 5; 10; 15; 20; 25—the values stored in the range A1:A5 used for the Number1 argument). If the argument is not valid, Excel displays an error description on the right side of the argument box.

The bottom of the Function Arguments dialog box displays a description of the function and a description of the argument containing the insertion point. As you enter arguments, the bottom of the dialog box also displays the results of the function, such as 75.

> **TIP** **#Name?**
>
> If you enter a function and #NAME? displays in the cell, you might have mistyped the function name. To avoid this problem, select the function name from the Formula AutoComplete list as you type the function name, or use the Insert Function dialog box. You can type a function name in lowercase letters. If you type the name correctly, Excel converts the name to all capital letters when you press Enter, indicating that you spelled the function name correctly.

Inserting Basic Math and Statistics Functions

Excel includes commonly used math and statistical functions that you can use for a variety of calculations. For example, you can insert functions to calculate the total amount you spend on dining out in a month, the average amount you spend per month downloading music from iTunes®, your highest electric bill, and your lowest time to run a mile this week.

Calculate a Total with the SUM Function

STEP 1 ≫   The *SUM function* totals values in two or more cells and displays the result in the cell containing the function. This function is more efficient to create when you need to add the values contained in three or more cells. For example, to add the contents of cells A2 through A14, you could enter =A2+A3+A4+A5+A6+A7+A8+A9+A10+A11+A12+A13+A14, which is time-consuming and increases the probability of entering an inaccurate cell reference, such as entering a cell reference twice or accidentally leaving out a cell reference. Instead, you should use the SUM function, =SUM(A2:A14).

=SUM(number 1, [number 2],...)

Formulas and Functions

TIP | Function Syntax

In this text, the function syntax lines are highlighted. Brackets [ ] indicate optional arguments; however, do not actually type the brackets when you enter the argument.

The SUM function contains one required argument (Number1) that represents a range of cells to add. The range, such as A2:A14, specifies the first and last cells containing values to SUM. Excel will sum all cells within that range. The Number2 optional argument is used when you want to sum values stored in nonadjacent cells or ranges, such as =SUM(A2:A14,F2:F14). The ellipsis in the function syntax indicates you can add as many additional ranges as desired, separated by commas.

TIP | Avoiding Functions for Basic Formulas

Do not use a function for a basic mathematical expression. For example, although =SUM(B4/C4) produces the same result as =B4/C4, the SUM function is not needed to perform the basic arithmetic division. Furthermore, someone taking a quick look at that formula might assume it performs addition instead of division. Use the most appropriate, clear-cut formula, =B4/C4.

To insert the SUM function (for example, to sum the values in the range A2:A14), do one of the following:

- Type =SUM(A2:A14) and press Enter.
- Type =SUM(and drag to select the range A2:A14 with the mouse. Type the ending #) and press Enter.
- Click in cell A15, click Sum in the Editing group on the HOME tab, press Enter to select the suggested range or type (or drag to select) A2:A14, and then press Enter.
- Click in cell A15, click Sum in the Function Library group on the FORMULAS tab, press Enter to select the suggested range or type A2:A14, and then press Enter.

Figure 14 shows the result of using the SUM function in cell D2 to total scores (898).

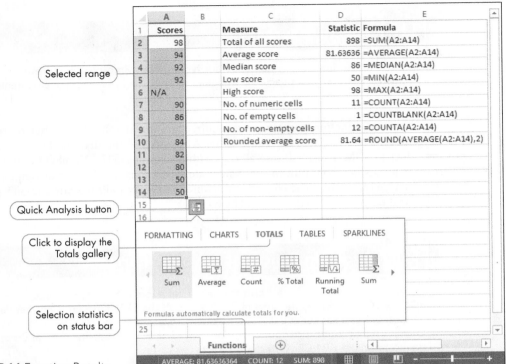

FIGURE 14 Function Results

 **Sum Arrow**

If you click Sum, Excel inserts the SUM function. However, if you click the Sum arrow in the Editing group on the Home tab or in the Function Library group on the Formulas tab, Excel displays a list of basic functions to select: Sum, Average, Count Numbers, Max, and Min. If you want to insert another function, select More Functions from the list.

Find Central Tendency with AVERAGE and MEDIAN

STEP 2 ▶▶ People often describe data based on central tendency, which means that values tend to cluster around a central value. Excel provides two functions to calculate central tendency: AVERAGE and MEDIAN. The **AVERAGE function** calculates the arithmetic mean, or average, for the values in a range of cells. You can use this function to calculate the class average on a biology test or the average number of points scored per game by a basketball player. In Figure 14, =AVERAGE(A2:A14) in cell D3 returns 81.63636 as the average test score. The AVERAGE function ignores empty cells and cells containing N/A or text.

=AVERAGE(number 1,[number2],…)

STEP 3 ▶▶ The **MEDIAN function** finds the midpoint value, which is the value that one half of the data set is above or below. The median is particularly useful because extreme values often influence arithmetic mean calculated by the AVERAGE function. In Figure 14, the two extreme test scores of 50 distort the average. The rest of the test scores range from 80 to 98. Cell D4 contains =MEDIAN(A2:A14). The median for test scores is 86, which indicates that half the test scores are above 86 and half the test scores are below 86. This statistic is more reflective of the data set than the average is. The MEDIAN function ignores empty cells and cells containing N/A or text.

=MEDIAN(number 1,[number 2],…)

Identify Low and High Values with MIN and MAX

STEP 4 » The *MIN function* analyzes an argument list to determine the lowest value, such as the lowest score on a test. Manually inspecting a range of values to identify the lowest value is inefficient, especially in large spreadsheets. If you change values in the range, the MIN function will identify the new lowest value and display it in the cell containing the MIN function. In Figure 14, =MIN(A2:A14) in cell D5 identifies that 50 is the lowest test score.

=MIN(number 1,[number 2],…)

The *MAX function* analyzes an argument list to determine the highest value, such as the highest score on a test. Like the MIN function, when the values in the range change, the MAX function will display the new highest value within the range of cells. In Figure 14, =MAX(A2:A14) in cell D6 identifies 98 as the highest test score.

=MAX(number 1,[number 2],…)

TIP Nonadjacent Ranges

You can use multiple ranges as arguments, such as finding the largest number within two nonadjacent (nonconsecutive) ranges. For example, you can find the highest test score where some scores are stored in cells A2:A14 and others are stored in cells K2:K14. Separate each range with a comma in the argument list, so that the formula is =MAX(A2:A14,K2:K14).

Identify the Total Number with COUNT Functions

Excel provides three basic count functions—COUNT, COUNTBLANK and COUNTA—to count the cells in a range that meet a particular criterion. The *COUNT function* tallies the number of cells in a range that contain values you can use in calculations, such as numerical and date data, but excludes blank cells or text entries from the tally. In Figure 14, the selected range spans 13 cells; however, =COUNT(A2:A14) in cell D7 returns 11, the number of cells that contain numerical data. It does not count the cell containing the text *N/A* or the blank cell.

The *COUNTBLANK function* tallies the number of cells in a range that are blank. In Figure 14, =COUNTBLANK(A2:A14) in cell D8 identifies that one cell in the range A2:A14 is blank. The *COUNTA function* tallies the number of cells in a range that are not blank, that is, cells that contain data, whether a value, text, or a formula. In Figure 14, =COUNTA(A2:A14) in cell D9 returns 12, indicating the range A2:A14 contains 12 cells that contain some form of data. It does not count the blank cell.

=COUNT(number 1,[number 2],…)
=COUNTBLANK(number 1,[number 2],…)
=COUNTA(number 1,[number 2],…)

TIP Status Bar Statistics: Average, Count, and Sum

When you select a range of cells containing values, by default Excel displays the average, count, and sum of those values on the status bar (see Figure 14). You can customize the status bar to show other selection statistics, such as the minimum and maximum values for a selected range. To display or hide particular selection statistics, right-click the status bar and select the statistic.

Perform Calculations with Quick Analysis Tools

Excel 2013 contains a new feature called *Quick Analysis*, which is a set of analytical tools you can use to apply formatting, create charts or tables, and insert basic functions. When you select a range of data, the Quick Analysis button displays in the bottom-right corner of the selected range. Click the Quick Analysis button to display the Quick Analysis gallery and select the analytical tool to meet your needs.

Figure 14 shows the TOTALS options so that you can sum, average, or count the values in the selected range. Select % Total to display the percentage of the grand total of two or more columns. Select Running Total to provide a cumulative total at the bottom of multiple columns.

Use Other Math and Statistical Functions

In addition to the functions you have learned in this chapter, Excel provides more than 100 other math and statistical functions. Table 2 lists and describes some of these functions that you might find helpful in your business, education, and general statistics courses.

TABLE 2   Math and Statistical Functions

Function Syntax	Description
=ABS(number)	Displays the absolute (i.e., positive) value of a number.
=FREQUENCY(data_array,bins_array)	Counts how often values appear in a given range.
=INT(number)	Rounds a value number down to the nearest whole number.
=MODE.SNGL(number1,[number2],…)	Displays the most frequently occurring value in a list.
=RANK.AVG(number,ref,[order])	Identifies a value's rank within a list of values; returns an average rank for identical values.
=RANK.EQ(number,ref,[order])	Identifies a value's rank within a list of values; the top rank is identified for all identical values.
=ROUND(number,num_digits)	Rounds a value to a specific number of digits. Rounds numbers of 5 and greater up and those less than 5 down.

 TIP   Round Versus Decrease Decimal Points

When you click Decrease Decimal in the Number group to display fewer or no digits after a decimal point, Excel still stores the original value's decimal places so that those digits can be used in calculations. The ROUND function changes the stored value to its rounded state.

Nest Functions as Arguments

A *nested function* occurs when one function is embedded as an argument within another function. Each function has its own set of arguments that must be included. For example, cell D10 in Figure 14 contains =ROUND(AVERAGE(A2:A14),2). The ROUND function requires two arguments: number and num_digits.

The AVERAGE function is nested in the *number* argument of the ROUND function. AVERAGE(A2:A14) returns 81.63636. That value is then rounded to two decimal places, indicated by 2 in the *num_digits* argument. The result is 81.64. If you change the second argument from 2 to 0, such as =ROUND(AVERAGE(A2:A14),0), the result would be 82.

Using Date Functions

Because Excel treats dates as serial numbers, you can perform calculations using dates. For example, assume today is January 1, 2016, and you graduate on May 6, 2016. To determine how many days until graduation, subtract today's date from the graduation date. Excel uses the serial numbers for these dates (42370 and 42494) to calculate the difference of 126 days.

Insert the TODAY Function

STEP 5 »

The **TODAY *function*** displays the current date, such as 6/14/2016, in a cell. Excel updates the function results when you open or print the workbook. The TODAY() function does not require arguments, but you must include the parentheses. If you omit the parentheses, Excel displays #NAME? in the cell with a green triangle in the top-left corner of the cell. When you click the cell, an error icon appears that you can click for more information.

`=TODAY()`

Insert the NOW Function

The **NOW *function*** uses the computer's clock to display the date and military time, such as 6/14/2016 15:30, that you last opened the workbook. (Military time expresses time on a 24-hour period where 1:00 is 1 a.m. and 13:00 is 1 p.m.) The date and time will change every time the workbook is opened. Like the TODAY function, the NOW function does not require arguments, but you must include the parentheses. Omitting the parentheses creates a #NAME? error.

`=NOW()`

TIP | Update the Date and Time

Both the TODAY and NOW functions display the date/time the workbook was last opened or last calculated. These functions do not continuously update the date and time while the workbook is open. To update the date and time, press F9 or click the Formulas tab and click *Calculate now* in the Calculation group.

Use Other Date & Time Functions

Excel contains a variety of other date functions. You can use these functions to calculate when employees are eligible for certain benefits, what the date is six months from now, or what day of the week a particular date falls on. Table 3 describes and Figure 15 shows examples of some date functions.

TABLE 3 Date Functions

Function Syntax	Description
=DATE(year,month,day)	Returns the serial number for a date.
=DAY(serial_number)	Displays the day (1–31) within a given month for a date or its serial number.
=EDATE(start_date,months)	Displays the serial number using the General format of a date a specified number of months in the future (using a positive value) or past (using a negative value). Displays the actual future or past date in Short Date format.
=EOMONTH(start_date,months)	Identifies the serial number of the last day of a month using General format or the exact last day of a month using Short Date format for a specified number of months from a date's serial number.
=MONTH(serial_number)	Returns the month (1–12) for a serial number, where 1 is January and 12 is December.
=WEEKDAY(serial_number, [return_type])	Identifies the weekday (1–7) for a serial number, where 1 is Sunday and 7 is Saturday (the default with no second argument); can specify a second argument for different numbers assigned to weekdays (see Help).
=YEAR(serial_number)	Identifies the year for a serial number.
=YEARFRAC(start_date,end_date,[basis])	Calculates the fraction of a year between two dates based on the number of whole days.

	A	B	C	D	E	F
1	Inputs:	7	11	2016	10/17/2016	
2						
3	Description			Format	Result	Formula
4	Today's Date			Short Date	10/17/2016	=TODAY()
5	Today's Date			Other Date	October 17, 2016	=TODAY()
6	Today's Date and Military Time			Date/Time	10/17/2016 17:15	=NOW()
7	Serial # of Date			General	42562	=DATE(D1,B1,C1)
8	Serial # of Date			Short Date	7/11/2016	=DATE(D1,B1,C1)
9	Day within the Month			General	17	=DAY(E4) or =DAY(TODAY())
10	Serial # of Date 3 Months in Future			General	42752	=EDATE(E4,3)
11	Date 3 Months in Future			Short Date	1/17/2017	=EDATE(E4,3)
12	Date 3 Years in Future			Short Date	10/17/2019	=EDATE(E4,3*12)
13	Date 2 Months Ago			Short Date	8/17/2016	=EDATE(E4,-2)
14	Serial # of Date 6 Months in Future			General	42746	=EDATE(DATE(D1,B1,C1),6)
15	Serial # of Last Day in 6 Months			General	42855	=EOMONTH(E4,6) or =EOMONTH(TODAY())
16	Last Day of 6 Months in Future			Short Date	4/30/2017	=EOMONTH(E4,6) or =EOMONTH(TODAY())
17	Month Number (where 6=June)			General	10	=MONTH(E5) or =MONTH(TODAY())
18	Week day (1=Sunday; 7=Saturday)			General	2	=WEEKDAY(E4)
19	Week day (1=Monday; 7=Sunday)			General	1	=WEEKDAY(E4,2)
20	Year for a Serial Date			General	2016	=YEAR(E4) or =YEAR(TODAY())
21	Fraction of Year 7/11/2016-10/17/2016			General	0.266666667	=YEARFRAC(DATE(D1,B1,C1),E1)

FIGURE 15 Date Function Examples

You can nest a date function inside another date function, such as =DAY(TODAY()). This nested function TODAY() first identifies today's date, and from that date, the DAY function identifies the day of the month. In Figure 15, cell E21 contains =YEARFRAC(DATE(D1,B1,C1),E1). The DATE function is nested to combine values in three cells (D1, B1, and C1) to build a date (7/11/2016). Excel finds the number of days between that date and 10/17/2016, the date stored in cell E1. From there, the YEARFRAC function calculates the fraction of a year (26.667%) between those two dates. Had 7/11/2016 been stored as a date in a single cell, the formula would simplify to something like =YEARFRAC(D1,E1).

TIP   Date Functions and Arithmetic Operations

You can combine date functions with arithmetic operations. For example, you sign a lease on June 14, 2016, for three years. The starting date is stored in cell E4. What date does your lease expire? Enter =EDATE(E4,3*12)-1 to calculate the expiration date. The first argument, E4, is the cell containing the start date, and the second argument, 3*12, equals three years containing 12 months each, or 36 months. (In an actual worksheet, you should store the value 36 in a cell instead of typing numbers in the argument.) That result is June 14, 2019, but the lease actually expires the day before. So you must then subtract 1 from the function result to calculate the June 13, 2019, date.

Quick
Concepts ✓

1. What visual features help guide you through typing a function directly in a cell?

2. What type of data do you enter in a Function Arguments dialog box, and what are four things the dialog box tells you?

3. What is the difference between the AVERAGE and MEDIAN functions?

4. What is a nested function, and why would you create one?

5. Provide three examples of using date functions to determine something specific.

Hands-On Exercises

2 Function Basics

The Townsend Mortgage Company's worksheet contains an area in which you must enter summary statistics. In addition, you need to include today's date and identify the year in which each mortgage will be paid off.

Skills covered: Use the SUM Function • Use the AVERAGE Function • Use the MEDIAN Function • Use the MIN, MAX, and COUNT Functions • Use the TODAY and YEAR Functions

STEP 1 ≫ USE THE SUM FUNCTION

The first summary statistic you need to calculate is the total value of the houses bought by the borrowers. You will use the SUM function. Refer to Figure 16 as you complete Step 1.

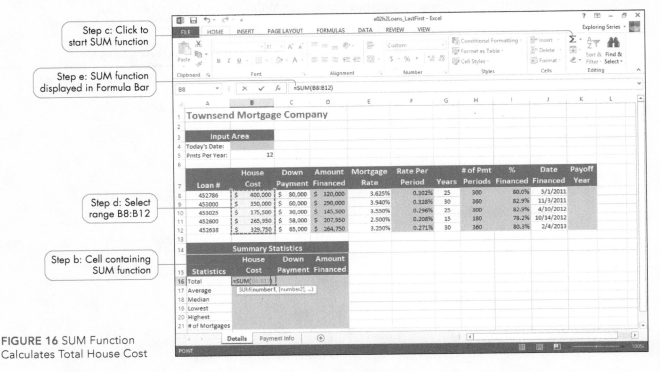

FIGURE 16 SUM Function Calculates Total House Cost

a. Open *e02h1Loans_LastFirst* if you closed it at the end of Hands-On Exercise 1 and save it as **e02h2Loans_LastFirst**, changing *h1* to *h2*.

b. Make sure the Details worksheet is active and click **cell B16**, the cell where you will enter a formula for the total house cost.

c. Click **Sum** in the Editing group on the HOME tab.

> **TROUBLESHOOTING:** Click the main part of the Sum command. If you click the Sum arrow, select Sum.

Excel anticipates the range of cells containing values you want to sum based on where you enter the formula—in this case, A8:D15. This is not the correct range, so you must enter the correct range.

d. Select the **range B8:B12**, the cells containing house costs.

As you use the semi-selection process, Excel enters the range in the SUM function.

> **TROUBLESHOOTING:** If you entered the function without changing the arguments, repeat steps b–d or edit the arguments in the Formula Bar by deleting the default range, typing B8:B12 between the parentheses and pressing Enter.

e. Click **Enter** (the checkmark between the Name Box and Formula Bar) and save the workbook.

Cell B16 contains the function = SUM(B8:B12), and the result is $1,521,200.

STEP 2 ≫ USE THE AVERAGE FUNCTION

Before copying the functions to calculate the total down payments and amounts financed, you want to calculate the average house cost bought by the borrowers in your list. Refer to Figure 17 as you complete Step 2.

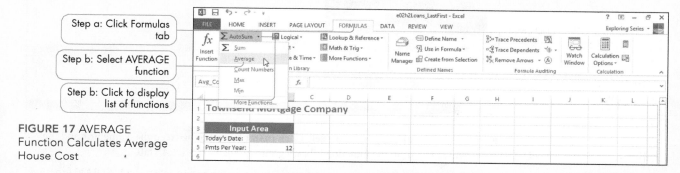

Step a: Click Formulas tab

Step b: Select AVERAGE function

Step b: Click to display list of functions

FIGURE 17 AVERAGE Function Calculates Average House Cost

a. Click the **FORMULAS tab** and click **cell B17**, the cell where you will display the average cost of the houses.

b. Click the **Sum arrow** in the Function Library group and select **Average**.

Excel selects cell B15, which is the total cost of the houses. You need to change the range.

> **TROUBLESHOOTING:** Sum, like some other commands in Excel, contains two parts: the main command icon and an arrow. Click the main command icon when instructed to click Sum to perform the default action. Click the arrow when instructed to click the Sum arrow for additional options. If you accidentally clicked Sum instead of the arrow, press Esc to cancel the SUM function from being completed and try step b again.

c. Select the **range B8:B12**, the cells containing the house costs.

The function is =AVERAGE(B8:B12).

d. Press **Enter**, make **cell B18** the active cell, and save the workbook.

The average house cost is $304,240.

STEP 3 ⟫ USE THE MEDIAN FUNCTION

You realize that extreme house costs may distort the average. Therefore, you decide to identify the median house cost to compare it to the average house cost. Refer to Figure 18 as you complete Step 3.

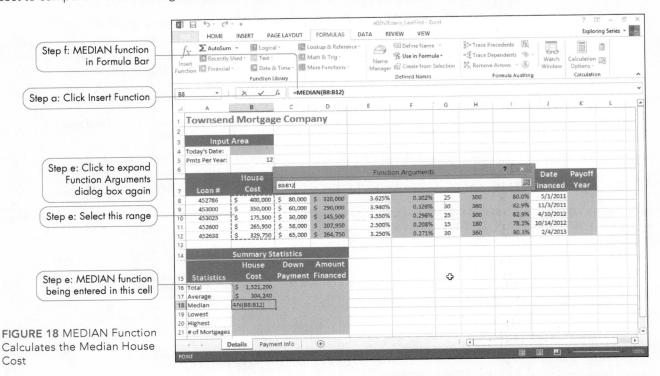

FIGURE 18 MEDIAN Function Calculates the Median House Cost

a. Make sure **cell B18** is the active cell. Click **Insert Function** between the Name Box and the Formula Bar, or in the Function Library group on the FORMULAS tab.

The Insert Function dialog box opens. Use this dialog box to select the MEDIAN function since it is not available on the Ribbon.

b. Type **median** in the **Search for a function box** and click **Go**.

Excel displays a list of functions in the *Select a function* list. The MEDIAN function is selected at the top of the list; the bottom of the dialog box displays the syntax and the description.

c. Read the MEDIAN function's description and click **OK**.

The Function Arguments dialog box opens. It contains one required argument, Number1, representing a range of cells containing values. It has an optional argument, Number2, which you can use if you have nonadjacent ranges that contain values.

d. Click the **collapse button** to the right of the Number1 box.

You collapsed the Function Arguments dialog box so that you can select the range.

e. Select the **range B8:B12** and click the **expand button** in the Function Arguments dialog box.

The Function Arguments dialog box expands, displaying B8:B12 in the Number1 box.

f. Click **OK** to accept the function arguments and close the dialog box. Save the workbook.

Half of the houses purchased cost more than the median, $329,750, and half of the houses cost less than this value. Notice the difference between the median and the average: The average is lower because it is affected by the lowest-priced house, $175,500.

Hands-On Exercise 2

96

Erica wants to know the least and most expensive houses so that she can analyze typical customers of the Townsend Mortgage Company. You will use the MIN and MAX functions to obtain these statistics. In addition, you will use the COUNT function to tally the number of mortgages in the sample. Refer to Figure 19 as you complete Step 4.

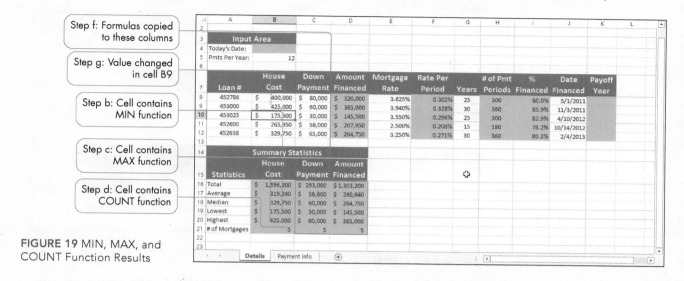

Step f: Formulas copied to these columns

Step g: Value changed in cell B9

Step b: Cell contains MIN function

Step c: Cell contains MAX function

Step d: Cell contains COUNT function

FIGURE 19 MIN, MAX, and COUNT Function Results

a. Click **cell B19**, the cell to display the cost of the lowest-costing house.

b. Click the **Sum arrow** in the Function Library group, select **Min**, select the **range B8:B12**, and then press **Enter**.

   The MIN function identifies that the lowest-costing house is $175,500.

c. Click **cell B20**, if necessary. Click the **Sum arrow** in the Function Library group, select **Max**, select the **range B8:B12**, and then press **Enter**.

   The MAX function identifies that the highest-costing house is $425,000.

d. Click **cell B21**, if necessary. Type **=COUNT(B8:B12)** and press **Enter**.

   As you type the letter *C*, Formula AutoComplete suggests functions starting with *C*. As you continue typing, the list of functions narrows. After you type the beginning parenthesis, Excel displays the function ScreenTip, indicating the arguments for the function. The range B8:B12 contains five cells.

e. Select the **range B16:B21**.

   You want to select the range of original statistics to copy the cells all at one time to the next two columns.

f. Drag the fill handle to the right by two columns to copy the functions. Click **cell D21**.

   Because you used relative cell references in the functions, the range changes from =COUNT(B8:B12) to =COUNT(D8:D12).

g. Change the value in **cell B9** to **425000**. Save the workbook.

   The results of several formulas and functions change, including the total, average, and max house costs.

STEP 5 ≫ USE THE TODAY AND YEAR FUNCTIONS

You have two date functions (TODAY and YEAR) to enter to complete the first worksheet. The TODAY function will display today's date, and you will use the YEAR function in a formula to calculate the payoff year for each mortgage. Refer to Figure 20 as you complete Step 5.

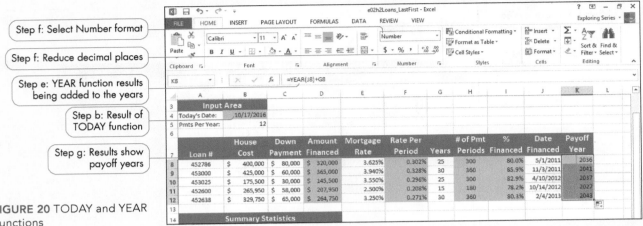

Step f: Select Number format

Step f: Reduce decimal places

Step e: YEAR function results being added to the years

Step b: Result of TODAY function

Step g: Results show payoff years

FIGURE 20 TODAY and YEAR Functions

a. Click **cell B4**, the cell to contain the current date.

b. Click **Date & Time** in the Function Library group, select **TODAY** to display the Function Arguments dialog box, and then click **OK** to close the dialog box.

The Function Arguments dialog box opens, although no arguments are necessary for this function. Excel inserts the current date in Short Date format, such as 1/2/2016, based on the computer system's date.

c. Click **cell K8**, click **Date & Time** in the Function Library group, scroll through the list, and then select **YEAR**.

The Function Arguments dialog box opens so that you can enter the argument, a serial number for a date.

d. Click **cell J8** to enter it in the **Serial_number box**. Click **OK**.

The function returns 2011, the year the first mortgage was taken out. However, you want the year the mortgage will be paid off. The YEAR function returns the year from a date. You need to add the years to the result of the function to calculate the year that the borrower will pay off the mortgage.

e. Press **F2** to edit the formula stored in **cell K8**. With the insertion point on the right side of the closing parenthesis, type **+G8** and press **Ctrl+Enter**.

Pressing Ctrl+Enter is the alternative to clicking Enter by the Formula Bar. It keeps the current cell as the active cell. The results show a date: 7/28/1905. You need to apply the Number format to display the year.

f. Click the **HOME tab**, click the **Number Format arrow** in the Number group, and then select **Number**. Decrease the number of decimal places to show the value as a whole number.

You applied the Number format instead of the Comma format because although the Comma format is correct for quantities, such as 2,036 units, it is not appropriate for the year 2036.

g. Copy the formula down the Payoff Year column.

h. Save the workbook. Keep the workbook open if you plan to continue with the next Hands-On Exercise. If not, close the workbook and exit Excel.

Logical, Lookup, and Financial Functions

As you prepare complex spreadsheets using functions, you will frequently use three function categories: logical, lookup and reference, and finance. Logical functions test the logic of a situation and return a particular result. Lookup and reference functions are useful when you need to look up a value in a list to identify the applicable value. Financial functions are useful to anyone who plans to take out a loan or invest money.

In this section, you will learn how to use the logical, lookup, and financial functions.

Determining Results with the IF Function

STEP 3 ▶▶

The most common logical function is the *IF function*, which returns one value when a condition is met or is true and returns another value when the condition is not met or is false. For example, a company gives a $500 bonus to employees who sold *over* $10,000 in merchandise this week, but no bonus to employees who did not sell over $10,000 in merchandise. Figure 21 shows a worksheet containing the sales data for three representatives and their bonuses, if any.

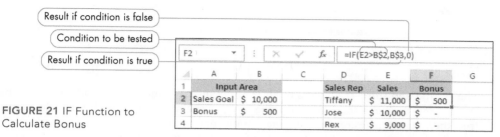

FIGURE 21 IF Function to Calculate Bonus

The IF function has three arguments: (1) a condition that is tested to determine if it is either true or false, (2) the resulting value if the condition is true, and (3) the resulting value if the condition is false.

=IF(logical_test,value_if_true,value_if_false)

You might find it helpful to create two flowcharts to illustrate an IF function. First, construct a flowchart that uses words and numbers to illustrate the condition and results. For example, the left flowchart in Figure 22 illustrates the condition to see if sales are greater than $10,000, and the $500 bonus if the condition is true or $0 if the condition is false. Then, create a second flowchart similar to the one on the right side of Figure 22 that replaces the words and values with actual cell references. Creating these flowcharts can help you construct the IF function that is used in cell F2 in Figure 21.

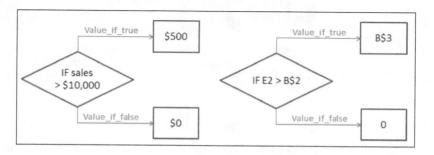

FIGURE 22 Flowcharts Illustrating IF Function

Design the Logical Test

The first argument for the IF function is the logical test. The *logical test* is a formula that contains either a value or an expression that evaluates to true or false. The logical expression is typically a binary expression, meaning that it requires a comparison between at least two variables, such as the values stored in cells E2 and B2. Table 4 lists and describes the logical operators to make the comparison in the logical test.

In Figure 21, cell F2 contains an IF function where the logical test is E2>B$2 to determine if Tiffany's sales in cell E2 are greater than the sales goal in cell B2. The reference to cell B2 can be mixed B$2 or absolute $B$2. Either way, copying the function down the column will compare each sales representative's sales with the $10,000 value in cell B2.

TABLE 4	Logical Operators
Operator	**Description**
=	Equal to
<>	Not equal to
<	Less than
>	Greater than
<=	Less than or equal to
>=	Greater than or equal to

Design the Value_If_True and Value_If_False Arguments

The second and third arguments of an IF function are value_if_true and value_if_false. When Excel evaluates the logical test, the result is either true or false. If the logical test is true, the value_if_true argument executes. If the logical test is false, the value_if_false argument executes. Only one of the last two arguments is executed; both arguments cannot be executed, because the logical test is either true or false but not both.

The value_if_true and value_if_false arguments can contain text, cell references, formulas, or constants (not recommended unless –1, 1, or 0). In Figure 21, cell F2 contains an IF function in which the value_if_true argument is B$3 and the value_if_false argument is 0. Because the logical test (E2>B$2) is true—that is, Tiffany's sales of $11,000 are greater than the $10,000 goal—the value_if_true argument is executed, and the result displays $500, the value that is stored in cell B3.

Jose's sales of $10,000 are not *greater than* $10,000, and Rex's sales of $9,000 are not *greater than* $10,000. Therefore, the value_if_false argument is executed and returns no bonus in cells F3 and F4.

 At Least Two Possible Right Answers

Every IF function can have at least two right solutions to produce the same results. For example, if the logical test is E2<=B$2 for Figure 21, the value_if_true is 0, and the value_if_false is B$3.

Create Other IF Functions

Figure 23 illustrates several IF functions, how they are evaluated, and their results. The input area contains values that are used in the logical tests and results. You can create this worksheet with the input area and IF functions to develop your understanding of how IF functions work.

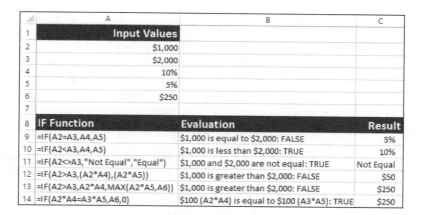

FIGURE 23 Sample IF Functions

	A	B	C
1	**Input Values**		
2	$1,000		
3	$2,000		
4	10%		
5	5%		
6	$250		
7			
8	**IF Function**	**Evaluation**	**Result**
9	=IF(A2=A3,A4,A5)	$1,000 is equal to $2,000: FALSE	5%
10	=IF(A2<A3,A4,A5)	$1,000 is less than $2,000: TRUE	10%
11	=IF(A2<>A3,"Not Equal","Equal")	$1,000 and $2,000 are not equal: TRUE	Not Equal
12	=IF(A2>A3,(A2*A4),(A2*A5))	$1,000 is greater than $2,000: FALSE	$50
13	=IF(A2>A3,A2*A4,MAX(A2*A5,A6))	$1,000 is greater than $2,000: FALSE	$250
14	=IF(A2*A4=A3*A5,A6,0)	$100 (A2*A4) is equal to $100 (A3*A5): TRUE	$250

- **Cell A9.** The logical test A2=A3 compares the values in cells A2 and A3 to see if they are equal. Because $1,000 is not equal to $2,000, the logical test is false. The value_if_false argument is executed, which displays 5%, the value stored in cell A5.

- **Cell A10.** The logical test A2<A3 determines if the value in cell A2 is less than the value in A3. Because $1,000 is less than $2,000, the logical test is true. The value_if_true argument is executed, which displays the value stored in cell A4, which is 10%.

- **Cell A11.** The logical test A2<>A3 determines if the values in cells A2 and A3 are not equal. Because $1,000 and $2,000 are not equal, the logical test is true. The value_if_true argument is executed, which displays the text *Not Equal*.

- **Cell A12.** The logical test A2>A3 is false. The value_if_false argument is executed, which multiplies the value in cell A2 ($1,000) by the value in cell A5 (5%) and displays $50. The parentheses in the value_if_true (A2*A4) and value_if_false (A2*A5) arguments are optional. They are not required but may help you read the function arguments better.

- **Cell A13.** The logical test A2>A3 is false. The value_if_false argument, which contains a nested MAX function, is executed. The MAX function, MAX(A2*A5,A6), multiplies the values in cells A2 ($1,000) and A5 (5%) and returns the higher of the product ($50) and the value stored in cell A6 ($250).

- **Cell A14.** The logical test A2*A4=A3*A5 is true. The contents of cell A2 ($1,000) are multiplied by the contents of cell A4 (10%) for a result of $100. That result is then compared to the result of A3*A5, which is also $100. Because the logical test is true, the function returns the value of cell A6 ($250).

 TIP **Using Text in Formulas**

You can use text within a formula. For example, you can build a logical test comparing the contents of cell A1 to specific text, such as A1="Input Values". The IF function in cell A11 in Figure 23 uses "Not Equal" and "Equal" in the value_if_true and value_if_false arguments. When you use text in a formula or function, you must enclose the text in quotation marks. However, do not use quotation marks around formulas, cell references, or values.

 TIP **Nest Functions in IF Functions**

You can nest functions in the logical test, value_if_true, and value_if_false arguments of the IF function. When you nest functions as arguments, make sure the nested function contains the required arguments for it to work and that you nest the function in the correct argument to calculate accurate results. For example, cell C13 in Figure 23 contains a nested MAX function in the value_if_false argument.

Logical, Lookup, and Financial Functions • Excel 2013

Using Lookup Functions

You can use lookup and reference functions to look up values to perform calculations or display results. For example, when you order merchandise on a Web site, the Web server looks up the shipping costs based on weight and distance, or at the end of a semester, your professor uses your average, such as 88%, to look up the letter grade to assign, such as B+.

Create the Lookup Table

A *lookup table* is a range containing a table of values or text that can be retrieved. The table should contain at least two rows and two columns, not including headings. Figure 24 illustrates a college directory with three "columns." The first column contains professors' names. You look up a professor's name in the first column to see his or her office (second "column") and phone extension (third "column").

Brazil, Estivan	GT 218b	7243
Fiedler, Zazilia	CS 417	7860
Lam, Kaitlyn	SC 124a	7031
Rodriquez, Lisa	GT 304	7592
Yeung, Bradon	CS 414	7314

FIGURE 24 College Directory Lookup Table Analogy

It is important to plan the table so that it conforms to the way in which Excel can utilize the data in it. Excel cannot interpret the structure of Table 5. To look up a value in a range (such as the range 80–89), you must arrange data from the lowest to the highest value and include only the lowest value in the range (such as 80) instead of the complete range. If the values you look up are *exact* values, you can arrange the first column in any logical order. The lowest value for a category or in a series is the **breakpoint**. The first column contains the breakpoints—such as 60, 70, 80, and 90—or the lowest values to achieve a particular grade. The lookup table contains one or more additional columns of related data to retrieve. Table 6 shows how to construct the lookup table in Excel.

TABLE 5	Grading Scale		TABLE 6	Grades Lookup Table
Range	**Grade**		**Range**	**Grade**
90–100	A		0	F
80–89	B		60	D
70–79	C		70	C
60–69	D		80	B
Below 60	F		90	A

Understand the VLOOKUP Function Syntax

STEP 1 ›› The ***VLOOKUP function*** accepts a value, looks the value up in a vertical lookup table, and returns a result. Use VLOOKUP to search for exact matches or for the nearest value that is less than or equal to the search value, such as assigning a B grade for an 87% class average. The VLOOKUP function has the following three required arguments and one optional argument: (1) lookup_value, (2) table_array, (3) col_index_number, and (4) range_lookup.

=VLOOKUP(lookup_value,table_array,col_index_number,[range_lookup])

Figure 25 shows a partial grade book that contains a vertical lookup table, as well as the final scores and letter grades. The function in cell F3 is =VLOOKUP(E3,$A$3:$B$7,2).

Formulas and Functions

Value (final score) to look up

Table array range

Use second column within the table to return letter grade

FIGURE 25 VLOOKUP Function for Grade Book

	F3			✕ ✓	fx	=VLOOKUP(E3,$A$3:$B$7,2)	

	A	B	C	D	E	F	G
1	Grading Scale			Partial Gradebook			
2	Breakpoint	Grade		Names	Final Score	Letter Grade	
3	0	F		Abbott	85	B	
4	60	D		Carter	69	D	
5	70	C		Hon	90	A	
6	80	B		Jackson	74	C	
7	90	A		Miller	80	B	
8				Nelsen	78	C	

The *lookup value* is the cell reference of the cell that contains the value to look up. The lookup value for the first student is cell E3, which contains 85. The *table array* is the range that contains the lookup table: $A$3:$B$7. The table array range must be absolute and cannot include column labels for the lookup table. The *column index number* is the column number in the lookup table that contains the return values. In this example, the column index number is 2.

> # TIP Using Values in Formulas
>
> You know to avoid using values in formulas because the input values in a worksheet cell might change. However, the value 2 is used in the col_index_number argument of the VLOOKUP function. The 2 refers to a particular column within the lookup table and is an acceptable use of a number within a formula.

Understand How Excel Processes the Lookup

Here is how the VLOOK function works:

1. The function identifies the value-stored cell used as the lookup value argument.
2. Excel searches the first column of the lookup table until it (a) finds an exact match (if possible) or (b) identifies the correct range if the lookup table contains breakpoints for range.
3. If Excel finds an exact match, it returns the value stored in the column designated by the column index number on that same row. If breakpoints are used and the lookup value is larger than the breakpoint, it looks to the next breakpoint to see if the lookup value is larger than that breakpoint also. When Excel detects that the lookup value is not greater than the next breakpoint, it stays on that row. It then uses the column index number to identify the column containing the value to return for the lookup value. Because Excel goes sequentially through the breakpoints, it is mandatory that the breakpoints are arranged from the lowest value to the highest value for ranges.

In Figure 25, the VLOOKUP function assigns letter grades based on final scores. Excel identifies the lookup value (85 in cell E3) and compares it to the values in the first column of the lookup table (range A3:B7). It tries to find an exact match of 85; however, the table contains breakpoints rather than every conceivable score. Because the lookup table is arranged from the lowest to the highest breakpoints, Excel detects that 85 is greater than the 80 breakpoint but is not greater than the 90 breakpoint. Therefore, it stays on the 80 row. Excel looks at the second column (column index number of 2) and returns the letter grade of B. The B grade is then stored in cell F3.

Use the Range_Lookup Argument

Instead of looking up values in a range, you can look up a value for an exact match using the optional range_lookup argument in the VLOOKUP function. By default, the range_lookup is set implicitly to TRUE, which is appropriate to look up values in a range. Omitting the optional argument or typing TRUE in it enables the VLOOKUP function to find the closest match in the table to the lookup value.

To look up an exact match, enter FALSE in the range_lookup argument. For example, if you are looking up product numbers, you must find an exact match to display the price. The function would look like this: =VLOOKUP(D15,$A$1:$B$50,2,FALSE). The function returns a value for the first lookup value that matches the first column of the lookup table. If no exact match is found, the function returns #N/A.

Nest Functions Inside the VLOOKUP Function

You can nest functions as arguments inside the VLOOKUP function. For example, Figure 26 illustrates shipping amounts that are based on weight and location (Boston or Chicago). In the VLOOKUP function in cell C3, the lookup_value argument looks up the weight of a package in cell A3. That weight (14 pounds) is looked up in the table_array argument, which is $E$3:$G$5. To determine which column of the lookup table to use, an IF function is nested as the column_index_number argument. The nested IF function compares the city stored in cell B3 to the text *Boston*. If cell B3 contains *Boston*, it returns 2 to use as the column_index_number to identify the shipping value for a package that is going to Boston. If cell B3 does not contain *Boston* (i.e., the only other city in this example is *Chicago*), the column_index_number is 3.

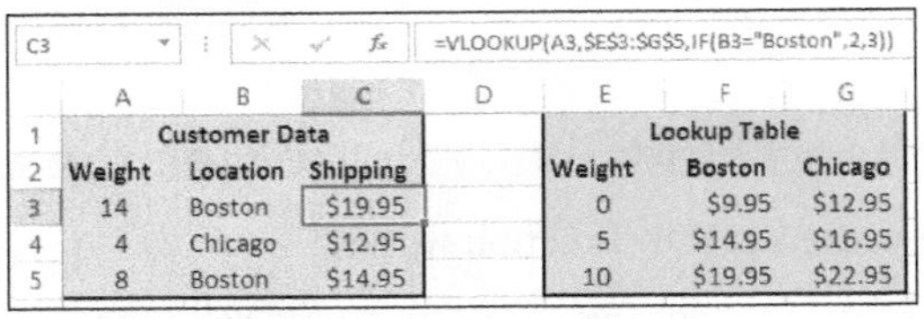

FIGURE 26 IF Function
Nested in VLOOKUP Function

Use the HLOOKUP Function

You can design a lookup table horizontally where the first row contains the values for the basis of the lookup or the breakpoints, and additional rows contain data to be retrieved. With a horizontal lookup table, use the **HLOOKUP function**. Table 7 shows how the grading scale would look as a horizontal lookup table.

TABLE 7	Horizontal Lookup Table			
0	60	70	80	90
F	D	C	B	A

The syntax is almost the same as the syntax for the VLOOKUP function, except the third argument is row_index_number instead of col_index_number.

=HLOOKUP(lookup_value,table_array,row_index_number,[range_lookup])

Calculating Payments with the PMT Function

STEP 2» Excel contains several financial functions to help you perform calculations with monetary values. If you take out a loan to purchase a car, you need to know the monthly payment, which depends on the price of the car, the down payment, and the terms of the loan, in order to determine if you can afford the car. The decision is made easier by developing the worksheet in Figure 27 and by changing the various input values as indicated.

B9		✕ ✓	f_x	=PMT(B6,B8,-B3)	

◢	A	B	C	D
1	Purchase Price	$25,999.00		
2	Down Payment	$ 5,000.00		
3	Amount to Finance	$20,999.00		
4	Payments per Year	12		
5	Interest Rate (APR)	3.500%		
6	Periodic Rate (Monthly)	0.292%		
7	Term (Years)	5		
8	No. of Payment Periods	60		
9	Monthly Payment	$ 382.01		
10				

FIGURE 27 Car Loan Worksheet

Creating a loan model helps you evaluate options. You realize that the purchase of a $25,999 car is prohibitive because the monthly payment is $382.01. Purchasing a less expensive car, coming up with a substantial down payment, taking out a longer-term loan, or finding a better interest rate can decrease your monthly payments.

The *PMT function* calculates payments for a loan with a fixed amount at a fixed periodic rate for a fixed time period. The PMT function uses three required arguments and up to two optional arguments: (1) rate, (2) nper, (3) pv, (4) fv, and (5) type.

=PMT(rate,nper,pv,[fv],[type])

The *rate* is the periodic interest rate, the interest rate per payment period. If the annual percentage rate (APR) is 12% and you make monthly payments, the periodic rate is 1% (12%/12 months). With the same APR and quarterly payments, the periodic rate is 3% (12%/4 quarters). Divide the APR by the number of payment periods in one year. However, instead of dividing the APR by 12 within the PMT function, calculate the periodic interest rate in cell B6 in Figure 27 and use that calculated rate in the PMT function.

The *nper* is the total number of payment periods. The term of a loan is usually stated in years; however, you make several payments per year. For monthly payments, you make 12 payments per year. To calculate the nper, multiply the number of years by the number of payments in one year. Instead of calculating the number of payment periods in the PMT function, calculate the number of payment periods in cell B8 and use that calculated value in the PMT function.

The *pv* is the present value of the loan. The result of the PMT function is a negative value because it represents your debt. However, you can display the result as a positive value by typing a minus sign in front of the present value cell reference in the PMT function.

Quick Concepts

1. Describe the three arguments for an IF function.

2. How should you structure a vertical lookup table if you need to look up values in a range?

3. What are the first three arguments of a PMT function? Why would you have to divide by or multiply an argument by 12?

Hands-On Exercises

Watch the Video for this Hands-On Exercise!

MyITLab®
HOE3 Training

3 Logical, Lookup, and Financial Functions

Erica wants you to complete another model that she might use for future mortgage data analysis. As you study the model, you realize you need to incorporate logical, lookup, and financial functions.

Skills covered: Use the VLOOKUP Function • Use the PMT Function • Use the IF Function

STEP 1 ≫ USE THE VLOOKUP FUNCTION

Rates vary based on the number of years to pay off the loan. Erica created a lookup table for three common mortgage years, and she entered the current APR. The lookup table will provide efficiency later when the rates change. You will use the VLOOKUP function to display the correct rate for each customer based on the number of years of the respective loans. Refer to Figure 28 as you complete Step 1.

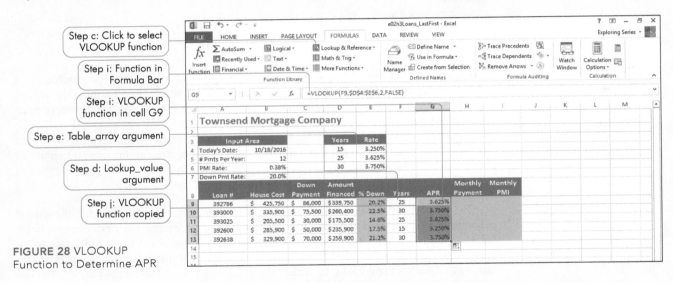

FIGURE 28 VLOOKUP Function to Determine APR

a. Open *e02h2Loans_LastFirst* if you closed it at the end of Hands-On Exercise 2 and save it as **e02h3Loans_LastFirst**, changing *h2* to *h3*.

b. Click the **Payment Info worksheet tab** to display the worksheet containing the data to complete. Click **cell G9**, the cell that will store the APR for the first customer.

c. Click the **FORMULAS tab**, click **Lookup & Reference** in the Function Library group, and then select **VLOOKUP**.

   The Function Arguments dialog box opens.

d. Click **F9** to enter F9 in the **Lookup_value box**.

   Cell F9 contains the value you need to look up from the table: 25 years.

> **TROUBLESHOOTING:** If you cannot see the cell you need to use in an argument, click the Function Arguments dialog box title bar and drag the dialog box on the screen until you can see and click the cell you need for the argument. Alternatively, you can click the collapse button to the right of the argument box to collapse the dialog box so that you can select the range. After selecting the range, click the expand button to expand the dialog box.

Hands-On Exercise 3

e. Press **Tab** and select the **range D4:E6** in the **Table_array box**.

This is the range that contains that data for the lookup table. The Years values in the table are arranged from lowest to highest. Do **not** select the column labels for the range.

Anticipate what will happen if you copy the formula down the column. What do you need to do to ensure that the cell references always point to the exact location of the table? If your answer is to make the table array cell references absolute, then you answered correctly.

f. Press **F4** to make the range references absolute.

The Table_array box now contains $D$4:$E$6.

g. Press **Tab** and type **2** in the **Col_index_num box**.

The second column of the lookup table contains the APRs that you want to return and display in the cells containing the formulas.

h. Press **Tab** and type **False** in the **Range_lookup box**.

You want the formula to display an error if an incorrect number of years has been entered. To ensure an exact match to look up in the table, you enter *False* in the optional argument.

i. Click **OK**.

The VLOOKUP function looks up the first person's years (25), finds an exact match in the first column of the lookup table, and then returns the corresponding APR, which is 3.625%.

j. Copy the formula down the column and save the workbook.

Spot check the results to make sure the function returned the correct APR based on the number of years.

STEP 2 ›› USE THE PMT FUNCTION

The worksheet now has all the necessary data for you to calculate the monthly payment for each loan: the APR, the number of years for the loan, the number of payment periods in one year, and the initial loan amount. You will use the PMT function to calculate the monthly payment, which includes paying back the principal amount with interest. This calculation does not include escrow amounts, such as property taxes or insurance. Refer to Figure 29 as you complete Step 2.

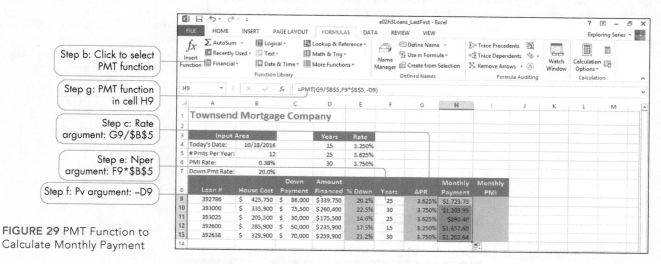

Step b: Click to select PMT function

Step g: PMT function in cell H9

Step c: Rate argument: G9/$B$5

Step e: Nper argument: F9*$B$5

Step f: Pv argument: −D9

FIGURE 29 PMT Function to Calculate Monthly Payment

a. Click **cell H9**, the cell that will store the payment for the first customer.

b. Click **Financial** in the Function Library group, scroll through the list, and then select **PMT**.

> **TROUBLESHOOTING:** Make sure you select PMT, not PPMT. The PPMT function calculates the principal portion of a particular monthly payment, not the total monthly payment itself.

The Function Arguments dialog box opens.

c. Type **G9/B5** in the **Rate box**.

Think about what will happen if you copy the formula. The argument will be G10/B6 for the next customer. Are those cell references correct? G10 does contain the APR for the next customer, but B6 does not contain the correct number of payments in one year. Therefore, you need to make B5 an absolute cell reference because the number of payments per year does not vary.

d. Press **F4** to make the reference to cell B5 absolute.

e. Press **Tab** and type **F9*$B$5** in the **Nper box**.

You calculate the nper by multiplying the number of years by the number of payments in one year. You must make B5 an absolute cell reference so that it does not change when you copy the formula down the column.

f. Press **Tab** and type **-D9** in the **Pv box**.

The bottom of the dialog box indicates that the monthly payment is 1723.73008 or $1,723.73.

> **TROUBLESHOOTING:** If the payment displays as a negative value, you probably forgot to type the minus sign in front of the D9 reference in the Pv box. Edit the function and type the minus sign in the correct place.

g. Click **OK**. Copy the formula down the column and save the workbook.

STEP 3 ≫ USE THE IF FUNCTION

Lenders often want borrowers to have a 20% down payment. If borrowers do not put in 20% of the cost of the house as a down payment, they pay a private mortgage insurance (PMI) fee. PMI serves to protect lenders from absorbing loss if the borrower defaults on the loan, and it enables borrowers with less cash to secure a loan. The PMI fee is about 0.38% of the amount financed. Some borrowers have to pay PMI for a few months or years until the balance owed is less than 80% of the appraised value. The worksheet contains the necessary values input area. You need to use the IF function to determine which borrowers must pay PMI and how much they will pay. Refer to Figure 30 as you complete Step 3.

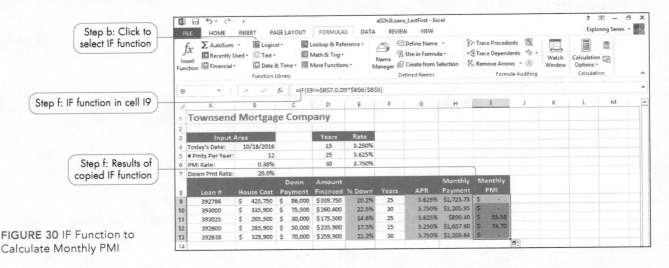

FIGURE 30 IF Function to Calculate Monthly PMI

a. Click **cell I9**, the cell that will store the PMI, if any, for the first customer.

b. Click **Logical** in the Function Library group and select **IF**.

The Function Arguments dialog box opens. You need to enter the three arguments.

c. Type **E9>=$B$7** in the **Logical_test box**.

The logical test compares the down payment percentage to see if the customer's down payment is at least 20%, the threshold stored in B7, of the amount financed. The customer's percentage cell reference needs to be relative so that it will change when you copy it down the column; however, cell B7 must be absolute because it contains the threshold value.

d. Press **Tab** and type **0** in the **Value_if_true box**.

If the customer makes a down payment that is at least 20% of the purchase price, the customer does not pay PMI. The first customer paid 20% of the purchase price, so he or she does not have to pay PMI.

e. Press **Tab** and type **D9*$B$6/$B$5** in the **Value_if_false box**.

If the logical test is false, the customer must pay PMI, which is calculated by dividing the yearly PMI (0.38%) by 12 and multiplying the result by the amount financed.

f. Click **OK** and copy the formula down the column.

The third and fourth customers must pay PMI because their respective down payments were less than 20% of the purchase price.

TROUBLESHOOTING: If the results are not as you expected, check the logical operators. People often mistype < and > or forget to type = for >= situations. Correct any errors in the original formula and copy the formula again.

---

g. Save the workbook. Keep the workbook open if you plan to continue with the next Hands-On Exercise. If not, close the workbook and exit Excel.

Range Names

To simplify entering ranges in formulas, you can use range names. A ***range name*** is a word or string of characters assigned to one or more cells. Think of range names in this way: Your college identifies you by your student ID; however, your professors call you by an easy-to-remember name, such as Micah or Vanessa. Similarly, instead of using cell addresses, you can use descriptive range names in formulas. Going back to the VLOOKUP example shown in Figure 25, you can assign the range name *Grades* to cells A3:B7 and modify the VLOOKUP function to be =VLOOKUP(E3,Grades,2), using the range name *Grades* in the formula. Another benefit of using range names is that they are absolute references, which helps ensure accuracy in your calculations.

In this section, you will work with range names. First, you will learn how to create and maintain range names. Then you will learn how to use a range name in a formula.

Creating and Maintaining Range Names

Each range name within a workbook must be unique. For example, you cannot assign the name *COST* to ranges on several worksheets or on the same sheet. After you create a range name, you might need to change its name or range. If you no longer need a range name, you can delete it. You can also insert in the workbook a list of range names and their respective cell ranges for reference.

Create a Range Name

STEP 1 ▶ A range name can contain up to 255 characters, but it must begin with a letter or an underscore. You can use a combination of upper- or lowercase letters, numbers, periods, and underscores throughout the range name. A range name cannot include spaces or special characters. You should create range names that describe the range of cells being named, but names cannot be identical to the cell contents. Keep the range names short to make them easier to use in formulas. Table 8 lists acceptable and unacceptable range names.

TABLE 8 Range Names	
Name	Description
Grades	Acceptable range name
COL	Acceptable abbreviation for cost-of-living
Tax_Rate	Acceptable name with underscore
Commission Rate	Unacceptable name; cannot use spaces in names
Discount Rate %	Unacceptable name; cannot use special symbols and spaces
2016_Rate	Unacceptable name; cannot start with a number
Rate_2016	Acceptable name with underscore and numbers

To create a range name, select the range you want to name and do one of the following:

- Click in the Name Box, type the range name, and then press Enter.
- Click the FORMULAS tab, click Define Name in the Defined Names group to open the New Name dialog box (see Figure 31), type the range name in the Name Box, and then click OK.
- Click the FORMULAS tab, click Name Manager in the Defined Names group to open the Name Manager dialog box, click New, type the range name in the Name Box, click OK, and then click Close.

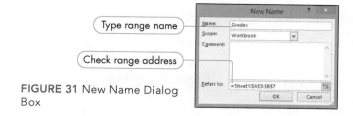

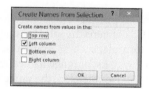

FIGURE 31 New Name Dialog Box

You can create several range names at the same time if your worksheet includes ranges with values and descriptive labels. To do this, select the range of cells containing the labels that you want to become names and the cells that contain the values to name, click *Create from Selection* in the Defined Named group on the Formulas tab, and then select an option in the *Create Names from Selection* dialog box (see Figure 32).

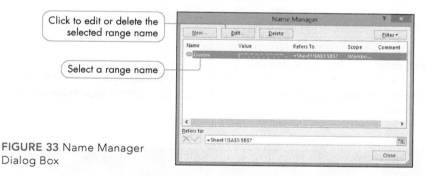

FIGURE 32 Create Names from Selection Dialog Box

Edit or Delete a Range Name

STEP 2 ≫ Use the Name Manager dialog box to edit, delete, and create range names. To open the Name Manager dialog box shown in Figure 33, click Name Manager in the Defined Names group on the Formulas tab. To edit a range or range name, click the range name in the list and click Edit. In the Edit Name dialog box, make your edits and click OK.

FIGURE 33 Name Manager Dialog Box

To delete a range name, open the Name Manager dialog box, select the name you want to delete, click Delete, and then click OK in the confirmation message box.

If you change a range name, any formulas that use the range name reflect the new name. For example, if a formula contains =cost*rate and you change the name rate to tax_rate, Excel updates the formula to be =cost*tax_rate. If you delete a range name and a formula depends on that range name, Excel displays #NAME?—indicating an Invalid Name Error.

Insert a Table of Range Names

STEP 4 ≫ You can document a workbook by inserting a list of range names in a worksheet. To insert a list of range names, click *Use in Formula* in the Defined Names group on the Formulas tab and select Paste Names. The Paste Name dialog box opens (see Figure 34), listing all range names in the current workbook. Click Paste List to insert a list of range names in alphabetical order. The first column contains a list of range names, and the second column contains the worksheet names and range locations.

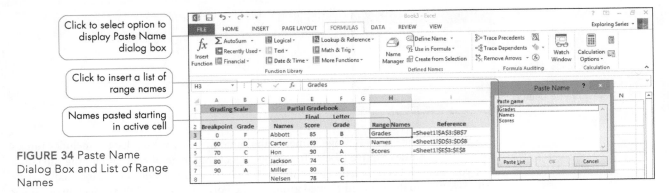

Click to select option to display Paste Name dialog box

Click to insert a list of range names

Names pasted starting in active cell

FIGURE 34 Paste Name Dialog Box and List of Range Names

Using Range Names in Formulas

STEP 3 >> You can use range names in formulas instead of cell references. For example, if cell C15 contains a purchase amount, and cell C5 contains the sales tax rate, instead of typing =C15*C5, you can type the range names in the formula, such as =purchase*tax_rate. When you type a formula, Formula AutoComplete displays a list of range names, as well as functions, that start with the letters as you type (see Figure 35). Double-click the range name to insert it in the formula.

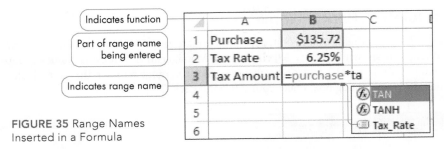

Indicates function

Part of range name being entered

Indicates range name

FIGURE 35 Range Names Inserted in a Formula

Another benefit of using range names is that if you have to copy the formula, you do not have to make the cell reference absolute in the formula. Furthermore, if you share your workbook with others, range names in formulas help others understand what values are used in the calculations.

TIP | Go to a Range Name

Use the Go To dialog box to go to the top-left cell in a range specified by a range name.

Quick Concepts

1. What is a range name?

2. List at least five guidelines and rules for naming a range.

3. What is the purpose of inserting a list of range names in a worksheet? What is contained in the list, and how is it arranged?

Formulas and Functions

Hands-On Exercises

Watch the Video
for this Hands-
On Exercise!

MyITLab®
HOE4 Training

4 Range Names

You decide to simplify the VLOOKUP function by using a range name for the APR rates lookup table instead of the actual cell references. After creating a range name, you will modify some range names Erica created and create a list of range names.

Skills covered: Create a Range Name • Edit and Delete Range Names • Use a Range Name in a Formula • Insert a List of Range Names

STEP 1 ≫ CREATE A RANGE NAME

You want to assign a range name to the lookup table of years and APRs. Refer to Figure 36 as you complete Step 1.

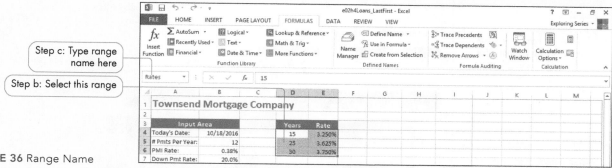

FIGURE 36 Range Name

a. Open *e02h3Loans_LastFirst* if you closed it at the end of Hands-On Exercise 3 and save it as **e02h4Loans_LastFirst**, changing *h3* to *h4*.

b. Make sure the **Payment Info worksheet tab** is active. Select **range D4:E6** (the lookup table).

c. Click in the **Name Box**, type **Rates**, and then press **Enter**. Save the workbook.

STEP 2 ≫ EDIT AND DELETE RANGE NAMES

You noticed that Erica added some range names. You will use the Name Manager dialog box to view and make changes to the range names, such as reducing the length of two range names and deleting another range name. Refer to Figure 37 as you complete Step 2.

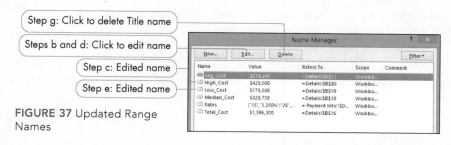

FIGURE 37 Updated Range Names

a. Click **Name Manager** in the Defined Names group on the FORMULAS tab.

   The Name Manager dialog box opens.

b. Select **Highest_House…** and click **Edit** to open the Edit Name dialog box.

c. Type **High_Cost** in the **Name Box** and click **OK**.

d. Select **Lowest_House...** and click **Edit**.

e. Type **Low_Cost** in the **Name Box** and click **OK**.

f. Select **Title** in the Name Manager dialog box.

This range name applies to a cell containing text, which does not need a name as it cannot be used in calculations. You decide to delete the range name.

g. Click **Delete**, read the warning message box, and then click **OK** to confirm the deletion of the Title range name.

h. Click **Close** and save the workbook.

STEP 3 ⟫ USE A RANGE NAME IN A FORMULA

You will modify the VLOOKUP function by replacing the existing Table_array argument with the range name. This will help Erica interpret the VLOOKUP function. Refer to Figure 38 as you complete Step 3.

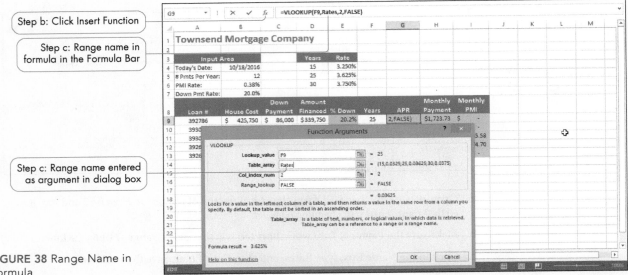

FIGURE 38 Range Name in Formula

a. Click **cell G9**, the cell containing the VLOOKUP function.

b. Click **Insert Function** between the Name Box and the Formula Bar to open the Function Arguments dialog box.

The Table_array argument contains $D$4:$E$6, the absolute reference to the lookup table.

c. Select **$D$4:$E$6** in the **Table_array box**, type **Rates**, and then click **OK**.

The new function is =VLOOKUP(F9,Rates,2,FALSE).

d. Copy the updated formula down the column and save the workbook.

The results are the same as they were when you used the absolute cell references. However, the formulas are shorter and easier to read with the range names.

Before submitting the completed workbook to Erica, you want to create a documentation worksheet that lists all of the range names in the workbook. Refer to Figure 39 as you complete Step 4.

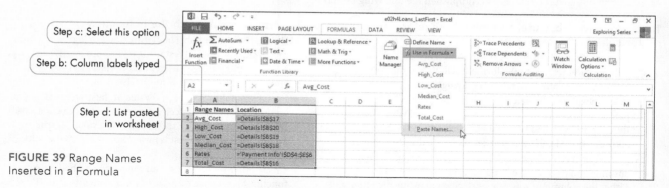

FIGURE 39 Range Names Inserted in a Formula

a. Click **New sheet** to the right of the worksheet tabs and double-click the default sheet name, **Sheet1**. Type **Range Names** and press **Enter**.

You inserted and renamed the new worksheet to reflect the data you will add to it.

b. Type **Range Names** in **cell A1** and type **Location** in **cell B1**. Bold these headings.

These column headings will display above the list of range names.

c. Click **cell A2**, click **Use in Formula** in the Defined Names group on the FORMULAS tab, and then select **Paste Names**.

The Paste Name dialog box opens, displaying all of the range names in the workbook.

d. Click **Paste List**.

Excel pastes an alphabetical list of range names starting in cell A2. The second column displays the locations of the range names.

e. Increase the widths of columns A and B to fit the data.

f. Save and close the workbook, and submit based on your instructor's directions.

TIP List of Range Names

When you paste range names, the list will overwrite any existing data in a worksheet, so consider pasting the list in a separate worksheet. If you add, edit, or delete range names, the list does not update automatically. To keep the list current, you would need to paste the list again.

After reading this chapter, you have accomplished the following objectives:

1. **Use relative, absolute, and mixed cell references in formulas.**
   - Use a relative cell address: A relative reference indicates a cell's location relative to the formula cell. When you copy the formula, the relative cell reference changes.
   - Use an absolute cell reference: An absolute reference is a permanent pointer to a particular cell, indicated with $ before the column letter and row number, such as $B$5. When you copy the formula, the absolute cell reference does not change.
   - Use a mixed cell reference: A mixed reference contains part absolute and part relative reference, such as $B5 or B$5. Either the column or row reference changes, while the other remains constant when you copy the formula.

2. **Correct circular references.**
   - A circular reference occurs when a formula refers to the cell containing the formula. The status bar indicates the location of a circular reference.

3. **Insert a function.**
   - A function is a predefined formula that performs a calculation. It contains the function name and arguments. Formula AutoComplete, function ScreenTips, and the Insert Function dialog box help you select and create functions. The Function Arguments dialog box guides you through entering requirements for each argument.

4. **Insert basic math and statistics functions.**
   - Calculate the total with the SUM function: The SUM function calculates the total of a range of values. The syntax is =SUM(number1,[number2],...).
   - Find central tendency with AVERAGE and MEDIAN: The AVERAGE function calculates the arithmetic mean of values in a range. The MEDIAN function identifies the midpoint value in a set of values.
   - Identify low and high values with MIN and MAX: The MIN function identifies the lowest value in a range, whereas the MAX function identifies the highest value in a range.
   - Identify the total number with COUNT functions: The COUNT function tallies the number of cells in a range, whereas the COUNTBLANK function tallies the number of blank cells in a range.
   - Use other math and statistical functions: Excel contains other math and statistical functions, such as MODE.
   - Nest functions as arguments: You can nest one function inside another function's argument, such as nesting the AVERAGE function inside the ROUND function: =ROUND(AVERAGE(A2:A14),2).

5. **Use date functions.**
   - Insert the TODAY function: The TODAY function displays the current date.
   - Insert the NOW function: The NOW function displays the current date and time.
   - Use other date functions: Excel contains a variety of date and time functions.

6. **Determine results with the IF function.**
   - Design the logical test: The IF function is a logical function that evaluates a logical test using logical operators, such as <, >, and =, and returns one value if the condition is true and another value if the condition is false.
   - Design the value_if_true and value_if_false arguments: The arguments can contain cell references, text, or calculations. If a logical test is true, Excel executes the value_if_true argument. If a logical test is false, Excel executes the value_if_false argument.
   - Create other IF functions: You can nest or embed other functions inside one or more of the arguments of an IF function to create more complex formulas.

7. **Use lookup functions.**
   - Create the lookup table: Design the lookup table using exact values or the breakpoints for ranges. If using breakpoints, the breakpoints must be in ascending order.
   - Understand the VLOOKUP syntax: The VLOOKUP function contains the required aruguments lookup_value, table_array, and col_index_num and one optional argument, range_lookup.
   - Understand how Excel processes the lookup: The VLOOKUP function looks up a value for a particular record, compares it to a lookup table, and returns a result in another column of the lookup table.
   - Use the range_lookup argument: If an exact match is required, the optional fourth argument should be FALSE; otherwise, the fourth argument can remain empty.
   - Nest functions inside the VLOOKUP function: You can nest functions inside one or more arguments.
   - Use the HLOOKUP function: The HLOOKUP function looks up values by row (horizontally) rather than by column (vertically).

8. **Calculate payments with the PMT function.**
   - The PMT function calculates periodic payments for a loan with a fixed interest rate and a fixed term. The PMT function requires the periodic interest rate, the total number of payment periods, and the original value of the loan.

9. **Create and maintain range names.**
   - Create a range name: A range name may contain letters, numbers, and underscores, but must start with either a letter or an underscore.
   - Edit or delete a range name: Use the Name Manager dialog box to edit, create, or delete range names.
   - Insert a table of range names: The first column contains an alphabetical list of range names, and the second column contains a list of their ranges.

10. **Use range names in formulas.**
    - You can use range names in formulas to make the formulas easier to interpret by using a descriptive name for the value(s) contained in a cell or range.

Key Terms Matching

Match the key terms with their definitions. Write the key term letter by the appropriate numbered definition.

a. Absolute cell reference
b. Argument
c. AVERAGE function
d. Circular reference
e. COUNT function
f. IF function
g. Logical test
h. Lookup table
i. MAX function
j. MEDIAN function
k. MIN function

l. Mixed cell reference
m. NOW function
n. PMT function
o. Range name
p. Relative cell reference
q. SUM function
r. Syntax
s. TODAY function
t. VLOOKUP function

1. _____ A set of rules that governs the structure and components for properly entering a function.

2. _____ Displays the current date.

3. _____ Indicates a cell's specific location; the cell reference does not change when you copy the formula.

4. _____ Occurs when a formula directly or indirectly refers to itself.

5. _____ An input, such as a cell reference or value, needed to complete a function.

6. _____ Identifies the highest value in a range.

7. _____ Tallies the number of cells in a range that contain values.

8. _____ Looks up a value in a vertical lookup table and returns a related result from the lookup table.

9. _____ A range that contains data for the basis of the lookup and data to be retrieved.

10. _____ Calculates the arithmetic mean, or average, of values in a range.

11. _____ Identifies the midpoint value in a set of values.

12. _____ Displays the current date and time.

13. _____ Evaluates a condition and returns one value if the condition is true and a different value if the condition is false.

14. _____ Calculates the total of values contained in two or more cells.

15. _____ Calculates the periodic payment for a loan with a fixed interest rate and fixed term.

16. _____ Indicates a cell's location from the cell containing the formula; the cell reference changes when the formula is copied.

17. _____ Contains both an absolute and a relative cell reference in a formula; the absolute part does not change but the relative part does when you copy the formula.

18. _____ A word or string of characters that represents one or more cells.

19. _____ An expression that evaluates to true or false.

20. _____ Displays the lowest value in a range.

Multiple Choice

1. If cell D15 contains the formula =$C$5*D$15, what is the D15 in the formula?

    (a) Relative reference

    (b) Absolute reference

    (c) Circular reference

    (d) Range name

2. What function would most appropriately accomplish the same thing as =(B5+C5+D5+E5+F5)/5?

    (a) =SUM(B5:F5)/5

    (b) =AVERAGE(B5:F5)

    (c) =MEDIAN(B5:F5)

    (d) =COUNT(B5:F5)

3. When you start =AV, what displays a list of functions and defined names?

    (a) Function ScreenTip

    (b) Formula AutoComplete

    (c) Insert Function dialog box

    (d) Function Arguments dialog box

4. A formula containing the entry =$B3 is copied to a cell one column to the right and two rows down. How will the entry appear in its new location?

    (a) =$B3

    (b) =B3

    (c) =$C5

    (d) =$B5

5. Cell B10 contains a date, such as 1/1/2016. Which formula will determine how many days are between that date and the current date, given that the cell containing the formula is formatted with Number Format?

    (a) =TODAY()

    (b) =CURRENT()-B10

    (c) =TODAY()-B10

    (d) =TODAY()+NOW()

6. Given that cells A1, A2, and A3 contain values 2, 3, and 10, respectively, and B6, C6, and D6 contain values 10, 20, and 30, respectively, what value will be returned by the function =IF(B6>A3,C6*A1,D6*A2)?

    (a) 10

    (b) 40

    (c) 60

    (d) 90

7. Given the function =VLOOKUP(C6,$D$12:$F$18,3), the entries in:

    (a) Range D12:D18 are in ascending order.

    (b) Range D12:D18 are in descending order.

    (c) The third column of the lookup table must be text only.

    (d) Range D12:D18 contain multiple values in each cell.

8. The function =PMT(C5,C7,-C3) is stored in cell C15. What must be stored in cell C5?

    (a) APR

    (b) Periodic interest rate

    (c) Loan amount

    (d) Number of payment periods

9. Which of the following is *not* an appropriate use of the SUM function?

    (a) =SUM(B3:B45)

    (b) =SUM(F1:G10)

    (c) =SUM(A8:A15,D8:D15)

    (d) =SUM(D15-C15)

10. Which of the following is *not* an acceptable range name?

    (a) FICA

    (b) Test_Weight

    (c) Goal for 2016

    (d) Target_2015

Practice Exercises

1 Blue Canadian Skies Airlines

You are an analyst for Blue Canadian Skies Airlines, a regional airline headquartered in Victoria. Your assistant developed a template for you to store daily flight data about the number of passengers per flight. Each regional aircraft can hold up to 70 passengers. You need to calculate the occupancy rate (the percent of each flight that is occupied), daily statistics (such as total number of passengers, averages, least full flights, etc.), and weekly statistics per flight number. This exercise follows the same set of skills as used in Hands-On Exercises 1 and 2 in the chapter. Refer to Figure 40 as you complete this exercise.

FIGURE 40 Blue Canadian Skies Airlines

a. Open *e02p1Flights* and save it as **e02p1Flights_LastFirst**.

b. Click **cell D6**, the cell to display the occupancy percent for Flight 4520 on Sunday, and do the following:

- Type **=C6/$C$2** and click **Enter** (the checkmark between the Name Box and the Formula Bar). The occupancy rate of Flight 4520 is 85.7%.
- Double-click the **cell D6 fill handle** to copy the formula down the column.

c. Click **cell D7**. When you copy a formula, Excel also copies the original cell's format. The cell containing the original formula did not have a bottom border, so when you copied the formula down the column, Excel formatted it to match the original cell with no border. To reapply the border, click **cell D15**, click the **Border arrow** in the Font group on the HOME tab, and then select **Bottom Border**.

d. Select the **range D6:D15**, click **Copy**, click **cell F6**, and then click **Paste**. The formula in cell F6 is =E6/$C$2. The first cell reference changes from C6 to E6, maintaining its relative location from the pasted formula. $C$2 remains absolute so that the number of passengers per flight is always divided by the value stored in cell C2. The copied range is still in the Clipboard. Paste the formula into the remaining % Full columns (columns H, J, L, N, and P). Press **Esc**.

e. Clean up the data by deleting *0.0%* in cells, such as H7. The 0.0% is misleading, as it implies the flight was empty; however, some flights do not operate on all days. Check your worksheet against the *Daily Flight Information* section in Figure 40.

f. Calculate the total number of passengers per day by doing the following:

- Click **cell C18** and click **Sum** in the Editing group.
- Select the **range C6:C15** and press **Enter**.

g. Calculate the average number of passengers per day by doing the following:
- Click **cell C19**, click the **Sum arrow** in the Editing group, and then select **Average**.
- Select the **range C6:C15** and click **Enter** (the checkmark between the Name Box and the Formula Bar).

h. Calculate the median number of passengers per day by doing the following:
- Click **cell C20**.
- Click **Insert Function**, type **median** in the **Search for a function box**, and then click **Go**.
- Click **MEDIAN** in the **Select a function box** and click **OK**.
- Select the **range C6:C15** to enter it in the **Number1 box** and click **OK**.

i. Calculate the least number of passengers on a daily flight by doing the following:
- Click **cell C21**, click the **Sum arrow** in the Editing group, and then select **Min**.
- Select the **range C6:C15** and press **Enter**.

j. Calculate the most passengers on a daily flight by doing the following:
- Click **cell C22** if necessary, click the **Sum arrow** in the Editing group, and then select **Max**.
- Select the **range C6:C15** and press **Enter**.

k. Calculate the number of flights for Sunday by doing the following:
- Click **cell C23** if necessary, click the **Sum arrow** in the Editing group, and then select **Count Numbers**.
- Select the **range C6:C15** and press **Enter**.

l. Calculate the average, median, least full, and most full percentages in **cells D19:D22**. Format the values with Percent Style with zero decimal places. Do not copy the formulas from column C to column D, as that will change the borders. Select **cells C18:D23**, copy the range, and then paste in these cells: **E18, G18, I18, K18, M18**, and **O18**. Press **Esc** after pasting.

m. Create a footer with your name on the left side, the sheet name code in the center, and the file name code on the right side.

n. Save and close the workbook, and submit based on your instructor's directions.

2 Steggel Consulting Firm Salaries

You work in the Human Resources Department at Steggell Consulting Firm. You are preparing a model to calculate bonuses based on performance ratings, where ratings between 1 and 1.9 do not receive bonuses, ratings between 2 and 2.9 earn $100 bonuses, ratings between 3 and 3.9 earn $250 bonuses, ratings between 4 and 4.9 earn $500 bonuses, and ratings of 5 or higher earn $1,000 bonuses. In addition, you need to calculate annual raises based on years employed. Employees who have worked five or more years earn a 3.25% raise; employees who have not worked at least five years earn a 2% raise. This exercise follows the same set of skills as used in Hands-On Exercises 1–4 in the chapter. Refer to Figure 41 as you complete this exercise.

a. Open *e02p2Salary* and save it as **e02p2Salary_LastFirst**.

b. Click **cell B4**, click the **FORMULAS tab**, click **Date & Time** in the Function Library group, select **TODAY**, and then click **OK** to enter today's date in the cell.

c. Enter a formula to calculate the number of years employed by doing the following:
- Click **cell C11**, click **Date & Time** in the Function Library group, scroll through the list, and then select **YEARFRAC**.
- Click **cell A11** to enter the cell reference in the **Start_date box**.
- Press **Tab** and click **cell B4** to enter the cell reference in the **End_date box**.
- Press **F4** to make **cell B4** absolute and click **OK**. (Although you could have used the formula =($B$4-A11)/365 to calculate the number of years, the YEARFRAC function provides better accuracy because it accounts for leap years and the divisor 365 does not. The completed function is =YEARFRAC(A11,$B$4).
- Double-click the **cell C11 fill handle** to copy the YEARFRAC function down the Years Employed column. Your results will differ based on the date contained in cell B4.

Practice Exercises

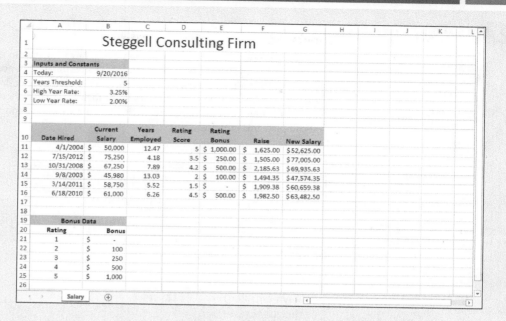

	A	B	C	D	E	F	G
1			Steggell Consulting Firm				
2							
3	**Inputs and Constants**						
4	Today:	9/20/2016					
5	Years Threshold:	5					
6	High Year Rate:	3.25%					
7	Low Year Rate:	2.00%					
8							
9							
10	Date Hired	Current Salary	Years Employed	Rating Score	Rating Bonus	Raise	New Salary
11	4/1/2004	$ 50,000	12.47	5	$ 1,000.00	$ 1,625.00	$52,625.00
12	7/15/2012	$ 75,250	4.18	3.5	$ 250.00	$ 1,505.00	$77,005.00
13	10/31/2008	$ 67,250	7.89	4.2	$ 500.00	$ 2,185.63	$69,935.63
14	9/8/2003	$ 45,980	13.03	2	$ 100.00	$ 1,494.35	$47,574.35
15	3/14/2011	$ 58,750	5.52	1.5	$ -	$ 1,909.38	$60,659.38
16	6/18/2010	$ 61,000	6.26	4.5	$ 500.00	$ 1,982.50	$63,482.50
17							
18							
19	**Bonus Data**						
20	Rating		Bonus				
21	1	$	-				
22	2	$	100				
23	3	$	250				
24	4	$	500				
25	5	$	1,000				
26							

Salary

FIGURE 41 Steggell Consulting Firm

d. Enter the breakpoint and bonus data for the lookup table by doing the following:
- Click **cell A21**, type **1**, and then press **Ctrl+Enter**.
- Click the **HOME tab**, click **Fill** in the Editing group, and then select **Series**. Click **Columns** in the *Series in* section, leave the **Step value** at **1**, type **5** in the **Stop value box**, and then click **OK**.
- Click **cell B21**. Enter **0, 100, 250, 500**, and **1000** down the column. The cells have been formatted with Accounting Number Format with zero decimal places.
- Select **range A21:B25**, click in the **Name Box**, type **Bonus**, and then press **Enter**.

e. Enter the bonus based on rating by doing the following:
- Click **cell E11** and click the **FORMULAS tab**.
- Click **Lookup & Reference** in the Function Library group and select **VLOOKUP**.
- Type **D11** in the **Lookup_value box**, type **Bonus** in the **Table_array box**, type **2**, and then click **OK**. The completed function is =VLOOKUP(D11,Bonus,2).
- Double-click the **cell E11 fill handle** to copy the formula down the Rating Bonus column.

f. Enter the raise based on years employed by doing the following:
- Click **cell F11**, click **Logical** in the Function Library group, and then select **IF**.
- Type **C11>=$B$5** to compare the years employed to the absolute reference of the five-year threshold in the **Logical_test box**.
- Press **Tab** and type **B11*$B$6** to calculate a 3.25% raise for employees who worked five years or more in the **Value_if_true box**.
- Press **Tab** and type **cell B11*$B$7** to calculate a 2% raise for employees who worked less than five years in the Value_if_false box. Click **OK**. The completed function is =IF(C11>=$B$5,B11*$B$6,B11*$B$7).
- Double-click the **cell F11 fill handle** to copy the formula down the Raise column.

g. Click **cell G11**. Type **=B11+E11+F11** to add the current salary, the bonus, and the raise to calculate the new salary. Double-click the **cell G11 fill handle** to copy the formula down the column.

h. Create a footer with your name on the left side, the sheet name code in the center, and the file name code on the right side.

i. Save and close the workbook, and submit based on your instructor's directions.

3 New Car Loan

After obtaining a promotion at work, you want to buy a luxury car, such as a Lexus or Infinity. Before purchasing a car, you want to create a worksheet to estimate the monthly payment based on the purchase price (including accessories, taxes, and license plate), APR, down payment, and years. You will assign range names and use range names in the formulas to make them easier to analyze. This exercise follows the same set of skills as used in Hands-On Exercises 1–4 in the chapter. Refer to Figure 42 as you complete this exercise.

	A	B	C
1	Car Loan		
2			
3	**Inputs**		
4	Cost of Car*	45000	
5	Down Payment	10000	
6	APR	0.0399	
7	Years	5	
8	Payments Per Year	12	
9	*Includes taxes, etc.		
10			
11	**Outputs**		
12	Loan	=Cost-Down	
13	Monthly Payment	=PMT(APR/Months,Years*Months,-Loan)	
14	Total to Repay Loan	=Years*Months*Payment	
15	Total Interest Paid	=Repaid-Loan	
16			

FIGURE 42 Car Loan

a. Open *e02p3CarLoan* and save it as **e02p3CarLoan_LastFirst**.

b. Name the input values by doing the following:

- Select the **range A4:B8**.
- Click the **FORMULAS tab** and click **Create from Selection** in the Defined Names group.
- Make sure *Left column* is selected and click **OK**.
- Click each input value cell in the **range B4:B8** and look at the newly created names in the Name Box.

DISCOVER

c. Edit the range names by doing the following:

- Click **Name Manager** in the Defined Names group.
- Click **Cost_of_Car**, click **Edit**, type **Cost**, and then click **OK**.
- Change *Down_Payment* to **Down**.
- Change *Payments_Per_Year* to **Months**.
- Click **Close** to close the Name Manager.

d. Name the output values in the **range A12:B15** using the *Create from Selection* method you used in step b to assign names to the empty cells in the range B12:B15. However, you will use the range names as you build formulas in the next few steps. Edit the range names using the same approach you used in step c.

- Change *Monthly_Payment* to **Payment.**
- Change *Total_Interest_Paid* to **Interest**.
- Change *Total_to_Repay_Loan* to **Repaid**.
- Click **Close** to close the Name Manager.

e. Enter the formula to calculate the amount of the loan by doing the following:
- Click **cell B12**. Type **=Cos** and double-click **Cost** from the Function AutoComplete list. If the list does not appear, type the entire name **Cost**.
- Press - and type **do**, and then double-click **Down** from the Function AutoComplete list.
- Press **Enter** to enter the formula =Cost-Down.

f. Calculate the monthly payment of principal and interest by doing the following:
- Click the **FORMULAS tab**. Click **cell B13**. Click **Financial** in the Function Library group, scroll down, and then select **PMT**.
- Type **APR/Months** in the **Rate box**.
- Press **Tab** and type **Years*Months** in the **Nper box**.
- Press **Tab**, type **-Loan** in the **Pv box**, and then click **OK**. The completed function is =PMT(APR/Months,Years*Months,-Loan).

DISCOVER

g. Enter the total amount to repay loan formula by doing the following:
- Click **cell B14**. Type = to start the formula.
- Click **Use in Formula** in the Defined Names group and select **Years**.
- Type *, click **Use in Formula** in the Defined Names group, and then select **Months**.
- Type *, click **Use in Formula** in the Defined Names group, and then select **Payment**.
- Press **Enter**. The completed formula is =Years*Months*Payment.

h. Use the skills from step g to enter the formula =**Repaid-Loan** in **cell B15**.

i. Select the **range B12:B15**, click the **HOME tab**, and then click **Accounting Number Format** in the Number group.

j. Select the option to center the worksheet data between the left and right margins in the Page Setup dialog box.

k. Create a footer with your name on the left side, the sheet name code in the center, and the file name code on the right side.

l. Right-click the **Car sheet tab**, select **Move or Copy** from the menu, click **(move to end)** in the *Before sheet* section, click the **Create a copy check box**, and then click **OK**. Rename the Car (2) sheet **Formulas**.

m. Make sure the Formulas sheet is active. Click the **FORMULAS tab** and click **Show Formulas** in the Formula Auditing group. Widen column B to display entire formulas.

n. Click the **PAGE LAYOUT tab** and click the **Gridlines Print check box** and the **Headings Print check box** in the Sheet Options group to select these two options.

o. Insert a new sheet, name it **Names**, type **Range Name** in **cell A1**, and then type **Location** in cell **B1**. Apply bold to these column labels. Click **cell A2**, click the **FORMULAS tab**, click **Use in Formula**, select **Paste Names**, and then click **Paste List** to paste an alphabetical list of range names in the worksheet. Adjust the column widths. Apply the same Page Setup settings and footer to the Formulas and Cars worksheets.

p. Save and close the workbook, and submit based on your instructor's directions.

1 Metropolitan Zoo Gift Shop Weekly Payroll

ANALYSIS CASE

As manager of the gift shop at the Metropolitan Zoo, you are responsible for managing the weekly payroll. Your assistant developed a partial worksheet, but you need to enter the formulas to calculate the regular pay, overtime pay, gross pay, taxable pay, withholding tax, FICA, and net pay. In addition, you want to total pay columns and calculate some basic statistics. As you construct formulas, make sure you use absolute and relative cell references correctly in formulas and avoid circular references.

a. Open the *e02m1Payroll* workbook and save it as **e02m1Payroll_LastFirst**.

b. Study the worksheet structure and read the business rules in the Notes section.

c. Use IF functions to calculate the regular pay and overtime pay based on a regular 40-hour workweek in **cells E5** and **F5**. Pay overtime only for overtime hours. Calculate the gross pay based on the regular and overtime pay. Abram's regular pay is $398. With 8 overtime hours, Abram's overtime pay is $119.40.

d. Create a formula in **cell H5** to calculate the taxable pay. Multiply the number of dependents by the deduction per dependent and subtract that from the gross pay. With two dependents, Abram's taxable pay is $417.40.

e. Use a VLOOKUP function in **cell I5** to identify and calculate the federal withholding tax. With a taxable pay of $417.40, Abram's tax rate is 25% and the withholding tax is $104.35. The VLOOKUP function returns the applicable tax rate, which you must then multiply by the taxable pay.

f. Calculate FICA in **cell J5** based on gross pay and the FICA rate and calculate the net pay in **Cell K5**.

g. Calculate the total regular pay, overtime pay, gross pay, taxable pay, withholding tax, FICA, and net pay on row 17.

h. Copy all formulas down their respective columns.

i. Apply **Accounting Number Format** to the **range C5:C16**. Apply **Accounting Number Format** to the first row of monetary data and to the total row. Apply **Comma Style** to the monetary values for the other employees. Underline the last employee's monetary values and use the Format Cells dialog box to apply **Double Accounting Underline** for the totals.

j. Insert appropriate functions to calculate the average, highest, and lowest values in the Summary Statistics area (the **range I21:K23**) of the worksheet.

DISCOVER

k. At your instructor's discretion, use Help to learn about the FREQUENCY function. The Help feature contains sample data for you to copy and practice in a new worksheet to learn about this function. You can close the practice worksheet containing the Help data without saving it. You want to determine the number (frequency) of employees who worked less than 20 hours, between 20 and 29 hours, between 30 and 40 hours, and over 40 hours. **Cells J28:J31** list the ranges. You need to translate this range into correct values for the Bin column in **cells I28:I31** and enter the FREQUENCY function in **cells K28:K31**. The function should identify one employee who worked between 0 and 19 hours and six employees who worked more than 40 hours.

l. Apply other page setup formats as needed.

m. Insert a new sheet named **Overtime**. List the number of overtime hours for the week. Calculate the yearly gross amount spent on overtime assuming the same number of overtime hours per week. Add another row with only half the overtime hours (using a formula). What is your conclusion and recommendation on overtime? Format this worksheet.

n. Insert a footer with your name on the left side, the sheet name code in the center, and the file name code on the right side of both worksheets.

o. Save and close the workbook, and submit based on your instructor's directions.

2 Mortgage Calculator

As a financial consultant, you work with people who are planning to buy a new house. You want to create a worksheet containing variable data (the price of the house, down payment, date of the first payment, and borrower's credit rating) and constants (property tax rate, years, and number of payments in one year). Borrowers pay 0.5% private mortgage insurance (PMI) on the loan amount if they do not make at least a 20% down payment. A borrower's credit rating determines the required down payment percentage and APR. For example, a person with an excellent credit rating may make only a 5% down payment with a 3.25% APR loan. A person with a fair credit rating will make a 15% down payment and have a higher APR at 5.25%. Your worksheet needs to perform various calculations. The filled cells in column F indicate cells containing formulas, not values. Refer to Figure 43 as you complete this exercise.

	A	B	C	D	E	F
1			Mortgage Calculator			
2						
3	Inputs				Intermediate Calculations	
4	Negotiated Cost of House		$ 375,000.00		APR Based on Credit Rating	3.25%
5	Additional Down Payment		$ 5,000.00		Min Down Payment Required	$ 18,750.00
6	Date of First Payment		5/1/2016		Annual Property Tax	$ 2,812.50
7	Credit Rating		Excellent		Annual PMI	$ 1,756.25
8						
9	Constants				Outputs	
10	Property Tax Rate		0.75%		Total Down Payment	$ 23,750.00
11	Down Payment to Avoid PMI		20.00%		Amount of the Loan	$351,250.00
12	PMI Rate		0.50%		Monthly Payment (P&I)	$1,528.66
13	Term of Loan in Years		30		Monthly Property Tax	234.38
14	# of Payments Per Year		12		Monthly PMI	146.35
15					Total Monthly Payment	$ 1,909.39
16	Credit	Down Payment	APR		Date of Last Payment	4/1/2046
17	Excellent	5%	3.25%			
18	Good	10%	3.50%			
19	Fair	15%	4.25%			
20	Poor	20%	5.25%			
21						

FIGURE 43 Mortgage Data

a. Start a new Excel workbook, save it as **e02m2Loan_LastFirst**, rename Sheet1 **Payment**, add a new sheet, and then rename it **Range Names**.

b. Select the **Payment sheet**, type **Mortgage Calculator** in **cell A1**, and then merge and center the title on the first row in the **range A1:F1**. Apply bold, **18 pt size**, and **Gold, Accent 4, Darker 25% font color**.

c. Create and format the Inputs and Constants areas by doing the following:
   - Type the labels in the **range A3:A20**. For each label, such as *Negotiated Cost of House*, merge the cells, such as the **range A4:B4**, and apply **Align Text Left**. You will have to merge cells for nine labels.
   - Enter and format the *Inputs* and *Constants* values in column C.

d. Create the lookup table in the **range A16:C20** to use the credit ratings to identify the appropriate required percentage down payment and the respective APR by doing the following:
   - Type **Credit**, **Down Payment**, and **APR** in the **range A16:C16**.
   - Type the four credit ratings in the first column, the required down payment percentages in the second column, and the respective APRs in the third column.
   - Format the percentages, apply **Align Text Right**, and then indent the percentages in the cells as needed.

e. Assign range names to cells containing individual values in the Inputs and Constants sections. Do *not* use the *Create from Selection* feature because the labels are stored in merged cells. Assign a range name to the lookup table.

f. Type labels in the *Intermediate Calculations* and *Outputs* sections in column E and assign a range name to each cell in the **ranges F4:F7** and **F10:F12**. Widen column E as needed.

g. Enter formulas in the *Intermediate Calculations* and *Outputs* sections using range names to calculate the following:

- **APR** based on the borrower's credit rating by using a lookup function. Include the range_lookup argument to ensure an *exact match*. For example, a borrower who has an Excellent rating gets a 3.25% APR.
- **Minimum down payment required** amount by using a lookup function and calculation. Include the range_lookup argument to ensure an *exact match*. For example, a borrower who has an Excellent rating is required to pay a minimum of 5% down payment of the negotiated purchase price. Multiply the function results by the negotiated cost of the house. Hint: The calculation comes after the closing parenthesis.
- **Annual property tax** based on the negotiated cost of the house and the annual property tax rate.
- **Annual PMI**. If the borrower's total down payment (required and additional) is 20% or higher of the negotiated purchase price (multiply the cost by the PMI avoidance percentage), PMI is zero. If the total down payment is less than 20%, the borrower has to pay PMI based on multiplying the amount of the loan by the PMI rate.
- **Total down payment**, which is sum of the required minimum down payment (calculated previously) and any additional down payment entered in the Inputs section.
- **Amount of the loan**, which is the difference between the negotiated cost of the house and the total down payment.
- **Monthly payment** of principal and interest using the PMT function.
- **Monthly property tax**, the **monthly PMI**, and the **total monthly payment**.
- **Last payment date** using the EDATE function. The function's second argument must calculate the correct number of months based on the total length of the loan. For example, if the first payment date is 5/1/2016, the final payment date is 4/1/2046 for a 30-year loan. The last argument of the function must subtract 1 to ensure the last payment date is correct. If the last payment date calculated to 5/1/2046, you would be making an extra payment.

h. Format each section with fill color, bold, underline, number formats, borders, and column widths as shown in the figure.

i. Paste a list of range names in the Range Names worksheet. Insert a row above the list and type and format column labels above the two columns in the list of range names.

j. Center the worksheet data horizontally between the left and right margins.

k. Insert a footer with your name on the left side, the sheet name code in the center, and the file name code on the right side of both sheets.

l. Save and close the workbook, and submit based on your instructor's directions.

3 Professor's Grade Book

You are a teaching assistant for Dr. Denise Gerber, who teaches an introductory C# programming class at your college. One of your routine tasks is to enter assignment and test grades into the grade book. Now that the semester is almost over, you need to create formulas to calculate category averages, the overall weighted average, and the letter grade for each student. In addition, Dr. Gerber wants to see general statistics, such as average, median, low, and high for each graded assignment and test, as well as category averages and total averages. Furthermore, you need to create the grading scale on the documentation worksheet and use it to display the appropriate letter grade for each student.

a. Open *e02m3Grades* and save it as **e02m3Grades_LastFirst**.

b. Use breakpoints to enter the grading scale in the correct structure on the Documentation worksheet and name the grading scale range **Grades**. The grading scale is as follows:

95+	A
90–94.9	A–
87–89.9	B+
83–86.9	B
80–82.9	B–
77–79.9	C+
73–76.9	C
70–72.9	C–
67–69.9	D+
63–66.9	D
60–62.9	D–
0–59.9	F

c. Calculate the total lab points earned for the first student in **cell T8** in the Grades worksheet. The first student earned 93 lab points.

d. Calculate the average of the two midterm tests for the first student in **cell W8**. The student's midterm test average is 87.

e. Calculate the assignment average for the first student in **cell I8**. The formula should drop the lowest score before calculating the average. Hint: You need to use a combination of three functions: SUM, MIN, and COUNT. The argument for each function for the first student is B8:H8. Find the total points and subtract the lowest score. Then divide the remaining points by the number of assignments minus 1. The first student's assignment average is 94.2 after dropping the lowest assignment score.

f. Calculate the weighted total points based on the four category points (assignment average, lab points, midterm average, and final exam) and their respective weights (stored in the **range B40:B43**) in **cell Y8**. Use relative and absolute cell references as needed in the formula. The first student's total weighted score is 90.

g. Use a VLOOKUP function to calculate the letter grade equivalent in **cell Z8**. Use the range name in the function. The first student's letter grade is A–.

h. Copy the formulas down their respective columns for the other students.

i. Name the passing score threshold in **cell B5** with the range name **Passing**. Use an IF function to display a message in the last grade text column based on the student's semester performance. If a student earned a final score of 70 or higher, display *Enroll in CS 202*. Otherwise, display *RETAKE CS 101*. Remember to use quotation marks around the text arguments.

j. Calculate the average, median, low, and high scores for each assignment, lab, test, category average, and total score. Display individual averages with no decimal places; display category and final score averages with one decimal place. Display other statistics with no decimal places.

k. Insert a list of range names in the designated area in the Documentation worksheet. Complete the documentation by inserting your name, today's date, and a purpose statement in the designated areas.

DISCOVER

l. At your instructor's discretion, add a column to display each student's rank in the class. Use Help to learn how to insert the RANK function.

m. Select page setup options as needed to print the Grades worksheet on one page.

n. Insert a footer with your name on the left side, the sheet name code in the center, and the file name code on the right side of each worksheet.

o. Save and close the workbook, and submit based on your instructor's directions.

4 Facebook and YouTube

COLLABORATION CASE

FROM SCRATCH

Social media extends past friendships to organizational and product "fan" pages. Organizations such as Lexus, Pepsi, and universities create pages to provide information about their organizations. Some organizations even provide product details, such as the Lexus ES350. Facebook includes a wealth of information about Microsoft Office products. People share information, pose questions, and reply with their experiences.

a. Log in to your Facebook account. If you do not have a Facebook account, sign up for one and add at least two classmates as friends. Search for Microsoft Excel and click **Like**.

b. Review postings on the Microsoft Excel wall. Notice that some people post what they like most about Excel or how much it has improved their productivity. Post a note about one of your favorite features about Excel that you have learned so far or how you have used Excel in other classes or on the job. Start Word and, using the Snipping Tool, insert a screenshot of your posting. Save the document as **e02t1_LastFirst**.

c. Click the **Discussions link** on the Microsoft Excel Facebook page and find topics that relate to IF or VLOOKUP functions. Post a response to one of the discussions. Take a screenshot of your posting and insert it into your Word document.

d. Create a team of three students. Create one discussion that asks people to describe their favorite use of any of the nested functions used in this chapter. Each team member should respond to the posting. Monitor the discussion and, when you have a few responses, capture a screenshot of the dialogue and insert it into your Word document.

e. Save and close the document. Submit it based on your instructor's directions.

f. Go to www.youtube.com and search for one of these Excel topics: absolute references, mixed references, semi-selection, IF function, VLOOKUP function, circular references, statistical functions shown in Table 2, date functions shown in Table 3, or range names.

g. Watch several video clips and find one of particular interest to you.

h. Post the URL on your Facebook wall. Specify the topic and describe why you like this particular video.

i. Watch videos from the links posted by other students on their Facebook walls. Comment on at least two submissions. Point out what you like about the video or any suggestions you have for improvement.

j. If required by your instructor, insert screenshots of your postings in a Word document. Save and submit based on your instructor's directions.

Beyond the Classroom

College Sports Scores

RESEARCH CASE ➡️

FROM SCRATCH

You want to create a spreadsheet to display data for your favorite college sports team. Conduct an Internet search to identify the game dates, your team's scores, the opponent, and the opponent's score for each game for the last complete season. Enter the data into a new workbook and save the workbook as **e02b2Sports_LastFirst**. Games are usually scheduled seven days apart. Enter this value on a second sheet, assign a range name, and then use the range name in a formula to calculate the game dates based on the original game date. In some instances, you may have to enter a date if more or fewer days exist between two game dates. In the fifth column, use an IF function to determine if your team won or lost each game; display either *Win* or *Lose*. In the sixth column, use an IF function to calculate by how many points your team won each game or display an empty string by entering "" in the value_if_false argument if your team lost.

Create a statistics area to calculate the average, median, low, and high scores for your team. Below the won-by points column, use two different count functions to count the number of games won and lost. Use Help to learn about the COUNTIF function and use this function to count the number of games won based on the number of *Win* entries. Use mixed references in the function's first argument, copy the function, and then edit the second argument of the copied COUNTIF function to calculate the number of games lost. The summary area should have four count functions. Add titles and column labels, format data within the columns, and then include the URL of where you got the data. Include a footer with your name on the left side, the date code in the center, and the file name code on the right side. Save and close the workbook, and submit based on your instructor's directions.

Park City Condo Rental

DISASTER RECOVERY ➕

You and some friends are planning a Labor Day vacation to Park City, Utah. You have secured a four-day condominium that costs $1,200. Some people will stay all four days; others will stay part of the weekend. One of your friends constructed a worksheet to help calculate each person's cost of the rental. The people who stay Thursday night will split the nightly cost evenly. To keep the costs down, everyone agreed to pay $30 per night per person for Friday, Saturday, and/or Sunday nights. Depending on the number of people who stay each night, the group may owe more money. Kyle, Ian, Isaac, and Daryl agreed to split the difference in the total rental cost and the amount the group members paid. Open *e02b3ParkCity*, address the circular reference error message that displays, and save the workbook as **e02b3ParkCity_LastFirst**.

Review the worksheet structure, including the assumptions and calculation notes at the bottom of the worksheet. Check the formulas and functions, making necessary corrections. With the existing data, the number of people staying each night is 5, 7, 10, and 10, respectively. The total paid given the above assumptions is $1,110, giving a difference of $90 to be divided evenly among the first four people. Kyle's share should be $172.50. In the cells containing errors, insert comments to describe the error and fix the formulas. Verify the accuracy of formulas by entering an IF function in **cell I1** to ensure the totals match. Nick, James, and Body inform you they can't stay Sunday night, and Rob wants to stay Friday night. Change the input accordingly. The updated total paid is now $1,200, and the difference is $150. Include a footer with your name on the left side, the date code in the center, and the file name code on the right side. Save and close the workbook, and submit based on your instructor's directions.

Interview Walkthough

After watching the video, create a workbook named **e02b4Interview_LastFirst** that lists five to seven common interview questions in the first column. In the second column, enter a percentage weight for each question. For example, the first question might count 5% of the total. The total weights should be 100%. Include columns to rate five interviewees on the questions using a scale of 1–5 where 1 is low and 5 is high. Incude a column label with a first name for each interviewee. At the bottom of the first interviewee's column, use the AVERAGE function with the argument to multiply that person's individual scores by their respective weights using relative and absolute references correctly. Copy the formula to the other candidates.

Add an input area for a minimum weighted score of 4.5. Assign a range name to the score. On the row below the weighted scores, add a row labeled *Second Interview?* Enter an IF function for the first candidate: If the weighted score is greater than or equal to 4.5, then display *Yes*; otherwise, display *No*. Copy the function for the other candidates. Include a footer with your name on the left side, the date code in the center, and the file name code on the right side. Save and close the workbook, and submit based on your instructor's directions.

You are a sales representative at the local fitness center, Health & Fitness Gym. Your manager expects each representative to track weekly new membership data, so you created a spreadsheet to store data. Membership costs are based on membership type. Clients can rent a locker for an additional annual fee. You are required to collect a down payment based on membership type, determine the balance, and then calculate the monthly payment based on a standard interest rate. In addition, you need to calculate general statistics to summarize for your manager. Spot-check results to make sure you created formulas and functions correctly.

Perform Preliminary Work

You need to open the starting workbook you created, acknowledge the existing circular reference error, and assign a range name to the membership lookup table. You will correct the circular reference error later.

a. Open the *e02c1Gym* workbook, click **Help**, read about circular references, close the Help window that displays, and then save the workbook as **e02c1Gym_LastFirst**.

b. Assign the name **Membership** to the **range A18:C20**.

c. Insert a function to display the current date in **cell B2**.

Calculate Cost, Annual Total, and Total Due

You are ready to calculate the basic annual membership cost and the total annual cost. The basic annual membership is determined based on each client's membership type, using the lookup table.

a. Insert a lookup function in **cell C5** to display the basic annual membership cost for the first client.

b. Use an IF function in **cell E5** to calculate the annual total amount, which is the sum of the basic cost and locker fees for those who rent a locker. For people who do not rent a locker, the annual cost is only the cost shown in column C. The Locker column displays *Yes* for clients who rent a locker and *No* for those who don't.

c. Calculate the total amount due in **cell G5** for the first client based on the annual total and the number of years in the contract.

d. Copy the three formulas down their respective columns.

Determine the Down Payment and Balance

You need to collect a down payment based on the type of membership for each new client. Then you must determine how much each client owes.

a. Insert a lookup function in **cell H5** to display the amount of down payment for the first client based on the membership type.

b. Find and correct the circular reference for the balance. The balance is the difference between the total due and the down payment.

c. Copy the two formulas for the rest of the clients.

Calculate the Monthly Payment

Clients pay the remainder by making monthly payments. Monthly payments are based on the number of years specified in the client's contract and a standard interest rate.

a. Insert the function in **cell J5** to calculate the first client's monthly payment, using appropriate relative and absolute cell references.

b. Copy the formula down the column.

c. Edit the formula by changing the appropriate cell reference to a mixed cell reference. Copy the formula down.

Finalize the Workbook

You need to perform some basic statistical calculations and finalize the workbook with formatting and page setup options.

a. Calculate totals on row 14.

b. Insert the appropriate functions in the *Summary Statistics* section of the worksheet: **cells H18:H22**. Format the payments with **Accounting Number Format** and format the number of new members appropriately.

c. Format the other column headings on rows 4 and 17 to match the fill color in the **range E17:H17**. Wrap text for the column headings.

d. Format the monetary values for Andrews and the total row with **Accounting Number Format**. Use zero decimal places for whole amounts and display two decimal places for the monthly payment. Apply **Comma Style** to the internal monetary values. Underline the values before the totals and apply **Double Accounting Underline** (found in the Format Cells dialog box) for the totals.

e. Set **0.3"** left and right margins and ensure the page prints on only one page.

f. Insert a footer with your name on the left side, the date code in the center, and the file name code on the right side.

g. Save and close the workbook, and submit based on your instructor's directions.

Glossary

Absolute cell reference A designation that provides a permanent reference to a specific cell. When you copy a formula containing an absolute reference, the cell reference in the copied formula does not change, regardless of where you copy the formula. An absolute cell reference appears with a dollar sign before both the column letter and the row number, such as $B$4.

Argument A variable or constant input, such as a cell reference or value, needed to complete a function. The entire group of arguments for a function is enclosed in parentheses.

AVERAGE function A statistical function that calculates the arithmetic mean, or average, of values in a range.

Breakpoint The lowest value for a specific category or series in a lookup table.

Circular reference A situation that occurs when a formula contains a direct or an indirect reference to the cell containing the formula.

Column index number The number of the column in the lookup table that contains the return values. Used as the third argument in a VLOOKUP or HLOOKUP function.

COUNT function A statistical function that tallies the number of cells in a range that contain values you can use in calculations, such as the numerical and date data, but excludes blank cells or text entries from the tally.

COUNTA function A statistical function that tallies the number of cells in a range that are not blank; that is, cells that contain data, whether a value, text, or a formula.

COUNTBLANK function A statistical function that tallies the number of cells in a range that are blank.

Formula AutoComplete A feature that displays a list of functions and defined names that match letters as you type a formula.

Function A predefined computation that simplifies creating a complex calculation and produces a result based on inputs known as arguments.

Function ScreenTip A small pop-up description that displays the arguments for a function as you enter it directly in a cell.

HLOOKUP function A lookup & reference function that looks up a value in a horizontal lookup table where the first row contains the values to compare with the lookup value.

IF function A logical function that evaluates a condition and returns one value if the condition is true and a different condition if the value is false.

Logical test An expression that evaluates to true or false; the first argument in an IF function.

Lookup table A range that contains data for the basis of the lookup and data to be retrieved. In a vertical lookup table, the first column contains a list of values to compare to the lookup value. In a horizontal lookup table, the first row contains a list of values to compare to the lookup value.

Lookup value The cell reference of the cell that contains the value to look up within a lookup table.

MAX function A statistical function that finds the highest value in a range.

MEDIAN function A statistical function that finds the midpoint value, which is the value that one half of the values in a list are above or below.

MIN function A statistical function that finds the lowest value in a range.

Mixed cell reference A designation that combines an absolute cell reference with a relative cell reference, such as $B4 or B$4.

Nested function A function that contains another function embedded inside one or more of its arguments.

NOW function A date & time function that uses the computer's clock to display the current date and time in a cell.

Nper The number of payment periods over the life of a loan or investment; the second argument in the PMT function.

PMT function A financial function in Excel that calculates the periodic loan payment.

Pv The present value of a loan or an annuity; the third argument in the PMT function and refers to the original amount of the loan.

Quick Analysis A tool that provides a fast way to analyze a selected range of data by inserting basic calculations, creating charts, converting the data to a table, or applying conditional formatting or other analytical features.

Range name A word or string of characters assigned to one or more cells. It can be up to 255 letters, characters, or numbers but must start with a letter or underscore and have no spaces or special symbols.

Rate The periodic interest rate; the percentage of interest paid for each payment period; the first argument in the PMT function.

Relative cell reference A designation that indicates a cell's relative location within the worksheet using the column letter and row number, such as B5. When a formula containing a relative cell reference is copied, the cell references in the copied formula change relative to the position of the copied formula.

SUM function A statistical function that calculates the total of values contained in two or more cells.

Syntax The rules that dictate the structure and components required to perform the necessary calculations in an equation or to evaluate expressions.

Table array The range that contains the body of the lookup table, excluding column labels. The first column must be in ascending order to find a value in a range, or it can be in any order to look up an exact value. It is the second argument within a VLOOKUP or HLOOKUP function.

TODAY function A date & time function that displays the current date in a cell.

VLOOKUP function A lookup & reference function that looks up a value and returns a related result from the lookup table.

Datasets and Tables

Managing Large Volumes of Data

OBJECTIVES | AFTER YOU READ THIS CHAPTER, YOU WILL BE ABLE TO:

1. Freeze rows and columns

2. Print large datasets

3. Design and create tables

4. Apply a table style

5. Sort data

6. Filter data

7. Use structured references and a total row

8. Apply conditional formatting

9. Create a new rule

CASE STUDY | Reid Furniture Store

Vicki Reid owns Reid Furniture Store in Portland, Oregon. She divided her store into four departments: Living Room, Bedroom, Dining Room, and Appliances. All merchandise is categorized into one of these four departments for inventory records and sales. Vicki has four sales representatives: Chantalle Desmarais, Jade Gallagher, Sebastian Gruenewald, and Ambrose Sardelis. The sales system tracks which sales representative processed each transaction.

The business has grown rapidly, and Vicki hired you to analyze the sales data in order to increase future profits. For example, which department generates the most sales? Who is the leading salesperson? Do most customers purchase or finance? Are sales promotions necessary to promote business, or will customers pay the full price?

You downloaded March 2016 data from the sales system into an Excel workbook. To avoid extraneous data that is not needed in the analysis, you did not include customer names, accounts, or specific product numbers. The downloaded file contains transaction numbers, dates, sales representative names, departments, general merchandise description, total price, payment type, transaction type, and the total price.

From Excel Chapter 4 of *Microsoft® Excel 2013 Comprehensive*, First edition. Mary Anne Poatsy, Keith Mulbery, Jason Davidson, Robert T. Grauer. Copyright © 2014 by Pearson Education, Inc. Published by Pearson Prentice Hall. All Rights Reserved. Download student resources at http://www.pearsonhighered.com/exploring.

Large Datasets

So far you have worked with worksheets that contain small datasets, a collection of structured, related data in a limited number of columns and rows. In reality, you will probably work with large datasets consisting of hundreds or thousands of rows and columns of data. When you work with small datasets, you can usually view most or all of the data without scrolling. When you work with large datasets, you probably will not be able to see the entire dataset onscreen even on a large, widescreen monitor set at high resolution. You might want to keep the column and row labels always in view, even as you scroll throughout the dataset. Figure 1 shows the Reid Furniture Store's March 2016 sales transactions. Because it contains a lot of transactions, the entire dataset is not visible. You could decrease the zoom level to display more transactions; however, doing so decreases the text size onscreen, making it hard to read the data.

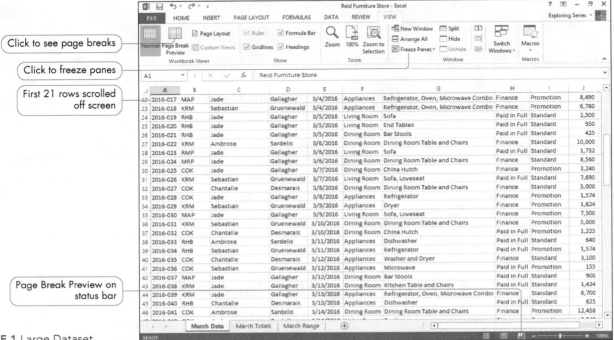

FIGURE 1 Large Dataset

As you work with larger datasets, realize that the data will not always fit on one page. You will need to preview the automatic page breaks and probably insert some manual page breaks in more desirable locations, or you might want to print only a selected range within the large dataset to distribute to others.

In this section, you will learn how to keep labels onscreen as you scroll through a large dataset. In addition, you will learn how to manage page breaks, print only a range instead of an entire worksheet, and print column labels at the top of each page of a large dataset.

TIP Go to a Specific Cell

You can navigate through a large worksheet by using the Go To command. Click Find & Select in the Editing group on the Home tab and select Go To (or press F5 or Ctrl+G) to display the Go To dialog box, enter the cell address in the Reference box, and then press Enter to go to the cell.

You can also click in the Name Box, type the cell reference, and then press Enter to go to a specific cell.

Freezing Rows and Columns

When you scroll to parts of a dataset not initially visible, some rows and columns disappear from view. When the row and column labels scroll off the screen, you may not remember what each column represents. You can keep labels onscreen by freezing them. *Freezing* is the process of keeping rows and/or columns visible onscreen at all times even when you scroll through a large dataset. Table 1 describes the three freeze options.

TABLE 1 Freeze Options	
Option	**Description**
Freeze Panes	Keeps both rows and columns above and to the left of the active cell visible as you scroll through a worksheet.
Freeze Top Row	Keeps only the top row visible as you scroll through a worksheet.
Freeze First Column	Keeps only the first column visible as you scroll through a worksheet.

STEP 1 » To freeze labels, click the View tab, click Freeze Panes in the Window group, and then select a freeze option. To freeze one or more rows and columns, use the Freeze Panes option. Before selecting this option, make the active cell one row below and one column to the right of the rows and columns you want to freeze. For example, to freeze the first five rows and the first column, make cell B6 the active cell before clicking the Freeze Panes option. As Figure 2 shows, Excel displays a horizontal line below the last frozen row (row 5) and a vertical line to the right of the last frozen column (column A). Unfrozen rows (such as rows 6–14) and unfrozen columns (such as columns B and C) are no longer visible as you scroll down and to the right, respectively.

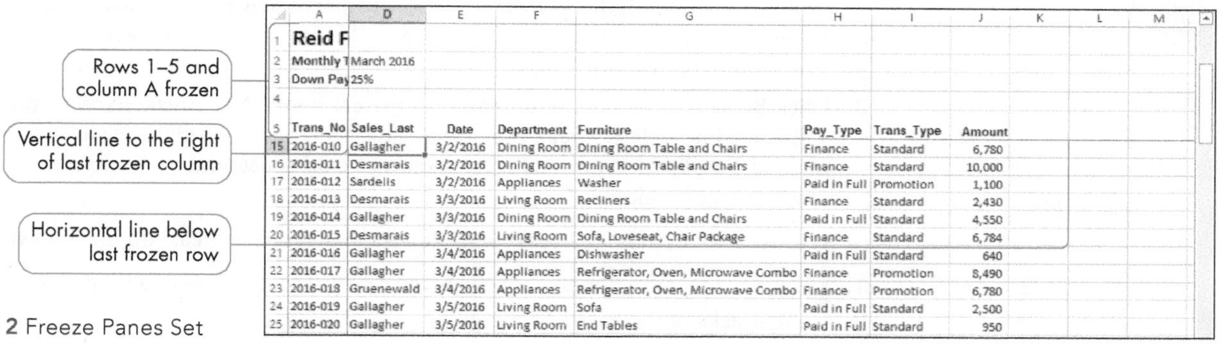

Rows 1–5 and column A frozen

Vertical line to the right of last frozen column

Horizontal line below last frozen row

FIGURE 2 Freeze Panes Set

To unlock the rows and columns from remaining onscreen as you scroll, click Freeze Panes in the Window group and select Unfreeze Panes, which only appears on the menu when you have frozen rows and/or columns. After you unfreeze the panes, the Freeze Panes option appears instead of Unfreeze Panes on the menu again.

When you freeze panes and press Ctrl+Home, the first unfrozen cell is the active cell instead of cell A1. For example, with column A and rows 1 through 5 frozen in Figure 2, pressing Ctrl+Home makes cell B6 the active cell. If you need to edit a cell in the frozen area, click the particular cell to make it active and edit the data.

Printing Large Datasets

For a large dataset, some columns and rows may print on several pages. Analyzing the data on individual printed pages is difficult when each page does not contain column and row labels. To prevent wasting paper, always use Print Preview. Doing so enables you to adjust page settings until you are satisfied with how the data will print.

The Page Layout tab (see Figure 3) contains options to help you prepare large datasets to print. Previously, you changed the page orientation, set different margins, and adjusted the scaling. In addition, you can manage page breaks, set the print area, and print titles.

Click to print titles
Click to insert a page break
Click to set print area

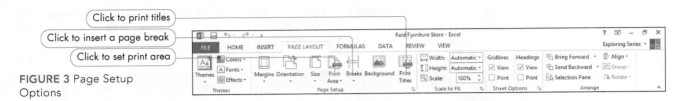

FIGURE 3 Page Setup Options

Display and Change Page Breaks

Based on the paper size, orientation, margins, and other settings, Excel identifies how much data can print on a page. Then it displays a *page break*, indicating where data will start on another printed page. To identify where these automatic page breaks will occur, click Page Break Preview on the status bar or in the Workbook Views group on the View tab. In Page Break Preview, Excel displays watermarks, such as *Page 1*, indicating the area that will print on a specific page. Blue dashed lines indicate where the automatic page breaks occur, and solid blue lines indicate manual page breaks.

If the automatic page breaks occur in undesirable locations, you can adjust the page breaks. For example, if you have a worksheet listing sales data by date, the automatic page break might occur within a group of rows for one date, such as between two rows of data for 3/14/2016. To make all rows for that date appear together, you can either insert a page break above the first data row for that date or decrease the margins so that all 3/14/2015 transactions fit at the bottom of the page. To do this, drag a page break line to the desired location.

Manual Page Break: Do the following to set a manual break at a specific location:

STEP 2»

1. Click the cell that you want to be the first row and column on a new printed page. For example, click cell A50 if you want cell A50 to start a new page. If you click cell D50, you create a page for columns A through C, and then column D starts a new page.
2. Click the PAGE LAYOUT tab.
3. Click Breaks in the Page Setup group and select Insert Page Break. Excel displays a solid blue line in Page Break Preview or a dashed line in Normal view to indicate the manual page breaks you set. Figure 4 shows a worksheet with both automatic and manual page breaks.

Remove a Manual Page Break: To remove a manual page break, do the following:

1. Click a cell below a horizontal page break or a cell to the right of a vertical page break.
2. Click Breaks in the Page Setup group and select Remove Page Break.

Reset Page Breaks: To reset all page breaks back to the automatic page breaks, do the following:

1. Click Breaks in the Page Setup group.
2. Select Reset All Page Breaks.

Datasets and Tables

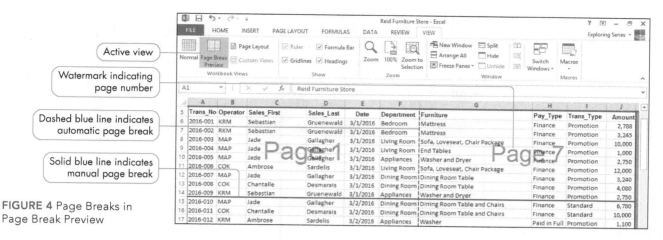

Active view

Watermark indicating
page number

Dashed blue line indicates
automatic page break

Solid blue line indicates
manual page break

FIGURE 4 Page Breaks in
Page Break Preview

Set and Clear a Print Area

The default Print settings send an entire dataset on the active worksheet to the printer. However, you might want to print only part of the worksheet data. If you display the worksheet in Page Break view, you can identify which page(s) you want to print. Then click the File tab and select Print. Type the number(s) of the page(s) you want to print. For example, to print page 2 only, type 2 in the Pages text box and in the *to* text box.

You can further restrict what is printed by setting the **_print area_**, which is the range of cells that will print. For example, you might want to print only an input area or just the transactions that occurred on a particular date. To set a print area, do the following:

STEP 3 ≫

1. Select the range you want to print.
2. Click the PAGE LAYOUT tab and click Print Area in the Page Setup group.
3. Select Set Print Area.

In Page Break Preview, the print area has a white background and solid blue border; the rest of the worksheet has a gray background (see Figure 5). In Normal view or Page Layout view, the print area is surrounded by thin gray lines.

Dark blue lines indicate
boundaries in Page Break
Preview

Click to set print area

Gray background indicates
nonprinting area in Page
Break Preview

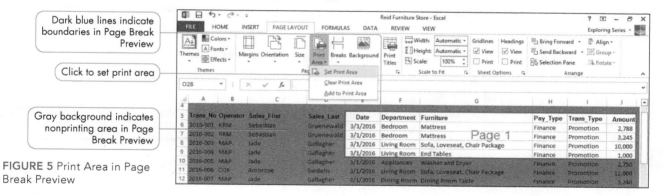

FIGURE 5 Print Area in Page
Break Preview

To add print areas where each print area will print on a separate page, select the range you want to print, click Print Area, and then select *Add to Print Area*. To clear the print area, click Print Area in the Page Setup group and select Clear Print Area.

> ### TIP | Print a Selection
>
> Another way to print part of a worksheet is to select the range you want to print. Click the File tab and click Print. Click the first arrow in the *Settings* section and select Print Selection.

Print Titles

STEP 4 » When you print large datasets, it is helpful that every page contains descriptive column and row labels. When you click Print Titles in the Page Setup group on the Page Layout tab, Excel opens the Page Setup dialog box with the Sheet tab active so that you can select which row(s) and/or column(s) to repeat on each printout (see Figure 6).

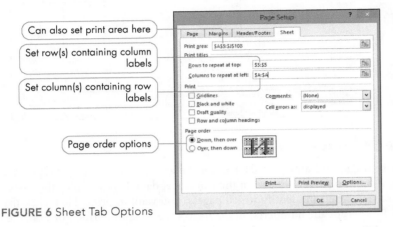

Can also set print area here

Set row(s) containing column labels

Set column(s) containing row labels

Page order options

FIGURE 6 Sheet Tab Options

To print the column labels at the top of each page, select the row(s) that contain the labels or titles (such as row 5) in the *Rows to repeat at top* box to display $5:$5. To print the row labels at the left side of each page, select the column(s) that contain the labels or titles (such as column A) in the *Columns to repeat at left* box to display AA.

Control Print Page Order

Print order is the sequence in which the pages are printed. By default, the pages print in this order: top-left section, bottom-left section, top-right section, and bottom-right section. However, you might want to print the entire top portion of the worksheet before printing the bottom portion. To change the print order, open the Page Setup dialog box, click the Sheet tab, and then select the desired *Page order* option (see Figure 6).

Quick Concepts

1. What is the purpose of freezing panes in a worksheet?

2. Why would you want to insert page breaks instead of using the automatic page breaks?

3. What steps should you take to ensure that column labels display on each printed page of a large dataset?

Hands-On Exercises

Watch the Video
for this Hands-
On Exercise!

MyITLab®
HOE1 Training

1 Large Datasets

You want to review the large dataset that shows the March 2016 transactions for Reid Furniture Store. You will need to view the data and adjust some page setup options so that you can print necessary labels on each page.

Skills covered: Freeze Rows and Columns • Manage Page Breaks • Set and Clear a Print Area • Print Titles

STEP 1 ≫ FREEZE ROWS AND COLUMNS

Before printing the March 2016 transaction dataset, you want to view the data. The dataset contains more rows than will display onscreen at the same time. You decide to freeze the column and row labels to stay onscreen as you scroll through the transactions. Refer to Figure 7 as you complete Step 1.

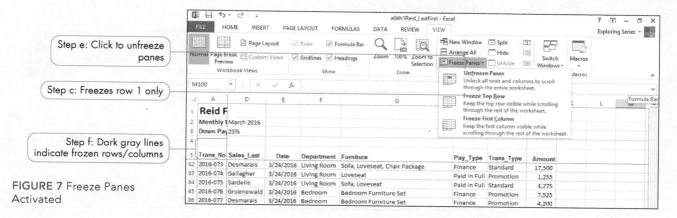

FIGURE 7 Freeze Panes Activated

a. Open *e04h1Reid* and save it as **e04h1Reid_LastFirst**.

> **TROUBLESHOOTING:** If you make any major mistakes in this exercise, you can close the file, open *e04h1Reid* again, and then start this exercise over.

The workbook contains three worksheets: March Data (for Hands-On Exercises 1–3), March Totals (for Hands-On Exercise 4), and March Range (for Hands-On Exercise 5).

b. Press **Page Down** four times to scroll through the dataset. Then press **Ctrl+Home** to go back to the top of the worksheet.

After you press Page Down, the column labels in row 5 scroll off the screen, making it challenging to remember what type of data are in some columns.

c. Click the **VIEW tab**, click **Freeze Panes** in the Window group, and then select **Freeze Top Row**.

A dark gray horizontal line displays between rows 1 and 2.

d. Press **Page Down** to scroll down through the worksheet.

As rows scroll off the top of the Excel window, the first row remains frozen onscreen. The title by itself is not helpful; you need to freeze the column labels as well.

e. Click **Freeze Panes** in the Window group and select **Unfreeze Panes**.

f. Click **cell B6**, the cell below the row and one column to the right of what you want to freeze. Click **Freeze Panes** in the Window group and select **Freeze Panes**.

Excel displays a vertical line between columns A and B, indicating that column A is frozen, and a horizontal line between rows 5 and 6, indicating the first five rows are frozen.

g. Press **Ctrl+G**, type **M100** in the **Reference box** of the Go To dialog box, and then click **OK** to make cell M100 the active cell. Save the workbook.

Rows 6 through 81 and columns B and C are not visible because they scrolled off the screen.

> **TROUBLESHOOTING:** Your screen may differ from Figure 7 due to different Windows resolution settings. If necessary, continue scrolling right and down until you see columns and rows scrolling offscreen.

STEP 2 ≫ MANAGE PAGE BREAKS

You plan to print the dataset so that you and Vicki Reïd can discuss the transactions in your weekly meeting. Because the large dataset will not fit on one page, you want to see where the automatic page breaks are and then insert a manual page break. Refer to Figure 8 as you complete Step 2.

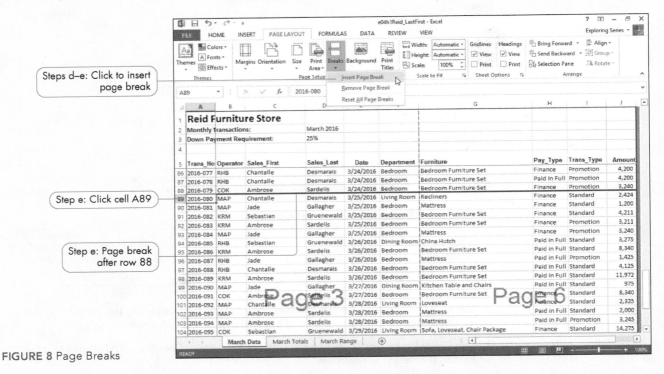

FIGURE 8 Page Breaks

a. Press **Ctrl+Home** to move to **cell B6**, the first cell in the unfrozen area. Click the **VIEW tab**, if necessary, and click **Page Break Preview** in the Workbook Views group or on the status bar.

Excel displays blue dashed lines to indicate the automatic page breaks.

b. Scroll down until you see row 44 below the frozen column labels.

The automatic horizontal page break is between rows 46 and 47 (or between rows 45 and 46). You do not want transactions for a particular day to span between printed pages, so you need to move the page break up to keep all 3/13/2016 transactions together.

c. Click **cell A45**, the first cell containing 3/13/2016 data and the cell to start the top of the second page.

d. Click the **PAGE LAYOUT tab**, click **Breaks** in the Page Setup group, and then select **Insert Page Break**.

You inserted a page break between rows 44 and 45 so that the 3/13/2016 transactions will be on one page.

e. Click **cell A89**, click **Breaks** in the Page Setup group, and then select **Insert Page Break**. Save the workbook.

You inserted a page break between rows 88 and 89 to keep the 3/25/2016 transactions on the same page.

TIP | Using the Mouse Pointer to Move Page Breaks

To use the mouse pointer to adjust a page break, position the mouse pointer on the page break line to see the two-headed arrow and drag the line to where you want the page break to occur.

STEP 3 ≫ SET AND CLEAR A PRINT AREA

You want to focus on the transactions for only March 1, 2016. To avoid printing more data than you need, you will set the print area to print transactions for only that day. Refer to Figure 9 as you complete Step 3.

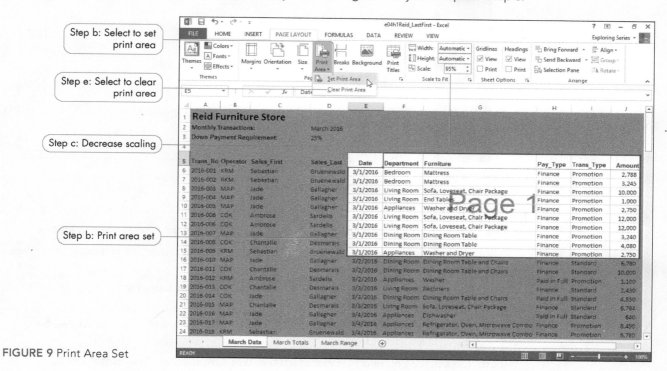

FIGURE 9 Print Area Set

a. Scroll up to see the first row of March data. Select the **range E5:J15**, the range of data for March 1, 2016.

b. Click the **PAGE LAYOUT tab**, if necessary, click **Print Area** in the Page Setup group, and then select **Set Print Area**.

Excel displays the print area with a solid blue border. A dotted blue line displays between columns I and J, indicating an automatic page break. The rest of the worksheet displays with a gray background.

c. Click **cell E5** and click the **Scale arrow** down one time in the *Scale to Fit* group.

The selected print area will print on one page.

Hands-On Exercise 1

d. Press **Ctrl+P** to see that only the print area will print. Press **Esc**.

e. Click **Print Area** in the Page Setup group and select **Clear Print Area**. Save the workbook.

STEP 4 ≫ PRINT TITLES

Only the first page will print both row and column labels. Pages 2 and 3 will print the remaining row labels, Page 4 will print the remaining column labels, and Pages 5 and 6 will not print either label. You want to make sure the column and row labels print on all pages. To do this, you will print titles. Refer to Figure 10 as you complete Step 4.

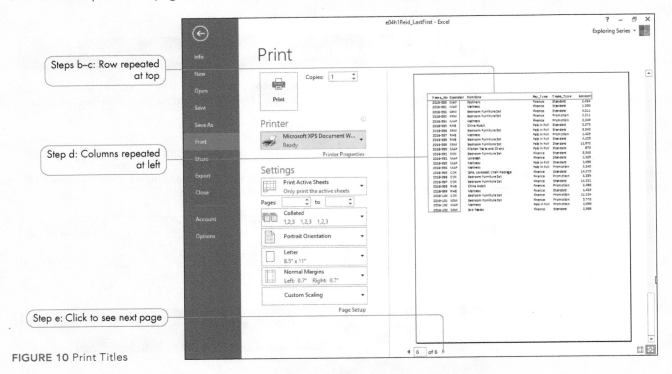

FIGURE 10 Print Titles

a. Click **Print Titles** in the Page Setup group.

The Page Setup dialog box opens, displaying the Sheet tab.

b. Click the **Collapse Dialog box button** on the right side of the *Rows to repeat at top* box.

Clicking the *Collapse Dialog box* button reduces the dialog box so that you can select a range in the worksheet easily.

c. Click the **row 5 heading** and click the **Collapse Dialog box button** within the Page Setup: Rows to repeat at top dialog box.

You selected the fifth row, which contains the column labels, and expanded the Page Setup dialog box back to its full size.

d. Click in the **Columns to repeat at left box**, type **A:B**, and then click **Print Preview**.

e. Click **Next Page** at the bottom of the Microsoft Office Backstage view. Click **Next Page** until the sixth page displays.

Figure 10 shows a preview of the sixth page. The column labels and the first two columns appear on all pages.

f. Click the **Back arrow** in the top-left corner of the Microsoft Office Backstage view.

g. Save the workbook. Keep the workbook onscreen if you plan to continue with the next Hands-On Exercise. If not, close the workbook and exit Excel.

Hands-On Exercise 1

Excel Tables

All organizations maintain lists of data. Businesses maintain inventory lists, educational institutions maintain lists of students and faculty, and governmental entities maintain lists of contracts. Although more complicated related data should be stored in a database-management program, such as Access, you can maintain structured lists in Excel tables. A *table* is a structured range that contains related data organized in such a way as to facilitate data management and analysis. Although you can manage and analyze a range of data, a table provides many advantages over a range of data:

- Column headings remain onscreen without having to use Freeze Panes.
- Filter arrows are available for efficient sorting and filtering.
- Table styles easily format table rows and columns with complementary fill colors.
- Calculated columns where the formulas copy down the columns automatically are available to create and edit.
- Calculated total row enables the user to implement a variety of summary functions.
- Structured references can be used instead of cell references in formulas.
- Table data can export to a SharePoint list.

In this section, you will learn table terminology and rules for structuring data. You will create a table from existing data, manage records and fields, and remove duplicates. Then you will apply a table style to format the table.

Designing and Creating Tables

A table is a group of related data organized in a series of rows and columns that is managed independently from any other data on the worksheet. Each column represents a *field*, which is an individual piece of data, such as last names or quantities sold. Each field should represent the smallest possible unit of data. For example, instead of a Name field, separate name data into First Name and Last Name fields. Instead of one large address field, separate address data into Street Address, City, State, and ZIP Code fields. Separating data into the smallest units possible enables you to manipulate the data in a variety of ways for output. Each row in a table represents a *record*, which is a collection of related data about one entity. For example, all data related to one particular transaction form a record in the Reid Department Store worksheet.

You should plan the structure before creating a table. The more thoroughly you plan, the fewer changes you will have to make to the table after you create it. To help plan your table, follow these guidelines:

- Enter field (column) names on the top row.
- Keep field names short, descriptive, and unique. No two field names should be identical.
- Format the field names so that they stand out from the data.
- Enter data for each record on a row below the field names.
- Do not leave blank rows between records or between the field names and the first record.
- Delete any blank columns between fields in the dataset.
- Make sure each record has something unique, such as a transaction number or ID.
- Insert at least one blank row and one blank column between the table and other data, such as the main titles. When you need multiple tables in one workbook, a best practice is to place each table on a separate worksheet.

Create a Table

STEP 1 » When your worksheet data are structured correctly, you can easily create a table. To create a table from existing data, do the following:

1. Click within the existing range of data.
2. Click the INSERT tab and click Table in the Tables group. The Create Table dialog box opens (see Figure 11), prompting you to enter the range of data.
   - If Excel does not correctly predict the range, select the range for the *Where is the data for your table?* box.
   - If the existing range contains column labels, select the *My table has headers* check box.
3. Click OK to create the table.

FIGURE 11 Create Table Dialog Box

TIP | Quick Analysis Table Creation

You can also create a table by selecting a range, clicking the Quick Analysis button, clicking TABLES (see Figure 12) in the Quick Analysis gallery, and then clicking Table. While Quick Analysis is efficient for tasks such as creating a chart, it may take more time to create a table because you have to select the entire range first. Some people find that it is faster to create a table from the Insert tab.

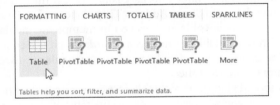

FIGURE 12 Quick Analysis Gallery

After you create a table, the Table Tools Design tab displays. Excel applies the default Table Style Medium 2 style to the table, and each cell in the header row has arrows, also called *filtering arrows* or *filtering buttons* in Excel Help (see Figure 13). This text uses the term *filter arrows* for consistency. Excel assigns a name to each table, such as Table 1. You can change the table name by clicking in the Table Name box in the Properties group, typing a new name using the same rules you applied when assigning range names, and then pressing Enter.

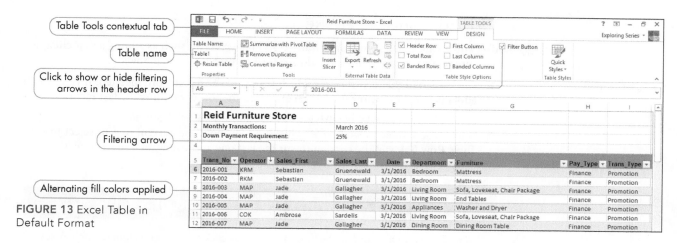

Table Tools contextual tab

Table name

Click to show or hide filtering arrows in the header row

Filtering arrow

Alternating fill colors applied

FIGURE 13 Excel Table in Default Format

Instead of converting a range to a table, you can create a table structure first and add data to it later. Select an empty range and follow the previously listed steps to create the range for the table. The default column headings are Column1, Column2, and so on. Click each default column heading and type a descriptive label. Then enter the data into each row of the newly created table.

TIP | Converting a Table to a Range

To convert a table back to a range, click within the table range, click the Table Tools Design tab, click *Convert to Range* in the Tools group, and then click Yes in the message box asking, *Do you want to convert the table to a normal range?*

Add and Delete Fields

STEP 2

After creating a table, you might want to add a new field. For example, you might want to add a field for product numbers to the Reid Furniture Store transaction table. To insert a field:

1. Click in any data cell (but not the cell containing the field name) in a field that will be to the right of the new field. For example, to insert a new field between the fields in columns A and B, click any cell in column B.
2. Click the HOME tab and click the Insert arrow in the Cells group.
3. Select *Insert Table Columns to the Left*.

TIP | Adding a New Field on the Right Side of a Table

If you want to add a field at the end of the right side of a table, click in the cell to the right of the last field name and type a label. Excel will extend the table to include that field and will format the cell as a field name.

You can also delete a field if you no longer need any data for that particular field. Although deleting records and fields is easy, you must make sure not to delete data erroneously. If you accidentally delete data, click Undo immediately. To delete a field, do the following:

1. Click a cell in the field that you want to delete.
2. Click the Delete arrow in the Cells group on the HOME tab.
3. Select Delete Table Columns.

Add, Edit, and Delete Records

After you create a table, you might want to add new records, such as adding a new client or a new item to an inventory table. To add a record to a table, do the following:

1. Click a cell in the record below which you want the new record inserted. If you want to add a new record below the last record, click the row containing the last record.
2. Click the HOME tab and click the Insert arrow in the Cells group.
3. Select Insert Table Rows Above to insert a row above the current row, or select Insert Table Row Below if the current row is the last one and you want a row below it.

> **TIP Adding a New Record at the End of a Table**
>
> You can also add a record to the end of a table by clicking in the row immediately below the table and typing. Excel will extend the table to include that row as a record in the table and will apply consistent formatting.

You might need to change data for a record. For example, when a client moves, you need to change the client's address and phone number. You edit data in a table the same way you edit data in a regular worksheet cell.

Finally, you can delete records. For example, if you maintain an inventory of artwork in your house and sell a piece of art, delete that record from the table. To delete a record from the table:

1. Click a cell in the record that you want to delete.
2. Click the HOME tab and click the Delete arrow in the Cells group.
3. Select Delete Table Rows.

Remove Duplicate Rows

A table might contain duplicate records, which can give false results when totaling or performing other calculations on the dataset. For a small table, you might be able to detect duplicate records by scanning the data. For large tables, it is more difficult to identify duplicate records by simply scanning the table with the eye. To remove duplicate records, do the following:

1. Click within the table and click the DESIGN tab.
2. Click Remove Duplicates in the Tools group to display the Remove Duplicates dialog box (see Figure 14).
3. Click Select All to set the criteria to find a duplicate for every field in the record and click OK. If you select individual column(s), Excel looks for duplicates in the specific column(s) only and deletes all but one record of the duplicated data. Excel will display a message box informing you of how many duplicate rows it removed.

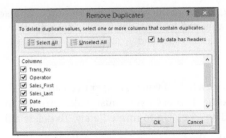

FIGURE 14 Remove Duplicates Dialog Box

Applying a Table Style

STEP 5

Excel applies a table style when you create a table. *Table styles* control the fill color of the header row (the row containing field names) and rows of records. In addition, table styles specify bold and border lines. You can change the table style to a color scheme that complements your organization's color scheme or to emphasize data the header rows or columns. Click Quick Styles in the Table Styles group to display the Table Styles gallery (see Figure 15). To see how a table style will format your table using Live Preview, position the pointer over a style in the Table Styles gallery. After you identify a style you want, click it to apply it to the table.

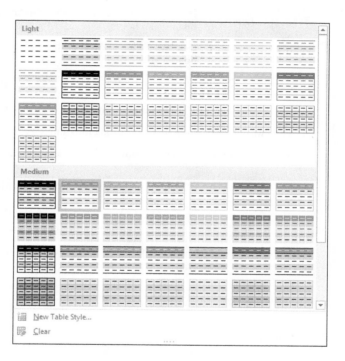

FIGURE 15 Table Styles Gallery

After you select a table style, you can control what the style formats. The Table Style Options group contains check boxes to select specific format actions in a table. Table 2 lists the options and the effect of each check box. Avoid overformatting the table. It is not good to apply so many formatting effects that the message you want to present with the data is obscured or lost.

TABLE 2 Table Style Options

Check Box	Action
Header Row	Displays the header row (field names) when checked; removes field names when not checked. Header Row formatting takes priority over column formats.
Total Row	Displays a total row when selected. Total Row formatting takes priority over column formats.
First Column	Applies a different format to the first column so that the row headings stand out. First Column formatting takes priority over Banded Rows formatting.
Last Column	Applies a different format to the last column so that the last column of data stands out; effective for aggregated data, such as grand totals per row. Last Column formatting takes priority over Banded Rows formatting.
Banded Rows	Displays alternate fill colors for even and odd rows to help distinguish records.
Banded Columns	Displays alternate fill colors for even and odd columns to help distinguish fields.
Filter Button	Displays a filter button on the right side of each heading in the header row.

Quick Concepts

1. List at least four guidelines for planning a table in Excel.

2. Why would you convert a range of data into an Excel table?

3. What are six options you can control after selecting a table style?

Hands-On Exercises

Watch the Video
for this Hands-
On Exercise!

MyITLab®
HOE2 Training

2 Excel Tables

You want to convert the March data to a table. As you review the table, you will delete the unnecessary Operator field, add two new fields, insert a missing furniture sale transaction, and remove duplicate transactions. Finally, you will enhance the table appearance by applying a table style.

Skills covered: Create a Table • Add and Delete Fields • Add Records • Remove Duplicate Rows • Apply a Table Style

STEP 1 ›› CREATE A TABLE

Although the Reid Furniture Store's March transaction data are organized in an Excel worksheet, you know that you will have additional functionality if you convert the range to a table. Refer to Figure 16 as you complete Step 1.

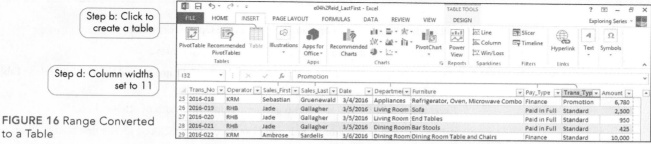

Step b: Click to create a table

Step d: Column widths set to 11

FIGURE 16 Range Converted to a Table

a. Open *e04h1Reid_LastFirst* if you closed it at the end of Hands-On Exercise 1 and save it as **e04h2Reid_LastFirst**, changing *h1* to *h2*. Click **Normal** on the status bar.

b. Click in any cell within the transactional data, click the **INSERT tab**, and then click **Table** in the Tables group.

The Create Table dialog box opens. The *Where is the data for your table?* box displays =$A$5:$I$112. Keep the *My table has headers* check box selected so that the headings on the fifth row become the field names for the table.

c. Click **OK** and click **cell A5**.

Excel creates a table from the data range and displays the DESIGN tab, filter arrows, and alternating fill colors for the records. The columns widen to fit the field names, although the wrap text option is still applied to those cells.

d. Set column width to **11** for the Sales_First, Sales_Last, Department, Pay_Type, and Trans_Type fields.

e. Unfreeze the panes and scroll through the table. Save the workbook.

With a regular range of data, column labels scroll off the top of the screen if you do not freeze panes. When you scroll within a table, the table's header row remains onscreen by moving up to where the Excel column (letter) headings usually display (see Figure 16).

STEP 2 >> ADD AND DELETE FIELDS

The original range included a column for the data entry operators' initials. You will delete this column because you do not need it for your analysis. In addition, you want to add a field to display down payment amounts in the future. Refer to Figure 17 as you complete Step 2.

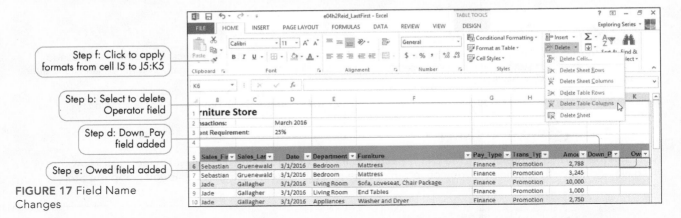

Step f: Click to apply formats from cell I5 to J5:K5

Step b: Select to delete Operator field

Step d: Down_Pay field added

Step e: Owed field added

FIGURE 17 Field Name Changes

a. Click **cell B25** or any cell containing a value in the Operator column.

You need to make a cell active in the field you want to remove.

b. Click the **HOME tab**, click the **Delete arrow** in the Cells group, and then select **Delete Table Columns**.

Excel deletes the Operator column and may adjust the width of other columns.

c. Adjust the widths of columns E, F, and G as necessary. Click **cell J5**, the first blank cell on the right side of the field names.

d. Type **Down_Pay** and press **Ctrl+Enter**.

Excel extends the table formatting to column J automatically. A filter arrow appears for the newly created field name, and alternating fill colors appear in the rows below the field name. The fill color is the same as the fill color for other field names; however, the font color is White, Background 1, instead of Black Text 1.

e. Click **cell K5**, type **Owed**, and then press **Ctrl+Enter**.

f. Click **cell I5**, click **Format Painter** in the Clipboard group, and then select the **range J5:K5** to copy the format. Save the workbook.

Hands-On Exercise 2

STEP 3 ≫ ADD RECORDS

As you review the March 2016 transaction table, you notice that two transactions are missing: 2016-68 and 2016-104. After finding the paper invoices, you are ready to add records with the missing transaction data. Refer to Figure 18 as you complete Step 3.

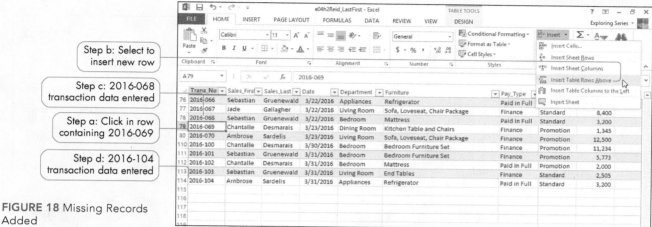

Step b: Select to insert new row

Step c: 2016-068 transaction data entered

Step a: Click in row containing 2016-069

Step d: 2016-104 transaction data entered

FIGURE 18 Missing Records Added

a. Click **cell A78** or any cell within the table range on row 78.

The missing record 2016-68 needs to be inserted between 2016-67 on row 77 and 2016-69 on row 78.

b. Click the **HOME tab**, click the **Insert arrow** in the Cells group, and then select **Insert Table Row Above**.

Excel inserts a new table row on row 78, between the 2016-67 and 2016-69 transactions.

c. Enter the following data in the respective fields on the newly created row.

2016-68, Sebastian, Gruenewald, 3/22/2016, Bedroom, Mattress, Paid in Full, Standard, 3200

d. Click **cell A114** and enter the following data in the respective fields. Save the workbook.

2016-104, Ambrose, Sardelis, 3/31/2016, Appliances, Refrigerator, Paid in Full, Standard, 1500

When you start typing 2016-104 in the row immediately below the last record, Excel immediately includes and formats row 114 as part of the table. Review Figure 18 to ensure you inserted the records in the correct locations. Rows 81–109 are hidden to display both new records in one screenshot.

You noticed that the 2016-006 transaction is duplicated on rows 11 and 12 and that the 2016-118 transaction is duplicated on rows 24 and 25. You think the table may contain other duplicate rows. To avoid having to look at the entire table row by row, you want to have Excel find and remove the duplicate rows for you. Refer to Figure 19 as you complete Step 4.

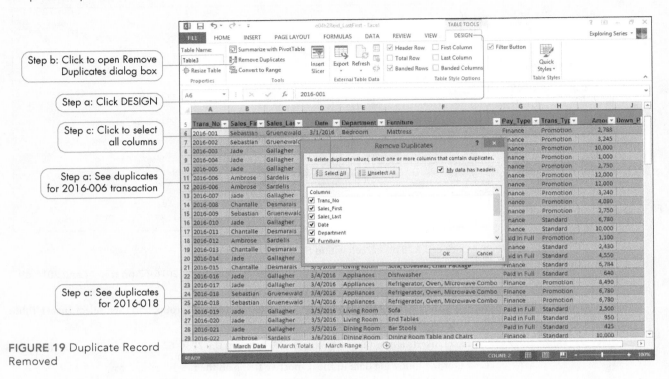

FIGURE 19 Duplicate Record Removed

a. Scroll to see rows 11 and 12. Click the **DESIGN tab**.

The records on rows 11 and 12 are identical. Rows 24 and 25 are also duplicates. You need to remove the extra rows.

b. Click **Remove Duplicates** in the Tools group.

The Remove Duplicates dialog box opens.

c. Click **Select All**, make sure the **My data has headers check box** is selected, and then click **OK**.

Excel displays a message box indicating *5 duplicate records found and removed; 104 unique values remain.*

d. Click **OK** in the message box. Press **Page Down** until you see the last record. Save the workbook.

Transaction 2016-104 is located on row 109 after the duplicate records are removed.

STEP 5 >> APPLY A TABLE STYLE

Now that you have finalized the fields and added missing records to the March 2016 transaction table, you want to apply a table style to format the table. Refer to Figure 20 as you complete Step 5.

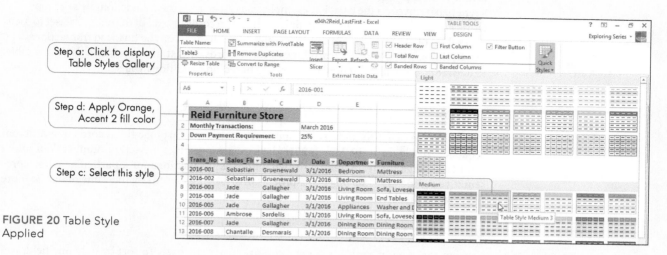

Step a: Click to display Table Styles Gallery

Step d: Apply Orange, Accent 2 fill color

Step c: Select this style

FIGURE 20 Table Style Applied

a. Click the **DESIGN tab** and click **Quick Styles** in the Table Styles group to open the Table Styles gallery.

b. Position the mouse pointer over the fourth style on the second row in the *Light* section.

   Live Preview shows the table with the Table Style Light 10 style but does not apply it.

c. Click **Table Style Medium 3**, the third style on the first row in the *Medium* section.

   Excel formats the table with the Table Style Medium 3, which applies Orange, Accent 2 fill color to the header row and Orange, Accent 2, Lighter 80% fill color to every other record.

d. Press **Ctrl_Home** to go to cell A1. Select the **range A1:C1**, click the **Fill Color arrow** in the Font group on the HOME tab, and then click **Orange, Accent 2**.

   You applied a fill color for the title to match the fill color of the field names on the header row in the table.

e. Save the workbook. Keep the workbook onscreen if you plan to continue with the next Hands-On Exercise. If not, close the workbook and exit Excel.

Table Manipulation

You have a variety of options to manipulate table data, in addition to managing fields, adding records, and applying table styles. You can arrange the records in different sequences to get different perspectives on the data. For example, you can arrange the transactions by sales representative. Furthermore, you can display only particular records instead of the entire dataset to focus on a subset of the data. For example, you might want to focus on the financed transactions.

In this section, you will learn how to sort records by text, numbers, and dates in a table. In addition, you will learn how to filter data based on conditions you set.

Sorting Data

Table data are easier to understand and work with if you arrange the records in a different sequence. In Figure 1, the March 2016 data are arranged by transaction number. You might want to arrange the transactions so that all of the transactions for a particular sales representative are together. *Sorting* is the process of arranging records by the value of one or more fields within a table.

Sort One Field

STEP 1 » You can sort data in a table or a regular range in a worksheet. To sort by only one field, you can use any of the following methods for either a range of data or a table:

- Click in a cell within the field you want to sort and click Sort & Filter in the Editing group on the HOME tab.
- Click in a cell within the field you want to sort and click *Sort A to Z*, *Sort Z to A*, or Sort in the Sort & Filter group on the DATA tab.
- Right-click the field to sort, point to Sort on the shortcut menu, and then select the type of sort you want.
- Click the filter arrow in the header row and select the desired sort option.

Table 3 lists sort options by data type.

TABLE 3   Sort Options

Data Type	Options	Explanation
Text	Sort A to Z	Arranges data in alphabetical order.
	Sort Z to A	Arranges data in reverse alphabetical order.
Dates	Sort Oldest to Newest	Displays data in chronological order, from oldest to newest.
	Sort Newest to Oldest	Displays data in reverse chronological order, from newest to oldest.
Values	Sort Smallest to Largest	Arranges values from the smallest value to the largest.
	Sort Largest to Smallest	Arranges values from the largest value to the smallest.
Color	Sort by Cell Color	Arranges data together for cells containing a particular fill color.
	Sort by Font Color	Arranges data together for cells containing a particular font color.

Sort Multiple Fields

STEP 2 » At times, sorting by only one field yields several records that have the same information. For example, the same last name or the same department could display several times. In those instances, you may want to add a sort on a second field. A second sort will help to uniquely identify a record. You might need both last name and first name to identify an individual. Using multiple level sorts enables like records in the primary sort to be further organized by additional sort levels. For example, you might want to sort by department, then by sales representative, and finally by sales amount. Excel enables you to sort data on 64 different levels. To perform a multiple level sort:

1. Click in any cell in the table.
2. Click Sort in the Sort & Filter group on the Data tab to display the Sort dialog box.
3. Select the primary sort level by clicking the *Sort by* arrow, selecting the field to sort by, and then clicking the Order arrow and selecting the sort order from the list.
4. Click Add Level, select the second sort level by clicking the *Then by* arrow, select the column to sort by, click the Order arrow, and then select the sort order from the list.
5. Continue to click Add Level and add sort levels until you have entered all sort levels. See Figure 21. Click OK.

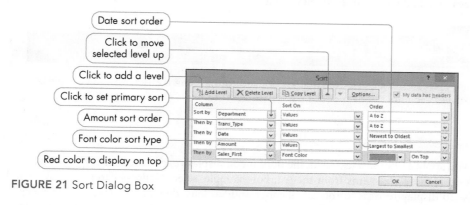

FIGURE 21 Sort Dialog Box

Create a Custom Sort

Excel arranges data in defined sequences, such as alphabetical order. For example, days of the week are sorted alphabetically: Friday, Monday, Saturday, Sunday, Thursday, Tuesday, and Wednesday. However, you might want to create a custom sort sequence. For example, you can create a custom sort to arrange days of the week in order from Sunday to Saturday.

To create a custom sort sequence:

1. Click Sort in the Sort & Filter group on the DATA tab.
2. Click the Order arrow and select Custom List to display the Custom Lists dialog box (see Figure 22).
3. Select an existing sort sequence in the *Custom lists* box, or select NEW LIST.
4. Click Add and type the entries in the desired sort sequence in the *List entries* box, pressing Enter between entries.
5. Click Add and click OK.

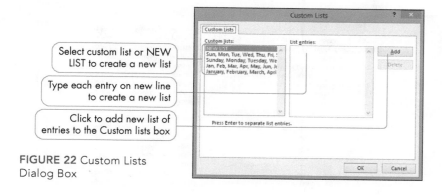

FIGURE 22 Custom Lists Dialog Box

Filtering Data

Filtering is the process of specifying conditions to display only those records that meet certain conditions. For example, you might want to filter the data to show transactions for only a particular sales representative. To filter records by a particular field, click the filter arrow for that field. The list displays each unique label, value, or date contained in the column. Deselect the (Select All) check box and click the check box for each value you want to include in the filtered results.

Often you will need to apply more than one filter to display the needed records. You can filter more than one field. Each additional filter is based on the current filtered data and further reduces a data subset. To apply multiple filters, click each field's filter arrow and select the values to include in the filtered data results.

TIP | Copying Before Filtering Data

Often, you need to show different filters applied to the same dataset. You can copy the worksheet and filter the data on the copied worksheet to preserve the original dataset.

Apply Text Filters

STEP 3 »

When you apply a filter to a text field, the filter menu displays each unique text item. You can select one or more text items from the list. For example, select Gallagher to show only her records. To display records for both Gallagher and Sardelis, deselect the (Select All) check mark and click the Gallagher and Sardelis check boxes. You can also select Text Filters to see a submenu of additional options, such as *Begins With*, to select all records for which the name begins with the letter G, for example.

Figure 23 shows the Sales_Last filter menu with two names selected. Excel displays records for these two reps only. The records for the other sales reps are hidden but not deleted. The filter arrow displays a filter icon, indicating which field is filtered. Excel displays the row numbers in blue, indicating that you applied a filter. The missing row numbers indicate hidden rows of data. When you remove the filter, all the records display again.

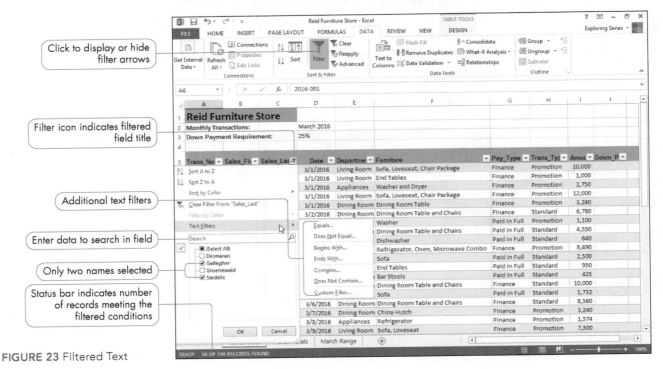

FIGURE 23 Filtered Text

Datasets and Tables

TIP | Filter Arrows

Click the Filter Button check box in the Table Style Options group on the Design tab to display or hide the filter arrows. For a range of data instead of a table, click Filter in the Sort & Filter group on the Data tab to display or hide the filter arrows.

Apply Number Filters

STEP 4 »

When you filter a field of numbers, you can select specific numbers. You might want to filter numbers by a range, such as numbers greater than $5,000 or numbers between $4,000 and $5,000. The submenu enables you to set a variety of number filters. In Figure 24, the amounts are filtered to show only those that are above the average amount. In this situation, Excel calculates the average amount as $4,512. Only records above that amount display.

If the field contains a large number of unique entries, you can click in the Search box and then type a value, text label, or date. Doing so narrows the visible list so that you do not have to scroll through the entire list. For example, if you enter $7, the list will display only values that start with $7.

FIGURE 24 Filtered Numbers

The Top 10 option enables you to specify the top records. Although the option name is Top 10, you can specify the number or percentage of records to display. For example, you can filter the list to display only the top five or the bottom 7%. Figure 25 shows the Top 10 AutoFilter dialog box. Click the first arrow to select either Top or Bottom, click the spin arrows to indicate a value, and then click the last arrow to select either Items or Percent.

FIGURE 25 Top 10 AutoFilter Dialog Box

Apply Date Filters

STEP 5 > When you filter a field of dates, you can select specific dates or a date range, such as dates after 3/15/2016 or dates between 3/1/2016 and 3/7/2016. The submenu enables you to set a variety of date filters. For more specific date options, point to Date Filters, point to *All Dates in the Period*, and then select a period, such as Quarter 2 or October. Figure 26 shows the Date Filter menu.

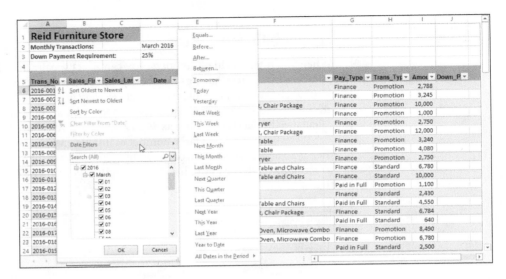

FIGURE 26 Filtered Dates

Apply a Custom Filter

If you select options such as *Greater Than* or *Before*, Excel displays the Custom AutoFilter dialog box (see Figure 27). You can also select Custom Filter from the menu to display this dialog box, which is designed for more complex filtering requirements.

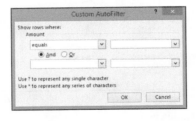

FIGURE 27 Custom AutoFilter Dialog Box

The dialog box indicates the column being filtered. To set the filters, click the arrows to select the comparison type, such as equals or contains. Click the arrow on the right to select a specific text, value, or date entry, or type the data yourself. For ranges of dates or values, click And, and then specify the comparison operator and value or date for the next condition row. For text, click Or. For example, if you want both Gallagher and Desmarais, you must select Or because each data entry contains either Gallagher or Desmarais but not both at the same time.

You can use wildcards to represent characters. For example, to select all states starting with New, type *New* * in the second box to obtain results such as New York or New Mexico. The asterisk (*) represents any number of characters. If you want a wildcard for only a single character, type the question mark (?).

Clear Filters

You can remove the filters from one or more fields to expand the dataset again. To remove only one filter and keep the other filters, click the filter arrow for the field from which you wish to clear the filter and select Clear Filter From.

To remove all filters and display all records in a dataset, do one of the following:

- Click Filter in the Sort & Filter group on the DATA tab.
- Click Sort & Filter in the Editing group on the HOME tab and select Filter.

Quick
Concepts

1. What is the purpose of sorting data in a table?

2. What are two ways to arrange (sort) dates?

3. List at least five ways you can filter numbers.

4. Assume you are filtering a list and want to display records for people who live in Boston or New York. What settings do you enter in the Custom AutoFilter dialog box for that field?

Hands-On Exercises

Watch the Video
for this Hands-
On Exercise!

MyITLab®
HOE3 Training

3 Table Manipulation

You want to start analyzing the March 2016 transactions for Reid Furniture Store by sorting and filtering data in a variety of ways to help you understand the transactions better.

Skills covered: Sort One Field • Sort Multiple Fields • Apply Text Filters • Apply a Number Filter • Apply a Date Filter

STEP 1 ≫ SORT ONE FIELD

First, you want to compare the number of transactions by sales rep, so you will sort the data by the Rep_Last field. After reviewing the transactions by sales reps, you want to arrange the transactions from the one with the largest purchase first to the smallest purchase last. Refer to Figure 28 as you complete Step 1.

Step b: Click to sort alphabetically by last name

Step c: Click to sort amount from largest to smallest

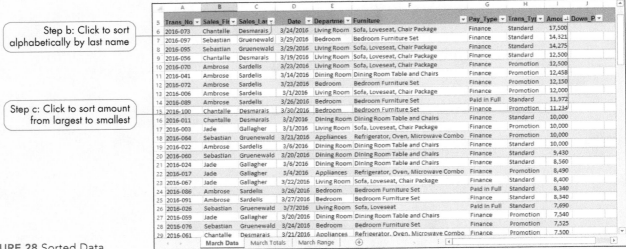

FIGURE 28 Sorted Data

a. Open *e04h2Reid_LastFirst* if you closed it at the end of Hands-On Exercise 2. Save it as **e04h3Reid_LastFirst**, changing *h2* to *h3*.

b. Click the **Sales_Last filter arrow** and select **Sort A to Z**.

Excel arranges the transactions in alphabetical order by last name, starting with Desmarais. Within each sales rep, records display in their original sequence by transaction number. If you scan the records, you can see that Gallagher completed the most sales transactions in March. The up arrow icon on the Sales_Last filter arrow indicates records are sorted in alphabetical order by that field.

TIP Name Sorts

Always check the data to determine how many levels of sorting you need to apply. If your table contains several people with the same last name but different first names, you would first sort by the Last Name field, then sort by First Name field. All the people with the last name Desmarais would be grouped together and further sorted by first name, such as Amanda and then Bradley.

c. Click the **Amount filter arrow** and select **Sort Largest to Smallest**. Save the workbook.

The records are no longer sorted by Sales_Last. When you sort by another field, Excel arranges the data for that field. In this case, Excel arranges the transactions from the one with the largest amount to the smallest amount, indicated by the down arrow icon in the Amount filter arrow.

STEP 2 >> SORT MULTIPLE FIELDS

You want to review the transactions by payment type (financed or paid in full). Within each payment type, you want to further compare the transaction type (promotion or standard). Finally, you want to compare costs within the sorted records by displaying the highest costs first. You will use the Sort dialog box to perform a three-level sort. Refer to Figure 29 as you complete Step 2.

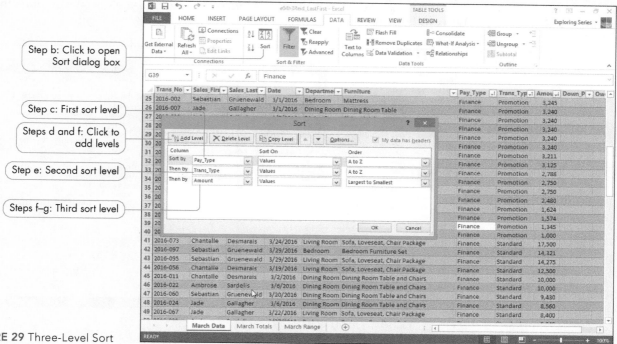

FIGURE 29 Three-Level Sort

a. Click inside the table and click the **DATA tab**.

Both the DATA and HOME tabs contain commands to open the Sort dialog box.

b. Click **Sort** in the Sort & Filter group to open the Sort dialog box.

c. Click the **Sort by arrow** and select **Pay_Type**. Click the **Order arrow** and select **A to Z**.

You start by specifying the column for the primary sort. In this case, you want to sort the records first by the Payment Type column.

d. Click **Add Level**.

The Sort dialog box adds the *Then by* row, which adds a secondary sort.

e. Click the **Then by arrow** and select **Trans_Type**.

The default order is A to Z, which will sort in alphabetical order by Trans_Type. Excel will first sort the records by the Pay_Type (Finance or Paid in Full). Within each Pay_Type, Excel will further sort records by Trans_Type (Promotion or Standard).

f. Click **Add Level** to add another *Then by* row. Click the second **Then by arrow** and select **Amount**.

g. Click the **Order arrow** for the Amount sort and select **Largest to Smallest**.

Within the Pay_Type and Trans_Type sorts, this will arrange the records with the largest amount first in descending order to the smallest amount.

h. Click **OK** and scroll through the records. Save the workbook.

Most customers finance their purchases instead of paying in full. For the financed transactions, more than half were promotional sales. For merchandise paid in full, a majority of the transactions were standard sales, indicating that people with money don't necessarily wait for a promotional sale to purchase merchandise.

STEP 3 ≫ APPLY TEXT FILTERS

Now that you know Jade Gallagher had the most transactions for March, you will filter the table to focus on her sales. You notice that she sells more merchandise from the Dining Room department, so you will filter out the other departments. Refer to Figure 30 as you complete Step 3.

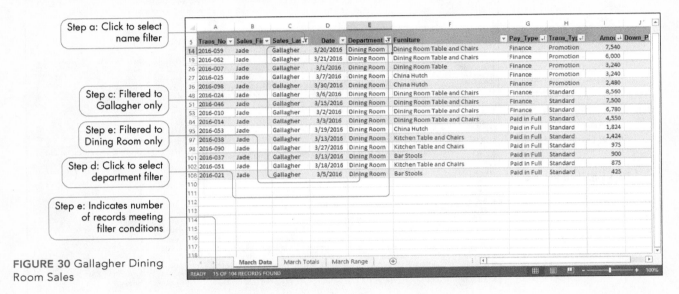

FIGURE 30 Gallagher Dining Room Sales

a. Click the **Sales_Last filter arrow**.

The (Select All) check box is selected.

b. Click the **(Select All) check box** to deselect all last names.

c. Click the **Gallagher check box** and click **OK**.

The status bar indicates that 33 out of 104 records meet the filtering condition. The Sales_Last filter arrow includes a funnel icon, indicating that this column is filtered.

d. Click the **Department filter arrow**.

e. Click the **(Select All) check box** to deselect all departments, click the **Dining Room check box** to focus on that department, and then click **OK**. Save the workbook.

The remaining 15 records show Gallagher's dining room sales for the month. The Department filter arrow includes a funnel icon, indicating that this column is also filtered.

STEP 4 >> APPLY A NUMBER FILTER

Vicki is considering giving a bonus to employees who sold the high-end dining room furniture during a specific time period (3/16/2016 to 3/31/2016). You want to determine if Jade Gallagher qualifies for this bonus. In particular, you are interested in how much gross revenue she generated for dining room furniture that cost at least $5,000 or more. Refer to Figure 31 as you complete Step 4.

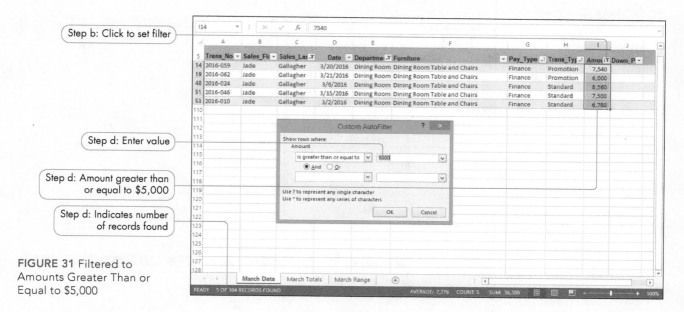

FIGURE 31 Filtered to Amounts Greater Than or Equal to $5,000

a. Select the **range I14:I108** of the filtered list and then view the status bar.

The average transaction amount is $3,754 with 15 transactions (i.e., 15 filtered records).

b. Click the **Amount filter arrow**.

c. Point to **Number Filters** and select **Greater Than Or Equal To**.

The Custom AutoFilter dialog box opens. The default comparison *is greater than or equal to* is displayed.

d. Type **5000** in the box to the right of *is greater than or equal to* and click **OK**. Save the workbook.

When typing numbers, you can type raw numbers such as 5000 or formatted numbers such as $5,000. Out of Gallagher's original 15 dining room transactions, only 5 transactions (one-third of her sales) were valued at $5,000 or more.

> **TROUBLESHOOTING:** If no records display or if too many records display, you might have entered 500000 or 500. Repeat steps b through d.

Hands-On Exercise 3

Finally, you want to study Jade Gallagher's sales records for the last half of the month. You will add a date filter to identify those sales records. Refer to Figure 32 as you complete Step 5.

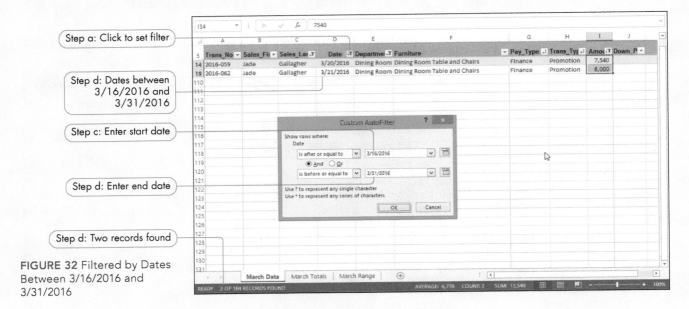

Step a: Click to set filter

Step d: Dates between 3/16/2016 and 3/31/2016

Step c: Enter start date

Step d: Enter end date

Step d: Two records found

FIGURE 32 Filtered by Dates Between 3/16/2016 and 3/31/2016

a. Click the **Date filter arrow**.

b. Point to **Date Filters** and select **Between**.

    The Custom AutoFilter dialog box opens. The default comparisons are *is after or equal to* and *is before or equal to*, ready for you to enter the date specifications.

c. Type **3/16/2016** in the box on the right side of *is after or equal to*.

    You specified the starting date of the range of dates to include. You will keep the *And* option selected.

d. Type **3/31/2016** in the box on the right side of *is before or equal to*. Click **OK**.

    Gallagher had only two dining room sales greater than $5,000 during the last half of March.

e. Save the workbook. Keep the workbook onscreen if you plan to continue with the next Hands-On Exercise. If not, close the workbook and exit Excel.

Hands-On Exercise 3

Table Aggregation

In addition to sorting and filtering tables to analyze the data, you might want to add fields that perform calculations using existing fields. For example, you might want to calculate a required down payment on the amount purchased. Furthermore, you might want to perform aggregate calculations, such as AVERAGE, for a field of numeric data.

In this section, you will learn how to insert structured references to build formulas within a table. In addition, you will learn how to add a row at the end of the table to display basic statistical calculations.

Using Structured References and a Total Row

Excel aids you in quantitative analysis. Your value to an organization increases with your ability to create sophisticated formulas, aggregate data in a meaningful way, and interpret those results. Although you can create complex formulas that you understand, you should strive to create formulas that other people can understand. Creating easy-to-read formulas helps you present self-documenting formulas that require less explanation on your part. When you create formulas for tables, you can use built-in functionality (such as structured references and a total row) that assists you in building understandable formulas.

Create Structured References in Formulas

Your experience in building formulas involves using cell references, such as =SUM(B1:B15) or =H6*$B$3, or range names, such as grades in =VLOOKUP(E5,grades,2). You can use cell references and range names in formulas to perform calculations in a table, as well as another type of reference for formulas in tables: structured references. A ***structured reference*** is a tag or use of a table element, such as a field heading, as a reference in a formula. Structured references in formulas clearly indicate which type of data is used in the calculations.

STEP 1 »

A structured reference requires brackets around column headings or field names, such as =[Amount]–[Down_Pay]. The use of field headings without row references in a structured formula is called an *unqualified reference*. Formula AutoComplete displays a list of field headings after you type the equal sign and the opening bracket (see Figure 33). Type or double-click the column name from the list and type the closing bracket. Excel displays a colored border around the referenced column. When you enter a formula using structured references, Excel copies the formula down the rest of the table column automatically, compared to typing references in formulas and manually copying the formula down a column.

	Date	Department	Furniture	Pay_Type	Trans_Type	Amount	Down_P	Owed
98	3/28/2016	Bedroom	Mattress	Paid in Full	Standard	2,000	=[	
99	3/28/2016	Bedroom	Mattress	Paid in Full	Promotion	3,245		Trans_No
100	3/29/2016	Living Room	Sofa, Loveseat, Chair Package	Finance	Standard	14,275		Sales_First
101	3/29/2016	Bedroom	Bedroom Furniture Set	Finance	Promotion	3,285		Sales_Last
102	3/29/2016	Bedroom	Bedroom Furniture Set	Finance	Standard	14,321		Date
103	3/30/2016	Dining Room	China Hutch	Finance	Promotion	2,480		Department
104	3/30/2016	Bedroom	Mattress	Finance	Standard	1,425		Furniture
105	3/30/2016	Bedroom	Bedroom Furniture Set	Finance	Promotion	11,234		Pay_Type
106	3/31/2016	Bedroom	Bedroom Furniture Set	Finance	Promotion	5,773		Trans_Type
107	3/31/2016	Bedroom	Mattress	Paid in Full	Promotion	2,000		Amount
108	3/31/2016	Living Room	End Tables	Finance	Standard	2,505		Down_Pay
109	3/31/2016	Appliances	Refrigerator	Paid in Full	Standard	1,500		Owed

Type =[to start structured reference

Formula AutoComplete displays field names

FIGURE 33 Structured Reference Creation

You can also use the semiselection process to create a formula. As you point to cells to enter a formula in a table, Excel builds a formula like this: =[@Amount]–[@Down_Pay], where the @ indicates the current row. If you use the semiselection process to create a formula outside the table, the formula includes the table and field names, such as =Table1 [@Amount]–Table1[@Down_Pay]. Table1 is the name of the table; Amount and Down_Pay are field names. This structured formula that includes references, such as table numbers, is called a *fully qualified structured reference*. When you build formulas *within* a table, you can use either unqualified or fully qualified structured references. If you need to use table data in a formula *outside* the table boundaries, you must use fully qualified structured references.

Add a Total Row

At times, aggregating data provides more meaningful quantitative interpretation than individual values. For regular ranges of data, you use basic statistical functions, such as SUM, AVERAGE, MIN, and MAX, to provide meaning for a dataset. An Excel table provides the advantage of being able to display a total row automatically without creating the aggregate function yourself. A **total row** displays below the last row of records in an Excel table and enables you to display summary statistics, such as a sum of values displayed in a column.

To display and use the total row:

STEP 2>>

1. Click the DESIGN tab.
2. Click Total Row in the Table Style Options group. Excel displays the total row below the last record in the table. Excel displays *Total* in the first column of the total row. Excel either sums or counts data for the last field, depending on the type of data stored in that field. If the last field consists of values, Excel sums the values. If the last field is text, Excel counts the number of records.
3. Click a cell in the total row, click that cell's total row arrow, and then select the function results that you desire. To add a summary statistic to another column, click in the empty cell for that field in the total row and click the arrow to select the desired function. Select None to remove the function.

Figure 34 shows the active total row with totals applied to the Amount, Down_Pay, and Owed fields. A list of functions displays to change the function for the last field.

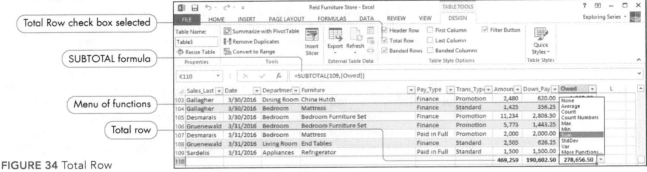

Total Row check box selected

SUBTOTAL formula

Menu of functions

Total row

FIGURE 34 Total Row

TIP Filtering Data and Subtotals

If you filter the data and display the total row, the SUBTOTAL function's 109 argument ensures that only the displayed data are summed; data for hidden rows are not calculated in the aggregate function.

The calculations on the total row use the SUBTOTAL function. The **SUBTOTAL function** calculates an aggregate value, such as totals or averages, for values in a range or database. If you click in a calculated total row cell, the SUBTOTAL function displays in the Formula Bar. The function for the total row looks like this: =SUBTOTAL(function_num,ref1). The function_num argument is a number that represents a function (see Table 4). The ref1 argument indicates the range of values to calculate. The SUBTOTAL function to total the values in the

Owed field would be =SUBTOTAL(109,[Owed]), where the number 109 represents the SUM function, and [Owed] represents the Owed field. A benefit of the SUBTOTAL function is that it subtotals data for filtered records, so you have an accurate total for the visible records.

=SUBTOTAL(function_num,ref1,...)

TABLE 4	SUBTOTAL Function Numbers	
Function	Database Number	Table Number
AVERAGE	1	101
COUNT	2	102
COUNTA	3	103
MAX	4	104
MIN	5	105
PRODUCT	6	106
STDEV	7	107
STDEVP	8	108
SUM	9	109
VAR	10	110
VARP	11	111

Quick Concepts

1. What is a structured reference? What is the general format for including a field name in a formula? Give an example.

2. What are the benefits of displaying a total row and selecting functions instead of adding functions yourself below a table?

4 Table Aggregation

You further analyze the March 2016 transactions for Reid Furniture Store: You want to calculate the required down payment amount and how much customers owe for their purchases. Finally, you will convert the table back to a range.

Skills covered: Create Structured References in Formulas • Add a Total Row • Convert a Table to a Range

STEP 1 ≫ CREATE STRUCTURED REFERENCES IN FORMULAS

To continue reviewing the March transactions, you need to calculate the required down payment for customers who financed their purchases. The required down payment is located above the table data so that you can change that value if needed. In addition, you want to calculate how much customers owe on their purchases if they did not pay in full. You will use structured formulas to perform these calculations. Refer to Figure 35 as you complete Step 1.

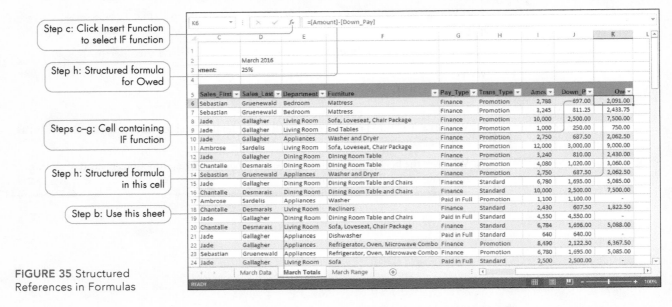

FIGURE 35 Structured References in Formulas

a. Open *e04h3Reid_LastFirst* if you closed it at the end of Hands-On Exercise 3. Save it as **e04h4Reid_LastFirst**, changing *h3* to *h4*.

b. Click the **March Totals worksheet tab** and make **cell J6** the active cell.

    To preserve the integrity of the sorting and filtering in case your instructor wants to verify your work, you will continue with an identical dataset on another worksheet.

c. Click **Insert Function** to open the Insert Function dialog box, select **IF** in the **Select a function list**, and then click **OK**.

d. Type [**Pay_Type**]="**Paid in Full**" in the **Logical_test box**.

    The logical test evaluates whether a customer paid in full, indicated in the Pay_Type field. Remember to type the brackets around the column label.

e. Type [**Amount**] in the **Value_if_true box**.

    If a customer pays in full, the down payment is the full amount.

Hands-On Exercise 4

f. Type [**Amount**]*$D$3 in the **Value_if_false box.**

If a customer does not pay in full, he or she must pay a required down payment. You use [Amount] to refer to the Amount field in the table. Enclose the field labels in brackets. The amount is multiplied by the absolute reference to D3, the cell containing the required down payment percentage. Make this cell reference absolute so that it does not change when Excel copies the formula down the Down_Pay column.

g. Click **OK** to enter the formula.

The formula looks like this in the Formula Bar: =IF([Pay_Type]= "Paid in Full",[Amount],[Amount]*$D$3). Because you are entering formulas in a table, Excel copies the formula down the column automatically. The first customer must pay a $697 down payment (25% of $2,788). The columns in the current worksheet have been formatted as Comma Style for you.

> **TROUBLESHOOTING:** If the results seem incorrect, check your function. Errors will result if you do not enclose the field names in brackets, if you have misspelled a field name, if you omit the quotation marks around *Paid in Full*, and so on. Correct any errors.

h. Click **cell K6**. Type the formula =[**Amount**]–[**Down_Pay**] and press **Enter**. Save the workbook.

The formula calculates how much customers owe if they finance their purchases. Excel copies the formula down the column.

STEP 2 ⟩⟩ ADD A TOTAL ROW

You want to see the monthly totals for the Amount, Down_Pay, and Owed columns. Instead of entering SUM functions yourself, you will add a total row. Refer to Figure 36 as you complete Step 2.

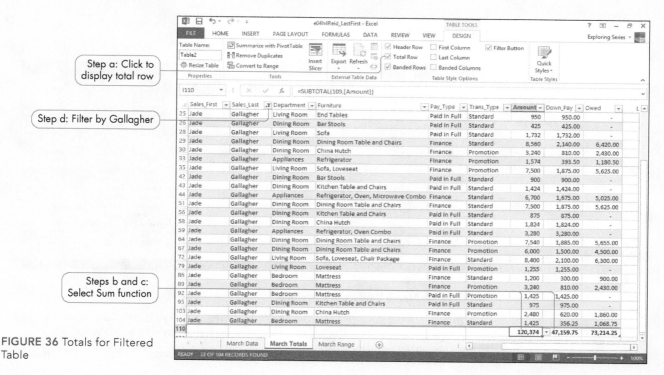

FIGURE 36 Totals for Filtered Table

a. Click the **DESIGN tab** and click **Total Row** in the Table Style Options group.

Excel displays the total row after the last record. It sums the last field of values automatically. The total amount customers owe is $278,656.50.

b. Click the **Down_Pay cell** in row 110, click the **total arrow**, and then select **Sum**.

You added a total to the Down_Pay field. The total amount of down payment collected is $190,602.50. The formula displays as =SUBTOTAL(109,[Down_Pay]) in the Formula Bar.

c. Click the **Amount cell** in row 110, click the **total arrow**, and then select **Sum**.

You added a total to the Amount column. The total amount of merchandise sales is $469,259. The formula displays as =SUBTOTAL(109,[Amount]) in the Formula Bar.

d. Filter by Gallagher again. Save the workbook.

The total row values change to display the totals for only Gallagher: $120,374 (Amount), 47,159.75 (Down_Pay), and 73,214.25 (Owed). This is an advantage of using the Total Row, which uses the SUBTOTAL function, as opposed to if you had inserted the SUM function manually. The SUM function would provide a total for all data in the column, not just the filtered data.

STEP 3 ›› CONVERT A TABLE TO A RANGE

Your last task for now is to convert a copy of the table to a range again so that you can apply other formats. Refer to Figure 37 as you complete Step 3.

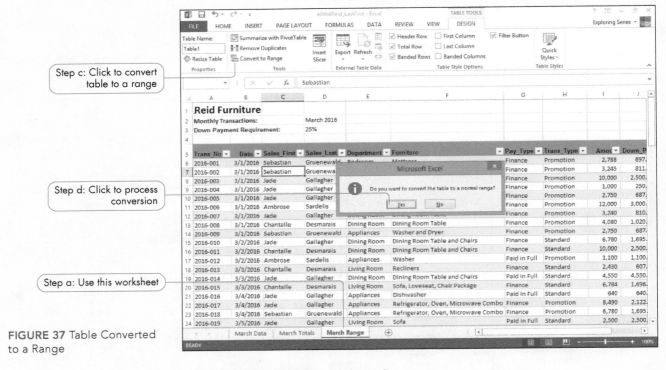

FIGURE 37 Table Converted to a Range

a. Click the **March Range worksheet tab**.

To preserve the integrity of the sorting and filtering in case your instructor wants to verify your work, you will continue with an identical dataset on another worksheet.

b. Click within the table and click the **DESIGN tab**, if necessary.

Hands-On Exercise 4

c. Click **Convert to Range** in the Tools group.

Excel displays a message box asking if you want to convert the table to a range.

d. Click **Yes**.

Excel converts the table to a range. The filter arrows disappear, and the Design tab no longer displays. The range is still formatted using a table style. The structured formula =[Amount]-[Down_Pay] in cell K6 changes to ='March Range'!$I$6:$I$109-'March Range'!$J$6:$J$109.

e. Save the workbook. Keep the workbook onscreen if you plan to continue with the next Hands-On Exercise. If not, close the workbook and exit Excel.

Conditional Formatting

You use table styles, or a variety of font, alignment, and number formats on the Home tab, to format a worksheet. You can also apply special formatting to cells that contain particular values or text using conditional formatting. ***Conditional formatting*** applies special formatting to highlight or emphasize cells that meet specific conditions. For example, a sales manager might want to highlight cells containing the top 10 sales amounts, or a professor might want to highlight test scores that fall below the average. You can also apply conditional formatting to point out data for a specific date or duplicate values in a range.

In this section, you will learn about the five conditional formatting categories and how to apply conditional formatting to a range of values based on a condition you set.

Applying Conditional Formatting

Conditional formatting helps you and your audience understand a dataset better because it adds a visual element to the cells. The term is called *conditional* because the formatting occurs when a condition is met. This is similar logic to the IF function you have used. Remember with an IF function, you create a logical test that is evaluated. If the logical or conditional test is true, the function produces one result. If the logical or conditional test is false, the function produces another result. With conditional formatting, if the condition is true, Excel formats the cell automatically based on that condition. If the condition is false, Excel does not format the cell. If you change a value in a conditionally formatted cell, Excel examines the new value to see if it should apply the conditional format.

Apply Conditional Formatting with the Quick Analysis Tool

When you select a range and click the Quick Analysis button, the FORMATTING options display in the Quick Analysis gallery. Position the mouse over a thumbnail to see how it will affect the selected range (see Figure 38). You can also apply conditional formatting by clicking Conditional Formatting in the Styles group on the Home tab.

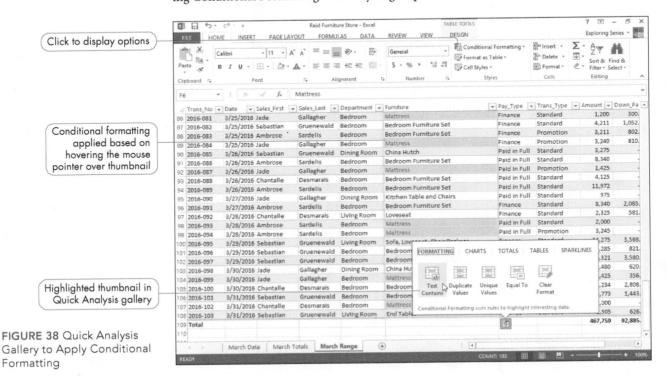

FIGURE 38 Quick Analysis Gallery to Apply Conditional Formatting

Datasets and Tables

Table 5 describes the conditional formatting options in the Quick Analysis gallery.

TABLE 5	Conditional Formatting Options in Quick Analysis Gallery
Options	**Description**
Text Contains	Formats cells that contain the text in the first selected cell. In Figure 38, the first selected cell contains Mattress. If a cell contains Mattress and Springs, Excel would format that cell also because it *contains* Mattress.
Duplicate Values	Formats cells that are duplicated in the selected range.
Unique Values	Formats cells that are unique; that is, no other cell in the selected range contains the same data.
Equal To	Formats cells that are exactly like the data contained in the first selected cell.
Clear Format	Removes the conditional formatting from the selected range.

Table 6 lists and describes a number of different conditional formats that you can apply if you want more specific rules.

TABLE 6	Conditional Formatting Options
Options	**Description**
Highlight Cells Rules	Highlights cells with a fill color, font color, or border (such as Light Red Fill with Dark Red Text) if values are greater than, less than, between two values, equal to a value, or duplicate values; text that contains particular characters; or dates when a date meets a particular condition, such as *In the last 7 days.*
Top/Bottom Rules	Formats cells with values in the top 10 items, top 10%, bottom 10 items, bottom 10%, above average, or below average. You can change the exact values to format the top or bottom items or percentages, such as top 5 or bottom 15%.
Data Bars	Applies a gradient or solid fill bar in which the width of the bar represents the current cell's value compared to other cells' values.
Color Scales	Formats different cells with different colors, assigning one color to the lowest group of values and another color to the highest group of values, with gradient colors to other values.
Icon Sets	Inserts an icon from an icon palette in each cell to indicate values compared to each other.

To apply a conditional format, select the cells for which you want to apply a conditional format, click the Home tab, click Conditional Formatting in the Styles group, and then select the conditional formatting category you want to apply.

Apply the Highlight Cells Rules

STEP 1 » The Highlight Cells Rules category enables you to apply a highlight to cells that meet a condition, such as a value greater than a particular value. This option contains predefined combinations of fill colors, font colors, and/or borders. This category is useful because it helps you identify and format automatically values of interest. For example, a weather tracker who developed a worksheet containing the temperatures for each day of a month might want to apply a conditional format to cells that contain temperatures between 70 and 75 degrees. To apply this conditional formatting, she would select Highlight Cells Rules and then select

Between. In the Between dialog box (see Figure 39), the weather tracker would type 70 in the *Format cells that are BETWEEN* box and 75 in the *and* box, select the type of conditional formatting, such as *Light Red Fill with Dark Red Text*, and then click OK to apply the formats.

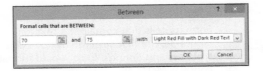

FIGURE 39 Between Dialog
Box

Figure 40 shows two columns of data that contain conditional formats. The Department column is conditionally formatted to highlight text with a Light Red Fill with Dark Red Text for cells that contain *Living Room*, and the Amount column is conditionally formatted to highlight with Red Border values between $5,000 and $10,000.

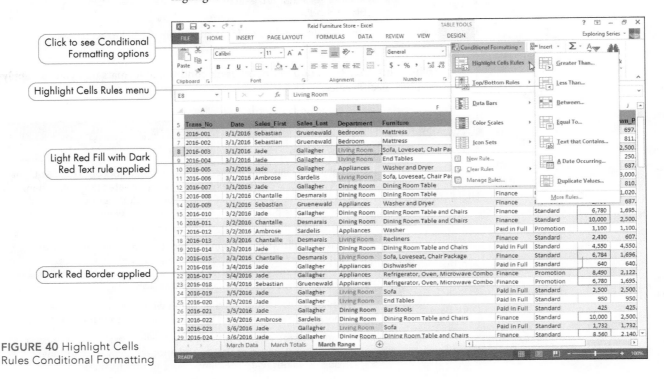

FIGURE 40 Highlight Cells
Rules Conditional Formatting

Specify Top/Bottom Rules

STEP 2 ≫ You might be interested in identifying the top five sales to reward the sales associates, or want to identify the bottom 15% of automobile dealers so that you can close underperforming locations. The Top/Bottom Rules category enables you to specify the top or bottom number, top or bottom percentage, or values that are above or below the average value in that range. In Figure 41, the Amount column is conditionally formatted to highlight the top five amounts. (Some rows are hidden so that all top five values display in the figure.) Although the menu option is Top 10 Items, you can specify the exact number of items to format.

Datasets and Tables

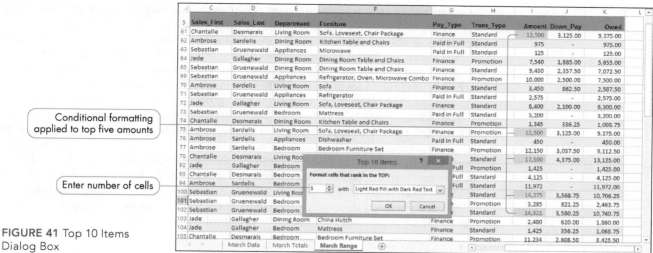

Conditional formatting applied to top five amounts

Enter number of cells

FIGURE 41 Top 10 Items Dialog Box

Display Data Bars, Color Scales, and Icon Sets

STEP 3

Data bars indicate the value of a cell relative to other cells (see Figure 42). The width of the data bar represents the value in a cell, with a wider bar representing a higher value and a narrower bar a lower value. Use data bar conditional formatting to identify high and low values. Excel locates the largest value and displays the widest data bar in that cell. Excel then finds the smallest value and displays the smallest data bar in that cell. Excel sizes the data bars for the remaining cells based on their values relative to the high and low values in the column. If you change the values, Excel updates the data bar widths. Excel uses the same color for each data bar, but each bar differs in size based on the value in the respective cells.

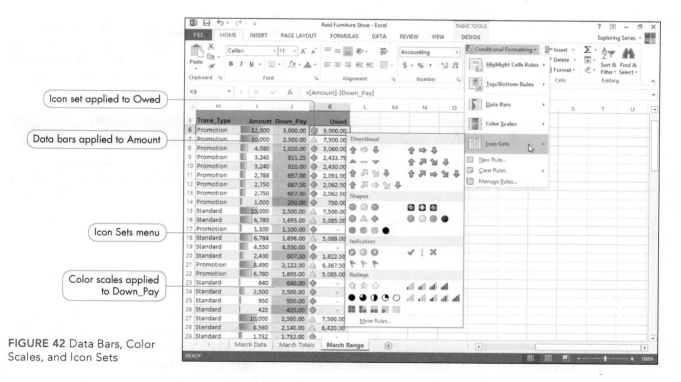

Icon set applied to Owed

Data bars applied to Amount

Icon Sets menu

Color scales applied to Down_Pay

FIGURE 42 Data Bars, Color Scales, and Icon Sets

Color scales format cells with different colors based on the relative value of a cell compared to other selected cells. You can apply a two- or three-color scale. This scale assists in comparing a range of cells using gradations of those colors. The shade of the color represents higher or lower values. In Figure 42, for example, the red color scales display for the lowest values, the green color displays for the highest values, and gradients of yellow and orange represent the middle range of values in the Down_Pay column. Use color scales to understand variation in the data to identify trends, for example, to view good stock returns and weak stock returns.

Icon sets are symbols or signs that classify data into three, four, or five categories, based on the values in a range. Excel determines categories of value ranges and assigns an icon to each range. In Figure 42, a three-icon set was applied to the Owed column. Excel divided the range of values between the lowest value $0 and the highest value of $13,125 into thirds. The red diamond icon displays for the cells containing values in the lowest third ($0 to $4,375), the yellow triangle icon displays for cells containing the values in the middle third ($4,376 to $8,750), and the green circle icon displays for cells containing values in the top third ($8,751 to $13,125). Most purchases fall into the lowest third.

TIP | Don't Overdo It!

Although conditional formatting helps identify trends, you should use this feature wisely. Apply conditional formatting when you want to emphasize important data. When you decide to apply conditional formatting, think about which category is best to highlight the data. Sometimes simple highlighting will suffice when you want to point out data meeting a particular condition; other times, you might want to apply data bars to point out relative differences among values. Finally, do not apply conditional formatting to too many columns.

Clear Rules

To clear conditional formatting from the entire worksheet, click Conditional Formatting in the Styles group on the Home tab, point to Clear Rules, and then select *Clear Rules from Entire Sheet*. To remove conditional formatting from a range of cells, select cells. Then click Conditional Formatting, point to Clear Rules, and then select *Clear Rules from Selected Cells*.

TIP | Sort and Filter Using Conditional Formatting

You can sort and filter by conditional formatting. For example, if you applied the Highlight Cells Rules conditional formatting, you can sort the column by color so that all cells containing the highlight appear first or last. To do this, display the filter arrows, click the arrow for the conditionally formatted column you wish to sort, point to Sort by Color, and then click the fill color or No Fill in the *Sort by Cell Color* area. If you applied the Icon Sets conditional formatting, you can filter by icon.

Creating a New Rule

The default conditional formatting categories provide a variety of options. Excel also enables you to create your own rules to specify different fill colors, borders, or other formatting if you do not want the default settings. Excel provides three ways to create a new rule:

- Click Conditional Formatting in the Styles group and select New Rule.
- Click Conditional Formatting in the Styles group, select Manage Rules to open the Conditional Formatting Rules Manager dialog box, and then click New Rule.
- Click Conditional Formatting in the Styles group, select a rule category such as Highlight Cells Rules, and then select More Rules.

Datasets and Tables

The New Formatting Rule dialog box opens (see Figure 43) so that you can define your new conditional formatting rule. First, select a rule type, such as *Format all cells based on their values*. The *Edit the Rule Description* section changes, based on the rule type you select. With the default rule type selected, you can specify the format style (2-Color Scale, 3-Color Scale, Data Bar, or Icon Sets). You can then specify the minimum and maximum values, the fill colors for color sets or data bars, or the icons for icon sets. After you edit the rule description, click OK to save your new conditional format.

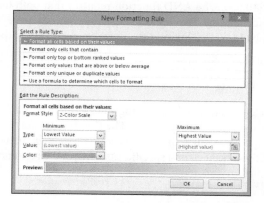

FIGURE 43 New Formatting Rule Dialog Box

If you select any rule type except the *Format all cells based on their values* rule, the dialog box contains a Format button. When you click Format, the Format Cells dialog box opens so that you can specify number, font, border, and fill formats to apply to your rule.

TIP   Format Only Cells That Contain

This option provides a wide array of things you can format: values, text, dates, blanks, no blanks, errors, or no errors. Formatting blanks is helpful to see where you are missing data, and formatting cells containing errors helps you find those errors quickly.

Use Formulas in Conditional Formatting

STEP 4 If you need to create a complex conditional formatting rule, you can select a rule that uses a formula to format cells. For example, you might want to format merchandise amounts of financed items *and* amounts that are $10,000 or more. Figure 44 shows the Edit Formatting Rule dialog box and the corresponding conditional formatting applied to cells.

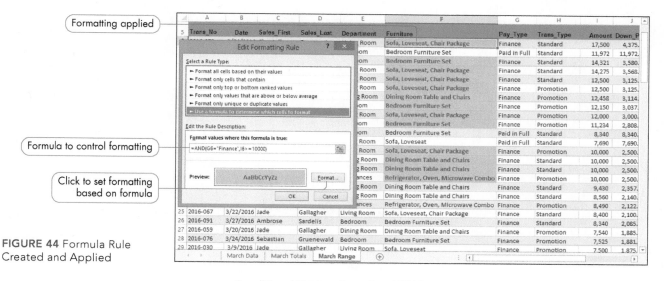

Formatting applied

Formula to control formatting

Click to set formatting based on formula

FIGURE 44 Formula Rule Created and Applied

To create a formula-based conditional formatting rule, select the data and create a new rule. In the New Formatting Rule dialog box, select *Use a formula to determine which cells to format* and type the formula, using cell references in the first row, in the *Format values where this formula is true* box. Excel applies the general formula to the selected range, substituting the appropriate cell reference as it makes the comparisons. In the Figure 44 example, =AND(G6="Finance",I6>=10000) requires that the text in the Pay_Type column (column F) contain *Finance* and the Amount column (column I) contain a value that is greater than or equal to $10,000. The AND function requires that both logical tests be met to apply the conditional formatting. Two logical tests are required; however, you can include additional logical tests. Note that *all* logical tests must be true to apply the conditional formatting.

= AND(logical1,logical2,…)

Manage Rules

To edit or delete conditional formatting rules you create, click Conditional Formatting in the Styles group and select Manage Rules. The Conditional Formatting Rules Manager dialog box opens (see Figure 45). Click the *Show formatting rules for* arrow and select from current selection, the entire worksheet, or a specific table. Select the rule and click Edit Rule or Delete Rule.

FIGURE 45 Conditional Formatting Rules Manager Dialog Box

Quick Concepts

1. How is conditional formatting similar to an IF function?

2. What conditional formatting would be helpful to identify the three movies with the highest revenue playing at theaters?

3. How is data bar conditional formatting helpful when reviewing a column of data?

Hands-On Exercises

5 Conditional Formatting

Vicki Reid wants to review the transactions with you. She is interested in Sebastian Grunewald's sales record and the three highest transaction amounts. In addition, she wants to compare the down payment amounts visually. Finally, she wants you to analyze the amounts owed for sales completed by Sebastian.

Skills covered: Highlight Cells Rules • Specify Top/Bottom Rules • Display Data Bars • Use a Formula in Conditional Formatting

STEP 1 ›› HIGHLIGHT CELLS RULES

You want to identify Sebastian's sales for March 2016 without filtering the data. You will apply a conditional format to apply a fill and font color so that cells containing his first name stand out. Refer to Figure 46 as you complete Step 1.

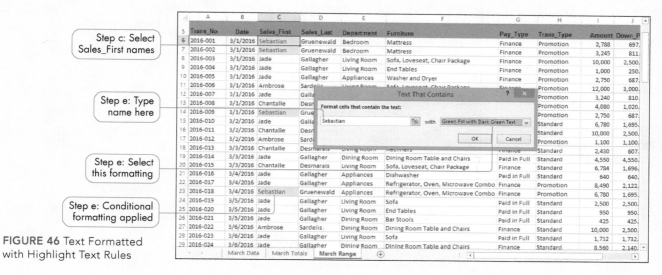

FIGURE 46 Text Formatted with Highlight Text Rules

a. Open *e04h4Reid_LastFirst* if you closed it at the end of Hands-On Exercise 4. Save the workbook as **e04h5Reid_LastFirst**, changing *h4* to *h5*.

b. Select **row headings 6 through 109** in the March Range worksheet. Click the **HOME tab**, if necessary, click the **Fill Color arrow**, and then select **No Fill**.

   You removed the previous table style with banded rows. This will avoid having too many fill colors when you apply conditional formatting rules.

c. Select the **range C6:C109**, which is the column containing the sales representatives' first names.

d. Click **Conditional Formatting** in the Styles group, point to *Highlight Cells Rules*, and then select **Text that Contains**.

   The Text That Contains dialog box opens.

e. Type **Sebastian** in the box, click the **with arrow**, and then select **Green Fill with Dark Green Text**. Click **OK**. Deselect the range and save the workbook.

   Excel formats only cells that contain Sebastian with the fill and font color.

While the range is selected, you can apply another conditional format, such as Light Yellow with Dark Yellow text for another first name.

STEP 2 ≫ SPECIFY TOP/BOTTOM RULES

Vicki is now interested in identifying the highest three sales transactions in March. Instead of sorting the records, you will use the Top/Bottom Rules conditional formatting. Refer to Figure 47 as you complete Step 2.

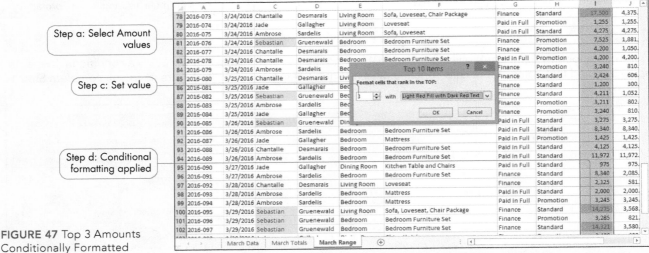

Step a: Select Amount values

Step c: Set value

Step d: Conditional formatting applied

FIGURE 47 Top 3 Amounts Conditionally Formatted

a. Select the **range I6:I109**, the range containing the amounts.

b. Click **Conditional Formatting** in the Styles group, point to *Top/Bottom Rules*, and then select **Top 10 Items**.

The Top 10 Items dialog box opens.

c. Click the spin arrow to display *3* and click **OK**.

d. Scroll through the worksheet to see the top three amounts. Save the workbook.

STEP 3 ≫ DISPLAY DATA BARS

Vicki wants to compare all of the down payments. Data bars would add a nice visual element as she compares down payment amounts. Refer to Figure 48 as you complete Step 3.

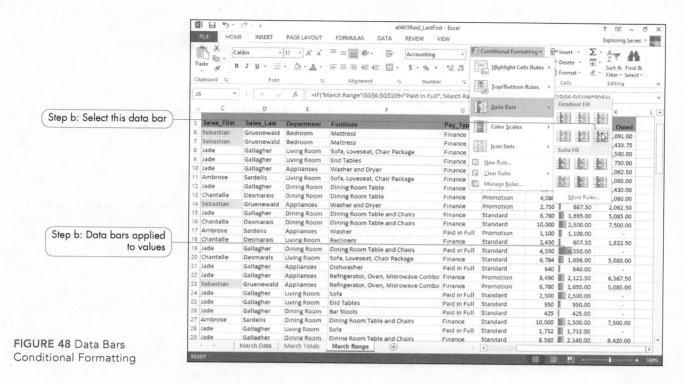

FIGURE 48 Data Bars
Conditional Formatting

a. Select the **range J6:J109**, which contains the down payment amounts.

b. Click **Conditional Formatting** in the Styles group, point to *Data Bars*, and then select **Purple Data Bar** in the *Gradient Fill* section. Scroll through the list and save the workbook.

   Excel displays data bars in each cell. The larger bar widths help Vicki quickly identify the largest down payments. However, the largest down payments are identical to the original amounts when the customers pay in full. This result illustrates that you should not accept the results at face value. Doing so would provide you with an inaccurate analysis.

STEP 4 ➤➤ USE A FORMULA IN CONDITIONAL FORMATTING

Vicki's next request is to analyze the amounts owed by Sebastian's customers. In particular, she wants to highlight the merchandise for which more than $5,000 is owed. To do this, you realize you need to create a custom rule that evaluates both the Sales_First column and the Owed column. Refer to Figure 49 as you complete Step 4.

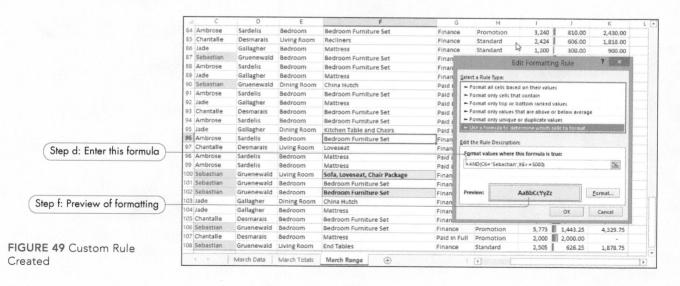

FIGURE 49 Custom Rule
Created

Hands-On Exercise 5

a. Select the **range F6:F109**, which contains the merchandise.

b. Click **Conditional Formatting** in the Styles group and select **New Rule**.

The New Formatting Rule dialog box opens.

c. Select **Use a formula to determine which cells to format**.

d. Type **=AND(C6="Sebastian",K6>5000)** in the **Format values where this formula is true box**.

Because you are comparing the contents of cell C6 to text, you must enclose the text within quotation marks.

e. Click **Format** to open the Format Cells dialog box.

f. Click the **Font tab**, if necessary, and then click **Bold** in the **Font style list**. Click the **Border tab**, click the **Color arrow**, select **Blue, Accent 5**, and then click **Outline**. Click the **Fill tab**, click **Blue, Accent 5, Lighter 80% background color** (the second color from the right on the first row below the first horizontal line), and then click **OK**.

Figure 49 shows the Edit Formatting Rule dialog box, but the options are similar to the New Formatting Rule dialog box.

g. Click **OK** in the New Formatting Rule dialog box and scroll through the list to see which amounts owed are greater than $5,000 for Sebastian only.

> **TROUBLESHOOTING:** If the results seem incorrect, click Conditional Formatting and select Manage Rules. Edit the rule you just created and make any corrections to the formula.

h. Save and close the workbook, and submit based on your instructor's directions.

Chapter Objectives Review

After reading this chapter, you have accomplished the following objectives:

1. **Freeze rows and columns.**
   - The Freeze Panes setting freezes the row(s) above and the column(s) to the left of the active cell. When you scroll, those rows and columns remain onscreen.
   - Use Unfreeze Panes to clear the frozen rows and columns.

2. **Print large datasets.**
   - Display and change page breaks: Display the data in Page Break Preview to see the automatic page breaks. Dashed blue lines indicate automatic page breaks. You can insert manual page breaks, indicated by solid blue lines.
   - Set and clear a print area: If you do not want to print an entire worksheet, select a range and set a print area.
   - Print titles: Select rows to repeat at top and/or columns to repeat at left to print the column and row labels on every page of a printout of a large dataset.
   - Control print page order: You can control the sequence in which the pages will print.

3. **Design and create tables.**
   - A table is a structured range that contains related data. Tables have several benefits over regular ranges. The column labels, called *field names*, display on the first row of a table. Each row is a complete set of data for one record.
   - You should plan a table before you create it. Create unique field names on the first row of the table and enter data below the field names, avoiding blank rows.
   - Create a table: You can create a table from existing data. Excel applies the Table Style Medium 2 format and assigns a name, such as Table1, to the table. When the active cell is within a table, the Table Tools Design tab displays.
   - Add and delete fields: You can insert and delete table rows and columns to adjust the structure of a table.
   - Add, edit, and delete records: You can add table rows, edit records, and delete table rows.
   - Remove duplicate rows: Use the Remove Duplicates dialog box to remove duplicate records in a table. Excel will display a dialog box telling you how many records are deleted.

4. **Apply a table style.**
   - Table styles control the fill color of the header row and records within the table.

5. **Sort data.**
   - Sort one field: You can sort text in alphabetical or reverse alphabetical order, values from smallest to largest or largest to smallest, and dates from oldest to newest or newest to oldest. Click the filter arrow and select the sort method from the list.
   - Sort multiple fields: Open the Sort dialog box and add column levels and sort orders.

   - Create a custom sort: You can create a custom sort for unique data, such as ensuring the months sort in sequential order rather than alphabetical order.

6. **Filter data.**
   - Filtering is the process of specifying conditions for displaying records in a table. Only records that meet those conditions display; the other records are hidden.
   - Apply text filters: A text filter can find exact text, text that does not equal a condition, text that begins with a particular letter, and so forth.
   - Apply number filters: A number filter can find exact values, values that do not equal a particular value, values greater than or equal to a value, and so on.
   - Apply date filters: You can set filters to find dates before or after a certain date, between two dates, yesterday, next month, and so forth.
   - Clear filters: If you do not need filters, you can clear the filters.

7. **Use structured references and a total row.**
   - Create structured references in formulas: A structured reference uses field names instead of cell references, such as =[Amount]–[Down Payment]. Field names must display in brackets within the formula.
   - Add a total row: You can display a total row after the last record. You can add totals or select a different function, such as Average.

8. **Apply conditional formatting.**
   - Apply conditional formatting with the Quick Analysis Tool: After selecting text, click FORMATTING on the Quick Analysis gallery to apply a conditional format.
   - Apply the highlight cells rules: This rule highlights cell contents with a fill color, font color, and/or border color where the contents match a particular condition.
   - Specify top/bottom rules: This rule enables you to highlight the top *x* number of items or percentage of items.
   - Display data bars, color scales, and icon sets: Data bars compare values within the selected range. Color scales indicate values that occur within particular ranges. Icon sets display icons representing a number's relative value compared to other numbers in the range.
   - Clear rules: If you no longer want conditional formatting applied, you can clear a rule.

9. **Create a new rule.**
   - You can create conditional format rules. The New Formatting Rule dialog box enables you to select a rule type.
   - Use formulas in conditional formatting: You can create rules based on content in multiple columns.
   - Manage rules: Use the Conditional Formatting Rules Manager dialog box to edit and delete rules.

Key Terms Matching

Match the key terms with their definitions. Write the key term letter by the appropriate numbered definition.

a. Color scale
b. Conditional formatting
c. Data bar
d. Field
e. Filtering
f. Freezing
g. Icon set
h. Page break
i. Print area

j. Print order
k. Record
l. Sorting
m. Structured reference
n. SUBTOTAL function
o. Table
p. Table style
q. Total row

1. _____ A conditional format that displays horizontal gradient or solid fill indicating the cell's relative value compared to other selected cells.

2. _____ The process of listing records or text in a specific sequence, such as alphabetically by last name.

3. _____ The process of specifying conditions to display only those records that meet those conditions.

4. _____ A set of rules that applies specific formatting to highlight or emphasize cells that meet specifications.

5. _____ A group of related fields representing one entity, such as data for one person, place, event, or concept.

6. _____ The rules that control the fill color of the header row, columns, and records in a table.

7. _____ An indication of where data will start on another printed page.

8. _____ A table row that appears below the last row of records in an Excel table and displays summary or aggregate statistics, such as a sum or an average.

9. _____ A conditional format that displays a particular color based on the relative value of the cell contents to the other selected cells.

10. _____ The sequence in which the pages are printed.

11. _____ A tag or use of a table element, such as a field label, as a reference in a formula. Field labels are enclosed in square brackets, such as [Amount] within the formula.

12. _____ A conditional format that displays an icon representing a value in the top third, quarter, or fifth based on values in the selected range.

13. _____ The range of cells within a worksheet that will print.

14. _____ A predefined formula that calculates an aggregate value, such as totals, for values in a range, a table, or a database.

15. _____ The smallest data element contained in a table, such as first name, last name, address, and phone number.

16. _____ A structure that organizes data in a series of records (rows), with each record made up of a number of fields (columns).

17. _____ The process of keeping rows and/or columns visible onscreen at all times even when you scroll through a large dataset.

Multiple Choice

1. You have a large dataset that will print on several pages. You want to ensure that related records print on the same page with column and row labels visible and that confidential information is not printed. You should apply all of the following page setup options *except* which one to accomplish this?

   (a) Set a print area.
   (b) Print titles.
   (c) Adjust page breaks.
   (d) Change the print page order.

2. You are working with a large worksheet. Your row headings are in column A. Which command(s) should be used to see the row headings and the distant information in columns X, Y, and Z?

   (a) Freeze Panes command
   (b) Hide Rows command
   (c) New Window command and cascade the windows
   (d) Split Rows command

3. Which statement is *not* a recommended guideline for designing and creating an Excel table?

   (a) Avoid naming two fields with the same name.
   (b) Ensure no blank columns separate data columns within the table.
   (c) Leave one blank row between records in the table.
   (d) Include field names on the first row of the table.

4. You have a list of all the employees in your organization. The list contains employee name, office, title, and salary. You want to list all employees in each office branch. The branches should be listed alphabetically, with the employee earning the highest salary listed first in each office. Which is true of your sort order?

   (a) Branch office is the primary sort and should be in A to Z order.
   (b) Salary is the primary sort and should be from highest to lowest.
   (c) Salary is the primary sort and should be from lowest to highest.
   (d) Branch office is the primary sort and should be in Z to A order.

5. You suspect a table has several identical records. What should you do?

   (a) Do nothing; a logical reason probably exists to keep identical records.
   (b) Use the Remove Duplicates command.
   (c) Look at each row yourself and manually delete duplicate records.
   (d) Find the duplicate records and change some of the data to be different.

6. Which check box in the Table Style Options group enables you to apply different formatting to the records in a table?

   (a) Header Row
   (b) Banded Rows
   (c) Banded Columns
   (d) Total Row

7. Which date filter option enables you to specify criteria for selecting a range of dates, such as between 3/15/2016 and 7/15/2016?

   (a) Equals
   (b) Before
   (c) All Dates in the Period
   (d) Between

8. You want to display a total row that identifies the oldest date in a field in your table. What function do you select from the list?

   (a) Max
   (b) Sum
   (c) Min
   (d) Count

9. What type of conditional formatting displays horizontal colors in which the width of the bar indicates relative size compared to other values in the selected range?

   (a) Color Scales
   (b) Icon Sets
   (c) Data Bars
   (d) Sparklines

10. When you select the _____ rule type, the New Formatting Rule dialog box does not show the Format button.

    (a) Format all cells based on their values
    (b) Format only cells that contain
    (c) Use a formula to determine which cells to format
    (d) Format only unique or duplicate values

1 Fiesta® Items and Replacement Values

FROM SCRATCH

Marie Maier has collected Fiesta dinnerware, manufactured by the Homer Laughlin China Company, since 1986. Between 1986 and 2012, the company produced 30 colors, each with a unique name. Marie created a table in Word that lists the name, number, year introduced, and year retired (if applicable) for each color. She created another table in Word that lists the item number, item, replacement value, and source of information for each item in her collection. Her main sources for replacement values are Homer Laughlin (www.fiestafactorydirect.com), Replacements, Ltd. (www.replacements.com), eBay (www.ebay.com), and two local antique stores. She needs your help to convert the data to Excel tables, apply table formatting, delete duplicate records, insert functions, and sort and filter the data. This exercise follows the same set of skills as used in Hands-On Exercises 1–3 in the chapter. Refer to Figure 50 as you complete this exercise.

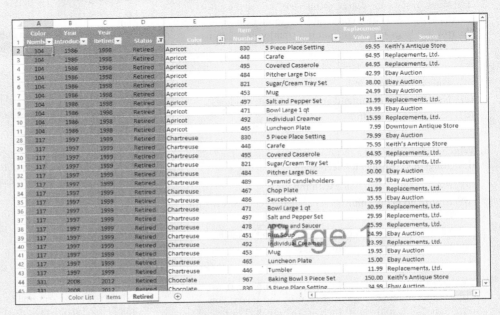

FIGURE 50 Fiesta® Collection

a. Open *e04p1Colors* in Word. Do the following to copy the Word table data into Excel and prepare the data to be used as a lookup table:
- Click the **table icon** in the top-left corner of the table and click **Copy** in the Clipboard group.
- Start a new Excel workbook, click the **Paste arrow** in the Clipboard group in Excel, and then select **Match Destination Formatting (M)**.
- Bold and horizontally center the labels on the first row. Center the data in the first, third, and fourth columns. Widen the second and third columns to fit the data.
- Select the **range A2:D31**, click in the **Name Box**, type **colors**, and then press **Enter** to assign a name to the selected range.
- Click **cell A2**, click **Sort & Filter** in the Editing group, and then select **Sort Smallest to Largest**. Remember that you must sort the first column in ascending order to use the table for an exact match for a VLOOKUP function.
- Save the Excel workbook as **e04p1Collection_LastFirst**. Close the Word document.

b. Open *e04p1Items* in Word. Select and copy the table, display the Excel workbook, add a new sheet, make sure **cell A1** is the active cell in the new sheet, and then paste the table in the same way you did in step a. Widen column E. Rename *Sheet2* **Items**. Close the Word document.

c. Click **cell A2** in the Items sheet, click the **VIEW tab**, click **Freeze Panes** in the Window group, and then select **Freeze Top Row**.

d. Press **Ctrl+End** to go to the last data cell. The first row is frozen so that the column labels remain onscreen. Press **Ctrl+Home** to go back to **cell A2**.

e. Click the **INSERT tab**, click **Table** in the Tables group, and then click **OK** in the Create Table dialog box.

f. Click **Quick Styles** in the Table Styles group and click **Table Style Medium 5**.

g. Click the **DATA tab**, click **Remove Duplicates** in the Data Tools group, and then click **OK** in the Remove Duplicates dialog box. Click **OK** in the message box that informs you that *12 duplicate values were found and removed; 356 unique values remain.*

h. Click **cell B2**, click the **HOME tab**, click the **Insert arrow** in the Cells group, and then select **Insert Table Columns to the Left**. Then insert two more columns to the left. Do the following to insert functions and customize the results in the three new table columns:

- Type **Year Introduced** in **cell B1**, **Year Retired** in **cell C1**, and **Color** in **cell D1**.
- Click **cell B2**, type **=VLOOKUP([Color Number],colors,3,False)**, and then press **Enter**. Excel copies the function down the Year Introduced column. This function looks up each item's color number using the structured reference [Color Number], looks up that value in the colors table, and then returns the year that color was introduced, which is in the third column of that table.
- Click **cell B2**, click **Copy**, click **cell C2**, and then click **Paste**. Change the *3* to **4** in the col_index_num argument of the pasted function. Excel copies the function down the Year Retired column. This function looks up each item's color number using the structured reference [Color Number], looks up that value in the colors table, and then returns the year that color was retired, if applicable, which is in the fourth column of that table. The function returns 0 if the retired cell in the lookup table is blank.

- Click the **FILE tab**, click **Options**, click **Advanced**, scroll down to the *Display options for this worksheet* section, click the **Show a zero in cells that have zero value check box** to deselect it, and then click **OK**. The zeros disappear. (This option hides zeros in the active worksheet. While this is not desirable if you need to show legitimate zeros, this worksheet is designed to avoid that issue.)
- Click **cell C2**, click **Copy**, click **cell D2**, and then click **Paste**. Change the *4* to **2** in the col_index_num argument of the pasted function. Excel copies the function down the Color column. This function looks up each item's color number using the structured reference [Color Number] to look up that value in the colors table and returns the color name, which is in the second column of that table.

i. Apply wrap text, horizontal centering, and **30.75 row height** to the column labels row. Adjust column widths. Center data horizontally in the Color Number, Year Introduced, Year Retired, and Item Number columns. Apply **Comma Style** to the Replacement Values. Deselect the data.

j. Click **Sort & Filter** in the Editing group and select **Custom Sort** to display the Sort dialog box. Do the following in the Sort dialog box:

- Click the **Sort by arrow** and select **Color**.
- Click **Add Level**, click the **Then by arrow**, and then select **Replacement Value**.
- Click the **Order arrow** and select **Largest to Smallest**. Click **OK**.

k. Right-click the **Items sheet tab**, select **Move or Copy**, click **(move to end)**, click the **Create a copy check box**, and then click **OK**. Rename the copied sheet **Retired**.

l. Make sure the active sheet is Retired. Insert a table column between the Year Retired and Color columns.

- Type **Status** in **cell D1** as the column label.
- Click **cell D2**, type **=IF([Year Retired]=0, "Current","Retired")**, and then press **Enter**. This function determines that if the cell contains a 0 (which is hidden), it will display the word *Current*. Otherwise, it will display *Retired*.

m. Click the **Status filter arrow**, deselect the **Current check box**, and then click **OK** to filter out the current colors and display only retired colors.

n. Click the **DESIGN tab** and click **Total Row** in the Table Style Options group. Press **Ctrl+End** to go to the total row, click the **Source total cell** (which contains a count of visible items), click the

Source total arrow, and then select **None**. Click **cell H358**, the *Replacement Value total* cell, click the **Replacement Value total arrow**, and then select **Sum**.

o. Prepare the Retired worksheet for printing by doing the following:
  - Set **0.2"** left and right page margins.
  - Select the **range E1:I358**, click the **PAGE LAYOUT tab**, click **Print Area** in the Page Setup group, and then select **Set Print Area**.
  - Click **Print Titles** in the Page Setup group, click the **Rows to repeat at top Collapse Dialog box button**, click the **row 1 header**, and then click the **Collapse Dialog box button**. Click **OK**.
  - Click the **VIEW tab** and click **Page Break Preview** in the Workbook Views group. Decrease the top margin to avoid having only one or two records print on the last page.

p. Create a footer with your name on the left side, the sheet name code in the center, and the file name code on the right side of each worksheet.

q. Save and close the workbook, and submit based on your instructor's directions.

2 Dentist Association Donation List

The Midwest Regional Dentist Association is planning its annual meeting in Lincoln, Nebraska, this spring. Several members donated items for door prizes at the closing general session. You will organize the list of donations and format it to highlight particular data for your supervisor, who is on the conference board of directors. This exercise follows the same set of skills as used in Hands-On Exercises 2–5 in the chapter. Refer to Figure 51 as you complete this exercise.

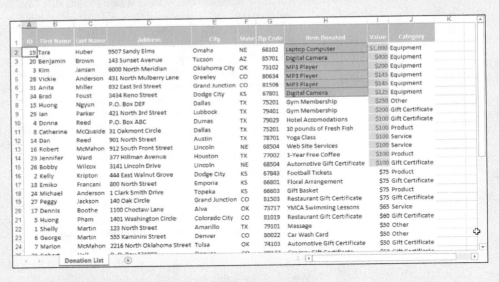

FIGURE 51 Donation List

a. Open *e04p2Donate* and save it as **e04p2Donate_LastFirst**.

b. Click the **DESIGN tab**, click **Remove Duplicates** in the Tools group, and then click **OK**. Click **OK** in the message box that tells you that Excel removed three duplicate records.

c. Click **Convert to Range** in the Tools group and click **Yes** in the message box.

d. Select the **range A2:J35**, click the **HOME tab**, click the **Fill Color arrow** in the Font group, and then select **No Fill** to remove the table fill colors.

e. Select the **range I2:I35**. Click **Conditional Formatting** in the Styles group, point to *Highlight Cells Rules*, and then select **Greater Than**. Type **99** in the **Format cells that are GREATER THAN box** and click **OK**.

f. Select **cells H2:H35**. Create a custom conditional format by doing the following:

- Click **Conditional Formatting** in the Styles group and select **New Rule**.
- Click **Use a formula to determine which cells to format**.
- Type **=(J2="Equipment")** in the **Format values where this formula is true box**. The basic condition is testing to see if the contents of cell J2 equal the word *Equipment*. You type *Equipment* in quotation marks because you are comparing text instead of a value.
- Click **Format**, click the **Fill tab** if necessary, and then click **Red, Accent 2, Lighter 60%** (sixth background color on the second row below the first horizontal line).
- Click the **Border tab**, click the **Color arrow**, click **Dark Red**, and then click **Outline**.
- Click **OK** in each dialog box.

DISCOVER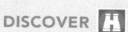

g. Click in the table to deselect the range. Click **Sort & Filter** in the Editing group and select **Custom Sort**. The dialog box may contain existing sort conditions for the State and City fields, which you will replace. Set the following sort conditions:

- Click the **Sort by arrow** and select **Item Donated**. Click the **Sort On arrow** and select **Cell Color**. Click the **Order arrow** and select the **RGB(146, 205, 220) fill color**. The fill color displays for the Order.
- Click the **Then by arrow** and select **Value**. Click the **Order arrow** and select **Largest to Smallest**.
- Click **OK**.

h. Select **Landscape orientation**, set appropriate margins, and then adjust column widths so that all the data will print on one page. Do not decrease the scaling.

i. Create a footer with your name on the left side, the sheet name code in the center, and the file name code on the right side.

j. Save and close the workbook, and submit based on your instructor's directions.

1 Biology Department Teaching Schedule

DISCOVER

As the department head of the biology department at a university, you prepare and finalize the faculty teaching schedule. Scheduling preparation takes time because you must ensure that you do not text faculty for different courses at the same time or double-book a classroom with two different classes. You downloaded the Spring 2015 schedule as a starting point and edited it to prepare the Spring 2016 schedule, and now you need to sort and filter the schedule to review it from several perspectives.

a. Open *e04m1Classes* and save it as **e04m1Classes_LastFirst**.

b. Freeze the panes so that the column labels do not scroll offscreen.

c. Convert the data to a table and name the table **Spring2016**.

d. Apply **Table Style Light 14** to the table.

e. Sort the table by Instructor, then Days, and then Start Time. Create a custom sort order for Days so that it appears in this sequence: MTWR, MWF, MW, M, W, F, TR, T, R. (The day abbreviations are as follows: M = Monday, T = Tuesday, W = Wednesday, R = Thursday, F = Friday.)

f. Remove duplicate records from the table. Excel should find and remove three duplicate records.

g. Copy the Faculty sheet, place the copied worksheet to the right of the Faculty sheet, and then rename the duplicate worksheet **Rooms**. Sort the data in the Rooms sheet by Room in ascending order, then by Days using the custom sort order you created in step e, and finally by Start Time from earliest to latest time.

h. Copy the Rooms sheet, place the copied worksheet to the right of the Rooms sheet, and then rename the duplicate worksheet **Prime Time**.

i. Filter the table in the Prime Time sheet to show only classes scheduled on any combination of Monday, Wednesday, and Friday. Include classes that meet four days a week (MTWR). Do not include any other combination of Tuesday or Thursday classes, though. Also filter the table by classes that start between 9:00 AM and 12:00 PM. The status bar indicates 20 of 75 records found.

j. Insert a field on the right side of the Credits field in the Faculty sheet. Type the label **Capacity**. Insert a lookup function that looks up the room number, compares it to the lookup table in the Room Capacity worksheet, and returns the room capacity. Make sure the function copies down the entire column.

k. Select the first three sheet tabs and set **0.2"** left and right margins, **Landscape orientation**, and **95% scaling**. Repeat the column labels on all pages. On the Faculty sheet, decrease some column widths so that the Capacity column will print on the same page as the other columns.

l. Display the Faculty sheet in Page Break Preview. Adjust any page breaks so that classes for a particular instructor do not split between pages.

m. Display the Rooms sheet in Page Break Preview. Adjust any page breaks so that classes for a particular room do not split between pages, if necessary. Set the worksheet to print 1 page wide and 3 pages tall.

n. Insert a footer with your name on the left side, the sheet name code in the center, and the file name code on the right side of all four sheets.

o. Save and close the workbook, and submit based on your instructor's directions.

2 Artwork

ANALYSIS CASE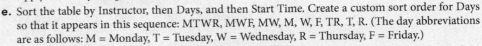

You work for a gallery that is an authorized Greenwich Workshop fine art dealer (www .greenwichworkshop.com). Customers in your area are especially fond of James C. Christensen's art. Although customers can visit the Web site to see images and details about his work, they have requested a list of all his artwork. Your assistant prepared a list of artwork: art, type, edition size, release date, and issue price. In addition, you included a column to identify which pieces are sold out at the publisher, indicating the rare, hard-to-obtain artwork that is available on the secondary market. You now want to convert the data to a table so that you can provide information to your customers.

a. Open *e04m2FineArt* and save it as **e04m2FineArt_LastFirst**.

b. Convert the data to a table and apply **Table Style Medium 5**.

c. Add a row (below the *The Yellow Rose* record) for this missing piece of art: **The Yellow Rose, Masterwork Canvas Edition, 50** edition size, **May 2009** release date, **$895** issue price. Enter **Yes** to indicate the piece is sold out.

d. Sort the table by Type in alphabetical order and then by release date from newest to oldest.

e. Add a total row that shows the largest edition size and the most expensive issue price. Delete the Total label in **cell A205**. Add a descriptive label in **cell C205** to reflect the content on the total row.

f. Create a custom conditional format for the Issue Price column with these specifications:

- 4 Traffic Lights icon set (Black, Red, Yellow, Green)
- Red icon when the number is greater than 1000
- Yellow icon when the number is less than or equal to 1000 and greater than 500
- Green icon when the number is less than or equal to 500 and greater than 250
- Black icon when the number is less than or equal to 250.

g. Filter the table by the Red Traffic Light conditional formatting icon.

h. Answer the questions in the range D211:D215 based on the filtered data.

i. Set the print area to print the **range C1:H205**, select the **first row to repeat at the top of each printout**, set **1"** top and bottom margins, set **0.3"** left and right margins, and then select **Landscape orientation**. Set the option to fit the data to 1 page.

j. Wrap text and horizontally center column labels and adjust column widths and row heights as needed.

k. Create a footer with your name on the left side, the sheet name code in the center, and the file name code on the right side.

l. Save and close the workbook, and submit based on your instructor's directions.

3 Party Music

COLLABORATION CASE

FROM SCRATCH

You are planning a weekend party and want to create a mix of music so that most people will appreciate some of the music you will play at the party. To help you decide what music to play, you have asked five classmates to help you create a song list. The entire class should decide on the general format, capitalization style, and sequence: song, musician, genre, year released, and approximate song length.

a. Conduct online research to collect data for your favorite 25 songs.

b. Enter the data into a new workbook in the format, capitalization style, and sequence that was decided by the class.

c. Save the workbook as **e04m3PlayList_LastFirst**.

d. Upload the file to a shared folder on SkyDrive or Dropbox that everyone in the class can access.

e. Download four workbooks from friends and copy and paste data from their workbooks into yours.

f. Convert the data to a table and apply a table style of your choice.

g. Detect and delete duplicate records. Make a note of the number of duplicate records found and deleted.

h. Sort the data by genre in alphabetical order, then by artist in alphabetical order, and then by release date with the newest year first.

i. Set a filter to hide songs that were released before 2000.

j. Display the total row and select the function to count the number of songs displayed.

k. Insert comments in the workbook to indicate which student's workbooks you used, the number of duplicate records deleted, and number of filtered records.

l. Save and close the workbook. Submit the workbook based on your instructor's directions.

Beyond the Classroom

Flight Arrival Status

RESEARCH CASE

FROM SCRATCH

As an analyst for an airport, you want to study the flight arrivals for a particular day. Select an airport and find its list of flight arrival data. Some airport websites do not list complete details, so search for an airport that does, such as Will Rogers World Airport or San Diego International Airport. Copy the column labels and arrival data (airline, flight number, city, gate, scheduled time, status, etc.) for one day and paste them in a new workbook. The columns may be in a different sequence from what is listed here. However, you should format the data as needed. Leave two blank rows below the last row of data and enter the URL of the Web page from which you got the data, the date, and the time. Save the workbook as **e04b2Flights_LastFirst**. Convert the list to a table and apply a table style.

Sort the table by scheduled time and then by gate number. Apply conditional formatting to the Status column to highlight cells that contain the text *Delayed* (or similar text). Add a total row to calculate the MODE for the gate number and arrival time. You must select **More Functions** from the list of functions in the total row and search for and select **MODE**. Change the label in the first column from *Total* to **Most Frequent**. Use Help to refresh your memory on how to nest an IF function inside another IF function. Add a calculated column on the right side of the table using a nested IF function and structured references to display *Late* if the actual time was later than the scheduled time, *On Time or Early* if the actual time was earlier or equal to the scheduled time, or *Incomplete* if the flight has not landed yet.

Name the worksheet **Arrival Time**. Copy the worksheet and name the copied worksheet **Delayed**. Filter the list by delayed flights. Include a footer with your name on the left side, the sheet name code in the center, and the file name code on the right side of both worksheets. Adjust the margins on both worksheets as necessary. Save and close the workbook, and submit based on your instructor's directions.

U.S. Population

DISASTER RECOVERY

A colleague at an advertising firm downloaded U.S. population information from the government Web site. In the process of creating tables, he made some errors and needs your help. Open *e04b3Populate* and save it as **e04b3Populate_LastFirst**. As you find the errors, document them on the Errors worksheet and make the corrections. Your documentation should include these columns: Error Number, Location, Problem, and Solution. Both tables in the U.S. Population worksheet should show grand total populations per year. The state table should be sorted by region and then by state. Your colleague wants to emphasize the top 15% state populations for the most recent year in the state table. The last column should show percentage changes from year to year, such as 0.6%. Your colleague wants to print only the state data. Select the sorted data population for one region at a time to compare to the regional totals in the first table to crosscheck the totals. For example, when you select the July 1, 2008, Midwest values in the second table, the status bar should display the same value as shown for the Midwest July 1, 2008, values in the first table. Create a footer with your name, the sheet name code, and the file name code. Save and close the workbook, and submit based on your instructor's directions.

Performance Evaluation

After watching the Performance Evaluation video, create a workbook that lists at least 10 performance traits mentioned in the video or other common performance traits, such as "arriving to work on time." Use the second column for a self-evaluation and the third column for manager evaluation. Below the list, create a description to describe ratings 1 through 5. For example, Exemplary—exceeds expectations is a 5, and Unacceptable—grounds for probation is a 1. Enter your own scores for each performance trait and enter scores based on your manager's review. Save the workbook as **e04b4Performance_LastFirst**.

Convert the list to a table and sort the table alphabetically by performance trait descriptions. Add a total row and select the AVERAGE function for the two ratings columns. Create a conditional formatting rule to highlight cells in the ratings columns for values less than 3. Insert three rows at the top for a title, your name, and the current date. Create a footer with your name on the left side, the date code in the center, and the filename code on the right side. Save and close the workbook, and submit based on your instructor's directions.

Capstone Exercise

You work at Mountain View Realty. A coworker developed a spreadsheet listing houses listed and sold during the past several months. She included addresses, location, list price, selling price, listing date, and date sold. You need to convert the data to a table. You will manage the large worksheet, prepare the worksheet for printing, sort and filter the table, include calculations, and then format the table.

Prepare the Large Worksheet as a Table

You will freeze the panes so that labels remain onscreen. You also want to convert the data to a table so that you can apply table options.

a. Open the *e04c1Houses* workbook and save it as **e04c1Houses_LastFirst**.

b. Freeze the first row on the Sales Data worksheet.

c. Convert the data to a table and apply the **Table Style Medium 17**.

d. Remove duplicate records.

Add Calculated Fields and a Total Row

The office manager asked you to insert a column to display the percentage of list price. The formula finds the sale price percentage of the list price. For example, if a house was listed at $100,000 and sells for $75,000, the percentage of list price is 75%. In some cases, the percentage is more than 100%. This happens when a bidding war occurs and buyers increase their offers, which results in the seller getting more than the list price.

a. Insert a new field to the right of the Selling Price field. Name the new field **Percent of List Price**.

b. Create a formula with structured references to calculate the percentage of the list price.

c. Format the field with **Percent Style** with one decimal place.

d. Insert a new field to the right of the Sale Date field. Name the new field **Days on Market**.

e. Create a formula with structured references to calculate the number of days on the market. Apply the **General number format** to the values.

f. Add a total row to display the average percentage of list price and average number of days on market. Format the average number of days on market as a whole number. Use an appropriate label for the total row.

Sort and Print the Table

To help the office manager compare house sales by city, you will sort the data. Then you will prepare the large table to print.

a. Sort the table by city in alphabetical order and add a second level to sort by days on market with the houses on the market the longest at the top within each city.

b. Adjust column widths so that the data are one page across (three pages total). Wrap the column labels.

c. Repeat the field names on all pages.

d. Change page breaks so that city data do not span between pages and change back to Normal view.

e. Add a footer with your name on the left side, the sheet name code in the center, and the file name code on the right side.

Copy and Filter the Data

The office manager needs to focus on houses that took longer than 30 days to sell within three cities. To keep the original data intact for the agents, you will copy the table data to a new sheet and use that sheet to display the filtered data.

a. Copy the Sales Data sheet and place the duplicate sheet to the right of the original sheet tab. Convert the table to a range of data and delete the average row.

b. Rename the duplicate worksheet **Filtered Data**.

c. Display the filter arrows for the data.

d. Filter the data to display the cities of Alpine, Cedar Hills, and Eagle Mountain.

e. Filter the data to display records for houses that were on the market 30 days or more.

Apply Conditional Formatting

To highlight housing sales to illustrate trends, you will apply conditional formatting. Because data are sorted by city, you will use an icon set to color-code the number of days on market. You will also apply data bar conditional formatting to the sale prices to help the office manager visualize the differences among the sales.

a. Apply the **3 Arrows (Colored) icon set** to the *Days on Market* values.

b. Apply the **Light Blue Data Bar conditional formatting** in the *Gradient Fill* section to the selling prices.

c. Create a new conditional format that applies yellow fill and bold font to values that contain 95% or higher for the *Percent of List Price* column.

d. Edit the conditional format you created so that it formats values 98% or higher.

Finalize the Workbook

You are ready to finalize the workbook by adding a footer to the new worksheet and saving the final workbook.

a. Add a footer with your name on the left side, the sheet name code in the center, and the file name code on the right side.

b. Remove all page breaks in the Filtered Data worksheet.

c. Select **Landscape orientation** and set appropriate margins so that the data will print on one page.

d. Save and close the workbook, and submit based on your instructor's directions.

Glossary

Color scale A conditional format that displays a particular color based on the relative value of the cell contents to the other selected cells.

Conditional formatting A set of rules that applies specific formatting to highlight or emphasize cells that meet specifications.

Data bar A conditional format that displays horizontal gradient or solid fill indicating the cell's relative value compared to other selected cells.

Field The smallest data element in a table, such as first name, last name, address, or phone number.

Filtering The process of specifying conditions to display only those records that meet those conditions.

Freezing The process of keeping rows and/or columns visible onscreen at all times even when you scroll through a large dataset.

Icon set A conditional format that displays an icon representing a value in the top third, quarter, or fifth based on values in the selected range.

Page break An indication where data will start on another printed page. The software inserts automatic page breaks based on data, margins, and paper size. Users can insert additional page breaks.

Print area The range of cells within a worksheet that will print.

Print order The sequence in which the pages are printed.

Record A group of related fields representing one entity, such as data for one person, place, event, or concept.

Sorting The process of listing records or text in a specific sequence, such as alphabetically by last name.

Structured reference A tag or use of a table element, such as a column label, as a reference in a formula. Column labels are enclosed in square brackets, such as [Amount], within the formula.

SUBTOTAL function A math or trig function that calculates the total of values contained in two or more cells; the first argument in the function specifies which aggregate function applies to the values in the range specified by the second argument.

Table An object used to store and organize data in a series of records (rows) with each record made up of a number of fields (columns).

Table style A named collection of color, font, and border design that can be applied to a table.

Total row A table row that displays below the last row of records in an Excel table, or in Datasheet view of a table or query, and displays summary or aggregate statistics, such as a sum or an average.

Excel

Subtotals, PivotTables, and PivotCharts

Summarizing and Analyzing Data

Yuri Arcurs/Shutterstock

OBJECTIVES AFTER YOU READ THIS CHAPTER, YOU WILL BE ABLE TO:

1. Subtotal data
2. Group and ungroup data
3. Create a PivotTable
4. Modify a PivotTable
5. Filter and slice a PivotTable
6. Create a calculated field
7. Format a PivotTable
8. Use PowerPivot Functionality
9. Create a PivotChart

CASE STUDY | Ivory Halls Publishing Company

You are the new Vice President of the Sociology Division at Ivory Halls Publishing Company. The sociology domain has many disciplines, such as introductory sociology, family, research, gender issues, and more. Ivory Halls publishes several textbooks in each discipline to appeal to a vast array of university professors and students.

Your assistant prepared a list of books, their disciplines, and other pertinent data. The current list is not easy to analyze. You need to organize the data so that you can study the sales trends by discipline and area. The list contains current editions of all sociology textbooks. Some books are brand new—in their first edition—while other books are in their 10th edition. All of the books on the list have publication dates between 2014 and 2017.

One of your first tasks in your new position is to analyze sales for all books published in the Sociology Division. To do this, you need to organize data so that you can group data by discipline and then insert subtotal rows. You will also use Excel's PivotTable tool to gain a variety of perspectives of aggregated data. Finally, you will create a PivotChart to depict the aggregated data visually.

From Excel Chapter 5 of *Microsoft® Excel 2013 Comprehensive*, First edition. Mary Anne Poatsy, Keith Mulbery, Jason Davidson, Robert T. Grauer. Copyright © 2014 by Pearson Education, Inc. Published by Pearson Prentice Hall. All Rights Reserved. Download student resources at http://www.pearsonhighered.com/exploring.

Subtotals and Outlines

When you use large datasets, you develop an appreciation for functionality that enables you to manage the data and quickly provide answers to imperative questions. Data alone are meaningless; data translated into meaningful information increase your knowledge so that you can make well-informed decisions. Previously, you used analytical tools such as sorting, filtering, conditional formatting, tables, and charts. These tools help translate raw data into information so that you can identify trends, patterns, and anomalies in a dataset. Now you are ready to explore other functionalities that help you consolidate and analyze large amounts of data.

In this section, you will learn how to insert subtotals for categories. Then you will learn how to group data to create an outline, collapse and expand groups within the outline, and ungroup data to return them to their original state.

Subtotaling Data

Decision makers often want to calculate subtotals by groups within large dataset. You can use the Subtotal feature to insert subtotal rows by categories for a regular data range.

For example, the Ivory Halls Publishing Company's dataset contains a list of sociology textbooks organized by discipline, such as Family. Textbooks are further classified by a specific area within the discipline. For example, the Family discipline contains specific areas such as *Family Interaction* and *Marriage and Family*. You can calculate the number of books sold and the total sales per area. Adding subtotals can help you identify which disciplines and which areas contribute the highest revenue for the company and which disciplines and areas produce the lowest revenue. You can then analyze the data to determine to continue publishing books in high-revenue–generating areas or discontinue the publication of books in low-selling areas. To add subtotals to a dataset, do the following:

STEP 1 ≫

1. Sort the data on a primary category (such as Discipline in the sociology textbook example) that has the same values, such as the same city, state, or department name for several records in one column. **NOTE: If the data are not sorted by a major category, the subtotaled results will not be correct.**
2. Convert the table to range (if the dataset is a table).
3. Click in the dataset and click the DATA tab.
4. Click Subtotal in the Outline group to open the Subtotal dialog box.
5. Click the *At each change in* arrow and select the column by which the data are sorted (see Figure 1). **NOTE: You must select the column by which you sorted data in Step 1.**
6. Click the *Use function* arrow and select the function you want to apply.
7. Select the appropriate column heading check boxes in the *Add subtotal to* list for each field you want to subtotal. You can use all functions for columns that contain numeric data. For text columns, you can only count the number of rows within the group.
8. Select any other check boxes you want to use and click OK.

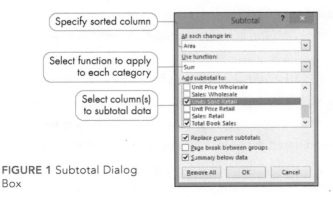

FIGURE 1 Subtotal Dialog Box

The dataset must be sorted by categorical labels. For example, the Sociology Textbooks dataset is sorted first by discipline. When you use the Subtotal feature, Excel inserts a *subtotal*, a row within the dataset containing at least one aggregated value when the category you specified in the *At a change in* option changes. For example, when Excel detects a change from Family to Introductory, a subtotal row is inserted on row 35 (see Figure 2). (NOTE: Subtotal rows for discipline are highlighted in yellow in the figure; however, the Subtotal feature does not add highlighting.) The subtotal of the number of Family discipline books sold at wholesale was 76,710, and the subtotal of the number of Introductory discipline books sold at wholesale was 179,415, indicating that the number of Introductory books sold is more than double the number of Family books sold. A grand total row is inserted at the end of the dataset to indicate the grand total values (not shown in the figure).

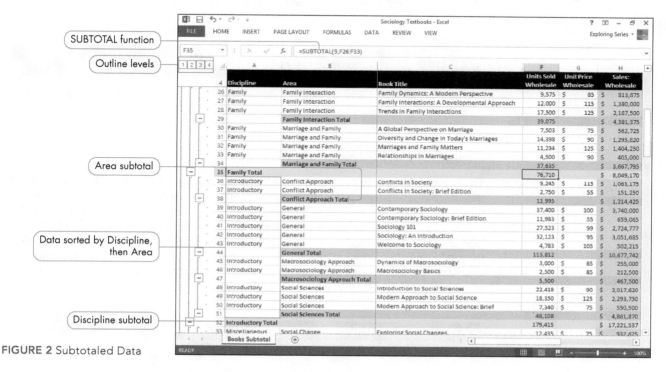

FIGURE 2 Subtotaled Data

Excel uses the SUBTOTAL function to calculate the subtotals. Cell F35 contains =SUBTOTAL(9,F26:F33) to sum the values in the range F26:F33. The first argument indicates which summary function is used to calculate the subtotal. Use 1-11 to summarize data including hidden values; use 101-111 to summarize visible data only. Table 1 lists some of the summary functions and their respective argument values. For example, 9 sums all values in the range specified in the second argument. If you create a subtotal to average the gross sales, the first argument in the function would be 1 instead of 9.

TABLE 1 SUBTOTAL Function_Num Argument		
Summary Function	Argument to Include Hidden Values	Argument to Ignore Hidden Values
AVERAGE	1	101
COUNT	2	102
COUNTA	3	103
MAX	4	104
MIN	5	105
SUM	9	109

Subtotals and Outlines • Excel 2013

Add a Second Level of Subtotals

You can add a second level of subtotals to a dataset. Adding a second level preserves the primary subtotals and adds another level of subtotals for subcategories. In the Sociology Textbook example, Figure 2 shows the discipline subtotals as well as the areas subcategory subtotals. To add a second level of subtotals while maintaining the existing subtotals, do the following:

STEP 2》
1. Perform a two-level sort based on primary and secondary categorical data.
2. Click the DATA tab and click Subtotal in the Outline group.
3. Click the *At a change in* arrow and specify the column that was used for the secondary sort.
4. Select the function and columns to be subtotaled.
5. Deselect the *Replace current subtotals* check box and click OK.

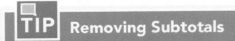
TIP **Removing Subtotals**

The subtotal rows are temporary. To remove them, display the Subtotals dialog box and click Remove All.

Collapse and Expand the Subtotals

STEP 3》
The Subtotal feature creates an ***outline***, a hierarchical structure of data. When a dataset contains a structured list, you can collapse or expand the categories after using the Subtotal feature. Table 2 explains the outline buttons that appear on the left side of the subtotaled data. Figure 3 shows a dataset that is collapsed to display the discipline subtotals and the grand total after the user clicked the outline button 2. The number of outline buttons depends on the total number of subtotals created. Because the data in Figure 2 contained discipline and area subtotals, four outline buttons appear in Figure 3. If the dataset contained only one level of subtotals, only three outline buttons would appear.

TABLE 2	Outline Buttons
Button	**Description**
1	Collapse outline to display the grand total only.
2	Display subtotals by the main subtotal category and the grand total.
3	Displays subtotals by the main subtotal category, the secondary subtotal category, and the grant total.
4	Display the entire list.
+	Expand an outline group to see its details.
−	Collapse an outline group to see its category name only.

Click to show category subtotals and grand total

Click to expand a particular area to show its details

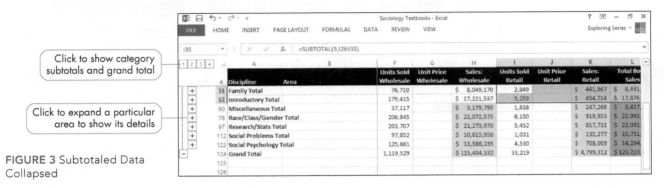

FIGURE 3 Subtotaled Data Collapsed

Subtotals, PivotTables, and PivotCharts

Grouping and Ungrouping Data

STEP 4 » The Subtotals feature outlines data into categories by rows. You can create outlines by columns of related data as well. For Excel to outline by columns, the dataset must contain formulas or aggregate functions. If Excel cannot create the outline, it displays the message box *Cannot create an outline*. To create an outline by columns, do the following:

1. Click the DATA tab.
2. Click the Group arrow in the Outline group.
3. Select Auto Outline.

For more control in creating an outline, you can create groups. *Grouping* is the process of joining rows or columns of related data together into a single entity. After you create groups in the dataset, you can click a collapse button (–) to collapse a group to show the outsider column or click the expand button (+) to expand groups of related columns to view the internal columns of data. Grouping enables you to hide raw data while you focus on key calculated results. To group data, do the following:

1. Select the rows or columns you want to group. For column groups, you often select columns containing details but not aggregate columns, such as totals or averages. (Rows are automatically grouped if you use the Subtotals feature.)
2. Click the DATA tab.
3. Click Group in the Outline group. If the Group dialog box opens, choose the option to group by columns or rows and click OK.

In Figure 4, Excel grouped the data by columns. Because the Units Sold Retail and Unit Price Retail columns are grouped, you can click the collapse button above Sales Retail to collapse the columns and focus on the Sales Retail column. Currently, some of the wholesale columns are hidden, showing only the Sales: Wholesale column. You can click the expand button above the Sales: Wholesale column to display the related wholesale columns.

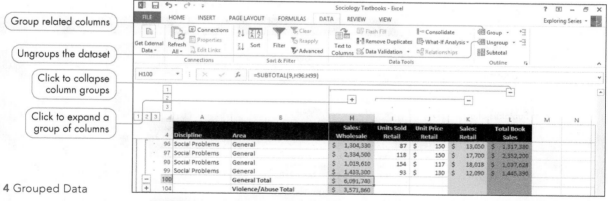

Group related columns
Ungroups the dataset
Click to collapse column groups
Click to expand a group of columns

FIGURE 4 Grouped Data

TIP Removing Groups

To remove groups, select all grouped columns or rows and click Ungroup in the Outline group.

Quick Concepts

1. Why must a dataset be sorted by a category before using the Subtotal feature? Within the Subtotal dialog box, which option do you set to match the column you used to sort the data?

2. Explain the SUBTOTAL function as it is used by the Subtotal feature.

3. How can you expand or collapse outlined groups of columns?

Hands-On Exercises

Watch the Video
for this Hands-
On Exercise!

MyITLab®
HOE1 Training

1 Subtotals and Outlines

As VP of the Sociology Division at Ivory Halls Publishing Company, you want to conduct a preliminary analysis of your current textbook offerings. Each textbook falls within a general discipline, and each discipline is divided into several areas. Details for each textbook include the title, current edition, and copyright year. The company tracks units sold, unit prices, and gross sales by two major types of sales: (1) wholesale sales to bookstores and (2) retail sales to individual consumers. You will organize the data and include area subtotals. Your assistant applied Freeze Panes to keep the column headings in row 4 and the disciplines and areas in columns A and B visible regardless of where you scroll.

Skills covered: Subtotal the Data • Add a Second Subtotal • Collapse and Expand the Subtotals • Group and Ungroup Data

STEP 1 ≫ SUBTOTAL THE DATA

Before you use the Subtotal feature, you must sort the data by discipline and then by area. After sorting the data, you will insert subtotals for each discipline. You want to see the totals for the wholesale sales, retail sales, and combined book sales. Refer to Figure 5 as you complete Step 1.

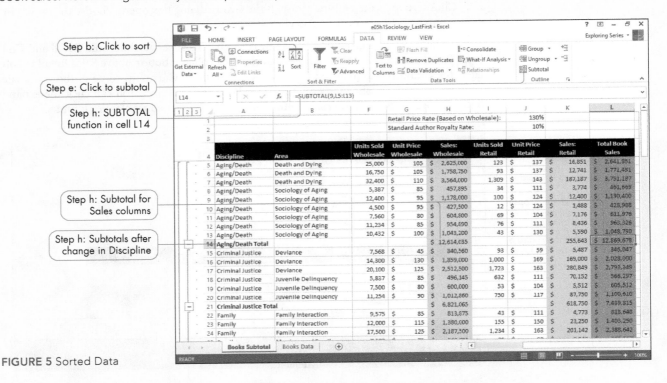

FIGURE 5 Sorted Data

a. Open *e05h1Sociology* and save it as **e05h1Sociology_LastFirst.**

> **TROUBLESHOOTING:** If you make any major mistakes in this exercise, you can close the file, open *e05h1Sociology* again, and then start this exercise over.

The workbook contains two worksheets: Books Subtotal for Hands-On Exercise 1 and Books Data for Hands-On Exercises 2–4.

Hands-On Exercise 1

b. Click the **DATA tab** and click **Sort** in the Sort & Filter group.

c. Click the **Sort by arrow** and select **Discipline** in the Sort dialog box.

d. Click **Add Level**, click the **Then by arrow**, and then select **Area**. Click **OK**.

Excel sorts the data by discipline in alphabetical order. Within each discipline, Excel sorts the data further by area. The data are sorted first by disciplines so that you can apply subtotals to each discipline.

e. Click **Subtotal** in the Outline group.

The Subtotal dialog box opens. The default *At each change in* is the Discipline column, and the default *Use function* is Sum. These settings are correct.

f. Click the **Sales: Wholesale check box** in the *Add subtotal to* section.

g. Click the **Sales: Retail check box** in the *Add subtotal to* section.

Excel selected the last column—Total Book Sales—automatically. You selected the other two sales columns to total. You will leave the *Replace current subtotals* and *Summary below data* check boxes selected.

h. Click **OK**. Scroll to the right to see the subtotals and click **cell L14** to see the SUBTOTAL function for the total book sales for the Aging/Death discipline. Save the workbook.

Excel inserts subtotal rows after each discipline category. The subtotal rows include labels and subtotals for the wholesale sales, retail sales, and book sales columns.

> **TROUBLESHOOTING:** If your subtotals do not match the totals in Figure 5, open the Subtotal dialog box, click Remove All, click OK, and repeat steps b through h again.

STEP 2 ≫ ADD A SECOND SUBTOTAL

Displaying subtotals by discipline helps you compare sales data better; however, you want to add another level to see subtotals for each area within each discipline. To insert two levels of subtotals, you must subtotal the primary category first (Discipline) and then add a subtotal to the second category (Area). As you use the Subtotal dialog box, you want to keep the original subtotals intact. Refer to Figure 6 as you complete Step 2.

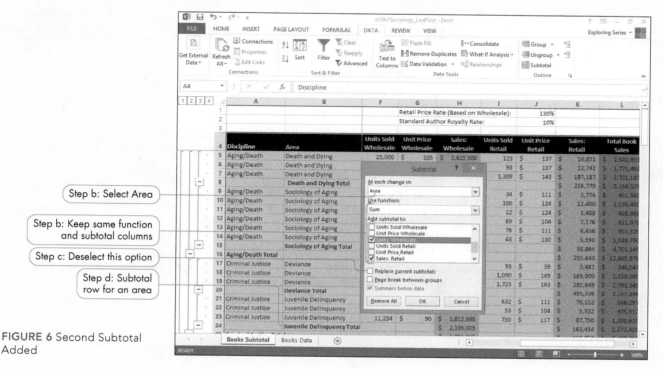

FIGURE 6 Second Subtotal Added

Hands-On Exercise 1

a. Click **Subtotal** in the Outline group to open the Subtotal dialog box again.

b. Click the **At each change in arrow** and select **Area**.

The *Use function* is still Sum, and Excel remembers the last columns you selected in the *Add subtotal to* section—Sales: Wholesale, Sales: Retail, and Total Book Sales.

c. Click the **Replace current subtotals check box** to deselect it.

Deselecting this check box will keep the discipline subtotals.

d. Click **OK** and click **cell L15**. Save the workbook.

Excel inserts subtotal rows after each area. The Formula Bar displays =SUBTOTAL(9,L9:L14). Your data have discipline subtotals and area subtotals within each discipline.

> **TROUBLESHOOTING:** If you subtotal the area first and then discipline, Excel adds several discipline subtotals, which repeat the area subtotals. That is why you must subtotal by the primary category first and then subtotal by the secondary category.

STEP 3 ≫ COLLAPSE AND EXPAND THE SUBTOTALS

You want to compare wholesale, retail, and book sales among the disciplines and then among areas within a discipline. Refer to Figure 7 as you complete Step 3.

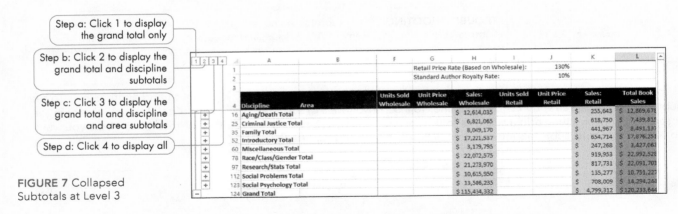

Step a: Click 1 to display the grand total only

Step b: Click 2 to display the grand total and discipline subtotals

Step c: Click 3 to display the grand total and discipline and area subtotals

Step d: Click 4 to display all

FIGURE 7 Collapsed Subtotals at Level 3

a. Click the **1** in the top-left outline area (to the left of the column headings).

You collapsed the outline to show the grand totals only.

b. Click the **2** in the top-left outline area.

You expanded the outline to show the grand and discipline subtotals. Which two disciplines had the highest wholesale and retail sales? Which discipline had the lowest total sales?

c. Click the **3** in the top-left outline area.

You expanded the outline to show the grand, discipline, and area subtotals (see Figure 7). Within the Introductory discipline, which area had the lowest sales? How do wholesale and retail sales compare? Are they proportionally the same within each area?

d. Click the **4** in the top-left outline area. Save the workbook.

You expanded the outline to show all details again. If you had not added the second subtotal, the outline would have had three levels instead of four.

You want to apply an outline to the columns so that you can collapse or expand the units sold and unit prices columns. Refer to Figure 8 as you complete Step 4.

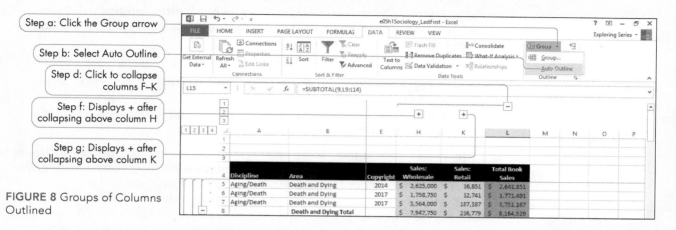

Step a: Click the Group arrow

Step b: Select Auto Outline

Step d: Click to collapse columns F–K

Step f: Displays + after collapsing above column H

Step g: Displays + after collapsing above column K

FIGURE 8 Groups of Columns Outlined

a. Click the **Group arrow** in the Outline group on the DATA tab.

   You want to see if Excel can create a column outline for you so that you do not have to select columns and group them individually.

b. Select **Auto Outline**.

   Excel displays the message box *Modify existing outline?* because it recognizes that an existing outline exists—the row subtotals outline.

c. Click **OK**.

   Excel maintains the outlined subtotals and adds column subtotals. Horizontal lines and collapse buttons appear above the columns. The formula in column H is =F5*G5, so Excel creates an outline for these columns. The formula in column K is =I5*J5, so Excel creates an outline for these columns. It also creates a hierarchical outline of columns F through K, since the formula in column L sums the values in columns H and K.

d. Click the **collapse (–) button** above column L.

   You collapsed columns F through K to display disciplines, areas, and total sales by title.

e. Click the **expand (+) button** above column L.

   You expanded the outline to show columns F through K again.

f. Click the **collapse (–) button** above column H.

   You collapsed the outline to hide columns F and G so you can focus on the wholesale sales without the distraction of the Units Sold or Unit Price columns.

g. Click the **collapse (–) button** above column K.

   You collapsed the outline to hide columns I and J so you can focus on the retail sales without the distraction of the Units Sold or Unit Price columns.

h. Save the workbook. Keep the workbook open if you plan to continue with Hands-On Exercise 2. If not, close the workbook and exit Excel.

PivotTable Basics

Analyzing large amounts of data is important for making solid decisions. Entering data is the easy part; retrieving data in a structured, meaningful way is more challenging. *Data mining* is the process of analyzing large volumes of data, using advanced statistical techniques, and identifying trends and patterns in the data. Managers use data-mining techniques to address a variety of questions, such as the following:

- What snack foods do customers purchase most when purchasing Pepsi® products?
- What age group from what geographic region downloads the most top 10 songs from iTunes?
- What hotel chain and rental car combinations are most popular among Delta Air Lines passengers flying into Salt Lake City?

Questions similar to those above help organizations prepare their marketing plans to capitalize on consumer spending patterns. The more you know about your customer demographics, the better you can focus your strategic plans to increase market share.

A *PivotTable* is a powerful, interactive data-mining feature that enables you to summarize and analyze data, especially helpful when working with large datasets. An advantage of using a PivotTable is that you can group data into one or more categories and perform a variety of calculations without altering the original dataset. The most important benefit of a PivotTable is that it is dynamic. You can easily and quickly *pivot*, or rearrange, data to analyze them from different viewpoints, such as expanding or collapsing details, organizing and grouping data differently, and switching row and column categories. Viewing the PivotTable from different perspectives helps you more easily identify trends and patterns among the variables in the data that might not be obvious from looking at the data from only one viewpoint.

In this section, you will learn how to create a PivotTable by organizing data into columns and rows to aggregate data.

Creating a PivotTable

Before you create a PivotTable, ensure the data source is well structured. Applying the rules for good table design is a start: Use meaningful column labels, ensure data accuracy, and avoid blank rows and columns in the dataset. To consolidate and aggregate data, at least one column must have duplicate values, such as the same city, state, or department name for several records. You then use these columns of duplicate values to create categories for organizing and summarizing data. Another column must have numeric values that can be aggregated to produce quantitative summaries, such as averages or sums.

Create a PivotTable from the Quick Analysis Gallery

You can create a PivotTable from the Quick Analysis gallery. A benefit of this method is that Excel displays recommended PivotTables based on the data. To create a PivotTable using Quick Analysis, do the following:

STEP 1 »
1. Select the entire dataset, including the field names (column labels).
2. Click the Quick Analysis button in the bottom-right corner of the selected range.
3. Click TABLES in the Quick Analysis gallery.
4. Position the mouse pointer over the PivotTable thumbnails to see a preview of the different recommended PivotTables (see Figure 9).
5. Click the PivotTable thumbnail to create the desired PivotTable.

Subtotals, PivotTables, and PivotCharts

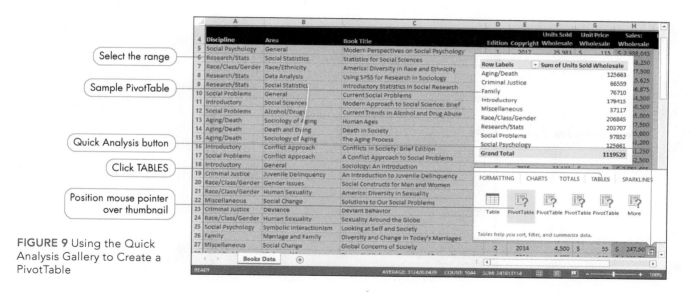

Select the range

Sample PivotTable

Quick Analysis button

Click TABLES

Position mouse pointer over thumbnail

FIGURE 9 Using the Quick Analysis Gallery to Create a PivotTable

TIP | **PivotTable or Subtotals?**

At first glance, PivotTables are similar to subtotals because they both produce subtotals, but PivotTables are more robust. PivotTables provide more flexibility than subtotals provide. If you need complex subtotals cross-referenced by two or more categories with filtering and other specifications, create a PivotTable.

Create a PivotTable from the Ribbon

You can also create a PivotTable by using commands on the Ribbon. The Insert tab contains PivotTable and Recommended PivotTables commands. If you click PivotTable, Excel displays the Create PivotTable dialog box so that you can create a blank PivotTable from scratch. However, if you click Recommended PivotTables, Excel displays a dialog box so that you can select from a gallery of PivotTables. This option is similar to using the Quick Analysis gallery. To create a recommended PivotTable using the Ribbon, do the following:

1. Click inside the dataset (the range of cells or table).
2. Click the INSERT tab and click Recommended PivotTables in the Tables group to open the Recommended PivotTables dialog box (see Figure 10).
3. Click a thumbnail in the gallery on the left side of the dialog box to see a preview of the PivotTable on the right side.
4. Click OK to create the desired PivotTable.

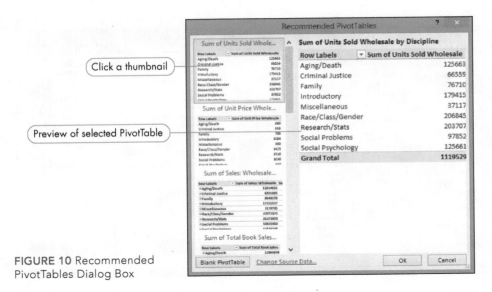

FIGURE 10 Recommended PivotTables Dialog Box

After you use the Recommended PivotTables dialog box or the Quick Analysis gallery, Excel creates a PivotTable on a new worksheet (see Figure 11). The ROWS area contains the category names of the summarized data. For example, each discipline, such as Family, is listed in only one row, regardless of how many times each category name appears in the original dataset.

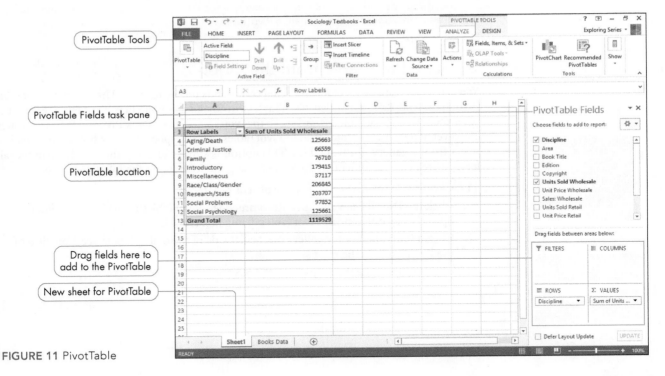

FIGURE 11 PivotTable

The PivotTable Fields task pane displays on the right side, and the PivotTable Tools Analyze and Design contextual tabs appear on the Ribbon. If you click outside the PivotTable, the contextual tabs and the task pane disappear. Click within the PivotTable to display these elements again.

PivotTable Fields Task Pane

If the PivotTable Fields task pane does not appear when you click inside a PivotTable, click the Show arrow on the Analyze tab, and then click Field List. This command is a toggle, so you can click it to show or hide task pane.

The **PivotTable Fields task pane** contains two sections. The *Choose fields to add to report* section lists all the fields or column labels from the original data source. You can click either drag a field to an area in the bottom of the task pane or click the check box to add the field to the PivotTable. Use the *Drag fields between areas below* section to arrange fields in one of the four PivotTable areas. Table 3 describes the areas of a PivotTable.

TABLE 3	Areas of a PivotTable
Area	**Description**
Filters Area	Filters the data to display results based on particular conditions you set.
Columns Area	Subdivides data into one or more additional categories.
Rows Area	Organizes and groups data into categories on the left side. Each group name occupies a single row.
Values Area	Displays summary statistics, such as totals or averages.

Modifying a PivotTable

After you create a PivotTable, you might want to modify it to see the data from a different perspective. For example, you might want to add fields to the rows, values, and columns areas of the PivotTable. In addition, you might want to collapse the PivotTable to show fewer details or expand it to show more details.

Add Rows

You can add fields to provide a more detailed analysis. For example, you might want to organize data by discipline by adding the Discipline field to the ROWS area in the PivotTable Fields task pane. To add a field as a row, do one of the following:

STEP 2 »
- Click the field's check box in the *Choose fields to add to report* section. Excel adds the field to a PivotTable area based on the type of data stored in the field. If the field contains text, Excel usually places that field in the ROWS area.
- Drag the field from the *Choose fields to add to report* section and drop it in the ROWS area.
- Right-click the field name in the *Choose fields to add to report* section and select *Add to Row Labels*.

Add Values

A PivotTable has meaning when you include quantitative fields, such as quantities and monetary values, to aggregate the data. For example, you might want to display the total wholesale sales for each discipline and area. To add values, do one of the following:
- Click the field's check box in the *Choose fields to add to report* section. Excel makes it the value aggregate, such as *Sum of Sales*.

- Drag the field from the *Choose fields to add to report* section and drop it in the VALUES area.
- Right-click the field name in the *Choose fields to add to report* section and select *Add to Values*.

Excel sums the values for each group listed in the ROWS area. For example, the total number of units sold wholesale for the Family discipline is 76,710. If you drag a text field, such as Book Title, to the VALUES area, Excel counts the number of records for each group listed in the ROWS area. In this case, Excel counts seven books in the Family discipline.

Add Columns

Although you can create subdivisions of data by adding more fields to the ROWS area, you might want to arrange the subdivision categories in columns. Doing so minimizes the redundancy of duplicating subdivision row labels and helps consolidate data. To subdivide data into columns, drag a field from the *Choose fields to add to report* section and drop it in the COLUMNS area. Excel updates the aggregated values by the combination of row and column categories.

Figure 12 shows a PivotTable that uses the Discipline field as rows, the *Sum of Units Sold Wholesale* field as values, and Copyright field as columns. Each discipline label and each copyright year label appears only once in the PivotTable. This added level of detail enables you to see the total sales for each discipline based on its copyright year. The PivotTable includes grand totals for each discipline and grand totals for each year.

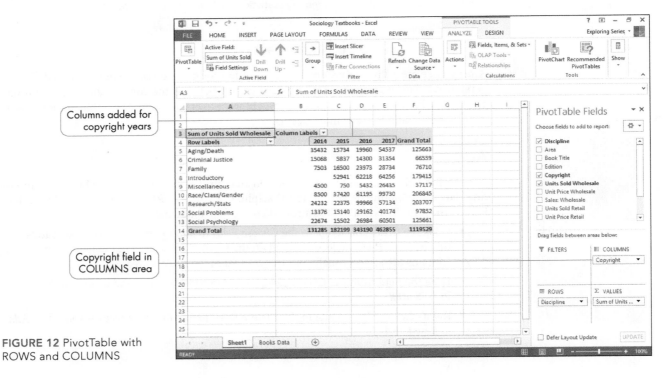

FIGURE 12 PivotTable with ROWS and COLUMNS

Collapse and Expand Items

If you include two fields as ROWS, the PivotTable displays more depth but may be overwhelming. You can hide or collapse the secondary field rows. For example, if the PivotTable contains both Discipline and Copyright row labels, you might want to collapse copyright years for some disciplines. The collapse and expand buttons display to the left of the row labels. If they do not, click Show and click the +/− buttons on the Analyze tab. Figure 13 shows the collapse and expand buttons.

Subtotals, PivotTables, and PivotCharts

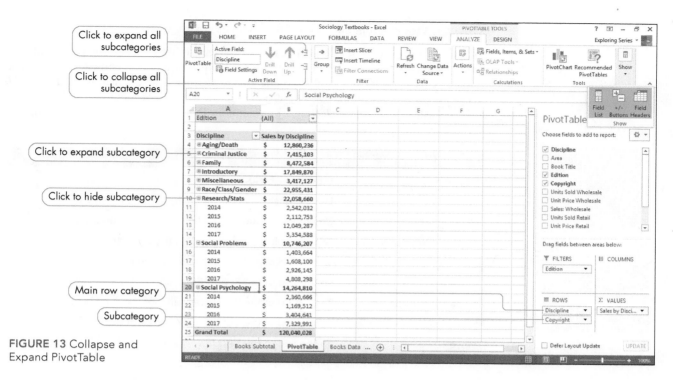

Click to expand all subcategories

Click to collapse all subcategories

Click to expand subcategory

Click to hide subcategory

Main row category

Subcategory

FIGURE 13 Collapse and Expand PivotTable

To hide the subcategories for a particular category, click the collapse button (−) on the left side of the specific category you wish to collapse. Excel hides the subcategories for that particular category and shows only the aggregated totals for the category. Continue collapsing other categories as needed to focus on a particular category's details.

To expand the subcategories again, click the expand button (+) on the left side of the category labels.

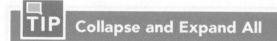

TIP Collapse and Expand All

You can collapse all categories at one time by clicking Collapse Field in the Active Field group on the Analyze tab. To expand all categories at one time, click Expand Field. This approach is faster than collapsing or expanding each category individually.

Remove Fields

You can remove fields to reduce the amount of data to analyze. To remove a field from the PivotTable, do one of the following:

STEP 3⟫

- Click the field name in the *Drag fields between areas below* section and select Remove Field.
- Deselect the check box next to the field name in the *Choose fields to add to report* section.
- Drag a field name in the *Drag fields between areas below* section outside the PivotTable Fields task pane.

Rearrange Fields

You can rearrange fields in a PivotTable to improve readability. For example, you might want more columns than rows, so you can switch the fields in the ROWS and COLUMNS areas in the task pane. To move a field from one area to another, drag the field in the *Drag fields between areas below* section. You can also change the location or hierarchy of the fields by clicking the field arrow and selecting a Move option. Table 4 explains the Move options.

TABLE 4 Move Options	
Option	**Moves the Field...**
Move Up	Up one position in the hierarchy within the same area
Move Down	Down one position in the hierarchy within the same area
Move to Beginning	To the beginning of all fields in the same area
Move to End	To the end of all fields in the same area
Move to Report Filter	To the end of the Report Filter area of the PivotTable
Move to Row Labels	To the end of the Row Labels area of the PivotTable
Move to Column Labels	To the end of the Column Labels area of the PivotTable
Move to Values	To the end of the VALUES area of the PivotTable

Change the Values Field Settings

Although Excel uses the SUM function as the default summary statistic for numerical fields, you can select a different function. For example, you might want to calculate the average, lowest, or highest value within each group, or identify the lowest sales for each discipline/copyright year combination to see if the older books have decreased sales. In addition to changing the summary statistic, you might want to change the column label that appears above the summary statistics. By default, words indicate the summary statistic function applied, such as *Sum of Total Sales by Book* or *Average of Total Sales by Book*, depending on the summary statistic applied to the values. Finally, you might need to format the aggregated values. To modify any of these value settings, do the following:

STEP 4 »

1. Click a value in the appropriate field in the PivotTable and click Field Settings in the Active Field group on the ANALYZE tab. Alternatively, click the field's arrow in the VALUES area of the task pane and select Value Field Settings. The Value Field Settings dialog box opens (see Figure 14).
2. Type the name you want to appear as the column label in the Custom Name box. For example, you might want the heading to appear as *Total Sales* instead of *Sum of Total Book Sales*.
3. Select the summary statistical function you want to use to summarize the values in the *Summarize value field by* list.
4. Click Number Format to open an abbreviated version of the Format Cells dialog box. Select a number type, such as Accounting, in the Category list; select other settings, such as number of decimal places in the *Decimal places* spin arrow; and then click OK.
5. Click OK in the Value Field Settings dialog box.

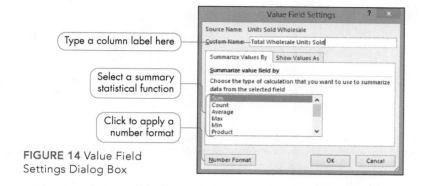

Type a column label here

Select a summary statistical function

Click to apply a number format

FIGURE 14 Value Field Settings Dialog Box

TIP **Multiple Summary Statistics**

You can display more than one function for a field. For example, you might want to show *both* the total book sales and the average book sales. To display multiple summary statistics, drag another copy of the same field to the VALUES area and set each value setting separately.

Refresh a PivotTable

Although PivotTables are powerful, they do not update automatically if you make any changes to the underlying data in the data source. For example, if you change a sales value or delete a row in the data source, the PivotTable does not reflect the changed data. Unfortunately, this causes PivotTable summary statistics to be outdated with inaccurate results. If you change the data source, you must update the PivotTable by doing the following:

STEP 5 ≫

1. Click in the PivotTable.
2. Click the ANALYZE tab.
3. Click Refresh in the Data group to refresh the current PivotTable only, or click the Refresh arrow and select Refresh All to refresh all PivotTables in the workbook.

If you want to ensure your PivotTable is up to date when you open the workbook, click the Analyze tab, click the PivotTable arrow on the left side of the Ribbon, select Options to open the PivotTable Options dialog box, click the Data tab, select *Refresh data when opening the file*, and then click OK.

Quick Concepts

1. What are the advantages of using a PivotTable instead of a subtotal?
2. What is the main benefit of creating a PivotTable using the Quick Analysis gallery or from the Recommended PivotTables dialog box over creating a blank PivotTable?
3. List the four areas of a PivotTable.

Hands-On Exercises

Watch the Video for this Hands-On Exercise!

MyITLab®
HOE2 Training

2 PivotTable Basics

After exhausting the possibilities of outlines and subtotals, you want to create a PivotTable to analyze the sociology book sales. You realize you can see the data from different perspectives, enabling you to have a stronger understanding of the sales by various categories.

Skills covered: Create a PivotTable • Add Rows, Values, and Columns • Remove and Rearrange Fields • Change the Values Field Settings • Refresh a PivotTable

---

STEP 1 ≫ CREATE A PIVOTTABLE

Because you want to keep the subtotals you created in the Books Subtotal worksheet, you will create a PivotTable from the Books Data worksheet. Refer to Figures 10 and 15 as you complete Step 1.

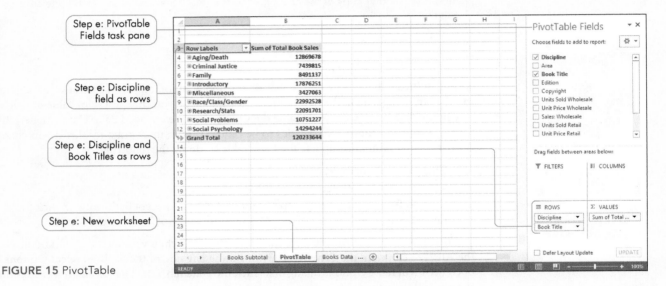

FIGURE 15 PivotTable

a. Open *e05h1Sociology_LastFirst* if you closed it at the end of Hands-On Exercise 1 and save it as **e05h2Sociology_LastFirst**, changing *h1* to *h2*.

b. Click the **Books Data worksheet tab**.

Excel does not let you create a PivotTable using subtotaled data. To preserve the subtotals you created in Hands-On Exercise 1, you will use the dataset in the Books Data worksheet.

c. Click in **cell A5**, click the **INSERT tab**, and then click **Recommended PivotTables** in the Tables group.

The Recommended PivotTables dialog box opens (see Figure 10).

d. Scroll the thumbnails of recommended PivotTables and click the **Sum of Total Book Sales by Discipline thumbnail**. (NOTE: Hover the mouse pointer over the thumbnails to see the full names.)

You selected this PivotTable to show the overall total book sales for each discipline. The dialog box shows a preview of the selected PivotTable.

Hands-On Exercise 2

214

e. Click **OK** and click within the PivotTable, if necessary. Rename Sheet1 as **PivotTable**. Save the workbook.

Excel inserts a new Sheet1 worksheet, which you renamed as PivotTable, with the PivotTable on the left side and the PivotTable Fields task pane on the right side (see Figure 15).

STEP 2 ›› ADD ROWS, VALUES, AND COLUMNS

You want to compare sales combinations by discipline, copyright year, and edition. The discipline field is already in the PivotTable, but you need to add the copyright year and edition fields. Refer to Figure 16 as you complete Step 2.

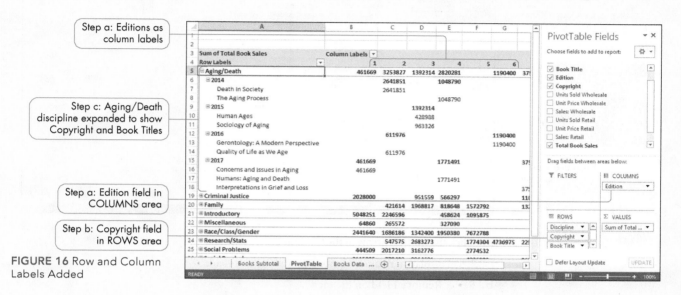

FIGURE 16 Row and Column Labels Added

a. Drag the **Edition field** to the COLUMNS area in the PivotTable Fields task pane.

Excel displays the total book sales by a combination of discipline and edition. This enables you to compare sales of current editions within each discipline. Blanks appear in the PivotTable when a discipline does not have a specific edition. For example, the Family discipline does not have any first-edition books currently being published.

b. Drag the **Copyright field** to be between the Discipline and Book Title fields in the ROWS area.

The Copyright and Book Titles are not showing because they are collapsed within the Discipline rows.

c. Click the **Aging/Death expand (+) button**. Save the workbook.

You expanded the Aging/Death discipline to show the copyright years and titles.

TIP Field ScreenTip

It may be confusing to see *Sum of Total...* in the VALUES box. Position the pointer over a field name in the area to see a ScreenTip with the full name, such as *Sum of Total Book Sales*.

Although it is informative to compare sales by edition, you think that the PivotTable contains too much detail, so you will remove the Edition field. In addition, the ROWS area contains the Book Titles field, but those data are collapsed; therefore, you will remove it as well. After you remove the fields, you will rearrange other fields to simplify the PivotTable. Refer to Figure 17 as you complete Step 3.

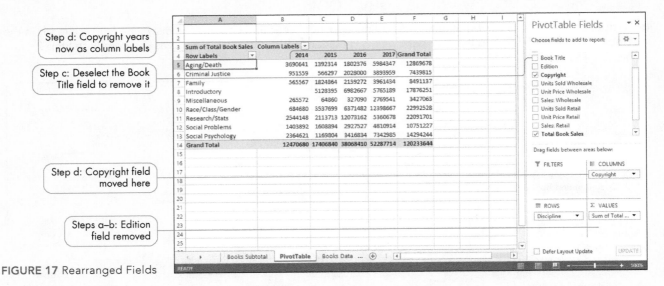

Step d: Copyright years now as column labels

Step c: Deselect the Book Title field to remove it

Step d: Copyright field moved here

Steps a–b: Edition field removed

FIGURE 17 Rearranged Fields

a. Click the **Edition arrow** in the Column Labels area.

Excel displays a menu of options to apply to this field.

b. Select **Remove Field** on the menu.

You removed the Edition field from the PivotTable. Instead of several sales columns, Excel consolidates the sales into one sales column. Although you find it helpful to have sales breakdowns by copyright year, you think the PivotTable will be easier to read if you move the Copyright field to the COLUMNS area.

c. Deselect the **Book Title check box** in the *Choose fields to add to report* section of the task pane.

You removed the Book Title field from the PivotTable.

d. Drag the **Copyright field** from the ROWS area to the COLUMNS area. Save the workbook.

This arrangement consolidates the data better. Instead of repeating the copyright years for each discipline, the copyright years are listed only once each at the top of the sales columns.

STEP 4 ≫ CHANGE THE VALUES FIELD SETTINGS

After selecting the PivotTable fields, you want to improve the appearance of the sociology textbook PivotTable. You will format the values for Accounting Number Format and replace the generic Row Labels description with a label that indicates the sociology disciplines. Refer to Figure 18 as you complete Step 4.

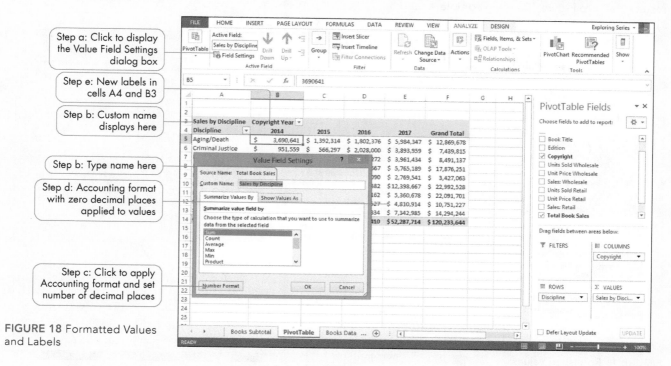

Step a: Click to display the Value Field Settings dialog box

Step e: New labels in cells A4 and B3

Step b: Custom name displays here

Step b: Type name here

Step d: Accounting format with zero decimal places applied to values

Step c: Click to apply Accounting format and set number of decimal places

FIGURE 18 Formatted Values and Labels

a. Click **cell B5** and click **Field Settings** in the Active Field group on the ANALYZE tab.

The Value Field Settings dialog box opens so that you can format the field.

b. Type **Sales by Discipline** in the **Custom Name box**.

Leave Sum as the selected calculation type in the *Summarize value field by* section.

c. Click **Number Format**.

Excel opens a Format Cells dialog box with only one tab: the Number tab.

d. Click **Accounting** in the Category list, change the **Decimal places value** to **0**, click **OK** in the Format Cells dialog box, and then click **OK** in the Value Field Settings dialog box.

You formatted the values with Accounting Number Format with no decimal places, and the heading *Sales by Discipline* appears in cell A3.

e. Type **Discipline** in **cell A4** and type **Copyright Year** in **cell B3**.

You replaced the generic *Row Labels* heading with *Discipline* to describe the contents of the first column, and you replaced the *Column Labels* heading with *Copyright Year*. Although you can create custom names for values, you cannot create custom names for row and column labels. However, you can edit the labels directly in the cells.

f. Select the **range B4:F4** and center the labels horizontally. Save the workbook.

Hands-On Exercise 2

STEP 5 >> REFRESH A PIVOTTABLE

After consulting with the Accounting Department, you realize that the retail prices are incorrect. The unit retail prices are based on a percentage of the wholesale price. The retail unit price is 30% more than the wholesale unit price, but it should be 25%. You will edit the input cell in the original worksheet and refresh the PivotTable to see the corrected results. Refer to Figure 19 as you complete Step 5.

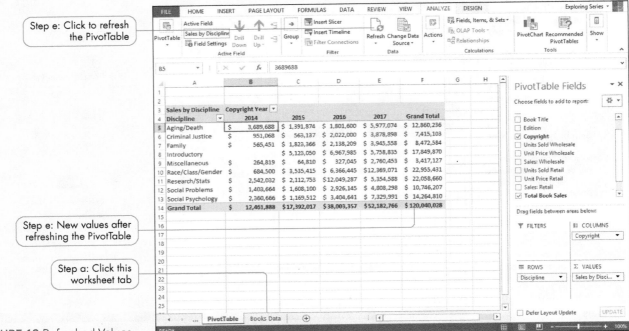

FIGURE 19 Refreshed Values

a. Click the **Books Data worksheet tab**.

   You need to locate and change the retail price percentage.

b. Click **cell J1**, the cell that contains the current retail price percentage.

c. Type **125%** and press **Enter**. Save the workbook to update the formula results on the Books Data worksheet.

> **TROUBLESHOOTING**: If the formula results in the Unit Price Retail, Sales: Retail, and Total Book Sales columns do not change after you edit the data in step c, the workbook may be set for manual calculation. To ensure that formulas update automatically, click the File tab, click Options, click Formulas, click Automatic as the Workbook Calculation setting, and then click OK.

d. Click the **PivotTable worksheet tab**.

   Notice that the PivotTable aggregate values did not change. The grand total is $120,233,644. You must refresh the PivotTable.

e. Click the **ANALYZE tab** and click **Refresh** in the Data group.

   Excel updates the PivotTable values based on the change you made in the Books Data worksheet.

f. Save the workbook. Keep the workbook open if you plan to continue with Hands-On Exercise 3. If not, close the workbook and exit Excel.

Hands-On Exercise 2

218

PivotTable Options

As you have experienced, PivotTables consolidate and aggregate large amounts of data to facilitate data analysis. You can customize the PivotTable for more in-depth analysis. In the previous section, you used the Analyze tab to display the Value Field Settings dialog box and refresh the PivotTable. However, the Analyze tab contains more ways for you to customize your PivotTable. For example, you can filter groups, display or hide particular groups temporarily, and add subtotals.

In this section, you will learn how to filter data in a PivotTable. In addition, you will create a calculated field and display subtotals.

Filtering and Slicing a PivotTable

By default, PivotTables display aggregated data for each category. However, you may want to set a filter to exclude particular categories or values. You can specify a particular field to use to filter the PivotTable. In addition, you can include slicers to easily set filters to designate which specific data to include in the PivotTable.

Add Filters

Although PivotTables consolidate data from the original data source into groups, the PivotTable might contain more details than you want. You can apply filters to show only a subset of the PivotTable. Drag a field to the FILTERS area in the task pane when you want to engage a filter based on a particular field. For example, you might want to filter the PivotTable to show only aggregates for first- and second-edition books. When you drag a field to the FILTERS area, Excel displays the field name in cell A1 with a filter arrow in cell B1. To set the filter, click the filter arrow and do one of the following and then click OK:

STEP 1 ▶

- Select the value in the list to filter the data by that value only.
- Click the *Select Multiple Items* check box if you want to select more than one value to filter the PivotTable. Then click the check boxes by each value you want to set (see Figure 20).
- Type a value in the Search box if the list is too long and you want to find a value quickly.

Only a subset of the data that meet those conditions appears in the PivotTable; Excel hides the unselected items.

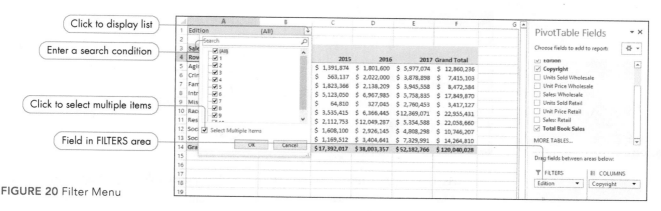

FIGURE 20 Filter Menu

Cell B1 displays (All) when no filter is enabled, the value if one filter is enabled, or (Multiple Items) if more than one item is selected. To remove the filter entirely, remove it from the FILTER area. To remove the filter temporarily, click the filter arrow in cell B1, select (All), and then click OK.

You can apply additional filters based on the row and column label groupings. For example, you can apply date filters to display summary statistics for data occurring within a particular time frame or apply filters for values within a designated range. To apply group filters, click the Row Labels or Column Labels arrow in the PivotTable and specify the settings (see Figure 21). Excel calculates the summary statistics based on the filtered data rather than the complete dataset.

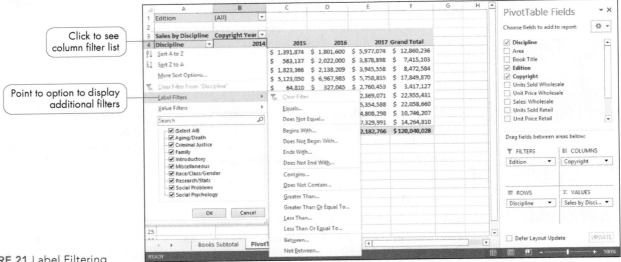

FIGURE 21 Label Filtering

Insert Slicers

You can insert a *slicer*, a small window containing one button for each unique item in a field so that you can filter the PivotTable quickly. Slicers are especially helpful to filter data when a PivotTable is based on multiple tables. The visual representation is easier to manipulate than adding more fields to the FILTERS area and then setting each field's filter through drop-down lists. To insert a slicer, do the following:

STEP 2 ▶

1. Click the ANALYZE tab.
2. Click Insert Slicer in the Filter group to display the Insert Slicers dialog box (see Figure 22).
3. Click one or more field check boxes to display one or more slicers and click OK.

FIGURE 22 Insert Slicers Dialog Box

Excel inserts slicers into the worksheet. You can manipulate a slicer by doing the following:

- **Move the Slicer.** Drag a slicer to move it onscreen.
- **Filter Data.** Click the slicer button to filter by the value represented by the button. Press Ctrl to select several slicers to apply additional filters. Excel highlights the item to make it clear how you filtered the PivotTable. For example, in Figure 23, the Discipline field is filtered by Family, Introductory, and Social Problems. Although

Subtotals, PivotTables, and PivotCharts

no filter has been enabled for the Edition field, the 6th and 9th edition buttons are unavailable because the three disciplines selected do not have books that are in their 6th or 9th editions.

- **Remove a Filter.** Click Remove Filter in the top-right corner of the slicer window.

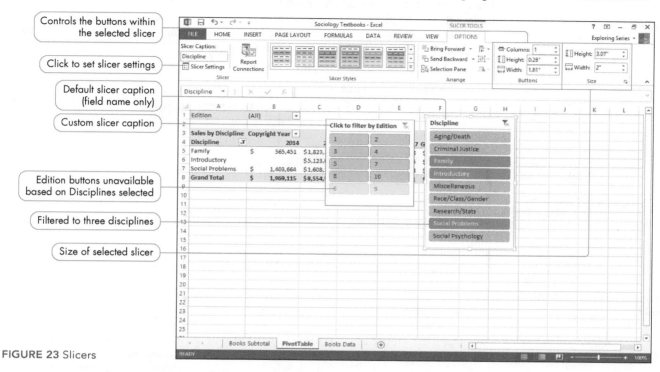

FIGURE 23 Slicers

Customize Slicers

When you select a slicer, the Slicer Tools Options tab displays so that you can customize a slicer. The default slicer caption displays the field name only. The **slicer caption** is text that displays in the header at the top of the slicer window. However, you can customize the slicer by changing its caption. In Figure 23, the left slicer's caption displays an instruction to the user, whereas the right slicer's caption displays the default field name. Table 5 lists and describes the commands on the Slicer Tools Options tab.

TABLE 5	Slicer Tools Commands
Group	**Commands**
Slicer	Enables you to change the slicer caption, display the Slicer Settings dialog box for further customization, and manage the PivotTable connected to the slicer. In Figure 23, the Edition slicer has been sorted in ascending order. The light blue items 6 and 9 do not apply to the selected disciplines.
Slicer Styles	Applies a style to the slicer by specifying the color of the filtered item in the slicer. For example, given the workbook theme, the default active filters appear in blue and unavailable items appear in light blue. In Figure 23, Slicer Style Dark 2 has been applied to the Discipline style.
Arrange	Specifies the slicer's placement in relation to other groups, such as placing a slicer on top of other slicers.
Buttons	Defines how many columns are displayed in the selected slicer and the height and width of each button inside the slicer. For example, the Edition slicer contains two columns, and the Discipline slicer contains one column in Figure 23.
Size	Sets the height and width of the slicer window. For example, the Discipline slicer's height is 3.07 " in Figure 23.

Creating a Calculated Field

You can create a *calculated field*, which is a user-defined field that does not exist in the original dataset. It derives its values based on performing calculations on other original dataset values. For example, you can create a calculated field that converts totals to percentages for easier relative comparison among categories, or you might want to create a calculated field that determines what the number of units a 10% increase in units sold for the upcoming year would be. To create a calculated field, do the following:

STEP 3 »

1. Select a cell within the PivotTable.
2. Click the PIVOTTABLE TOOLS ANALYZE tab.
3. Click Fields, Items, & Sets in the Calculations group and select Calculated Field to display the Insert Calculated Field dialog box (see Figure 24).

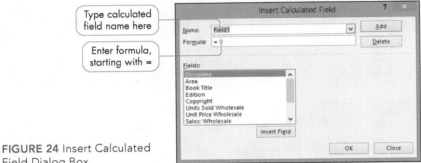

FIGURE 24 Insert Calculated Field Dialog Box

Type a descriptive label for the calculated field in the Name box. Build a formula starting with the equal sign (=). Instead of using cell references, insert the field names and other operands. For example ='Total Book Sales'*.1 calculates a 10% royalty amount on the total book sales. Click OK to insert the calculated field in the PivotTable. Format the numerical values in the calculated field column as needed.

Show Values as a Specific Calculation Result

In addition to creating calculated fields, you can apply built-in custom calculations that display relationships between values in rows and columns in the PivotTable. For example, you can show each value as a percentage of the grand total or each value's percentage of the row total. To display values in relation to others, do the following:

STEP 4 »

1. Click the field in the VALUES area of the task pane and select Value Field Settings (or click within the field in the PivotTable and click Field Settings in the Active Field group on the ANALYZE tab).
2. Click the Show Values As tab within the Value Field Settings dialog box.
3. Click the *Show values as* arrow and select the desired calculation type. Table 6 lists and describes some of the calculation options.
4. Click Number Format to set number formats, click OK to close the Format Cells dialog box, and then click OK to close the Value Field Settings dialog box.

Subtotals, PivotTables, and PivotCharts

TABLE 6 Calculation Options

Option	Description
% of Grand Total	Displays each value as a percentage of the grand total.
% of Column Total	Displays each value as a percentage of the respective column total. The values in each column total 100%.
% of Row Total	Displays each value as a percentage of the respective row total. The values in each row total 100%.
% of Parent Row Total	Displays values as: (value for the item) / (value for the parent item on rows).
Running Total	Displays values as running totals.
Rank Smallest to Largest	Displays the rank of values in a specific field where 1 represents the smallest value.
Rank Largest to Smallest	Displays the rank of values in a specific field where 1 represents the largest value.

Quick
Concepts

1. What is the purpose of applying a filter to a PivotTable? How do you apply a main filter and additional filters?

2. What is a slicer? What do the three different colors indicate in a slicer?

3. When would you create a calculated field in a PivotTable?

Hands-On Exercises

Watch the Video for this Hands-On Exercise!

MyITLab® HOE3 Training

3 PivotTable Options

The PivotTable you created has been beneficial for you to review sales data by discipline for each copyright year. In addition, you have used the PivotTable to compare grand total sales among disciplines and grand totals by copyright year. Now you want to extend your analysis. You will calculate author royalties from the sales and impose filters to focus your attention on each analysis.

Skills covered: Set Filters • Insert and Customize a Slicer • Create a Calculated Field • Show Values as Calculations

STEP 1 >> SET FILTERS

The level of success of the first two editions especially determines the likelihood of approving subsequent revisions and editions. To display aggregated sales for these editions, you need to set a filter to remove the other editions from being included in the calculated sales data. After you review the first- and second-edition data, you will enable additional filters to review books published in the past two years. Refer to Figure 25 as you complete Step 1.

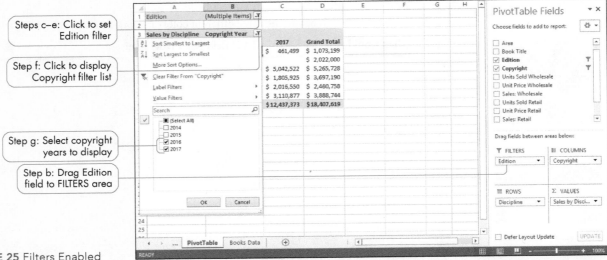

FIGURE 25 Filters Enabled

a. Open *e05h2Sociology_LastFirst* if you closed it at the end of Hands-On Exercise 2 and save it as **e05h3Sociology_LastFirst**, changing *h2* to *h3*.

> **TROUBLESHOOTING**: Click in the PivotTable to display the PivotTable Field task pane if necessary.

b. Make sure the PivotTable worksheet tab is active and drag the **Edition field** from the *Choose fields to add to report* section to the FILTERS area.

   You can now filter the PivotTable based on the Edition field. Cell A1 displays the field name, and cell B1 displays (All) and the filter arrow.

c. Click the **Edition filter arrow** in **cell B1** and click the **Select Multiple Items check box**.

   The list displays a check box for each item.

d. Click the **(All) check box** to deselect it.

Hands-On Exercise 3

224

e. Click the **1** and **2 check boxes** and click **OK**.

The summary statistics reflect sales data for only first- and second-edition publications. The filter arrow changes to a funnel icon in cell B1.

f. Click the **Copyright Year filter arrow** in **cell B3** and click the **(Select All) check box** to deselect it.

g. Click the **2016** and **2017 check boxes** and click **OK**.

Excel filters out data for years that do not meet the condition you set. The filter arrow changes to a funnel icon in cell B3.

h. Save the workbook.

STEP 2 >> INSERT AND CUSTOMIZE A SLICER

You might distribute the workbook to colleagues who are not as skilled in Excel as you are. To help them set their own filters, you insert slicers. Refer to Figure 26 as you complete Step 2.

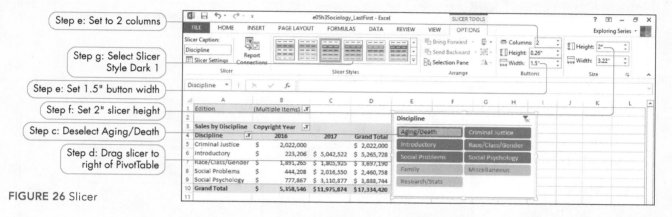

FIGURE 26 Slicer

a. Click **Insert Slicer** in the Filter group on the ANALYZE tab.

The Insert Slicers dialog box opens, listing each field name.

b. Click **Discipline** and click **OK**.

Excel inserts the Discipline slicer in the worksheet. Six slicer buttons are blue, indicating that those disciplines are selected. The grayed-out buttons at the bottom of the slicer indicate those disciplines are not applicable based on other engaged filters you set (first and second editions and 2016 and 2017 copyright years).

c. Press and hold **Ctrl** as you click **Aging/Death** in the Discipline slicer.

This deselects the Aging/Death discipline.

> **TROUBLESHOOTING**: Because several disciplines are selected, if you click Aging/Death instead of pressing Ctrl as you click it, you set Aging/Death as the only discipline. The others are filtered out. If this happens, immediately click Undo and repeat step c.

d. Drag the slicer to the right side of the PivotTable.

You moved the slicer so that it does not cover up data in the PivotTable.

e. Change the **Columns value** to **2** in the Buttons group on the SLICER TOOLS OPTIONS tab. Change the button **Width** to **1.5"** in the Buttons group.

The slicer now displays buttons in two columns. You changed the width of the buttons to 1.5" to display the full discipline names within the buttons.

Hands-On Exercise 3

f. Change the slicer **Height** to **2** in the Size group.

The slicer window is now only 2" tall.

g. Click the **More button** in the Slicer Styles group and click **Slicer Style Dark 1**. Save the workbook.

Based on the selected workbook theme, Slicer Style Dark 1 applies a dark blue fill color for selected disciplines, dark gray and black font for available but not currently selected disciplines, and light gray fill with medium gray font for nonapplicable disciplines.

STEP 3 ≫ CREATE A CALCULATED FIELD

You want to calculate the amount of the sales returned to the authors as royalties. Although the 10% royalty rate is stored in cell J2 in the Books Data worksheet, the value must be used in the calculated field because range names and cell references outside the PivotTable cannot be used. Refer to Figure 27 as you complete Step 3.

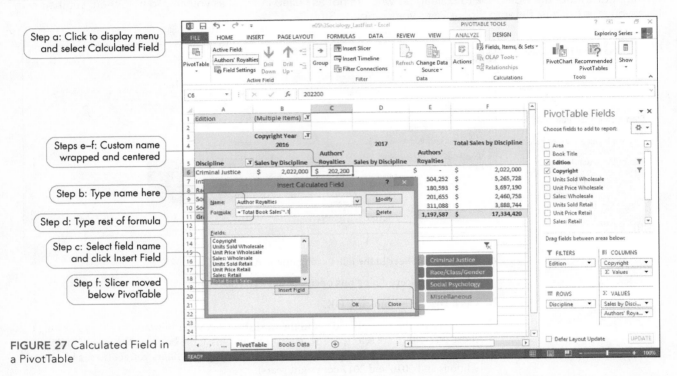

FIGURE 27 Calculated Field in a PivotTable

a. Click within the PivotTable, click the **ANALYZE tab**, click **Fields, Items, & Sets** in the Calculations group, and then select **Calculated Field**.

The Insert Calculated Field dialog box opens.

b. Type **Author Royalties** in the **Name box**.

c. Scroll down the Fields list, click **Total Book Sales**, and then click **Insert Field**.

Excel starts to build the formula, which is currently ='Total Book Sales'.

d. Type ***.1** at the end of the **Formula box** and click **OK**.

Excel adds Sum of Author Royalties calculated field columns, one for each copyright year category. It calculates the authors' royalties as 10% of the total sales for each copyright year.

e. Right-click the **Sum of Author Royalties heading** in **cell C5**, select **Value Field Settings**, type **Authors' Royalties** in the **Custom Name box**, and then click **OK**.

f. Move the slicer below the PivotTable. Select **cells C5** and **E5**, wrap text for field names, set **30** row height, **12** column widths, and center column labels.

g. Save the workbook.

Hands-On Exercise 3

STEP 4 >> SHOW VALUES AS CALCULATIONS

You want to see what copyright year generated the largest sales for each discipline, which discipline contributes the largest percentage of the total sociology sales, and which introductory book has the largest sales contribution within that discipline. Refer to Figure 28 as you complete Step 4.

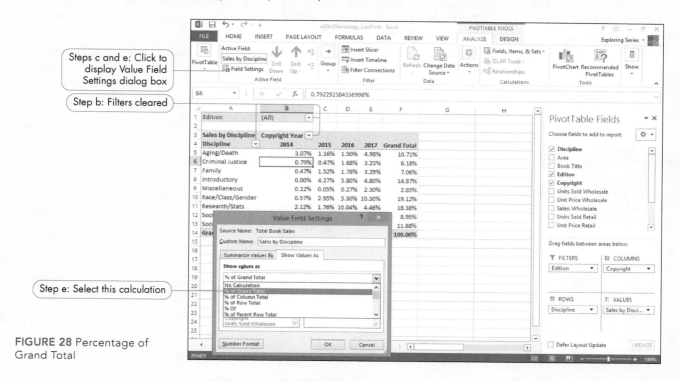

Steps c and e: Click to display Value Field Settings dialog box

Step b: Filters cleared

Step e: Select this calculation

FIGURE 28 Percentage of Grand Total

a. Right-click the **PivotTable worksheet tab**, select **Move or Copy**, click **Books Data** in the *Before sheet* list, click the **Create a copy check box**, and then click **OK**.

You copied the PivotTable worksheet to maintain the previous tasks you completed as evidence. You will work with the PivotTable (2) worksheet, which is the active worksheet.

b. Do the following to remove filters, slicer, and Authors' Royalties field:

- Click the **Edition filter** in **cell B1**, click the **(All) check box**, and then click **OK** to clear the Edition filter.
- Click the **Discipline filter** in **cell A5** and select **Clear Filter From "Discipline"**.
- Click the **Copyright Year filter** in **cell B3** and select **Clear Filter From "Copyright"**.
- Select the slicer and press **Delete**.
- Click the **Authors' Royalties** in the VALUES area of the task pane and select **Remove Field**.

c. Click within any value in the PivotTable, click the **ANALYZE tab**, and then click **Field Settings** in the Active Field group.

The Value Field Settings dialog box opens.

d. Click the **Show Values As tab**, click the **Show values as arrow**, select **% of Row Total**, and then click **OK**.

Excel displays each copyright year's values as percentages for that discipline. All disciplines except Introductory and Research/Stats had the highest percentage of sales for the books with a 2017 copyright. These two disciplines had their highest percentage of sales for books with a 2016 copyright.

Hands-On Exercise 3

e. Click the **Field Settings** in the Active Field group, click the **Show Values As tab** within the dialog box, select **% of Grand Total**, and then click **OK**.

See Figure 28. Each discipline's yearly value displays as a percentage of the total sales. Which discipline and for what copyright year produces the highest percentage of total sales? Answer: 2017 Race/Class/Gender with 10.30%, followed closely by the 2016 Research/Stats with 10.04%. In general, the Race/Class/Gender discipline contributed the highest percentage of the total sales with 19.12%.

f. Save the workbook and keep the workbook open if you plan to continue with Hands-On Exercise 4. If not, close the workbook and exit Excel.

PivotTable Design and PivotCharts

After you create and modify the structure of a PivotTable, you can focus on the overall appearance and format of the PivotTable. The PivotTable Tools Design tab enables you to control the position of grouped calculations and the PivotTable style. In addition to finalizing the PivotTable's appearance, you might want to create a PivotChart to depict the consolidated data in a visual form.

In this section, you will apply a different style to and change the layout of a PivotTable. In addition, you will create and format a PivotChart.

Formatting a PivotTable

Excel applies basic formatting to PivotTables. For example, it formats primary row labels in bold to distinguish those categories from the subcategories. In addition, the subtotals are bold to offset these values from the subcategory values. The PivotTable Tools Design tab contains commands for enhancing the format of a PivotTable (see Figure 29).

FIGURE 29 PivotTable Tools Design Tab

STEP 1 A PivotTable style controls bold formatting, font colors, shading colors, and border lines. To change the style, click the PivotTable Tools Design tab and click the More button in the PivotTable Styles group to display the PivotTable Styles gallery (see Figure 30). Select the most appropriate style that accentuates the data in your PivotTable. As you move the pointer over the gallery, Excel shows how that style will affect the PivotTable. Click a style to apply it to the PivotTable.

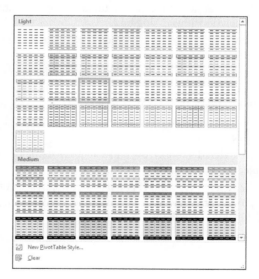

FIGURE 30 PivotTable Styles

After you apply a style, you can select which areas of the PivotTable are affected by the style. Select check boxes in the PivotTable Style Options group to apply formats to row headers, column headers, banded rows, and banded columns.

By default, the VALUES area consolidates data by showing subtotals for each category. You can customize the location of subtotals by clicking Subtotals in the Layout group on the

Design tab. For example, when the PivotTable is large, displaying the subtotals at the top of the group draws attention to the totals and enables you to scroll to view all of the supporting data if necessary. Table 7 describes the Subtotals options.

TABLE 7 PivotTable Subtotals Options	
Option	Description
Do Not Show Subtotals	Removes subtotals for each category but retains the category names and displays aggregated values for the subcategories.
Show All Subtotals at Bottom of Group	Displays category subtotals below the last subcategory value within each category. Subtotal labels and values appear in bold.
Show All Subtotals at Top of Group	Displays category subtotals at the top of the list on the same row as the category labels. This approach takes up fewer rows than Show All Subtotals at Bottom of Group.
Include Filtered Items in Totals	Includes values for filtered items in the total rows and columns. (Active only when a filter has been applied.)

Using PowerPivot Functionality

PowerPivot is a built-in add-in program in Excel 2013 that enables you to import millions of rows of data from multiple data sources, create a relationship between two or more related tables within one workbook (similar to creating relationships among tables in Access), and maintain connections. For example, one table contains sales representatives' names and IDs. A related table contains the sales dates and sales amounts but only the sales reps' IDs to avoid mistyping a person's name. You must create a relationship based on a common field (such as ID) between the tables. A *relationship* is an association between two related tables where both tables contain a related field of data, such as IDs.

After you create a relationship between tables, you can use PowerPivot to create a PivotTable from both tables. After you create the relationship, you can use the common field to display the sales reps' names instead of their IDs. To create a relationship, do the following:

1. Click the DATA tab and click Relationships in the Data Tools group to open the Manage Relationships dialog box.
2. Click New in the dialog box to open the Create Relationship dialog box (see Figure 31).
3. Click the Table arrow and select the name of the primary table. The primary table in this example is SALES.
4. Click the Column (Foreign) arrow and select the name of the column that contains a relationship to the related or lookup table. For example, the column that relates to the other table is REPS.
5. Click the Related Table arrow and select the name of the related or lookup table. For example, the related table is REPS.
6. Click the Related Column (Primary) arrow and select the name of the column that is related to the primary table. For example, the ID column relates to the Rep column in the SALES table. Click OK.

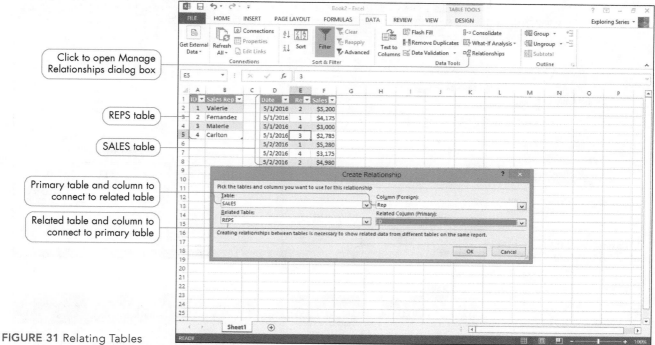

FIGURE 31 Relating Tables

Callout labels (left of figure):
- Click to open Manage Relationships dialog box
- REPS table
- SALES table
- Primary table and column to connect to related table
- Related table and column to connect to primary table

After you create a relationship between the tables, you can use PowerPivot to create a PivotTable based on the relationship. Do the following to create a PivotTable using two related tables:

1. Click within the primary table.
2. Click the INSERT tab and click PivotTable in the Tables group to open the Create PivotTable dialog box (see Figure 32).
3. Make sure the primary table name displays in the Table/Range box.
4. Click the *Add this data to the Data Model* check box and click OK.

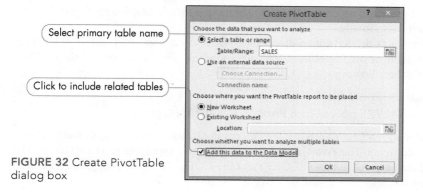

Callout labels:
- Select primary table name
- Click to include related tables

FIGURE 32 Create PivotTable dialog box

In the PivotTable Fields task pane, click ALL to display the names of all related tables. Then click the table names to display their field names. From there, you can arrange the fields in the different area boxes at the bottom of the task pane (see Figure 33).

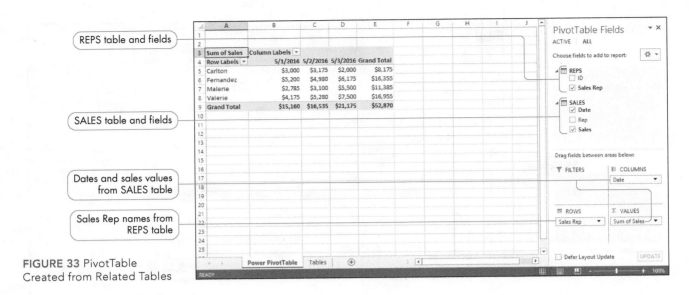

REPS table and fields

SALES table and fields

Dates and sales values
from SALES table

Sales Rep names from
REPS table

FIGURE 33 PivotTable
Created from Related Tables

TIP More Information on Power PivotTables

Look up the topic *What's new in PowerPivot in Excel 2013* to learn more about the PowerPivot functionality and how to create PivotTables from related tables. The Help menu also informs you which versions of Microsoft Office 2013 contain this feature and how you can enable it.

Creating a PivotChart

Charts display data visually. This visual representation may help you and your audience understand the data better than merely presenting the data in a spreadsheet. Although PivotTables help reduce the amount of data to analyze, PivotTables can be overwhelming. Another way to display a PivotTable's aggregated data is through a PivotChart. A **PivotChart** is an interactive graphical representation of the data in a PivotTable. A PivotChart presents the consolidated data visually.

A PivotChart is associated with a PivotTable. When you change the position of a field in either the PivotTable or the PivotChart, the corresponding object changes as well. To create a PivotChart, do the following:

1. Click inside the PivotTable.
2. Click the ANALYZE tab and click PivotChart in the Tools group.

Excel creates a PivotChart based on the current PivotTable settings—row labels, column labels, values, and filters. The PivotChart contains elements that enable you to set filters. The ROWS area changes to AXIS (CATEGORY) and the COLUMNS area changes to LEGEND (SERIES) when you select the PivotChart (see Figure 34).

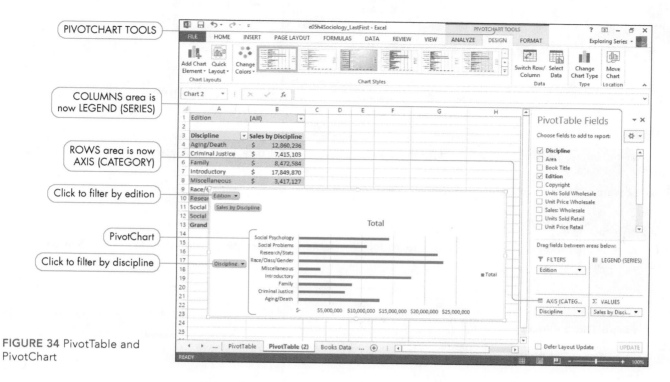

PIVOTCHART TOOLS

COLUMNS area is now LEGEND (SERIES)

ROWS area is now AXIS (CATEGORY)

Click to filter by edition

PivotChart

Click to filter by discipline

FIGURE 34 PivotTable and PivotChart

Although Excel creates the PivotChart based on the current PivotTable settings, you can change the settings using the PivotTable Field List. Click the FILTERS arrow and select values to filter the chart. Click the AXIS (CATEGORY) arrows to sort or filter the categories and subcategories in rows. Click the LEGEND (SERIES) to filter the chart representation based on the values. Changes you make to the PivotChart also affect the corresponding PivotTable. For example, if you apply a filter to the PivotChart, Excel also filters the PivotTable.

The Chart Tools Analyze tab contains the same options that you used to customize a PivotTable. In addition, the Actions group contains the Move Chart option so that you can move a PivotChart to a different worksheet.

The Chart Tools Design tab contains options to add a chart element, apply a layout, change colors, and apply a chart style. In addition, you can switch the data between the category axis and the legend, select the data used to create the chart, change the chart type, and move the chart to a different worksheet.

You can further customize PivotChart elements the same way you can customize regular charts—display data labels, change the fill color for a data series, display axis titles, and so forth. Use Help to learn more about customizing PivotCharts.

Quick Concepts

1. What types of specific elements can you select to be controlled by PivotTable styles?

2. What must be done to create a PivotTable from more than one table?

3. What replaces the ROWS and COLUMNS in the task pane when you create a PivotChart?

Hands-On Exercises

Watch the Video for this Hands-On Exercise!

MyITLab®
HOE4 Training

4 PivotTable Design and PivotCharts

You want to format the PivotTable to make it easier for you to analyze the sales data. In addition, you want to create a PivotChart to depict sales data.

Skills covered: Apply a PivotTable Style • Create a PivotChart

STEP 1 >> APPLY A PIVOTTABLE STYLE

To enhance the readability of the sociology textbook PivotTable, you will apply a style. Refer to Figure 35 as you complete Step 1.

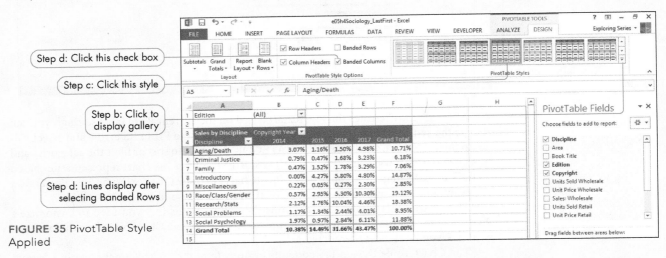

FIGURE 35 PivotTable Style Applied

a. Open *e05h3Sociology_LastFirst* if you closed it at the end of Hands-On Exercise 3 and save it as **e05h4Sociology_LastFirst**, changing *h3* to *h4*.

b. Make sure the PivotTable (2) sheet is active. Click a cell within the PivotTable, click the **DESIGN tab**, and then click the **More button** in the PivotTable Styles group.

The PivotTable Style gallery displays styles that you can apply.

c. Click **Pivot Style Medium 3** to apply a dark red style to the PivotTable.

d. Click the **Banded Columns check box** in the PivotTable Style Options group to add dark red vertical lines between the columns. Save the workbook.

STEP 2 >> CREATE A PIVOTCHART

You want to create a PivotChart to depict the sales data by discipline. Refer to Figure 36 as you complete Step 2.

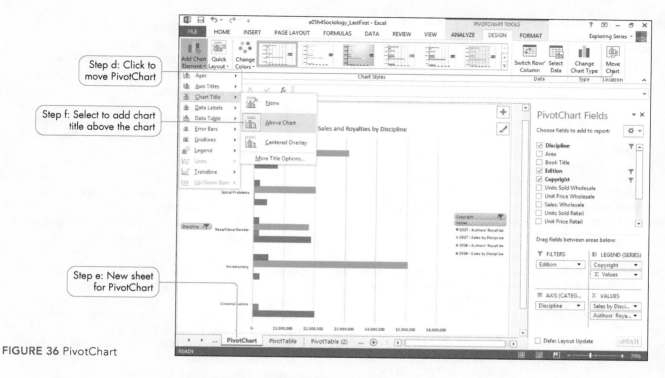

Step d: Click to move PivotChart

Step f: Select to add chart title above the chart

Step e: New sheet for PivotChart

FIGURE 36 PivotChart

a. Click the **PivotTable sheet tab** and click inside the PivotTable.

b. Click the **ANALYZE tab** and click **PivotChart** in the Tools group.

   The Insert Chart dialog box opens.

c. Click **Bar** and click **OK**.

   Excel creates a clustered bar PivotChart based on the PivotTable. Any changes you make to the PivotChart will also affect the PivotTable.

d. Click the **PIVOTCHART TOOLS DESIGN tab** and click **Move Chart** in the Location group.

   The Move Sheet dialog box opens.

e. Click **New sheet**, type **PivotChart**, and then click **OK**.

   The PivotChart is now on its own sheet.

f. Click the **DESIGN tab**, click **Add Chart Element**, point to *Chart Title*, and then select **Above Chart**.

   A Chart Title placeholder displays above the plot area in the PivotChart.

g. Type **Sales and Royalties by Discipline** and press **Enter**.

h. Save and close the workbook, and submit based on your instructor's directions.

Chapter Objectives Review

After reading this chapter, you have accomplished the following objectives:

1. Subtotal data.
- The Subtotal dialog box enables you to insert subtotals, such as sums or averages, based on sorted data. This feature detects changes between categories arranged in rows to insert the subtotal rows.
- Add a second level of subtotals: To keep the first level and add a second level, deselect the *Replace current* subtotals check box in the Subtotals dialog box.
- Collapse and expand the subtotals: Click the outline level buttons to collapse the subtotals to the grand total, grand total and subtotals, or entire dataset. Click a particular collapse button to collapse a category, or click an expand button to expand a particular category.

2. Group and ungroup data.
- If the data contain columns of formulas based on other columns and/or row subtotals, use the auto outline process to create an outline based on the data structure. You can then collapse and expand the outline as you review the data. If you no longer need grouped data, select and ungroup the data again.

3. Create a PivotTable.
- Create a PivotTable from the Quick Analysis Gallery: Select a range, click the Quick Analysis button, click TABLES, and click the desired PivotTable thumbnail.
- Create a PivotTable from the Ribbon: Use the Ribbon to create a blank PivotTable or to display the Recommended PivotTables dialog box to create a PivotTable.

4. Modify a PivotTable.
- Add rows and values: Drag fields to the ROWS and VALUES areas of the PivotTable Fields task pane to add row categories and columns of aggregated values.
- Add columns: Drag fields to the COLUMNS area to add additional columns of details.
- Collapse and expand items: Click the collapse button to collapse subcategory rows and click the expand button to expand a subcategory of details.
- Remove fields: Click a field name in the respective area of the task pane and select Remove Field.
- Rearrange fields: Drag fields from one area to another in the task pane to rearrange fields in the PivotTable.
- Change the value field settings: You can select a different function to calculate the statistics in the PivotTable. You can also apply number formatting and specify a custom column heading for value columns.

- Refresh a PivotTable: PivotTables do not update automatically if you change the original dataset. You must click Refresh to update the PivotTable.

5. Filter and slice a PivotTable.
- Add filters: Drag a field to the FILTERS area of the task pane and click the Filter arrow at the top of the PivotTable to set the filter conditions. You can also click the row labels arrow in cell A4 to set row filters and click the column arrow in cell B3 to set column filters.
- Insert slicers: A slicer is a small window containing the values for a particular field. You click buttons in the slicer to set filters for that particular field.
- Customize slicers: You can specify the slicer's style and size. You can specify how many columns of buttons appear in the slicer and the size of those buttons.

6. Create a calculated field.
- A calculated field is a user-defined field based on other fields. This field does not exist in the original dataset. You can use basic arithmetic operations, but you cannot use cell references or range names in the calculated field syntax.
- Show values as a specific calculation results: You can apply predefined calculations, such as *% of Grand Total*, for displaying the values in the PivotTable.

7. Format a PivotTable.
- The PivotTable Tools Design tab enables you to improve the appearance of a PivotTable by applying a PivotTable style. The style controls the fill color, bold formatting, and other formatting aspects of data in the PivotTable.

8. Use PowerPivot Functionality.
- You can create relationships between two or more related tables within one workbook. After creating the relationships, you can use PowerPivot to create a PivotTable that uses fields from the related tables.

9. Create a PivotChart.
- The PivotChart is similar to creating a regular chart, except it is based on the categories and structure of the PivotTable, not the original dataset. You can customize a PivotChart with the same methods you use to customize a regular chart. If you change fields or sort in either the PivotTable or the PivotChart, Excel automatically adjusts the corresponding pivot object.

Key Terms Matching

Match the key terms with their definitions. Write the key term letter by the appropriate numbered definition.

a. Calculated field
b. Columns area
c. Data mining
d. Filters area
e. Grouping
f. Outline
g. PivotChart
h. PivotTable

i. PivotTable Fields task pane
j. PowerPivot
k. Relationship
l. Rows area
m. Slicer
n. Slicer caption
o. Subtotal
p. Values area

1. _____ An association created between two tables where both tables contain a matching field.

2. _____ A hierarchical structure of data.

3. _____ A row within a dataset that displays the total or another statistic for a particular category.

4. _____ A process of joining related rows or columns of related data.

5. _____ The process of analyzing large volumes of data to identify patterns and trends.

6. _____ An organized structure that summarizes large amounts of data without altering the original dataset.

7. _____ A user-defined field that performs a calculation based on other fields in a PivotTable.

8. _____ A window listing all items in a field and enabling efficient filtering.

9. _____ Drag fields here to display categories horizontally in a PivotTable.

10. _____ Drag fields here to display data as aggregates, such as sums or averages.

11. _____ Drag fields here to be able to specify which values or content to include or exclude in the PivotTable.

12. _____ Drag fields here to add more vertical data to a PivotTable.

13. _____ A graphical representation of aggregated data derived from a PivotTable.

14. _____ A window that enables you to drag fields to particular areas to build and arrange data in a PivotTable.

15. _____ The label that appears at the top of a slicer window. By default, it displays the name of the field used.

16. _____ A built-in add-in program that enables users to create a PivotTable from multiple related tables.

Multiple Choice

1. A worksheet contains data for businesses that are sponsoring this year's Arts Festival. The worksheet contains these columns in this sequence: Business Name, Address, City, State, and Donation Amount. Data are sorted by State and then by City. What is the default *At a change in* setting within the Subtotal dialog box, and what would be a more appropriate setting?

   (a) Business Name (default field), Donation Amount (correct field)
   (b) Business Name (default field), State (correct field)
   (c) Donation Amount (default field), Address (correct field)
   (d) Address (default field), Donation Amount (correct field)

2. You created an outline for a dataset. What does the + button indicate to the left of a row heading?

   (a) You can add a new row at that location only.
   (b) One or more columns are hidden.
   (c) You can click it to collapse the details of that category.
   (d) You can click it to expand the details of that category.

3. A worksheet contains a PivotTable placeholder and the PivotTable Fields task pane. Where do you drag the State field if you want a list of each state in the first column of the PivotTable?

   (a) FILTERS area
   (b) COLUMNS area
   (c) ROWS area
   (d) VALUES area

4. You just created a slicer for the State field in a PivotTable. Which of the following does *not* characterize the initial slicer?

   (a) The slicer buttons are set to filter out all records.
   (b) The slicer caption is State.
   (c) The slicer contains one column of state names or abbreviations.
   (d) The slicer may display on top of the PivotTable data.

5. You created a PivotTable and made some changes to values in the original dataset from which the PivotTable was created. How does this affect the PivotTable?

   (a) The PivotTable updates automatically when you make changes to the dataset.
   (b) You must create a new PivotTable if you want updated results in a PivotTable.
   (c) Click the DATA tab and click Update to update the PivotTable to reflect changes you made in the dataset.
   (d) Click Refresh in the Data group on the ANALYZE tab to update the PivotTable.

6. You created a PivotTable to summarize salaries by department. What is the default summary statistic for the salaries in the PivotTable?

   (a) Average
   (b) Sum
   (c) Count
   (d) Max

7. What settings should you select for a PivotTable if you want to apply a different color scheme and display different fill colors for main category rows and horizontal lines within the PivotTable?

   (a) Banded Rows and Banded Columns check boxes
   (b) Banded Columns check box and a different PivotTable style
   (c) Banded Rows check box and a different PivotTable style
   (d) A different PivotTable style only

8. Which PivotTable calculated field is correctly constructed to calculate a 20% tip on a meal at a restaurant?

   (a) =Meal Cost * 20%
   (b) ='Meal Cost'*.2
   (c) ="Meal Cost"*.2
   (d) =B5*1.2

9. You have created a PivotChart showing sales by quarter by sales rep. Before presenting it to management, you notice the name of a rep who has since been fired. How do you remove this rep from the chart without deleting the data?

   (a) Filter the Sales Rep field in the PivotChart and deselect the employee's check box.
   (b) Make the employee's data points and axis titles invisible.
   (c) You cannot delete the rep from the chart without first deleting the data.
   (d) Hide that rep's row(s) in the underlying list, which automatically removes that rep from the chart.

10. Currently, the House Types field is in the Row Labels area, the Real Estate Agent field is in the Column Labels area, and Sum of List Prices is in the VALUES area. How can you modify the PivotTable to display the agent names as subcategories within the house types in the first column?

    (a) Drag the Real Estate Agent field from the Column Labels area and drop it above the House Types field in the Row Labels area.
    (b) Drag the House Types field from the ROWS area and drop it below the Real Estate Agent field in the COLUMNS area.
    (c) Drag the House Types field from the ROWS area to the FILTERS area and drag the Real Estate Agent field from the COLUMNS area to the ROWS area.
    (d) Drag the Real Estate Agent field from the COLUMNS area and drop it below the House Types field in the ROWS area.

Practice Exercises

1 The Men's Store

You work at the Men's Store, a men's department store in Cheyenne, Wyoming. You need to analyze a year's worth of transactions to determine which salesperson had the highest overall sales and which salesperson had the best sales in the Dress Shirts and Ties category. You will use the Subtotal feature and outline the list of transactions for the year. This exercise follows the same set of skills as used in Hands-On Exercise 1 in the chapter. Refer to Figure 37 as you complete this exercise.

FIGURE 37 Subtotals

	Order Date	Salesperson	Category	Sale Item	Total Amount
22			Accessories Total		$ 8,673.23
70			Casual wear Total		$ 32,870.22
101			Dress Shirts and Ties Total		$ 19,280.39
126			Sport Jackets and Slacks Total		$ 28,679.05
175			Suits Total		$ 71,981.32
188			Underwear Total		$ 1,024.91
189		Adams Total			$ 162,509.12
220			Accessories Total		$ 8,893.02
296			Casual Wear Total		$ 41,884.53
322			Dress Shirts and Ties Total		$ 12,167.17
360			Sport Jackets and Slacks Total		$ 41,201.04
408			Suits Total		$ 80,848.55
421			Underwear Total		$ 1,248.57
422		Baker Total			$ 186,287.88
443			Accessories Total		$ 6,327.99
489			Casual wear Total		$ 22,565.30
511			Dress Shirts and Ties Total		$ 9,878.98
535			Sport Jackets and Slacks Total		$ 24,945.13
576			Suits Total		$ 59,443.75
591			Underwear Total		$ 1,680.33
592		Davis Total			$ 124,841.48
613			Accessories Total		$ 8,595.89
654			Casual Wear Total		$ 19,318.44
687			Dress Shirts and Ties Total		$ 18,170.45
716			Sport Jackets and Slacks Total		$ 29,509.26
763			Suits Total		$ 68,558.25
772			Underwear Total		$ 785.42
773		Goodman Total			$ 144,917.71
774		Grand Total			$ 618,506.18

a. Open *e05p1MensStore* and save it as **e05p1MensStore_LastFirst**.

b. Sort the list by salesperson and then by category within salesperson.

c. Click the **DATA tab** and click **Subtotal** in the Outline group. Do the following in the Subtotal dialog box:
   - Click the **At each change in arrow** and select **Salesperson**.
   - Click the **Order Amount check box** and the **Sales Tax check box** in the *Add subtotal to* list.
   - Keep the *Total Amount* check box selected. Click **OK**.

d. Add a second-level subtotal by category by doing the following:
   - Click **Subtotal** in the Outline group.
   - Click the **At each change in arrow** and select **Category**.
   - Keep the *Order Total*, *Sales Tax*, and *Total Amount* check boxes selected.
   - Click the **Replace current subtotals check box** to deselect it. Click **OK**.

e. Click **2** to collapse the list to see the salesperson subtotals. Who had the highest order totals for the year? Who had the lowest order totals for the year?

f. Click **3** to expand the list to see category subtotals for each salesperson. Who had the highest dress shirts and tie sales for the year? Is this the same person who had the overall highest order totals for the year?

g. Click the **Group arrow** in the Outline group on the DATA tab and select **Auto Outline**. Click **OK** when prompted to modify the existing outline. Click the **collapse button** above column G to collapse the columns.

h. Create a footer with your name on the left side, the sheet name code in the center, and the file name code on the right side.

i. Save and close the workbook, and submit based on your instructor's directions.

Your college friend Cirio owns a successful Greek restaurant in Denver, Colorado. He tracks daily dinner revenue but needs your assistance to consolidate data for the entire year. Specifically, he wants to compare quarterly totals by weekday, and he wants to take a closer look at the fourth-quarter revenue. You will insert two functions to complete the main worksheet and then create a relationship between that table and a related table of weekday names. You will build a PivotTable and a PivotChart to help Cirio analyze the weekday revenue by quarters. This exercise follows the same set of skills as used in Hands-On Exercises 2–4 in the chapter. Refer to Figure 38 as you complete this exercise.

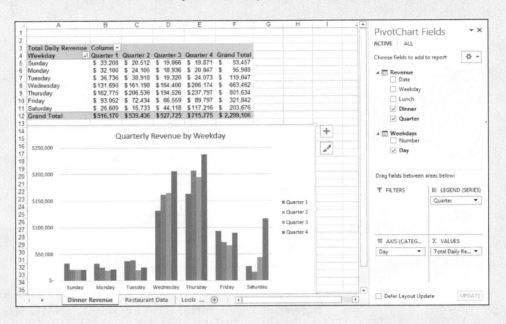

FIGURE 38 PivotTable and PivotChart

a. Open *e05p2Dinner* and save it as **e05p2Dinner_LastFirst**. Click the **Lookup Tables worksheet tab** to see the two datasets. The first dataset is a table named Weekdays that will be used to relate the day numbers (such as 2) with the names of the weekdays (such as Monday). The second dataset is a lookup table range-named Quarters so that you can create a VLOOKUP function to look up a value within a breakpoint, identified by month numbers, and return which quarter the month is in. For example, the fifth month (5) returns Quarter 2.

b. Create two formulas to calculate missing values by doing the following:
   - Click the **Restaurant Data worksheet tab**, click in **cell B2**, type **=WEEKDAY(A2)**, and then press **Enter**. For 1/1/2016, the WEEKDAY function returns 6, which represents Friday.
   - Click **cell E2**, type **=VLOOKUP(MONTH(A2),Quarters,2)**, and then press **Enter**. MONTH(A2) returns the month from the data in cell A2, which is 1. The VLOOKUP function looks up the month number in the lookup table that is range-named Quarters and returns the quarter of the year for that date. For example, months 1 through 3 return Quarter 1.

DISCOVER

c. Create a relationship between the Revenues table in the Restaurant Data worksheet and the Weekdays table in the Lookup Tables worksheet by doing the following:
   - Click the **DATA tab** and click **Relationships** in the Data Tools group to open the Manage Relationships dialog box.
   - Click **New** to open the Create Relationships dialog box.
   - Click the **Table arrow** and select **Revenue** (the main table). Click the **Column (Foreign) arrow** and select **Weekday**.
   - Click the **Related Table arrow** and select **Weekdays**. Click the **Related Column (Primary) arrow** and select **Number**.
   - Click **OK** to close the Create Relationships dialog box. Click **Close** to close the Manage Relationships dialog box.

Practice Exercises

d. Use PowerPivot to create a PivotTable using the related tables by doing the following:
- Click the **INSERT tab** and click **PivotTable** in the Tables group to open the Create PivotTable dialog box.
- Click the **Add this data to the Data Model check box** in the *Choose whether you want to analyze multiple tables* section. Click **OK**.
- Click **ALL** at the top of the PivotTable Fields task pane to display all table names.
- Click **Revenue** at the top of the task pane to display the fields for the Revenue table.
- Click the **Dinner** and **Quarter check boxes** in the task pane and drag **Quarter** from the ROWS area to the COLUMNS area.
- Scroll down, if necessary, and click **Weekdays** in the task pane to display the fields for the Weekdays table.
- Click the **Day check box** in the task pane to add this field to the ROWS area.

e. Modify the PivotTable by doing the following:
- Click the **Row Labels arrow** in **cell A4** and select **Sort A to Z**. (Note that this action sorts in sequential order by weekday, not alphabetical order by weekday name.)
- Click **cell A4**, type **Weekday**, and then press **Enter**.
- Click the **DESIGN tab**, click the **More button** in the PivotTable Styles group, and then click **Pivot Style Light 15**.

f. Format the values by doing the following:
- Click **cell B5**, click the **ANALYZE tab**, and then click **Field Settings** in the Active Field group.
- Type **Total Daily Revenue** in the **Custom Name box**.
- Click **Number Format**, click **Accounting**, click the **Decimal places spin arrow** to display *0*, click **OK** in the Format Cells dialog box, and then click **OK** in the Value Field Settings dialog box.
- Set a column width of **9** for column B.

g. Create a PivotChart from the PivotTable by doing the following.
- Click **PivotChart** in the Tools group on the ANALYZE tab and click **OK** in the Insert Chart dialog box to create a default column chart.
- Click the **DESIGN tab**, click **Quick Layout** in the Chart Layouts group, and then click **Layout 1**.
- Click the **Chart Title placeholder**, type **Quarterly Revenue by Weekday**, and then press **Enter**.
- Move the chart so that the top-left corner starts in **cell A14**. Resize the chart to extend through **cell H35**.
- Click the **ANALYZE tab**, click **Field Buttons** in the Show/Hide group, and then select **Hide All** to hide the buttons within the chart area.

h. Rename the Sheet1 worksheet **Dinner Revenue**. Create a footer with your name on the left side, the sheet name code in the center, and the file name code on the right side on each worksheet.

i. Save and close the workbook, and submit based on your instructor's directions.

3 Greek Restaurant Combined Revenue

Cirio needs to conduct additional revenue analysis. Now he wants you to create a PivotTable that displays the daily percentage of revenue that contributes to the total lunch and dinner revenues, respectively. Because he has a list of several ways to view the data, you decide to insert slicers so that Cirio can filter the PivotTable data himself. This exercise follows the same set of skills as used in Hands-On Exercises 2–4 in the chapter. Refer to Figure 39 as you complete this exercise.

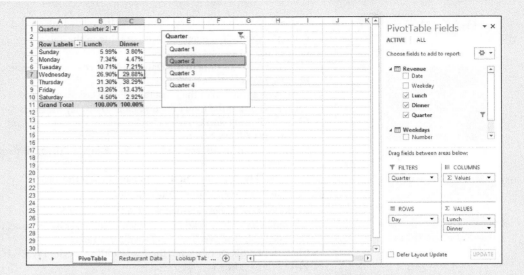

FIGURE 39 PivotTable and Slicers

a. Open *e05p3Revenue* and save it as **e05p3Revenue_LastFirst**.

b. Use PowerPivot to create a PivotTable using the related tables by doing the following:
   - Click the **INSERT tab** and click **PivotTable** in the Tables group to open the Create PivotTable dialog box.
   - Click the **Add this data to the Data Model check box** in the *Choose whether you want to analyze multiple tables* section. Click **OK**.
   - Click **ALL** at the top of the PivotTable Fields task pane to display all table names.
   - Click **Weekdays** at the top of the task pane to display the fields for the Weekday table.
   - Drag **Day** to the ROWS area.
   - Click **Revenue** in the task pane to display the fields for the Revenue table.
   - Drag the **Quarter field** to the FILTERS area.
   - Click the **Lunch** and **Dinner check boxes** to add them to the VALUES area.
   - Click the **Row Labels arrow** in **cell A3** and select **Sort A to Z**.

c. Display the daily revenue as a percentage of total weekly sales for lunch by doing the following:
   - Click **cell B4** and click **Field Settings** in the Active Field group to open the Value Field Settings dialog box.
   - Type **Lunch** in the **Custom Name box**.
   - Click the **Show Values As tab** in the dialog box, click the **Show Value As arrow**, and then select **% of Column Total**. Click **OK** in the Value Field Settings dialog box.
   - Apply the custom name **Dinner** to **cell C4** and show the values as *% of Column Total*. Click **OK** to close the dialog box.

d. Click **Insert Slicer** in the Filter group, click the **Quarter check box** in the Insert Slicer dialog box, and then click **OK**.

e. Move the slicer to the right of the PivotTable, click the **SLICER TOOLS OPTIONS tab**, enter **1.8** in the **Width box** in the Size group, and then enter **1.77** in the **Height box** in the Size group.

f. Click the **Quarter 2 slicer slice** to filter the PivotTable by the second quarter of the year.

g. Create a footer with your name on the left side, the sheet name code in the center, and the file name code on the right side on each worksheet.

h. Save and close the workbook, and submit based on your instructor's directions.

1 Mountain View Realty

ANALYSIS CASE

You are a real estate analyst who works for Mountain View Realty in the North Utah County area. You have consolidated a list of houses sold during the past few months and need to start analyzing the data. For a simple analysis, you will outline the data and use the Subtotal feature. Then you will create a PivotTable to give you a way to perform more in-depth analysis.

a. Open *e05m1RealEstate* and save it as **e05m1RealEstate_LastFirst**.

b. Make sure the Sales Subtotals worksheet is the active sheet. Insert a column between the Selling Price and Listing Date columns. Enter the heading **% of Asking Price** and double-click between the column G and H headings to increase the column width. Insert a formula in **cell G2** to calculate the selling price percentage of the asking price, format it with **Percent Style** with one decimal place, and then copy the formula down the column.

c. Enter the heading **Days on Market** on the right side of the last column and double-click between the column J and K headings to increase the column width. Calculate the number of days between the listing date and sale date. Copy the formula down the column.

d. Sort the list by city in alphabetical order, then by selling agent in alphabetical order, and finally by listing date in chronological order.

e. Use the Subtotal feature to calculate the average selling price, percentage of asking price, and days on market by city.

f. Apply an automatic outline to the columns. Collapse the outline to hide the listing and sale dates. Click the appropriate button to display the grand average and city average rows only. Format the average days on market to zero decimal places. Apply wrap text, **10.00** column width, and increased row height to **cells G1** and **J1**. Set a print area for the **range C1:J88**.

 g. Go to **cell C95** in the Sales Subtotals worksheet. Read the questions and provide the appropriate answers in the respective highlighted cells in the **range G96:G100**.

h. Click the **Sales Data worksheet** and create a PivotTable on a new worksheet. Name the new worksheet **PivotTable**.

i. Display the cities in the first row of the PivotTable, selling agents in the first column, and asking and selling prices in additional columns.

j. Modify the PivotTable. Display averages rather than sums with **Accounting Number Format** with zero decimal places. Pivot the data by placing the cities in columns and the selling agents in rows.

k. Add a group filter to display only Alpine and Cedar Hills.

l. Adjust column widths, wrap text as needed, insert a bottom border line below the city names, and then add a more descriptive label for the first column and any other columns that need more descriptive labels. Adjust row heights so that column labels fully display.

m. Go back to the Sales Data worksheet. You realize that a selling price is incorrect. Change the selling price for Number 40 from *$140,000* to **$1,400,000**. Refresh the PivotTable.

n. Create a footer with your name on the left side, the sheet name code in the center, and the file name code on the right side for the Sales Subtotals and the PivotTable worksheets. Adjust the margins and scaling to fit on one page.

o. Save and close the workbook, and submit based on your instructor's directions.

2 Fiesta® Collection

Your Aunt Laura has been collecting Fiesta dinnerware, a popular brand from the Homer Laughlin China Company, since 1986. You help her maintain an inventory. So far, you and Aunt Laura have created a table of color numbers, color names, year introduced, and year retired, if applicable. In a second table, you entered color numbers, item numbers, items, current value, and source. Previously, you helped her research current replacement costs from Homer Laughlin's Web site (www.hlchina.com), Replacements, Ltd. (www.replacements.com), and eBay (www.ebay.com); however, you believe the retired colors may be worth more now. Laura is especially interested in the values of retired colors so that she can provide this information for her insurance agent. You will build a PivotTable and add slicers to help her with the analysis.

a. Open *e05m2Fiesta* and save it as **e05m2Fiesta_LastFirst**.

b. Create a relationship between the Items table using the Color Number field and the Colors table using the Number field.

c. Create a blank PivotTable from within the Items table to analyze multiple tables. Place the PivotTable on a new worksheet and name the worksheet **Retired Colors**.

d. Display the names of both tables in the PivotTable Fields task pane.

e. Display the Color names as ROWS and the sum of the Replacement Value field as VALUES.

f. Add a FILTER to display aggregates for retired colors only. Note that current colors do not have a retirement date, so you must filter out the blanks.

g. Apply the **Pivot Style Medium 7**.

h. Format the values with **Accounting Number Format** with two decimal places. Create a custom heading named **Replacement Value**. Change *Row Labels* in **cell A3** to **Retired Colors**.

DISCOVER

i. Add a calculated field by doing the following:

- Display the Excel Options dialog box, click **Customize Ribbon** on the left side of the dialog box, click the **POWERPIVOT check box** in the *Customize the Ribbon* section on the right side, and then click **OK**.
- Use the Calculated Fields command to create a new calculated field.
- Enter the formula to multiply [Sum of Replacement Value] by 1.15.
- Type the custom name **Updated Replacement Values**. Word-wrap and center the label.
- Apply the same number format that you did for the Replacement Values column.

j. Add slicers for the Color field. Select these colors to display: **Apricot**, **Chartreuse**, **Lilac**, **Marigold**, **Pearl Gray**, and **Sapphire**.

k. Apply the **Slicer Style Light 6 style**.

l. Create a footer with your name on the left side, the sheet name code in the center, and the file name code on the right side of the Retired Colors worksheet.

m. Save and close the workbook, and submit based on your instructor's directions.

3 Facebook® Social Phenomenon

COLLABORATION CASE

FROM SCRATCH

Facebook has experienced phenomenal growth since its creation in 2004. What is it that has made Facebook a huge success story, starting a decade after many of the other Web company startups? To understand how people use Facebook, look at its applications. Work with another student to conduct this research, obtain data, and create PivotTables.

a. Open www.checkfacebook.com in a Web browser to read about Facebook's history.

b. Start a new Excel workbook and save it as **e05m3Facebook_LastFirst**.

c. Go to **http://statistics.allfacebook.com** and use this site to build a worksheet that lists at least 200 application leaders for 10 categories, two of which must be Business and Just For Fun. Each student should find 100 different application leaders. Use collaboration tools to make sure you and your team member use the same format and do not duplicate data.

d. Include data for these columns: Category, Name, Daily Average Use (DAU), Monthly Average Use (MAU), and Daily Growth.

e. Copy your team member's worksheet as a new worksheet in your workbook. Then create a third worksheet to combine the data. Name the sheets appropriately.

f. Format the data and headings appropriately in the combined worksheet.

g. Create a PivotTable based on the data to reflect one perspective of analysis. Format the values and apply desired filters.

h. Have your teammate copy the combined sheet and create his or her own PivotTable with a different perspective, formatting, and desired filters.

i. Discuss your analysis with your team member.

j. Create a footer with your name and your team member's name on the left side, sheet name code in the center, and the file name code on the right side of each worksheet.

k. Save and close the workbook, and submit based on your instructor's directions.

Mid-Level Exercises

Beyond the Classroom

Departing Flights

RESEARCH CASE

You want to research morning flight departures at Oklahoma City Will Rogers Airport. Find the airport's departing flight schedule and copy the morning departing flight information to a new worksheet. Name the workbook as **e05b2OKC_LastFirst**. Clean up the data after copying it. Name the worksheet as **Morning Departures**. Create a PivotTable using the *Count of Departing To by Airline* recommendation. Display the Status field as a column so that you can see canceled, on-time, and delayed flights. Add the Gate information as a secondary row label. Apply **PivotStyle Medium 13 style**. Type **Airlines and Gates** in cell A4. Type **Status** in **cell B3**. Adjust column widths as needed. Name the worksheet **PivotTable**.

Create a PivotChart from the original dataset. Use the Airline field as the Axis and the Flight # as the Value. Change the chart type to a pie chart. Add a chart title and percentage data labels. Adjust the chart size and location as needed. Name the sheet as **PivotChart**. Create a footer with your name, the sheet name code, and the file name code on each worksheet. Save and close the workbook, and submit based on your instructor's directions.

Innovative Game Studio

DISASTER RECOVERY

You work as an assistant to Terry Park, the producer for a video game studio in Phoenix, Arizona. The company produces games for the PlayStation®, Xbox®, and Wii™ consoles. The producer tracks salaries and performance for everyone on a particular team, which consists of artists, animators, programmers, and so forth. Terry tried to create a PivotTable to organize the data by department and then by title within department. He also wants to display total salaries by these categories and filter the data to show aggregates for team members who earned only Excellent and Good performance ratings. In addition, he wants to see what the percentages of total salaries for each job title are of each department's budget. For example, the total salary for Senior Artists is $263,300. That represents 50.27% of the Art Department's salary budget for Excellent- and Good-rated employees. However, the percentages are not displayed correctly. Terry called you in to correct his PivotTable.

Open *e05b3Games* and save it as **e05b3Games_LastFirst**. Identify the errors and make a list of these errors starting on row 41 in the PivotTable worksheet. Correct the errors and improve the format, including a medium Pivot Style, throughout the PivotTable. Create a footer with your name, the sheet name code, and the file name code. Save and close the workbook, and submit based on your instructor's directions.

Job Fair

SOFT SKILLS CASE

FROM SCRATCH

You are ready to help your college create a worksheet to organize the companies that will participate. Create a list of companies, the cities in which they are located, and the number of active openings they are advertising. Include any other details that help classify the companies. Sort the list by a major classification and then display subtotals to indicate the total number of jobs by classification. Save the workbook as **e05b4JobFair_LastFirst**. Create a footer with your name, the sheet name code, and the file name code. Save and close the workbook, and submit based on your instructor's directions.

Capstone Exercise

You are an analyst for an authorized Greenwich Workshop® fine art dealer (www.greenwichworkshop.com). Customers are especially fond of James C. Christensen's art. You prepared a list of artwork: art, type, edition size, release date, issue price, and estimated current market value. Studying the data will help you discuss value trends with art collectors.

Sort, Subtotal, and Outline Data

You need to organize data to facilitate using the Subtotal feature. Then you will further outline the list so that you can collapse and expand groups.

a. Open *e05c1FineArt* and save it as **e05c1FineArt_LastFirst**.

b. Click the **Subtotals worksheet**. Sort the data by type and further sort it by the name of the art, both in alphabetical order.

c. Use the Subtotal feature to identify the highest Issue Price and Est. Value.

d. Select and group the first and last name columns.

e. Collapse the names created by the grouping.

f. Study the list to see the Est. Value in each type.

Create a PivotTable

Although creating an outline and subtotaling data are helpful for an initial analysis of the artwork values, you will create a PivotTable for further analysis.

a. Click the **Christensen worksheet** and create a blank PivotTable from the data.

b. Use the Type, Release Date, and Issue Price fields, enabling Excel to determine where the fields go.

c. Remove the Release Date field. Add the Est. Value field.

Format the PivotTable

You will calculate averages within each art type. You will format the values and provide clear headings in the PivotTable.

a. Modify the value fields to determine the average issue price and average estimated market value by type.

b. Insert a calculated field to determine percent change in values by type.

c. Format the three columns of values appropriately, using whole numbers for dollar values and two decimal places for percentages.

d. Edit the custom names for the values columns. Apply these formats to the three values column headings: wrap text, center horizontally, **30** row height, and **9.7** column widths.

e. Enter appropriate labels for the first column and the grand total label.

Filter the PivotTable and Apply a Style

You want to focus on average values for sold-out art because these pieces typically increase in value on the secondary market. In addition, you want to narrow the list to particular types. After filtering the data, you will apply a style.

a. Set a filter to display only sold-out art (indicated by *Yes*).

b. Set a Type filter to *omit* Hand Colored Print, Limited Edition Hand Colored Print, Open Edition Print, and Poster types.

c. Apply **Pivot Style Medium 5**.

d. Display banded columns and banded rows.

Create a PivotChart

To help interpret the consolidated values of the art, you want to create a PivotChart. You realize that displaying both monetary values and percentages on the same chart is like mixing apples and oranges. If you modify the PivotChart, you will change the PivotTable; therefore, you will create a PivotChart from the original data source.

a. Use the Christensen worksheet to create a PivotChart.

b. Use the Type, Issue Price, and Est. Value fields. Find the average issue price and average estimated value.

c. Set filters as you did for the first PivotTable.

d. Apply formatting as you did for the first PivotTable.

e. Change the chart type to **Bar**.

f. Move the PivotChart below the PivotTable, resize the PivotChart, and hide the field buttons in the PivotChart.

g. Insert an appropriate chart title reflecting the contents and the filter. Set a **12-pt font size** for the chart title.

h. Set the upper limit of the value axis to **2000** if needed.

i. Sort the PivotTable in such a way that its effect on the PivotChart is to display the category labels alphabetically.

j. Type **Art Type** in **cell A3** and type **Overall Averages** in **cell A13**.

Finalizing Your Workbook

You need to finalize your workbook.

a. Rename the first PivotTable worksheet **PivotTable**.

b. Rename the second PivotTable/PivotChart worksheet **PivotChart**.

c. Select landscape orientation and adjust the top and bottom margins for the Subtotals worksheet.

d. Create a footer on all four worksheets with your name, the sheet name code, and the file name code.

e. Save and close the workbook, and submit based on your instructor's directions.

Glossary

Calculated field A user-defined field that performs an arithmetic calculation based on other fields in a PivotTable.

Columns area The region in which to place a field that will display labels to organize data vertically in a PivotTable.

Data mining The process of analyzing large volumes of data to identify patterns and trends.

Filters area The region in which to place a field so that the user can then filter the data by that field in a PivotTable or PivotChart.

Grouping (1) The process of joining rows or columns of related data into a single entity so that groups can be collapsed or expanded for data analysis. (2) The process of selecting worksheets to perform the same action at the same time.

Outline A hierarchical structure of data organized so that groups can be expanded to show details or collapsed to show high-level structure.

PivotChart A graphical representation of data in a PivotTable.

PivotTable An interactive organization of data that consolidates and aggregates data by categories that can be sorted, filtered, and calculated.

PivotTable Fields task pane A window that enables a user to specify what fields are used from a dataset and how to organize the data in columns, rows, values, and filters.

PowerPivot A PivotTable functionality in which two or more related tables can be used to extract data into a PivotTable.

Relationship A connection between two or more tables using a common field, such as an ID field.

Rows area The region in which to place a field that will display labels to organize data horizontally in a PivotTable.

Slicer A window listing all items in a field so that the user can click button to filter data by that particular item or value.

Slicer caption The text or field name that appears as a header or title at the top of a slicer to identify the data in that field.

Subtotal An aggregate calculation, such as SUM or AVERAGE, that applies for a subcategory of related data within a larger dataset.

Values area The range in which to place a field that will display aggregates, such as SUM, for categories of data in a PivotTable.

Access

Introduction to Access

Finding Your Way Through an Access Database

OBJECTIVES AFTER YOU READ THIS CHAPTER, YOU WILL BE ABLE TO:

1. Understand database fundamentals

2. Use an existing database

3. Sort table data on one or multiple fields

4. Create, modify, and remove filters

5. Know when to use Access or Excel to manage data

6. Understand relational power

7. Create a database

CASE STUDY | Managing a Business in the Global Economy

Northwind Traders* is an international gourmet food distributor that imports and exports specialty foods from around the world. Northwind's products include meats, seafood, dairy products, beverages, and produce. Keeping track of customers, vendors, orders, and inventory is a critical task. The owners of Northwind have just purchased an order-processing database created with Microsoft Office Access 2013 to help manage their customers, suppliers, products, and orders.

You have been hired to learn, use, and manage the database. Northwind's owners are willing to provide training about their business and Access. They expect the learning process to take about three months. After three months, your job will be to support the order-processing team as well as to provide detail and summary reports to the sales force as needed. Your new job at Northwind Traders will be a challenge, but it is also a good opportunity to make a great contribution to a global company. Are you up to the task?

*Northwind Traders was created by the Microsoft Access Team as a sample database for Access 2003. Access 2013 does not include a sample database, so you will use a modified version of Northwind Traders. The names of companies, products, people, characters, and/or data are fictitious.

From Access Chapter 1 of *Exploring Microsoft® Access 2013 Comprehensive*, First edition. Mary Anne Poatsy, Cynthia Krebs, Eric Cameron, Jerri Williams, Robert T. Grauer. Copyright © 2014 by Pearson Education, Inc. Published by Pearson Prentice Hall. All Rights Reserved. Download student resources at http://www.pearsonhighered.com/exploring.

Databases Are Everywhere!

A *database* is a collection of data organized as meaningful information that can be accessed, managed, stored, queried, sorted, and reported. You probably participate in data collection and are exposed to databases on a regular basis. For example, your community college or university uses a database to store registration data. When you enrolled at your institution, you created a profile that was saved in a database. When you registered for this course, your data was entered into a database. If you have a bank account, have a Social Security card, have a medical history, or have booked a flight with an airline, your information is stored in a record in a database.

If you use the Internet, you probably use databases often because the Internet can provide you with easy access to databases. For example, when you shop online or check your bank statement online, you connect to a database. Even when you type a search phrase into Google and click Search, you are using Google's massive database with all of its stored Web page references and keywords. Look for something on Amazon, and you are searching Amazon's database to find a product that you might want to buy. Need a new driver for golfing? Log on to Amazon, search for "golf clubs driver" (see Figure 1), and find the right driver with your preferred loft, hand orientation, flex, shaft material, and price range. All of this information is stored in Amazon's products database.

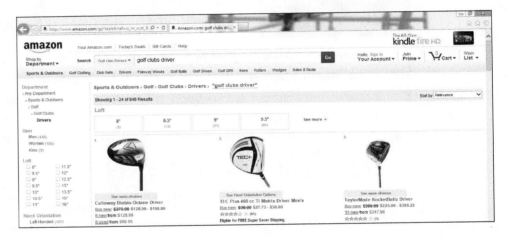

FIGURE 1 Amazon Web Site

Photo: Copyright © 2013 Amazon.com, Inc.

Organizations rely on data to conduct daily operations, regardless of whether the organization exists as a profit or not-for-profit environment. Organizations maintain data about their customers, employees, orders, volunteers, activities, and facilities. Organizations maintain data about their customers, employees, orders, volunteers, activities, and facilities, and this data needs to be stored, organized, and made available for analysis. *Data* and *information* are two terms that are often used interchangeably. However, when it comes to databases, the two terms mean different things. *Data* is what is entered into a database. *Information* is the finished product that is produced by the database. Data is converted to information by selecting, calculating, sorting, or summarizing records. Decisions in an organization are usually based on information produced by a database, rather than raw data.

In this section, you will learn the fundamentals of organizing data in a database, explore what Access database objects are and what their purpose is, and examine the Access interface.

Understanding Database Fundamentals

People use databases to store collections of data. A *database management system (DBMS)* is a software system that provides the tools needed to create, maintain, and use a database. Database management systems make it possible to access and control data and display the information in a variety of formats such as lists, forms, and reports. *Access* is the database management system included in the Office 2013 Professional suite and the Office 2013 Professional Academic suite. Access is a valuable decision-making tool that many organizations are using. Advanced Access users and software developers can even use Microsoft Access to develop software applications for specific solutions to the needs of organizations. For example, a health organization uses Access to track and understand disease reports.

Organize Information in a Database and Recognize Access Objects

STEP 2»

An Access database is a structured collection of *objects*, the main components that are created and used to make the database function. The main object types in an Access database are listed below and discussed in the following paragraphs.

- Tables
- Forms
- Queries
- Reports
- Macros
- Modules

The objects that make up an Access database are available from the ***Navigation Pane***. The Navigation Pane is an Access interface element that organizes and lists the database objects in an Access database. You will learn about the object types and their benefits in the remainder of this section. Later you will learn to create and use these objects.

The foundation of every database is a ***table***, the object in which data, such as a person's name or a product number, is stored. The other objects in a database are based on one or more underlying tables. To understand how an Access database works and how to use Access effectively, you should learn the structure of a table. Tables organize data into columns and rows. Columns display a *field*, the smallest data element of a table. For example, in the Northwind database, a table containing information about customers would include a Customer ID field. Another field would contain the Company Name. Fields may be required or optional—a contact name may be required, for example, but a contact title may be optional.

Each row in a table contains a ***record***, a complete set of all the fields (data elements) about one person, place, event, or concept. A customer record, for example, would contain all of the fields about a single customer, including the Customer ID, the Company Name, Contact Name, Contact Title, Address, City, etc. Figure 2 shows the Northwind database with the Customers table selected in the Navigation Pane. The Customers table is open and shows the records of Northwind customers in the table rows. Each record contains multiple fields, with the field name displaying at the top of each column.

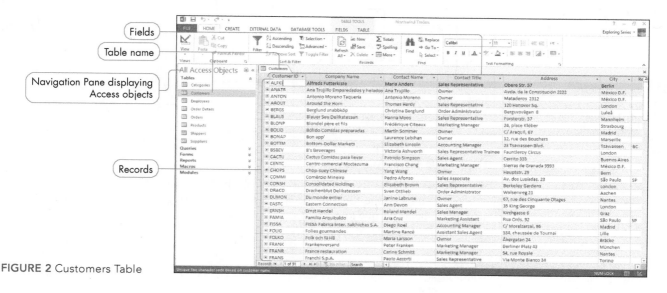

FIGURE 2 Customers Table

A *form* is an object that gives a user a way of entering and modifying data in databases. Forms enable you to enter, modify, or delete table data. They enable you to manipulate data in the same manner that you would in a table. The difference is that you can create a form that will limit the user to viewing only one record at a time. This helps the user to focus on the data being entered or modified and also provides for more reliable data entry. As an Access user, you will add, delete, and edit records in Form view. As the Access designer, you will create and edit the form structure.

A *query* is a question that you ask about the data in your database. For example, how many of our customers live in Boston? The answer is shown in the query results. A query can be used to display only records that meet certain conditions and only the fields that you require. In addition to helping you find and retrieve data that meets the conditions that you specify, you can use a query to update or delete records and to perform predefined or custom calculations with your data.

A *report* contains professional-looking formatted information from underlying tables or queries. Reports enable you to print the information in your database and are an effective way to present database information. You have control over the size and appearance of everything in a report. Access provides different views for designing, modifying, and running reports.

Two other object types, macros and modules, are used less frequently unless you are a power Access user. A *macro* object is a stored series of commands that carry out an action. You can create a macro to automate simple tasks by selecting an action from a list of macro actions. A *module* is similar to a macro, as it is an object that adds functionality to a database, but modules are written using the VBA (Visual Basic for Applications) programming language.

Figure 3 displays the different object types in Access with the foundation object—the table—in the center of the illustration. The purpose each object serves is explained underneath the object name. The flow of information between objects is indicated by single arrowhead arrows if the flow is one direction only. Two arrowhead arrows indicate that the flow goes both directions. For example, you can use forms to view, add, delete, or modify data from tables.

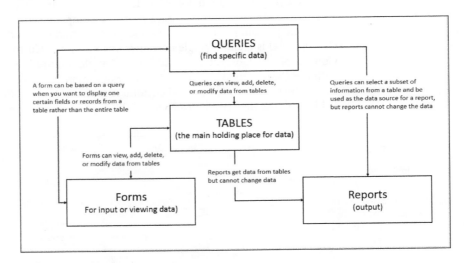

FIGURE 3 Object Types and Flow of Information

Examine the Access Interface

While Access includes the standard elements of the Microsoft Office applications interface such as the title bar, the Ribbon, the Home tab, the Backstage view, and scroll bars, it also includes elements unique to Access.

The Access Ribbon has five tabs that will always display, as well as contextual tabs that appear only when particular objects are open. The File tab leads to the Backstage view, which gives you access to a variety of database tools such as Save, Save As, Compact and Repair, Backup Database, and Print. The Home tab, the default Access tab, contains basic editing functions, such as cut and paste, filtering, find and replace, and most formatting actions. This tab also contains the features that enable you to work with record creation and deletion, totals, and spelling.

The Create tab contains all the tools used to create new objects in a database whereas the External Data tab contains all of the operations used to facilitate data import and export. Finally, the Database Tools tab contains the feature that enables users to create relationships between tables and enables use of the more advanced features of Access, such as setting relationships between tables, analyzing a table or query, and migrating data to SharePoint.

On the left side of the screen, you will see the Navigation Pane. The Navigation Pane organizes and lists all of the objects that are needed to make the current database function. You can open any object by double-clicking the object's name in the list. You can also open an object by right-clicking the object name and selecting Open from the shortcut menu. Right-clicking provides other options, such as renaming the object, cutting the object, and copying the object.

Most databases contain multiple tables, queries, forms, and reports. By default, the objects display in groups by object type in the Navigation Pane. If you wish, you can collapse the contents of an object group by clicking the group heading or the double arrows to the right of the group heading. To expand the contents of an object group that has been hidden, click the heading again or click the double arrows to the right of the group heading again. If you wish to change the way objects are grouped in the Navigation Pane, click the list arrow on the Navigation Pane title bar and select your preferred configuration of the available options.

By default, Access uses a Tabbed Documents interface. That means that each object that is open has its own tab beneath the Ribbon and to the right of the Navigation Pane. You can switch between open objects by clicking a tab to make that object active. Figure 4 shows the Access interface for the Northwind Traders database, which was introduced in the Case Study at the beginning of the chapter. The Navigation Pane is grouped by object type. The Tables and Reports groups in the Navigation Pane are expanded. The Table Tools contextual tab displays because the Employees table is open. The Employees table shows the records for nine employees. The employee records contain multiple fields about each employee, including the employee's Last Name, First Name, Hire Date, Region, and so on. Occasionally a field does not contain a value for a particular record. For example, one of the employees, Nancy Davolio, has not been assigned a title yet. The value of that field is missing. Access shows a blank cell when data is missing.

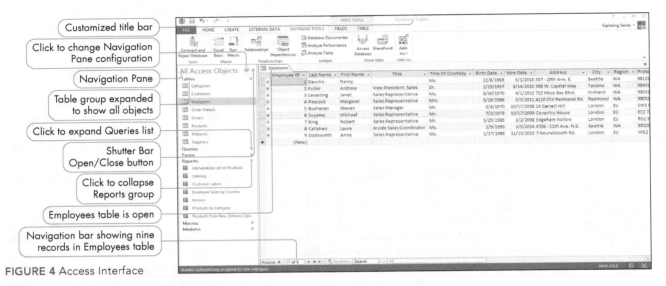

Customized title bar

Click to change Navigation Pane configuration

Navigation Pane

Table group expanded to show all objects

Click to expand Queries list

Shutter Bar Open/Close button

Click to collapse Reports group

Employees table is open

Navigation bar showing nine records in Employees table

FIGURE 4 Access Interface

Explore Access Views

Access provides two different ways to view a table: the Datasheet view and the Design view. To switch between views:

- Click the HOME tab and click View in the Views group to toggle between the current view and the previous view.
- Click the HOME tab, click the View arrow in the Views group, and then select the view you want to use.
- Right-click the object tab and select the view you want to use.
- Right-click the object in the Navigation Pane and select the view you want to use.
- Click one of the view shortcuts in the lower-right corner of the Access window.

The *Datasheet view* is a grid containing fields (columns) and records (rows), similar to an Excel spreadsheet. You can view, add, edit, and delete records in the Datasheet view. Figure 5 shows the Datasheet view for the Northwind Customers table. Each row contains a record for a specific customer. Click the *record selector* at the beginning of a row to select the record. Each column represents a field or one attribute about a customer. Click the *field selector*, or column heading, to select a column.

Customers table is open

Pencil in record selector indicates the record is being edited

Navigation bar indicates record 9 of 91 customers in the table is selected

Datasheet view

FIGURE 5 Customers Table in Datasheet View

The navigation bar at the bottom of Figure 5 shows that the Customers table has 91 records and that record number 9 is the current record. The vertical scroll bar on the right side of the window displays only when the table contains more records than can appear in the window at one time. Similarly, the horizontal scroll bar at the bottom of the window displays only when the table contains more fields than can appear in the window at one time.

The pencil symbol to the left of Record 9 indicates that the data in that record is being edited and that changes have not yet been saved. The pencil symbol disappears when you move to another record. It is important to understand that Access saves data automatically as soon as you move from one record to another. This may seem counterintuitive at first because other Office applications, such as Word and Excel, do not save changes and additions automatically.

Figure 6 shows the navigation buttons on the *navigation bar* that you use to move through the records in a table, query, or form. The buttons enable you to go to the first record, the previous record, the next record, or the last record. The button with the yellow asterisk is used to add a new (blank) record. You can also type a number directly into the current record field, and Access will take you to that record. Finally, the navigation bar enables you to find a record based on a single word. Type the word in the search box, and Access will locate the first record that contains the word.

Type in a single search word

Create a new (blank) record

Go to the last record

Go to the next record

Type in the record you want to go to

Go to the previous record

Go to the first record

FIGURE 6 Navigation Buttons

You can also use the Find command in the Find group on the Home tab to locate specific records within a table, form, or query. You can search for a single field or the entire record, match all or part of the selected field(s), move forward or back in a table, or specify a case-sensitive search. The Replace command can be used to substitute one value for another. Select Replace All if you want Access to automatically search for and replace every instance of a value without first checking with you. Be careful when using the Replace All option for global replacement, however, because unintended replacements are possible.

The *Design view* gives you a detailed view of the table's structure and is used to create and modify a table's design by specifying the fields it will contain, the fields' data types, and their associated properties. Data types define the type of data that will be stored in a field, such as short text, long text, numeric, currency, etc. For example, if you need to store the hire date of an employee, you would enter the field name Hire Date and select the Date/Time data type. The *field properties* define the characteristics of the fields in more detail. For example, for the field Hire Date, you could set a field property that requires a Short Date format.

Figure 7 shows the Design view for the Customers table. In the top portion, each row contains the field names, the data type, and an optional description for each field in the table. In the bottom portion, the Field Properties pane contains the properties (details) for each field. Click on a field, and the properties for that field will be displayed in the bottom portion of the Design view window.

Figure 7 also shows the primary key. The *primary key* is the field (or combination of fields) that uniquely identifies each record in a table. The CustomerID field is the primary key in the Customers table; it ensures that each record in the table can be distinguished from every other record. It also helps prevent the occurrence of duplicate records. Primary key fields may be numbers, letters, or a combination of both. In Figure 7, the primary key has an *AutoNumber* data type (a number that is generated by Access and is automatically incremented each time a record is added). Another example of a primary key is an automatically generated Employee ID.

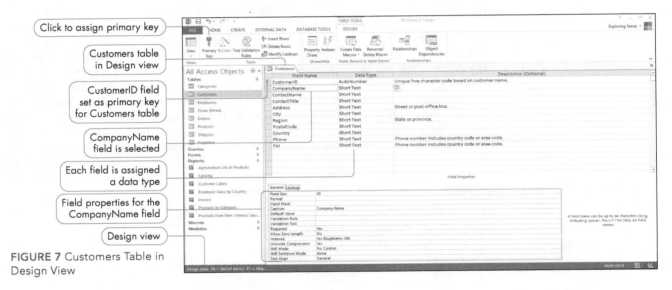

FIGURE 7 Customers Table in Design View

Open an Access File and Work with Content Security

STEP 1 ▷▷ When Access is first launched, the Backstage view displays. The left side of the view provides a list of databases you have recently used. Beneath the list of recently used databases is the Open Other Files option. Click Open Other Files to access the Open options. You will see a list of the places your account allows you to open a file from: a recent location, your SkyDrive account, your computer, or from any additional places you have added to your Places list. You can also add a new place by clicking the *Add a Place* option. If you select your SkyDrive or another place and the desired database is not in the recent list, you will need to click Browse to open the Open dialog box. Then you can locate and select the database and click Open.

If you are currently using Access and wish to open another database, do the following:

1. Click the FILE tab.
2. Click Open in Backstage view to access Open options.
3. Select the place where the database is stored.

Introduction to Access

4. Click Browse to open the Open dialog box.
5. Locate and select the database and click Open.

If you open a database from a location you have not designated as a trusted location or open a database that does not have a digital signature from a publisher you can trust, Access will display a message bar immediately below the Ribbon. The message bar displays a security warning designed to prevent you from opening a database that may contain harmful code that can be hidden in macros or VBA modules. Click the Enable Content button if you trust the database's source—it becomes a trusted location. After you click Enable Content, Access closes the database and reopens the file to enable the content. Access also adds the database to its list of trusted documents so you will not see the security message again. All content from this publisher and associated with this text can be trusted.

Using an Existing Database

Databases must be carefully managed to keep information accurate. Records need to be edited when changes occur and when new records are added, and records may need to be deleted on occasion. All of these processes are easily accomplished using Access. Managing a database also requires that you understand when data is saved and when you need to use the Save commands.

Understand the Difference Between Working in Storage and Memory

STEP 3>> The way Access performs its save function is different from the other Microsoft Office applications. Word, Excel, and PowerPoint all work primarily from memory. In those applications, your work is not automatically saved to your storage location. You must save your work. This could be catastrophic if you are working with a PowerPoint presentation and you forget to save it. If the power is lost, you may lose your presentation. Access, on the other hand, works primarily from storage. As you enter and update the data in an Access database, the changes are automatically saved to the storage location you specified when you saved the database. If a power failure occurs, you will lose only the changes to the record that you are currently editing.

When you make a change to a record's content in an Access table (for example, changing a customer's cell phone number), Access saves your changes as soon as you move the insertion point to a different record. However, you are required to save after you modify the design of a table, a query, a form, or a report. When you modify an object's design, such as widening a field display on the Customers form, and then close it, Access will prompt you with the message "Do you want to save changes to the design of form 'Customers'?" Click Yes to save your changes.

Also in Access, you can click Undo to reverse the most recent change (the phone number you just modified) to a single record immediately after making changes to that record. However, unlike other Office programs that enable multiple Undo steps, you cannot use Undo to reverse multiple edits in Access.

With an Access database file, several users can work in the same file at the same time. Databases are often located on company servers, making it easy to have multiple users working in the same database at the same time. As long as multiple users do not attempt to change the same record at the same time, Access will let these users access the database simultaneously. So one person can be adding records to the Customers table while another can be creating a query based on the Products table. Two users can even work on the same table as long as they are not working on the same record.

Add, Edit, and Delete Records

STEP 4 »

To add a new record, click New in the Records group on the Home tab or click *New (blank) record* on the navigation bar. In a table, you can also click the first column of the blank row beneath the last record. As soon as you begin typing, the asterisk record indicator changes to a pencil icon to show that you are in editing mode. Press Tab to move to the next column so that you can enter the data for the next field. Pressing Tab in the last column in the record saves the record and moves the insertion point to the next record. You can also press Shift+Enter at any time in the record to save the record. The easiest way to save the record is to press the up or down arrow on your keyboard, which moves you to another record. As soon as you move to another record Access automatically saves the changes to the record you created or changed.

To edit a record, tab to the field you want to modify and type the new data. When you start typing, you erase all existing data in the field because the entire field is selected. You can switch to Edit mode by pressing F2. In Edit mode, you will not automatically delete all the data in the field. Instead, you can position your insertion point and make the changes you want.

REFERENCE Keyboard Shortcuts for Entering Data

Keystroke	Result
Up arrow (↑)	Moves insertion point up one row.
Down arrow (↓)	Moves insertion point down one row.
Left arrow (←)	Moves insertion point left one field in the same row.
Right arrow (→)	Moves insertion point right one field in the same row.
Tab or Enter	Moves insertion point right one field in the same row.
Shift+Tab	Moves insertion point left one field in the same row.
Home	Moves insertion point to the first field in the current row.
End	Moves insertion point to the last field in the current row.
Page Up	Moves insertion point up one screen.
Page Down	Moves insertion point down one screen.
Ctrl+Home	Moves insertion point to the first field in the first row.
Ctrl+End	Moves insertion point to the last field in the last row.
Esc	Cancels any changes made in the current field while in Edit mode.
Ctrl+Z	Reverses the last edit.
Ctrl+semicolon (;)	Enters the current date.
Ctrl+Alt+Spacebar	Enters the default value of a field.
Ctrl+single quote	Enters the value from the same field in the previous record.
Ctrl+plus sign (+)	Moves to a new record row.
Ctrl+minus sign (−)	Deletes the current record.

STEP 5 »

To delete a record, click the row selector for the record you want to delete and click Delete in the Records group on the Home tab. You can also delete a selected record by pressing Delete on the keyboard, or by right-clicking the row selector and selecting Delete Record from the shortcut menu.

Introduction to Access

Save As, Compact and Repair, and Back Up Access Files

STEP 6 >>

The Backstage view gives you access to the Save As command. When you click the Save As command, you can choose the file type you want to save: the database or the current object. Having the option of saving the entire database or just a component of it distinguishes Access from Word, Excel, and PowerPoint. Those applications have only one thing being saved—the primary document, workbook, or presentation. Save Database As enables you to select whether you want to save the database in the default database format (Access 2007–2013 file format), in one of the earlier Access formats, or as a template. Save Object As enables you to make a copy of the current Access object or publish a copy of the object as a PDF or XPS file. A PDF or XPS file looks the same on most computers because these file types preserve the object's formatting. PDF and XPS files also have a small file size. You can also click Save on the Quick Access Toolbar to save an active object—clicking Save on the Quick Access Toolbar does not save the database.

To help you manage your database so that it operates efficiently and securely, Access provides two utilities to help protect the data within a database: ***Compact and Repair***, which reduces the size of the database, and ***Back Up Database***, which creates a duplicate copy of the database.

Databases have a tendency to expand with everyday use and may become corrupt, so Access provides the *Compact and Repair Database* utility. Entering data, creating queries, running reports, and adding and deleting objects will all cause a database file to expand. This growth may increase storage requirements and may also impact database performance. When you run the Compact and Repair utility, it creates a new database file behind the scenes and copies all the objects from the original database into the new one. As it copies the objects into the new file, Access removes temporary objects and unclaimed space due to deleted objects, which results in a smaller database file. *Compact and Repair* will also defragment a fragmented database file if needed. When the utility is finished copying the data, it deletes the original file and renames the new one with the same name as the original. This utility can also be used to repair a corrupt database. In most cases, only a small amount of data—the last record modified—will be lost during the repair process. You should compact your database every day. To compact and repair an open database, do the following:

1. Close all open objects in the database.
2. Click the FILE tab.
3. Click *Compact and Repair Database* in the Info options.

As an alternative, you can click the Database Tools tab and click *Compact and Repair Database* in the Tools group.

Databases Are Everywhere! • Access 2013

The Back Up Database utility makes a copy of the entire database to protect your database from loss or damage. Imagine what would happen to a firm that loses the orders placed but not shipped, a charity that loses the list of donor contributions, or a hospital that loses the digital records of its patients. Making backups is especially important when you have multiple users working with the database. When you use the Back Up Database utility, Access provides a file name for the backup that uses the same file name as the database you are backing up, an underscore, and the current date. This makes it easy for you to keep track of databases by the date they were created. To back up a database, do the following:

1. Click the FILE tab and click Save As.
2. Click Save Database As under File Types, if necessary.
3. Click Back Up Database under the Advanced group.
4. Click Save As. Revise the location and file name if you want to change either and click Save.

In Hands-On Exercise 1, you will work with the Northwind Traders database discussed in the Case Study at the beginning of the chapter. You open the database and examine the interface and Access views, organize information, work with records, and save, compact, repair, and back up the database.

Quick Concepts

1. Name the six objects in an Access database and briefly describe the purpose of each.
2. What is the difference between Datasheet view and Design view in a table?
3. What is meant by the statement "Access works from storage"?
4. What is the purpose of the *Compact and Repair* utility?

Hands-On Exercises

Watch the Video for this Hands-On Exercise!

MyITLab®
HOE1 Training

1 Databases Are Everywhere!

Northwind purchases food items from suppliers around the world and sells them to restaurants and specialty food shops. Northwind depends on the data stored in its Access database to process orders and make daily decisions. In your new position with Northwind Traders, you need to spend time getting familiar with the Access database. You will open Northwind's database, examine the Access interface, review the existing objects in the database, and explore Access views. You will add, edit, and delete records using both tables and forms. Finally, you will compact and repair, and back up the database.

Skills covered: Open an Access File and Work with Content Security • Examine the Access Interface, Explore Access Views, Organize Information in a Database, and Recognize Access Objects and Edit a Record and Understand the Difference Between Working in Storage and Memory • Add a Record • Delete a Record • Save As, Compact and Repair, and Back Up the Database

STEP 1 ≫ OPEN AN ACCESS FILE AND WORK WITH CONTENT SECURITY

This exercise introduces you to the Northwind Traders database. You will use this database to learn the fundamentals of working with database files. Refer to Figure 8 as you complete Step 1.

FIGURE 8 Message Bar Displaying Security Warning

a. Open Access, click **Open Other Files**, click **Computer**, and then click **Browse**. Navigate to the folder location designated by your instructor. Click *a01h1Traders* and click **Open**.

b. Click the **FILE tab**, click **Save As**, click **Save Database As**, and then verify *Access Database* is selected under *Database File Types*. Click **Save As** and save the file as **a01h1Traders_LastFirst**.

When you save files, use your last and first names. For example, as the Access author, I would save my database as *a01h1traders_KrebsCynthia*. The Security Warning message bar appears below the Ribbon, indicating that some database content is disabled.

c. Click **Enable Content** on the Security Warning message bar.

When you open an Access file from the student files associated with this text, you will need to enable the content. You may be confident of the trustworthiness of the files for this text. Keep the database open for the rest of the exercise.

STEP 2 ≫ EXAMINE THE ACCESS INTERFACE, EXPLORE ACCESS VIEWS, ORGANIZE INFORMATION IN A DATABASE, AND RECOGNIZE ACCESS OBJECTS

Now that you have opened Northwind Traders, you examine the Navigation Pane, objects, and views to become familiar with these fundamental Access features. Refer to Figure 9 as you complete Step 2.

Step e: Tabs showing open table objects

Step a: Expanded Tables group

Step f: Shutter Bar Open/Close button

Step h: Collapsed Forms group

Step g: Expanded Reports group

FIGURE 9 Access Navigation Pane and Open Objects

a. Scroll through the Navigation Pane and note the Access objects listed under each expanded group.

The Tables group and the Forms group are expanded, displaying all of the tables and forms objects. The Queries, Reports, Macros, and Modules groups are collapsed so that the objects in those groups are not displayed.

b. Right-click the **Customers table** in the Navigation Pane and select **Open**.

The Customers table opens. The Customers tab displays below the Ribbon indicating the table object is open. The data contained in the table displays. Each customer's record displays on a table row. The columns of the table display the fields that comprise the records. You are viewing the table in Datasheet view.

c. Click **View** in the Views group on the HOME tab.

The view of the Customers table switches to Design view. The top portion of the view displays each field that comprises a customer record, the field's data type, and an optional description of what the field should contain. The bottom portion of the view displays the field properties (attributes) for the selected field.

d. Click **View** in the Views group on the HOME tab again.

Because View is a toggle button, your view returns to the Datasheet view, which resembles an Excel worksheet.

e. Double-click **Employees** in the Navigation Pane Tables group and double-click **Products** in the same location.

The tabs for three table objects display below the Ribbon: Customers, Employees, and Products.

f. Click the **Shutter Bar Open/Close button** on the title bar of the Navigation Pane to contract the Navigation Pane. Click the button again to expand the Navigation Pane.

The Shutter Bar Open/Close button toggles to allow you to view more in the open object window, or to enable you to view your database objects.

g. Scroll down in the Navigation Pane and click **Reports**.

The Reports group expands, and all report objects display.

h. Click the arrows to the right of Forms in the Navigation Pane.

The Forms group collapses and individual form objects no longer display.

Hands-On Exercise 1

EDIT A RECORD AND UNDERSTAND THE DIFFERENCE BETWEEN WORKING IN STORAGE AND MEMORY

You need to learn to edit the data in the Northwind database, because data can change. For example, employees will change their address and phone numbers when they move, and customers will change their order data from time to time. Refer to Figure 10 as you complete Step 3.

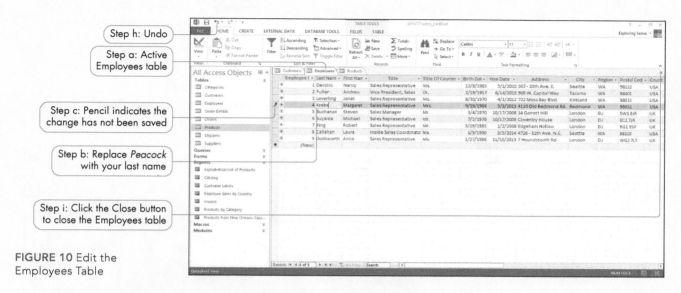

Step h: Undo

Step a: Active Employees table

Step c: Pencil indicates the change has not been saved

Step b: Replace *Peacock* with your last name

Step i: Click the Close button to close the Employees table

FIGURE 10 Edit the Employees Table

a. Click the **Employees tab** to activate the Employees table.

b. Click the **Last Name field** in the fourth row. Double-click **Peacock**; the entire name highlights. Type your last name to replace *Peacock*.

Your last name replaces Peacock. For example, as the Access author, my last name, Krebs, replaces Peacock.

c. Press **Tab** to move to the next field in the fourth row. Replace *Margaret* with your first name and press **Tab**.

Your first name replaces Margaret. For example, as the Access author, my first name, Cynthia, replaces Margaret. You have made changes to two fields in the same record. The pencil symbol in the row selector box indicates that the record has not yet been saved.

d. Click **Undo** on the Quick Access Toolbar.

Your first and last names revert back to *Margaret Peacock* because you have not yet left the record.

e. Type your first and last names again to replace *Margaret Peacock*. Press **Tab**.

You should now be in the title field and your title, *Sales Representative*, is selected. The record has not been saved, as indicated by the pencil symbol in the row selector box.

f. Click anywhere in the third row where Janet Leverling's data is stored.

The pencil symbol disappears, indicating your changes have been saved.

g. Click the **Address field** in the first record, Nancy Davolio's record. Select the entire address and then type **4004 East Morningside Dr**. Click anywhere on the second record, Andrew Fuller's record.

h. Click **Undo**.

Nancy Davolio's address reverts back to 507- 20th Ave. E. However, the Undo command is now faded. You can no longer undo the change that you made replacing Margaret Peacock's name with your own.

Hands-On Exercise 1

i. Click the **Close (X) button** at the top of the table to close the Employees table.

> The Employees table closes. You are not prompted to save your changes; they have already been saved for you because Access works in storage, not memory. If you reopen the Employees table, you will see your name in place of Margaret Peacock's name.

> **TROUBLESHOOTING:** If you click the Close (X) button on the title bar at the top right of the window and accidentally close the database, locate the file and double-click it to reopen the file.

STEP 4 ➤➤ ADD A RECORD

You need to add new products to the Northwind database because the company is adding a new line of products. Refer to Figure 11 as you complete Step 4.

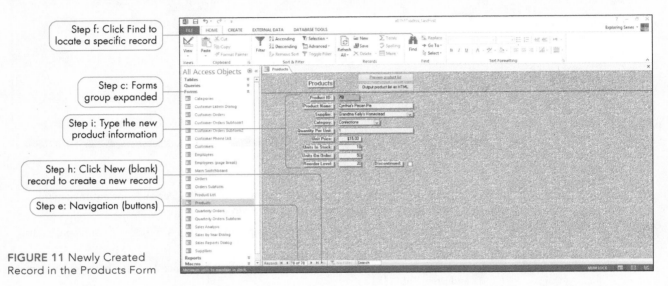

Step f: Click Find to locate a specific record

Step c: Forms group expanded

Step i: Type the new product information

Step h: Click New (blank) record to create a new record

Step e: Navigation (buttons)

FIGURE 11 Newly Created Record in the Products Form

a. Right-click the **Customers tab** and click **Close All**.

b. Click the **Tables group** in the Navigation Pane to collapse it and collapse the **Reports group**.

c. Click the **Forms group** in the Navigation Pane to expand the list of available forms.

d. Double-click the **Products form** to open it.

e. Locate the navigation buttons at the bottom of the Access window. Practice moving from one record to the next. Click **Next record** and click **Last record**; click **Previous record** and click **First record**.

f. Click **Find** in the Find group on the HOME tab, type **Grandma** in the **Find What box**, click the **Match arrow**, and then select **Any Part of Field**. Click **Find Next**.

> You should see the data for Grandma's Boysenberry Spread. Selecting the Any Part of the Field option will return a match even if it is contained in the middle of a word.

g. Close the Find dialog box.

h. Click **New (blank) record** on the navigation bar.

Hands-On Exercise 1

i. Enter the following information for a new product.

Field Name	Value to Type
Product Name	*Your name*'s Pecan Pie
Supplier	Grandma Kelly's Homestead (click the arrow to select from the list of Suppliers)
Category	Confections (click the arrow to select from the list of Categories)
Quantity Per Unit	1
Unit Price	15.00
Units in Stock	18
Units on Order	50
Reorder Level	20
Discontinued	No (leave the check box unchecked)

As soon as you begin typing in the product name box, Access assigns a Product ID, in this case 78, to the record. The Product ID is used as the primary key in the Products table.

j. Click anywhere on the Pecan Pie record you just entered. Click the **FILE tab**, click **Print**, and then click **Print Preview**.

The first four records display in the Print Preview.

k. Click **Last Page** in the navigation bar and click **Previous Page** to show the new record you entered.

The beginning of the Pecan Pie record is now visible. The record continues on the next page.

l. Click **Close Print Preview** in the Close Preview group.

m. Close the Products form.

STEP 5 ⟫ DELETE A RECORD

To help you understand how Access stores data, you verify that the new product is in the Products table. You also attempt to delete a record. Refer to Figure 12 as you complete Step 5.

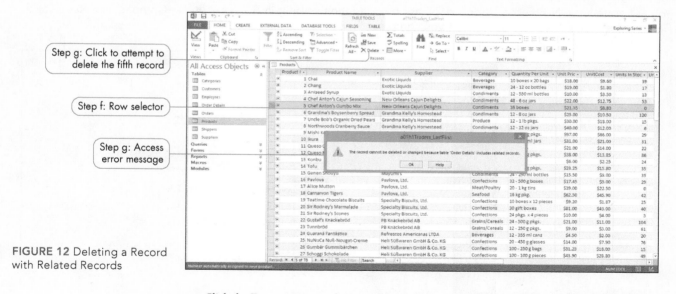

FIGURE 12 Deleting a Record with Related Records

a. Click the **Forms group** in the Navigation Pane to collapse it and expand the **Tables group**.

b. Double-click the **Products table** to open it.

c. Click **Last record** in the navigation bar.

The Pecan Pie record you entered in the Products form is listed as the last record in the Products table. The Products form was created from the Products table. Your newly created record, Pecan Pie, is stored in the Products table even though you added it using the form.

Hands-On Exercise 1

d. Navigate to the fifth record in the table, *Chef Anton's Gumbo Mix.*

e. Use the horizontal scroll bar to scroll right until you see the Discontinued field.

   The check mark in the Discontinued check box tells you that this product has been discontinued.

f. Click the **row selector** to the left of the fifth record.

   The row highlights with a red-colored border to show that it is selected.

g. Click **Delete** in the Records group and read the error message.

   The error message that displays tells you that you cannot delete this record because the table 'Order Details' has related records. (Customers ordered this product in the past.) Even though the product is now discontinued and no stock remains, it cannot be deleted from the Products table because related records exist in the Order Detail table.

h. Click **OK.**

i. Navigate to the last record and click the **row selector** to highlight the entire row.

j. Click **Delete** in the Records group. Read the warning.

   The warning box that appears tells you that this action cannot be undone. Although this product can be deleted because it was just entered and no orders were created for it, you do not want to delete the record.

k. Click **No.** You do not want to delete this record. Close the Products table.

TROUBLESHOOTING: If you clicked Yes and deleted the record, return to Step i. Reenter the information for this record. You will need it later in the lesson.

STEP 6 ≫ SAVE AS, COMPACT AND REPAIR, AND BACK UP THE DATABASE

You will protect the Northwind Traders database by using the two built-in Access utilities—Compact and Repair and Back Up Database. Refer to Figure 13 as you complete Step 6.

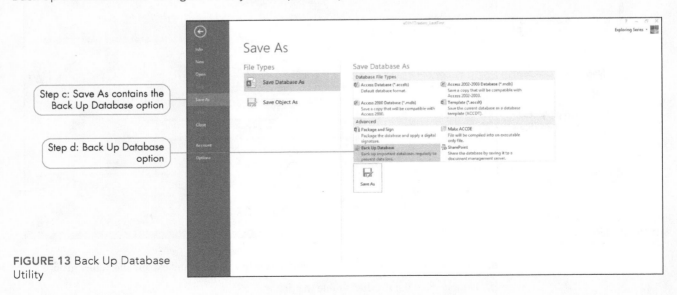

FIGURE 13 Back Up Database Utility

a. Click the **FILE tab** to open the Backstage view.

b. Click Compact & Repair Database.

   Using the *Compact and Repair* utility helps improve the performance of your database.

Hands-On Exercise 1

266

c. Click the **FILE tab**, click **Save As**, and then click **Save Database As** under *File Types*, if necessary.

d. Double-click **Back Up Database** under the Advanced group to open the **Save As** dialog box.

The backup utility assigns the default name by adding a date to your file name.

e. Verify the *Save in* folder displays the location where you want your file saved and click **Save**.

You just created a backup of the database after completing Hands-On Exercise 1. The original database *a01h1traders_LastFirst* remains onscreen.

f. Keep the database open if you plan to continue with Hands-On Exercise 2. If not, close the database and exit Access.

Sorts and Filters

Access provides you with many tools that you can use to change the order of information and to identify and extract only the data needed at the moment. For example, you might need to display information by customer name in alphabetical order. Or you might need to know which suppliers are located in New Orleans or which customers have outstanding orders that were placed in the last seven days. You might use that information to identify possible disruptions to product deliveries or customers who may need a telephone call to let them know the status of their orders.

In this section, you will learn how to sort information and to isolate records in a table based on certain criteria.

Sorting Table Data on One or Multiple Fields

You can change the order of information by sorting one or more fields. A *sort* lists records in a specific sequence, such as alphabetically by last name or by ascending EmployeeID. To sort a table on one criteria, do the following:

STEP 4 >>

1. Click in the field that you want to use to sort the records.
2. Click Ascending or Descending in the Sort & Filter group on the HOME tab.

Ascending sorts a list of text data in alphabetical order or a numeric list in lowest to highest order. *Descending* sorts a list of text data in reverse alphabetical order or a numeric list in highest to lowest order. Figure 14 shows the Customers table for a bank sorted in ascending order by state.

Click Ascending to apply an A–Z sort

Click Remove Sort to undo the A–Z sort

Customers sorted in ascending order by State

FIGURE 14 Customers Table Sorted by State

Access can sort records by more than one field. Access sorts multiple criteria by first sorting the column on the left. The column immediately to the right of that column is sorted next. Because of this, you must arrange your columns in this order. To move a column, select the column and hold down the left mouse button. A heavy black bar appears to the left of the column. Drag the column to the position where you want it for the multiple sort.

Creating, Modifying, and Removing Filters

In Hands-On Exercise 1, you added Pecan Pie to the Products table with a category of Confections, but you also saw many other products. Suppose you wanted to see a list of just the products in the Confections category. To obtain this list, you would open the Products table in Datasheet view and create a filter. A *filter* displays a subset of records based on specified criteria. A *criterion* (or criteria, plural) is a number, a text phrase, or an expression used to select records from a table. Therefore, to view a list of all Confections, you would need to filter the Category field of the Products table using Confections as the criterion.

You can use filters to analyze data quickly. Applying a filter does not delete any records; filters only *hide* records that do not match the criteria. Two types of filters are discussed in this section: *Filter by Selection* and *Filter by Form*.

Use, Modify, and Remove a Filter

Filter by Selection displays only the records that match a criterion you select. To use *Filter by Selection*, do the following:

STEP 1
1. Click in any field that contains the criterion on which you want to filter.
2. Click Selection in the Sort & Filter group on the HOME tab.
3. Select *Equals "criterion"* from the list of options.

Figure 15 displays a Customers table with 10 records. The records in the table are displayed in sequence according to the CustomerID, which is also the primary key (the field or combination of fields that uniquely identifies a record). The navigation bar at the bottom indicates that the active record is the first row in the table. *Owner* in the Job Title field is selected.

Click Selection to use *Filter by Selection*

Criterion set to Equals "Owner"

All job titles are displayed

10 customers are showing

FIGURE 15 Unfiltered Customers Table

Figure 16 displays a filtered view of the Customers table, showing records with the job title *Owner*. The navigation bar shows that this is a filtered list containing 4 records matching the criteria. (The Customers table still contains the original 10 records, but only 4 records are visible with the filter applied.)

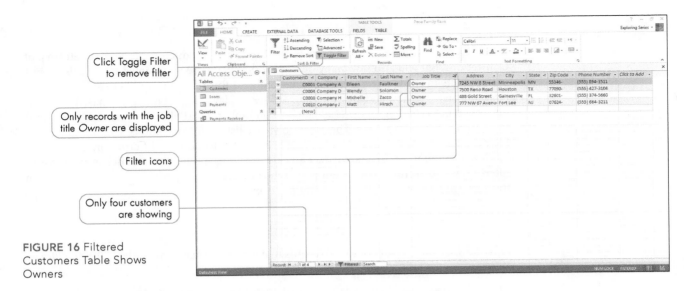

Click Toggle Filter to remove filter

Only records with the job title *Owner* are displayed

Filter icons

Only four customers are showing

FIGURE 16 Filtered Customers Table Shows Owners

Filter by Form is a more versatile method of selecting data because it enables you to display table records based on multiple criteria. When you use *Filter by Form*, all of the records are hidden and Access creates a blank form in a design grid. You see only field names with an arrow in the first field. Click on other fields and an arrow displays. Click an arrow and a list opens for you to use to specify your criterion. You can specify as many criteria as you need. When you apply the filter, Access displays the records that meet your criteria.

STEP 3 》

An advantage of using this filter method is that you can specify AND and OR logical operators. If you use the AND operator, a record is included in the results if all the criteria are true. If you use the OR operator, a record is included if at least one criterion is true. Another advantage of *Filter by Form* is that you can use a comparison operator. A **comparison operator** is used to evaluate the relationship between two quantities. For example, a comparison operator can determine if quantities are equal or not equal. If they are not equal, a comparison operator determines which one is greater than the other. Comparison operator symbols include: equal (=), not equal (<>), greater than (>), less than (<), greater than or equal to (>=), and less than or equal to (<=). To use *Filter by Form*, do the following:

1. Click Advanced in the Sort & Filter group on the HOME tab.
2. Click *Filter by Form*.
3. Click in the field you want to use as a criterion. Click the arrow to select the criterion from existing data.
4. Add additional criterion and comparison operators as needed.
5. Click Toggle Filter in the Sort & Filter group on the HOME tab to apply the filter.

In Figure 17, the Northwind Traders Products table is open. *Filter by Form* is set to select products with an inventory (Units in Stock) level greater than 30 (>30).

Introduction to Access

Click Advanced to access *Filter by Form*

Filter By Form

Filter set to display products with more than 30 units in stock

Add criteria by clicking the Or tab

FIGURE 17 Filter by Form Design Grid

The sort and filter operations can be done in any order; that is, you can sort a table first and apply a filter. Conversely, you can filter a table first to show only selected records and sort the filtered table to display the records in a certain order. It does not matter which operation is performed first.

STEP 2>> You can also filter the table further by applying a second, third, or more criteria. For example, in the Products table shown in Figure 17, you can apply *Filter by Form* by clicking in the Supplier cell, selecting Exotic Liquids from the list, and then applying the filter. Then you could click Beverages and apply *Filter by Selection* to display all the beverages supplied by Exotic Liquids. You can also click Toggle Filter at any time to remove all filters and display all the records in the table. Filters are a temporary method for examining table data. If you close the filtered table and reopen it, the filter will be removed and all of the records will be restored.

TIP Use Undo After Applying a Filter by Selection

You can apply one *Filter by Selection* to a table, and then a second, and then a third to display certain records based on three criteria. If you click Toggle Filter, all three filters will be removed. What if you only want the last filter removed? Click Undo to remove only the last filter. Click Undo again and remove the second-to-last filter. This feature will help you apply and remove multiple filters, one at a time.

Quick Concepts

1. What are the benefits of sorting the records in a table?

2. What is the purpose of creating a filter?

3. What is the difference between *Filter by Selection* and *Filter by Form*?

4. What is a comparison operator and how is it used in a filter?

Hands-On Exercises

Watch the Video
for this Hands-
On Exercise!

MyITLab®
HOE2 Training

2 Sorts and Filters

The sales manager at Northwind Traders needs quick answers to her questions about customer orders. You use the Access database to filter tables to answer these questions, then sort the records based on the manager's needs.

Skills covered: Use Filter by Selection with an Equal Condition • Use Filter by Selection with a Contains Condition • Use Filter by Form with a Comparison Operator • Sort a Table

STEP 1 ≫ USE FILTER BY SELECTION WITH AN EQUAL CONDITION

The sales manager asks for a list of customers who live in London. You use *Filter by Selection* with an equal condition to locate these customers. Refer to Figure 18 as you complete Step 1.

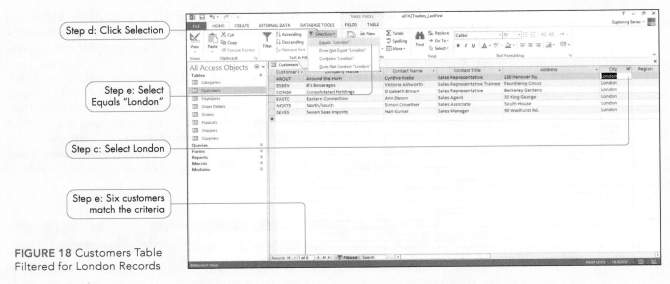

FIGURE 18 Customers Table Filtered for London Records

a. Open the *a01h1traders_LastFirst* database if you closed it after the last Hands-On Exercise and save it as **a01h2Traders_LastFirst**, changing *h1* to *h2*.

> **TROUBLESHOOTING:** If you make any major mistakes in this exercise, you can close the file, open *a01h1Traders_LastFirst* again, and then start this exercise over.

b. Double-click the **Customers table** in the Navigation Pane under *Tables*, navigate to record 4, and then replace *Thomas Hardy* with your name in the Contact Name field.

c. Scroll right until the City field is visible. The fourth record has a value of *London* in the City field. Click the field to select it.

d. Click **Selection** in the Sort & Filter group on the HOME tab.

e. Select **Equals "London"** from the menu. Note that six customers were located.

The navigation bar display shows that six records that meet the *London* criterion are available. The other records in the Customers table are hidden. The Filtered icon also displays on the navigation bar, indicating that the Customers table has been filtered.

f. Click **Toggle Filter** in the Sort & Filter group to remove the filter.

g. Click **Toggle Filter** again to reset the filter. Leave the Customers table open for the next step.

STEP 2 ≫ USE FILTER BY SELECTION WITH A CONTAINS CONDITION

The sales manager asks you to narrow the list of London customers so that it displays only Sales Representatives. To accomplish this task, you add a second layer of filtering using the *Filter by Selection* feature. Refer to Figure 19 as you complete Step 2.

FIGURE 19 Customers in London with the Contact Title *Sales Representative*

a. Click in any field in the Contact Title column that contains the value *Sales Representative*.

b. Click **Selection** in the Sort & Filter group and click **Contains "Sales Representative"**. Locate your name in the filtered table. Compare your results to those shown in Figure 19.

Three records match the criteria you set. You have applied a second layer of filtering to the customers in London. The second layer further restricts the display to only those customers who have the words *Sales Representative* contained in their titles.

> **TROUBLESHOOTING:** If you do not see the record for Victoria Ashworth, you selected *Equals "Sales Representative"* instead of *Contains "Sales Representative"*. Repeat steps a and b, making sure you select *Contains "Sales Representative"*.

c. Close the Customers table. Click **Yes** if a dialog box asks if you want to save the design changes to the Customers table.

STEP 3 ≫ USE FILTER BY FORM WITH A COMPARISON OPERATOR

You are asked to provide a list of records that do not match just one set of criteria. You are asked to provide a list of all extended prices less than $50 for a specific sales representative. Use *Filter by Form* to provide the information when two or more criteria are needed. You also preview the results in Print Preview to see how the list would print. Refer to Figure 20 as you complete Step 3.

Hands-On Exercise 2

273

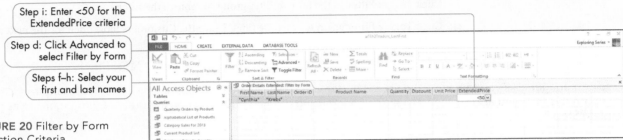

Step i: Enter <50 for the ExtendedPrice criteria

Step d: Click Advanced to select Filter by Form

Steps f–h: Select your first and last names

FIGURE 20 Filter by Form Selection Criteria

a. Click the **Tables group** in the Navigation Pane to collapse the listed tables.

b. Click the **Queries group** in the Navigation Pane to expand the list of available queries.

c. Locate and double-click the **Order Details Extended query** to open it.

This query contains information about orders. It has fields containing information about the sales person, the Order ID, the product name, the unit price, quantity ordered, the discount given, and an extended price. The extended price is a field used to total order information.

d. Click **Advanced** in the Sort & Filter group and select **Filter by Form** from the list.

All of the records are now hidden, and you see only field names and an arrow in the first field. Although you are applying *Filter by Form* to a query, you can use the same process as applying *Filter by Form* to a table. You are able to enter more than one criterion using *Filter by Form*.

e. Click in the first row under the First Name field, if necessary.

An arrow appears at the right of the box.

f. Click the **First Name arrow**.

A list of all available first names appears. Your name should be on the list. Figure 20 shows *Cynthia Krebs*, which replaced Margaret Peacock in Hands-On Exercise 1.

> **TROUBLESHOOTING:** If you do not see your name and you do see Margaret on the list, you probably skipped steps in Hands-On Exercise 1. Close the query without saving changes, return to the first Hands-On Exercise, and then rework it, making sure not to omit any steps. Then you can return to this location and work the remainder of this Hands-On Exercise.

g. Select your first name from the list.

h. Click in the first row under the Last Name field to reveal the arrow. Locate and select your last name by clicking it.

i. Scroll right until you see the Extended Price field. Click in the first row under the Extended Price field and type **<50**.

This will select all of the items that you ordered where the total was under $50. You ignore the arrow and type the expression needed.

j. Click **Toggle Filter** in the Sort & Filter group.

You have specified which records to include and have executed the filtering by clicking Toggle Filter. You should have 31 records that match the criteria you specified.

k. Click the **FILE tab**, click **Print**, and then click **Print Preview**.

You instructed Access to preview the filtered query results. The preview displays the query title as a heading. The current filter is applied, as well as page numbers.

l. Click **Close Print Preview** in the Close Preview group.

m. Close the Order Details Extended query. Click **Yes** if a dialog box asks if you want to save your changes.

Hands-On Exercise 2

TIP	**Deleting Filter by Form Criterion**

While working with *Filter by Selection* or *Filter by Form*, you may inadvertently save a filter. To view a saved filter, open the table or query that you suspect may have a saved filter. Click Advanced in the Sort & Filter group and click *Filter by Form*. If criteria appear in the form, then a filter has been saved. To delete a saved filter, toggle the filter, click Advanced, and then click Close All Filters. Close and save the table or query.

STEP 4 ≫ SORT A TABLE

The Sales Manager is pleased with your work; however, she would like some of the information to appear in a different order. You will now sort the records in the Customers table using the manager's new criteria. Refer to Figure 21 as you complete Step 4.

> Step i and j: Records are sorted by Country, then City

> Step c: Shutter Bar Open/Close button

> Steps i and j: Click Ascending to sort by Country, then City

FIGURE 21 Customers Table Sorted by Country, Then City

a. Click the **Queries group** in the Navigation Pane to collapse the listed queries.

b. Click the **Tables group** in the Navigation Pane to expand the list of available tables and double-click the **Customers table** to open it.

   This table contains information about customers. The table is sorted in alphabetical order by Company Name.

c. Click the **Shutter Bar Open/Close button** in the Navigation Pane to close the Navigation Pane.

   It will be easier to locate fields in the Customer table if the Navigation Pane is closed.

d. Click any field in the Customer ID column, the first field in the table. Click **Descending** in the Sort & Filter group on the HOME tab.

   Sorting in descending order on a character field produces a reverse alphabetical order.

e. Scroll right until you can see both the Country and City fields.

f. Click the **Country column heading**.

   The entire column is selected.

g. Click the **Country column heading** again and hold down the **left mouse button**.

   A thick dark blue line displays on the left edge of the Country field.

h. Check to make sure that you see the thick blue line. Drag the **Country field** to the left until the thick black line moves between the City and Region fields. Release the mouse and the Country field position moves to the right of the City field.

You moved the Country field next to the City field so that you can easily sort the table based on both fields. In order to sort by two or more fields, they need to be placed adjacent to each other.

i. Click any city name in the City field and click **Ascending** in the Sort & Filter group.

The City field displays the cities in alphabetical order.

j. Click any country name in the Country field and click **Ascending**.

The countries are sorted in alphabetical order. The cities within each country also are sorted alphabetically. For example, the customer in Graz, Austria, is listed before the customer in Salzburg, Austria.

k. Close the Customers table. Click **Yes** to save the changes to the design of the table.

l. Click the **Shutter Bar Open/Close button** in the Navigation Pane to open the Navigation Pane.

m. Click the **FILE tab** to open the Backstage view and click **Compact & Repair Database**.

n. Click the **FILE tab**, click **Save As**, and then click **Save Database As** in File Types, if necessary.

o. Double-click **Back Up Database** under the Advanced group to open the Save As dialog box.

p. Verify the *Save in* folder displays the location where you want your file saved and click **Save**.

q. Close the database and submit based on your instructor's directions. Leave Access open if you plan to continue with Hands-On Exercise 3. If not, exit Access.

Access Versus Excel, and Relational Databases

Both Access and Excel contain powerful tools that enable you to extract the information you need and arrange it in a way that makes it easy to analyze. An important part of becoming a proficient Office user is learning which of these applications to use to accomplish a task.

In this section, you will learn how to decide whether to use Access or Excel by examining the distinct advantages of each application. Ideally, the type of data and the type of functionality you require should determine which program will work best.

Knowing When to Use Access or Excel to Manage Data

You are probably familiar with working in an Excel spreadsheet. You type the column headings, enter the data, perhaps add a formula or two, and then add totals to the bottom. Once the data has been entered, you can apply a filter, sort the data, or start all over—similar to what you learned to do in Access with filters. It is true that you can accomplish many of the same tasks using either Excel or Access. Although the two programs have much in common, they each have distinct advantages. How do you choose whether to use Access or Excel? The choice you make may ultimately depend on how well you know Access. Users who know Excel only are more likely to use a spreadsheet even if a database would be better. When database features are used in Excel, they are generally used on data that is in one table. When the data is better suited to be on two or more tables, then using Access is preferable. Learning how to use Access will be beneficial to you because it will enable you to work more efficiently with large groups of data.

Select the Software to Use

A contact list (for example, name, address, phone number) created in Excel may serve your needs just fine in the beginning. Each time you enter a new contact, you can add another row to the bottom of your worksheet. You can sort the list by last name for easier look-up of names. In Excel, you can easily move an entire column, insert a new column, or copy and paste data from one cell to another. This is the "ease of use" characteristic of Excel.

If you need to expand the information in Excel to keep track of each time you contacted someone on your contact list, you may need an additional worksheet. This additional sheet would only list the contacts whom you have contacted and some information about the nature of the contact. Which contact was it? When was the contact made? Was it a phone contact or a face-to-face meeting? As you track these entries, your worksheet will contain a reference to the first worksheet using the contact name.

If a contact is deleted on the first worksheet, that contact's information will still remain on the second worksheet, unless someone remembers to remove it. Similarly, information could be added about a contact on the second worksheet without the contact being officially entered into the first worksheet. As the quantity and complexity of the data increase, the need to organize your data logically also increases.

Access provides built-in tools to help organize data better than Excel. One tool that helps Access organize data is the ability to create relationships between tables. A *relationship* is a connection between two tables using a field that is common to the two tables. The benefit of a relationship is the ability to efficiently combine data from related tables for the purpose of creating queries, forms, and reports. Relationships are the reason Access is referred to as a relational database.

Use Access

STEP 1 » Use Access to manage data when you:

- Require multiple related tables to store your data.
- Have a large amount of data.
- Need to connect to and retrieve data from external databases, such as Microsoft SQL Server.
- Need to group, sort, and total data based on various parameters.
- Have an application that requires multiple users to connect to one data source at the same time.

Use Excel

Use Excel to manage data when you:

- Need only one worksheet to handle all of your data.
- Have mostly numeric data—for example, you need to maintain an expense statement.
- Require subtotals and totals in your worksheet.
- Want to primarily run a series of "what if" scenarios on your data.
- Need to create complex charts and/or graphs.

Understanding Relational Power

In the previous section, we compared Excel worksheets to Access relational databases. Access has the ability to create relationships between two tables, whereas Excel does not. Access is known as a *relational database management system* (RDBMS); using an RDBMS, you can manage groups of data (tables) and set rules (relationships) between tables. When relational databases are designed properly, users can easily combine data from multiple tables to create queries, forms, and reports.

Good database design begins with grouping data into the correct tables. This practice, known as *normalization*, will take time to learn, but over time you will begin to understand the fundamentals. The design of a relational database management system is illustrated in Figure 22, which shows the table design of the Northwind Traders database. The tables have been created, the field names have been added, and the data types have been set. The diagram shows the relationships that were created between tables using *join lines*. Join lines enable you to create a relationship between two tables using a common field. Figure 22 also shows the join lines between related tables as a series of lines connecting common fields. For example, the Suppliers table is joined to the Products table using the common field SupplierID. If you examine some of the connections, you will see that the EmployeeID is linked to the Orders table by a join line. This means that you can produce a report displaying all orders for a customer and the employee who entered the order. The Orders table is joined to the Order Details table where the OrderID is the common field. The Products table is joined to the Order Details table where the ProductID is the common field. These table connections enable you to query the database for information stored in multiple tables. This feature gives the manager the ability to ask questions like "How many different beverages were shipped last week?" or "What was the total revenue generated from seafood orders last year?"

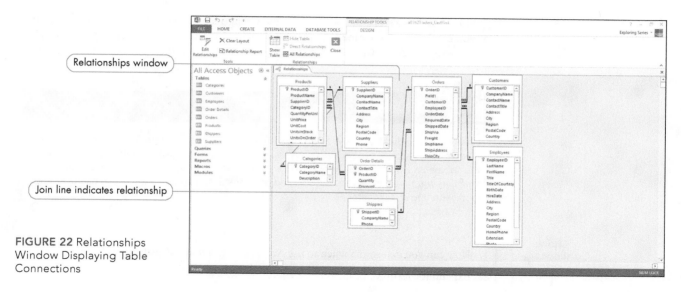

Relationships window

Join line indicates relationship

FIGURE 22 Relationships Window Displaying Table Connections

Use the Relationships Window

Relationships are set in the Relationships window by the database developer after the tables have been created but before any sample data is entered. The most common method of connecting two tables is to connect the primary key from one table to the foreign key of another. A *foreign key* is a field in one table that is also the primary key of another table. In the previous figure, Figure 22, the SupplierID (primary key) in the Suppliers table is joined to the SupplierID (foreign key) in the Products table. Remember, a primary key is a field that uniquely identifies each record in a table.

To create a relationship between two tables, follow these guidelines:

1. Click Relationships in the Relationships group on the DATABASE TOOLS tab.
2. Add the two tables that you want to join together to the Relationships window.
3. Drag the common field (e.g., SupplierID) from the primary table (e.g., Suppliers) onto the common field (e.g., SupplierID) of the related table (e.g., Products). The data types of the common fields must be the same.
4. Check the Enforce Referential Integrity check box.
5. Close the Relationships window.

STEP 2 | **TIP** **View Join Lines**

Databases with many tables with relationships may make it difficult to see the join lines between tables. Tables may be repositioned to make it easier to see the join lines. To reposition a table, drag the table by its table name to the new position.

Enforce Referential Integrity

STEP 3 Enforce referential integrity is one of three options you can select when setting a table relationship. When *enforce referential integrity* is checked, Access ensures that data cannot be entered into a related table unless it first exists in the primary table. For example, in Figure 22 you cannot enter a product into the Products table using a SupplierID that does not exist in the Suppliers table. This rule ensures the integrity of the data in the database and improves overall data accuracy. Referential integrity also prohibits users from deleting a record in one table if it has records in related tables.

In Hands-on Exercise 3, you examine the strengths of Access and Excel in more detail so that you can better determine when to use which application to complete a given task. You will also explore relationships between tables and learn about the power of relational data.

 Create Sample Data

When learning database skills, starting with a smaller set of sample data prior to entering all company records can be helpful. A small amount of data gives you the ability to check the tables and quickly see if your results are correct. Even though the data amounts are small, as you test the database tables and relationships, the results will prove useful as you work with larger data sets.

Quick Concepts

1. How can you determine when to use Access or Excel to manage data?

2. Explain the term RDBMS.

3. What is the purpose of a join line?

Hands-On Exercises

Watch the Video
for this Hands-
On Exercise!

MyITLab®
HOE3 Training

3 Access Versus Excel, and Relational Databases

In this exercise, you review the relationships set in the Northwind Traders database. This will help you learn more about the overall design of the database. Examining the relationships will also help you understand why Access rather than Excel is used by Northwind Traders for data management.

Skills covered: Know When to Use Access or Excel to Manage Data • Use the Relationships Window, Use Filter by Form with a Comparison Operator, and Reapply a Saved Filter • Enforce Referential Integrity

STEP 1 ≫ KNOW WHEN TO USE ACCESS OR EXCEL TO MANAGE DATA

In this exercise, you examine the connections between the tables in the Northwind Traders database and review the reasons that Access was selected as the application for this data. Refer to Figure 23 as you complete Step 1.

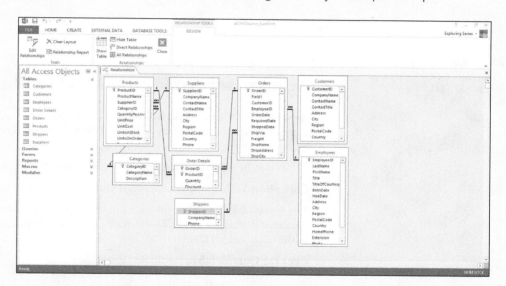

FIGURE 23 Relationships Window for the Northwind Database

a. Open the *a01h2Traders_LastFirst* database if you closed it after the last Hands-On Exercise and save it as **a01h3Traders_LastFirst**, changing *h2* to *h3*.

b. Click the **DATABASE TOOLS tab** and click **Relationships** in the Relationships group.

c. Examine the join lines showing the relationships that connect the various tables. For example, the Orders table is connected to the Order Details table.

Examining the number of tables in a database and their relationships is a good way to determine whether you need to use Excel or Access for your data. Because this data needs more than one table, involves a large amount of connected data, needs to group, sort, and total data based on various parameters, and needs to allow multiple users to connect to one data source at the same time, it is better to manipulate this data using Access rather than using Excel.

Use the Relationships window to move tables to make the join lines easier to view. To reinforce your filter skills, use *Filter by Form* to solve more complex questions about the Northwind data. After you retrieve the records, save the *Filter by Form* specifications so that you can reapply the filter later. Refer to Figure 24 as you complete Step 2.

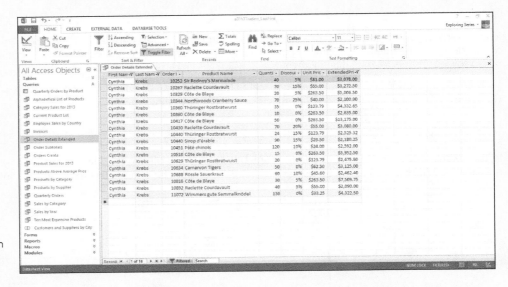

FIGURE 24 Query Results with Your Name and Extended Price >$2,000

a. Reposition the Shippers table beneath the Orders table by dragging it to the right by its table name. Reposition the Categories table beneath the Order Details table by dragging it to the right by its table name.

   Tables may be repositioned to make it easier to see the join lines creating the relationships.

b. Click **Show Table** in the Relationships group on the RELATIONSHIPS TOOLS DESIGN tab.

   The Show Table dialog box opens. It shows you the eight tables that are available in the database. If you look in the Relationships window, you will see that all eight tables are open in the relationships diagram.

c. Click the **Queries tab** in the Show Table dialog box.

   All of the queries created from the tables in the database are listed in the Show Table dialog box. You could add all of the queries to the Relationships window. Things might become cluttered, but you could tell at a glance from where the queries get their information.

d. Close the Show Table dialog box.

e. Click the **Shutter Bar Open/Close button** in the Navigation Pane to open the Navigation Pane, if necessary.

f. Click **All Access Objects** on the Navigation Pane and click **Tables and Related Views**.

   You now see each table and all the queries, forms, and reports that are based on each table. If a query is created using more than one table, it appears multiple times in the Navigation Pane.

g. Close the Relationships window. Save the changes to the design. Click **All Tables** on the Navigation Pane and click **Object Type**.

h. Collapse the Tables group in the Navigation Pane, expand the **Queries** group, and then double-click the **Order Details Extended query**.

i. Click **Advanced** in the Sort & Filter group, select **Filter by Form**, click in the first row under the Last Name field, and then select your last name.

Hands-On Exercise 3

j. Scroll right (or press **Tab**) until the Extended Price field is visible. Click in the first row in the Extended Price field and type **>2000**.

The Extended Price field shows the purchased amount for each item ordered. If an item sold for $15 and a customer ordered 10, the Extended Price would display $150.

k. Click **Toggle Filter** in the Sort & Filter group. Examine the filtered results.

Your comparison operator, >2000, identified 18 items ordered where the extended price exceeded $2,000.

l. Close the Order Details Extended query by clicking the **Close (X) button**. Click **Yes** to save changes.

m. Open the Order Details Extended query again.

The filter disengages when you close and reopen the object. However, because you opted to save the changes before closing, the filter has been stored with the query. You may reapply the filter at any time by clicking the Toggle Filter command (until the next filter replaces the current one).

n. Click **Toggle Filter** in the Sort & Filter group. Compare your results to Figure 24.

o. Save and close the query.

STEP 3 ≫ ENFORCE REFERENTIAL INTEGRITY

You need an additional relationship created between the Orders table and the Customers table. You create the relationship and enforce referential integrity. Refer to Figure 25 as you complete Step 3.

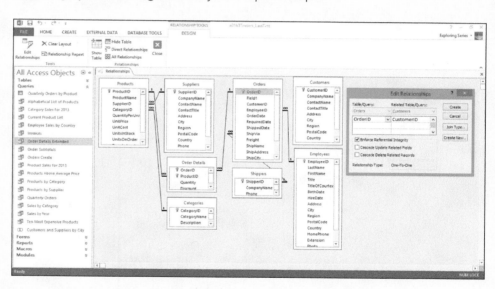

FIGURE 25 Relationship Created Between Orders Table and Customers Table

a. Click the **DATABASE TOOLS tab** and click **Relationships** in the Relationships group.

b. Locate the CustomerID field in the Orders table and drag it to the CustomerID field (primary key) in the Customers table.

The Edit Relationships dialog box opens. It shows that the Table/Query is from the Customers table and the related Table/Query comes from the Orders table. The relationship type is displayed at the bottom of the dialog box and indicates that this will be a One-To-Many relationship.

c. Click **Enforce Referential Integrity**.

Access will now ensure that data cannot be entered into the related table (Orders) unless it first exists in the primary table (Customers).

Hands-On Exercise 3

d. Click **Create**.

A join line displays between the Orders and Customers tables.

e. Click the **FILE tab** and click **Compact & Repair Database**. Click **Yes** if asked if you want to save changes to the layout of Relationships.

f. Click the **FILE tab**, click **Save As**, and then click **Save Database As** under *File Types* if necessary. Double-click **Back Up Database** in the Advanced group to open the Save As dialog box.

g. Verify the *Save in* folder displays the location where you want your backup file saved and click **Save**.

A duplicate copy of the database is saved with the default file name that is the original file name followed by the current date.

h. Exit Access.

Access Database Creation

Now that you have examined the fundamentals of an Access database and explored the power of relational databases, it is time to create one! In this section, you explore the benefits of creating a database using each of the methods discussed in the next section.

Creating a Database

When you first start Access, the Backstage view opens and provides you with three methods for creating a new database. These methods are:

- Creating a custom Web app
- Creating a blank desktop database
- Creating a database from a template

Creating a *custom Web app* enables you to create a database that you can build and then use and share with others through the Web. Creating a blank desktop database lets you create a database specific to your needs. Rather than starting from scratch by creating a blank desktop database, you may want to use a template to create a new database. An Access *template* is a predefined database that includes professionally designed tables, forms, reports, and other objects that you can use to jumpstart the creation of your database.

Figure 26 shows the options for creating a custom Web app, a blank desktop database, and multiple templates from which you can select the method for which you want to create a database.

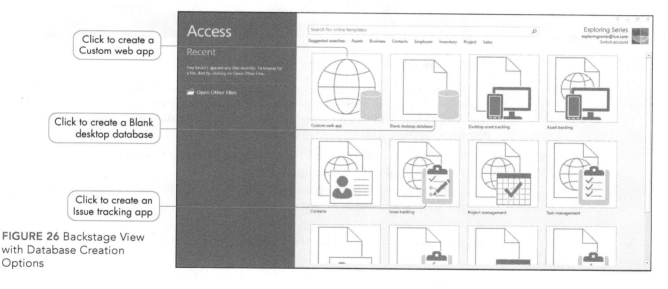

FIGURE 26 Backstage View with Database Creation Options

Create a Web Application Using a Template

Creating a Web app (application) is new in Access 2013. An Access Web app is a new type of database that lets you build a browser-based database application— you can create a database in the cloud that you and others can access and use simultaneously. This requires that you use a host server such as SharePoint (a Web application platform developed by Microsoft) or Office 365 (a cloud service edition of SharePoint).

To create a Web app, click *Custom web app* in the Backstage view, give your app a name, and then choose a location. Once you click Create, a blank database opens. You then create the tables that will serve as the foundation of your database. The easiest way to add a table is to use the Access library of Table Templates. Each of the templates in the library includes tables, fields, and views that you will need to create an app. Some templates also include related tables.

As an alternative to creating a Web app from scratch, you can select a Web app template from the Backstage view. These templates are fully functional Web databases. Click one of the Web app template tiles and an introduction screen appears that previews the datasheet, provides a description of the purpose of the datasheet, lets you know the download size of the database, and even displays how users like you have rated the database. You give the app a name and select the Web location where the app is to be saved. Finally, you create the app. When you have completed the database, click Launch App in the View group on the Home tab. You can then use it and share it on the Web. Figure 27 shows the introduction screen for the Asset tracking template. This template requires SharePoint so that you can share content with others.

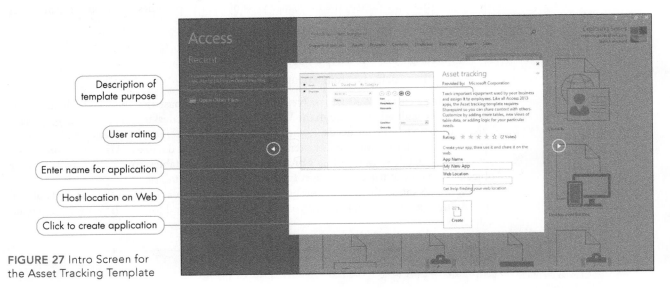

Description of template purpose

User rating

Enter name for application

Host location on Web

Click to create application

FIGURE 27 Intro Screen for the Asset Tracking Template

Create a Blank Desktop Database

To create a blank desktop database specific to your needs, click *Blank desktop database* in the Backstage view. Access opens to a blank table in Datasheet view where you can add data. You can refine the table in Design view. You would then create additional tables and objects as necessary. To create a blank desktop database, do the following:

1. Open Access or click the FILE tab to open the Backstage view and click New.
2. Click the *Blank desktop* database tile.
3. Enter the file name for the file in the text box, click the Browse button to navigate to the folder where you want to store the database file, and then click OK.
4. Click Create.
5. Enter data in the empty table that displays.

Create a Desktop Database Using a Template

Using a template to start a database saves you a great deal of creation time. Working with a template can also help a new Access user become familiar with database design. Templates are available from the Backstage view, where you can select from a variety of templates or search online for more templates.

Access also provides templates for desktop use. To create a desktop database from a template, do the following:

STEP 1 ▶
1. Open Access or click the FILE tab to open the Backstage view and click New.
2. Click the database template you want to use.
3. Enter the file name for the file in the text box, click the Browse button to navigate to the folder where you want to store the database file, and then click OK.

Introduction to Access

4. Click Create to download the template.
5. Open the database and click Enable Content in the Security Warning message bar if you trust the source of the database.

Once the database is open, you may see a Getting Started page that includes links you can use to learn more about the database. A new Access user can gain valuable information by watching any associated videos and clicking provided hyperlinks. When finished reviewing the learning materials, close the Getting Started page to view the database. Figure 28 displays the Getting Started page included with the *Desktop task management* template. Two videos are provided to aid you in using and modifying the database. Because this database contains a Contacts table, there is a hyperlink to a wizard that will import contacts from Microsoft Outlook (if you use Microsoft Outlook). Links are available that will connect you with experts, enable you to get free advice from a forum, and get more help from Microsoft .com. The Getting Started page also includes a button you can click to open a survey that provides feedback to Microsoft. Close the Getting Started page to return to the database.

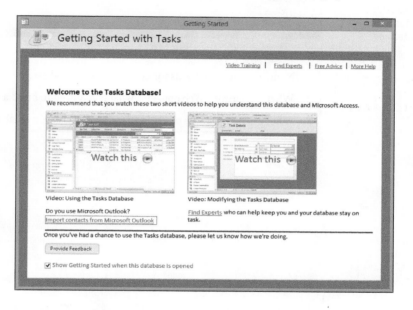

FIGURE 28 Getting Started Page for Desktop Task Management Template

STEP 2

Because you downloaded a template, some objects will have already been created. You can work with these objects just as you did in the first three sections of this chapter. For example, you can enter data directly into any existing table in the database by opening the table, clicking in the first empty field, typing the data, tabbing to the next empty field, and then typing the data for the next field. You can also open any form that is part of the down-loaded template and enter the data directly in the forms. Some templates will include queries and reports. Edit any object to meet your requirements.

STEP 3

Once the database is opened, review the objects listed in the Navigation Pane. Change the Navigation Pane category from Object Type to *Tables and Related Views* to become famil-iar with the relationships between the tables and other database objects. Note the tables and the objects that are based on them.

After noting the objects in the database, open the Relationships window to see the connections between them. Once you are familiar with the database design, you can enter your data.

Figure 29 displays the open Task Management database with the Navigation Pane set to display *Tables and Related Views*. The Tasks table displays with its related queries, forms, and reports. The Relationships window shows the relationship between the Contacts table and the Tasks table.

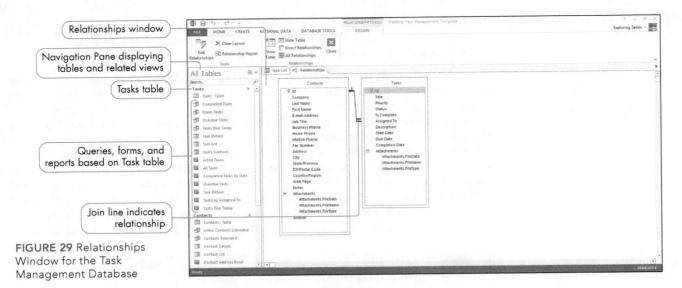

Relationships window

Navigation Pane displaying tables and related views

Tasks table

Queries, forms, and reports based on Task table

Join line indicates relationship

FIGURE 29 Relationships Window for the Task Management Database

Quick Concepts

1. Name the three methods for creating a new database.

2. What is a custom Web app, and what is required to build a custom Web app?

3. What are two benefits of using a template to create a database?

Hands-On Exercises

Watch the Video for this Hands-On Exercise!

MyITLab®
HOE4 Training

4 Access Database Creation

After working with the Northwind Traders database on the job, you decide to use Access to create a personal contact database. Rather than start from scratch, you use an Access Contact Manager desktop template to jumpstart your database creation. A Web app is not necessary because you do not want to share your contacts with others.

Skills covered: Create a Desktop Database Using a Template • Add Records to a Downloaded Desktop Database Template • Explore the Database Objects in a Downloaded Desktop Database Template

STEP 1 ≫ CREATE A DESKTOP DATABASE USING A TEMPLATE

You locate an Access desktop template that you can use to create your personal contact database. This template not only allows you to store names, addresses, telephone numbers, and other information, but also lets you categorize your contacts, send e-mail messages, and create maps of addresses. You download and save the template. Refer to Figure 30 as you complete Step 1.

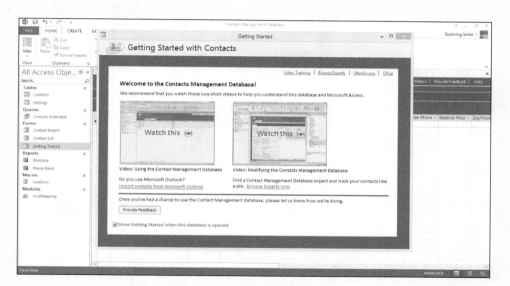

FIGURE 30 Desktop Contacts Intro Screen

a. Open Access. Scroll down until you see the *Desktop contacts* template and click the template tile.

   The Create Intro Screen page for the Desktop contacts database opens.

b. Click the **Browse icon** to navigate to the folder where you are saving your files, enter **a01h4Contacts_LastFirst** as the file name, and then click **OK**.

c. Click **Create** to download the template.

d. Click **Enable Content** on the Security Warning message bar.

   The *Getting Started with Contacts* page displays, providing you with videos you can watch to learn how to use and modify the database as well as other helpful links.

> **TROUBLESHOOTING:** If the Getting Started page does not display, click Getting Started in the Forms category on the Navigation Pane.

Hands-On Exercise 4

> **TROUBLESHOOTING:** The Getting Started page opens every time you open the Contacts Management database. To close this page until you want to view it again, clear the *Show Getting Started when this database is opened* check box at the bottom-left corner of the dialog box before closing the Getting Started page.

e. Close the Getting Started page.

The database displays with the Contact List table open.

STEP 2 ⟫ ADD RECORDS TO A DOWNLOADED DESKTOP DATABASE TEMPLATE

Because the database opens in the Contact List form, you decide to begin by entering a contact—your dentist—in the form. Refer to Figure 31 as you complete Step 2.

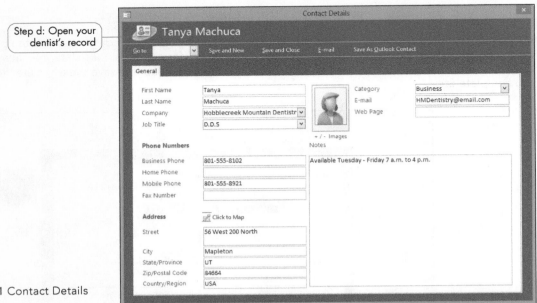

FIGURE 31 Contact Details Form

a. Click in the empty first field of the first row. Enter the following information, pressing **Tab** between each entry. Do not press Tab after entering the ZIP/Postal Code.

Field Name	Value to Type
First Name	Tanya
Last Name	Machuca
Company	Hobblecreek Mountain Dentistry
Job Title	D.D.S.
Category	Business (select from list)
E-mail Address	HMDentistry@email.com
Business Phone	801-555-8102
Home Phone	(leave blank)
Mobile Phone	801-555-8921
ZIP/Postal Code	84664

b. Click **Save and Close**.

c. Double-click **Contact List** in the Forms group on the Navigation Pane.

d. Click **Open** in the first field of Dr. Machuca's record.

Open is a hyperlink to a different form in the database. The Contact Details form opens, displaying Dr. Machuca's information. More fields are available for you to use to store information.

e. Enter the following additional information to the record:

Field Name	Value to Type
Street	56 West 200 North
City	Mapleton
State/Province	UT
Country/Region	USA
Notes	Available Tuesday - Friday 7 a.m. to 4 p.m.

f. Click the **Click to Map hyperlink** to view a map to Dr. Machuca's office. Close the map.

Bing displays a map to the address in the record. You can get directions, locate nearby businesses, and use many other options.

g. Click **Save and Close** in the top center of the form to close the Contact Details form.

The record is saved.

h. Click **New Contact** beneath the Contact List title bar.

The Contact Details form opens to a blank record.

i. Enter the following information for a new record, pressing **Tab** to move between fields. Some fields will be blank.

Field Name	Value to Type
First Name	Rowan
Last Name	Westmoreland
Company	Phoenix Aesthetics
Job Title	Aesthetician
Mobile Phone	801-555-2221
Street	425 North Main Street
City	Springville
State/Province	UT
ZIP/Postal Code	84663
Category	Personal
E-mail Address	Rowan55W5@email.com
Notes	Recommended by Michelle

j. Click **Save and Close**.

STEP 3 >> EXPLORE THE DATABASE OBJECTS IN A DOWNLOADED DESKTOP DATABASE TEMPLATE

You explore the objects created by the template so that you understand the organization of the database. Refer to Figure 32 as you complete Step 3.

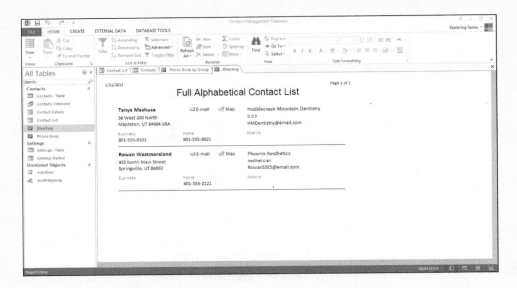

FIGURE 32 Directory Form

a. Double-click the **Contacts table** in the Navigation Pane to open it.

The information you entered using the Contact List form and the Contact Details form displays in the Contacts table.

b. Click the **Reports group** in the Navigation Pane to expand the list of reports, if necessary.

The list of reports contained in the database file opens.

c. Double-click **Phone Book** in the Navigation Pane to open it.

The Phone Book report opens displaying the contact name and phone information organized by category.

d. Double-click the **Directory report** in the Navigation Pane to open it.

The Directory report opens, displaying a full alphabetical contact list. The Directory report was designed to display more fields than the Phone Book, but it is not organized by category.

e. Click **All Access Objects** on the Navigation Pane and select **Tables and Related Views**.

You can now see the objects that are based on the Contacts table.

f. Right-click the **Directory report tab** and click **Close All**.

g. Exit Access and submit your work based on your instructor's directions.

Hands-On Exercise 4

Chapter Objectives Review

After reading this chapter, you have accomplished the following objectives:

1. **Understand database fundamentals.**
   - A database is a collection of data organized as meaningful information that can be accessed, managed, stored, queried, sorted, and reported.
   - Organize information in a database and recognize Access objects: An Access database is a structured collection of six types of objects—tables, forms, queries, reports, macros, and modules.
   - The foundation of a database is its tables, the objects in which data is stored. Each table in the database is composed of records, and each record is in turn comprised of fields.
   - The primary key in a table is the field (or combination of fields) that makes every record in a table unique.
   - Examine the Access interface: Objects are organized and listed in the Navigation Pane. Access also uses a Tabbed Documents interface in which each object that is open has its own tab.
   - Explore Access views: The Datasheet view enables the user to view, add, edit, and delete records, whereas the Design view is used to create and modify a table's design by specifying the fields it will contain, the fields' data types, and their associated properties.
   - Open an Access file and work with Content Security: When a database is opened from a location that has not been designated as a trusted location or that does not have a digital signature from a publisher you can trust, Access displays a message bar with a security warning. Click the Enable Content button if you trust the database's source.

2. **Use an existing database.**
   - Understand the difference between working in storage and memory: Access works primarily from storage. Records can be added, modified, or deleted in the database, and as the information is entered it is automatically saved.
   - Add, edit, and delete records: A pencil icon displays in the row selector box to indicate when you are in editing mode. Moving to another record or clicking Save on the Quick Access Toolbar saves the changes.
   - To add a new record, click *New (blank) record* on the navigation bar. To delete a record, click the row selector and click Delete in the Records group on the Home tab.
   - Save As, Compact and Repair, and Back Up Access files: *Compact and Repair* reduces the size of the database, and Back Up creates a duplicate copy of the database.

3. **Sort table data on one or multiple fields.**
   - Sorting changes the order of information, and information may be sorted by one or more fields.

4. **Create, modify, and remove filters.**
   - A filter is a set of criteria that is applied to a table to display a subset of records in that table.
   - *Filter by Selection* displays only the records that match the selected criteria.
   - *Filter by Form* displays records based on multiple criteria and enables the user to apply logical operators and use comparison operators.

5. **Know when to use Access or Excel to manage data.**
   - Use Access to manage data when you require multiple related tables to store your data; have a large amount of data; need to connect to and retrieve data from external databases; need to group, sort, and total data based on various parameters; and/ or have an application that requires multiple users to connect to one data source.
   - Use Excel to manage data when you need one worksheet to handle all of your data; have mostly numeric data; require subtotals and totals in your worksheet; want to primarily run a series of "what if" scenarios on your data; and/or need to create complex charts and/or graphs.

6. **Understand relational power.**
   - Use the Relationships window: A relationship is a connection between two tables using a common field. The benefit of a relationship is to efficiently combine data from related tables for the purpose of creating queries, forms, and reports.
   - Enforce referential integrity: Enforcing referential integrity when setting a table relationship ensures that data cannot be entered into a related table unless it first exists in the primary table.

7. **Create a database.**
   - Create a Web application using a template: Creating a custom Web app enables you to create a database that you can build and use and share with others through the Web.
   - Creating a blank desktop database: Creating a blank desktop database lets you create a database specific to your needs.
   - Create a desktop database using a template: A template is a predefined database that includes professionally designed tables, forms, reports, and other objects that you can use to jumpstart the creation of your database.

Key Terms Matching

Match the key terms with their definitions. Write the key term letter by the appropriate numbered definition.

a. Back Up Database
b. Compact and Repair
c. Custom Web app
d. Datasheet view
e. Design view
f. Field
g. Filter by Form
h. Filter by Selection
i. Form
j. Navigation Pane
k. Object

l. Primary key
m. Query
n. Record
o. Relational database management system (RDBMS)
p. Relationship
q. Report
r. Sort
s. Table
t. Template

1. _____ View that enables you to add, edit, and delete the records of a table.

2. _____ An Access object that enables you to enter, modify, or delete table data.

3. _____ An Access utility that reduces the size of the database and can repair a corrupt database.

4. _____ A main component that is created and used to make a database function.

5. _____ A filtering method that displays records based on multiple criteria

6. _____ A system that uses the relational model to manage groups of data (tables) and rules (relationships) between tables.

7. _____ A database that can be built, used, and shared with others through the use of a host server.

8. _____ An object that contains professional-looking formatted information from underlying tables or queries.

9. _____ An object used to store data, and the foundation of every database.

10. _____ An Access utility that creates a duplicate copy of the database.

11. _____ A predefined database that includes professionally designed tables, forms, reports, and other objects.

12. _____ A filtering method that displays only records that match selected criteria.

13. _____ A connection between two tables using a common field.

14. _____ A method of listing records in a specific sequence.

15. _____ View that enables you to create tables, add and delete fields, and modify field properties.

16. _____ An Access interface element that organizes and lists the database objects in a database.

17. _____ A question you ask that can help you find and retrieve table data meeting conditions you specify.

18. _____ The smallest data element in a table, such as first name, last name, address, or phone number.

19. _____ Complete set of all the fields (data elements) about one person, place, event, or concept.

20. _____ The field (or combination of fields) that uniquely identifies each record in a table.

1. Which sequence represents the hierarchy of terms, from smallest to largest?

   (a) Database, table, record, field

   (b) Field, record, table, database

   (c) Record, field, table, database

   (d) Field, record, database, table

2. You edit several records in an Access table. When should you execute the Save command?

   (a) Immediately after you edit a record

   (b) When you close the table

   (c) Once at the end of the session

   (d) Records are saved automatically; the save command is not required.

3. Which of the following is *not* true of an Access database?

   (a) Short Text, Number, AutoNumber, and Currency are valid data types.

   (b) Every record in a table has the same fields as every other record.

   (c) Every table in a database contains the same number of records as every other table.

   (d) Each table should contain a primary key; however, a primary key is not required.

4. Which of the following is *true* regarding the record selector box?

   (a) An orange border surrounds the record selector box and the active record.

   (b) A pencil symbol indicates that the current record already has been saved.

   (c) An asterisk indicates the first record in the table.

   (d) An empty square indicates that the current record is selected.

5. Which of the following will be accepted as valid during data entry?

   (a) Adding a record with a duplicate primary key

   (b) Entering text into a numeric field

   (c) Entering numbers into a text field

   (d) Omitting an entry in a required field

6. You have finished an Access assignment and wish to turn it in to your instructor for evaluation. As you prepare to transfer the file, you discover that it has more than doubled in size. You should:

   (a) Delete extra tables or reports or fields to make the file smaller.

   (b) Zip the database file prior to sending it to your instructor.

   (c) Compact and repair the database before sending it to your instructor.

   (d) Turn it in; the size does not matter.

7. Which of the following conditions is available through *Filter by Selection*?

   (a) Equals condition

   (b) Delete condition

   (c) AND condition

   (d) OR condition

8. An Employees table is open in Datasheet view. You want to sort the names alphabetically by last name and then by first name (e.g., Smith, Andrew). To do this, you must:

   (a) First sort ascending on first name and then on last name.

   (b) First sort descending on first name and then on last name.

   (c) First sort ascending on last name and then on first name.

   (d) First sort descending on last name and then on first name.

9. Which of the following is *not* true when creating relationships between tables?

   (a) Join lines create a relationship between two tables.

   (b) The common fields used to create a relationship must both be primary keys.

   (c) The data types of common fields must be the same.

   (d) Enforcing referential integrity ensures that data cannot be entered into a related table unless it first exists in the primary table.

10. All of the following statements are *true* about creating a database *except*:

    (a) Creating a custom Web app requires that you use a host server.

    (b) When creating a blank desktop database, Access opens to a blank table in Datasheet view.

    (c) Using a template to create a database saves time because it includes predefined objects.

    (d) The objects provided in a template cannot be modified.

1 Hotel Rewards

The Lakes Hotel and Conference Center caters to upscale business travelers and provides stylish hotel suites, sophisticated meeting and reception facilities, and state-of-the-art media equipment. The hotel is launching a rewards club to help the marketing department track the purchasing patterns of its most loyal customers. All of the hotel transactions will be stored in an Access database. Your task is to create a member table and enter sample customers. You will practice filtering on the table data. This exercise follows the same set of skills as used in Hands-On Exercises 1 and 2 in the chapter. Refer to Figure 33 as you complete this exercise.

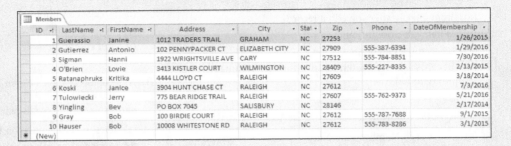

FIGURE 33 Enter Data into the Members Table

a. Open Access and click **Blank desktop database**.

b. Type **a01p1Rewards_LastFirst** in the **File Name box**. Click the **Browse icon**. Navigate to the location where you are saving your files in the File New Database dialog box, click **OK** to close the dialog box, and then click **Create** to create the new database.

c. Click **View** in the Views group on the TABLE TOOLS FIELDS tab to switch to Design view. Type **Members** in the **Save As dialog box** and click **OK**.

d. Type **LastName** under the ID field and press **Tab**. Accept **Short Text** as the Data Type. Type **FirstName** in the third row and press **Tab**. Accept **Short Text** as the Data Type.

e. Type the next five fields into the Field Name column: **Address**, **City**, **State**, **Zip**, and **Phone**. Accept **Short Text** as the Data Type for each of these fields.

f. Type **DateOfMembership** as the last Field Name and select **Date/Time** as the Data Type.

g. Click **View** in the Views group to switch to Datasheet view. Click **Yes** to save the table. Type the data as shown in Figure 33. Increase the column widths to fit the data as necessary. Press **Tab** to move to the next field.

h. Find a record that displays *Raleigh* as the value in the City field. Click **Raleigh** to select that data value.

i. Click **Selection** in the Sort & Filter group on the HOME tab. Select **Equals "Raleigh"**.

j. Find a record that displays *27612* as the value in the Zip field. Click **27612** to select that data value.

k. Click **Selection** in the Sort & Filter group on the HOME tab. Select **Equals "27612"**.

l. Click any value in the FirstName field. Click **Ascending** in the Sort & Filter group on the HOME tab. Click any value in the LastName field. Click **Ascending** in the Sort & Filter group on the HOME tab.

m. Click the **FILE tab**, click **Print**, and then click **Print Preview** to preview the sorted and filtered table.

n. Click **Close Print Preview** in the Close Preview group.

o. Close the table and save the changes.

p. Click the **FILE tab** and click **Compact and Repair Database** under *Advanced*.

q. Click the **FILE tab**, click **Save As**, and then double-click **Back Up Database**.

r. Click **Save** to accept the default backup file name with today's date.

s. Click the **FILE tab** and click **Exit** (to exit Access). Submit the database based on your instructor's directions.

The Custom Coffee Company provides coffee, tea, and snacks to offices in Miami. Custom Coffee also provides and maintains the equipment for brewing the beverages. The firm has a reputation for providing outstanding customer service. To improve customer service even further, the owner recently purchased an Access database to keep track of customers, orders, and products. This database will replace the Excel spreadsheets currently maintained by the office manager. The Excel spreadsheets are out of date, and they do not allow for data validation while data is being entered. The company hired you to verify and enter all the Excel data into the Access database. This exercise follows the same set of skills as used in Hands-On Exercises 1–3 in the chapter. Refer to Figure 34 as you complete this exercise.

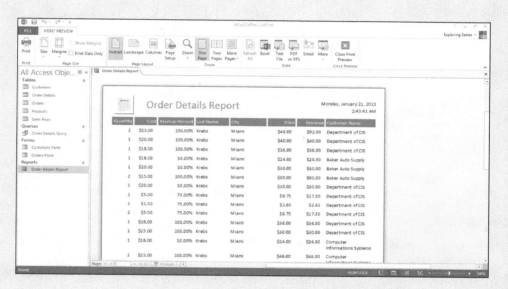

FIGURE 34 Order Details Report Filtered for *YourName* and *Miami*

a. Open the *a01p2Coffee* file and save the database as **a01p2Coffee_LastFirst**.

b. Click the **DATABASE TOOLS tab** and click **Relationships** in the Relationships group. Review the table relationships. Take note of the join line between the Customers and Orders tables.

c. Click **Close** in the Relationships group.

d. Double-click the **Sales Reps table** in the Navigation Pane to open it. Replace *YourName* with your name in both the LastName and FirstName fields. For example, as the Access author, I used the name Cynthia Krebs in place of FirstName LastName. Close the table by clicking the **Close (X) button** on the right side of the Sales Reps window.

e. Double-click the **Customers Form** to open it. Click **New (blank) record** in the navigation bar at the bottom of the window. Add a new record by typing the following information; press **Tab** after each field.

Customer Name:	*your name* Company
Contact:	*your name*
Email:	*yourname*@email.com
Address1:	123 Main St
Address2:	(leave blank)
City:	Miami
State:	FL
Zip Code:	33133
Phone:	(305) 555-1234

Fax:	(leave blank)
Service Start Date:	01/17/2016
Credit Rating:	A
Sales Rep ID:	2

Note the pencil in the top-left margin of the form window. This symbol indicates the new record has not been saved. Press **Tab**. The pencil symbol disappears, and the new customer is automatically saved to the table.

f. Close the Customers Form.

g. Double-click the **Orders Form** to open it. Click **New (blank) record** in the navigation bar at the bottom of the window. Add a new record by typing the following information:

Customer ID:	15 (Access will convert it to C0015)
Payment Type:	Cash (select using the arrow)
Comments:	Ship this order in 2 days
Product ID:	4 (Access will convert it to P0004)
Quantity:	2

h. Add a second product using the following information:

| Product ID: | 6 (Access will convert it to P0006) |
| Quantity: | 1 |

i. Close the form.

j. Double-click the **Order Details Report** to open it in Report view. Click your name in the Last Name field, click **Selection** in the Sort & Filter group, and then click **Equals "Your Name"**.

k. Right-click **Miami** in the City field and select **Equals "Miami"** from the shortcut menu.

l. Click the **FILE tab**, click **Print**, and then click **Print Preview**.

m. Click **Close Print Preview** in the Close Preview group. Close the report.

n. Click the **FILE tab** and click **Compact & Repair Database**.

o. Click the **FILE tab**, click **Save As**, and then double-click **Back Up Database**. Use the default backup file name.

p. Close Access. Submit based on your instructor's directions.

3 Camping Trip

FROM SCRATCH

You and your friends have decided to spend your annual reunion camping at the Wawona Campground in Yosemite National Park. Wawona Campground is an extremely popular campground. Campground reservations are available in blocks of one month at a time, up to five months in advance, on the 15th of each month at 7 AM Pacific time. Nearly all reservations are filled the first day they become available, usually within seconds or minutes after 7 AM. Realizing that making reservations is a high-priority, critical task, and that there are many other tasks that must be completed before you can have a successful trip, your group decides to use the Access Task Management Database to begin getting organized for their trip on September 15, 2015. Other tasks can be entered at a later time. This exercise follows the same set of skills as used in Hands-On Exercises 3 and 4 in the chapter. Refer to Figures 1.35–38 as you complete this exercise.

Practice Exercises

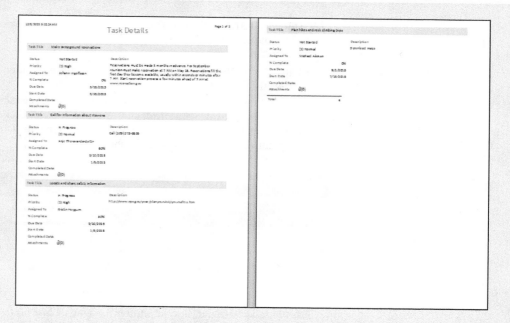

FIGURE 35 Task Details Report

a. Open Access and click the **Desktop task management template** in the Access Backstage view.

b. Type **a01p3Camping_LastFirst** in the **File name box**. Click the **Browse icon**. Navigate to the location where you are saving your files in the File New Database dialog box, click **OK** to close the dialog box, and then click **Create** to create the new database.

c. Click the **Watch this arrow** for the *Using the Tasks Database* template video on the left side of the Getting Started page. If the Getting Started page does not open, open the Getting Started form in the Forms group in the Navigation Pane. Click **Watch this>>** and watch the video. Close the video when you have finished watching it. Click **Close** again to return to the *Getting Started with Tasks* page.

d. Remove the check in the *Show Getting Started when this database is opened* check box so that the page does not automatically display in the future. If you want to view Getting Started again, you can click **Getting Started** in the Forms category on the Navigation Pane. Click the **Close (X) button**.

e. Click **Relationships** in the Relationships group on the DATABASE TOOLS tab and note the relationship between the Contacts table and the Tasks table. Close the Relationships window.

f. Double-click **Contact List** in the Forms category on the Navigation Pane. Type the information for each field in the Contact list form using the information displayed in Figure 36, pressing **Tab** between each field.

FIGURE 36 Contact List

g. Close the Contact List form. The Task List form displays because it was the form open when you downloaded the database.

> **TROUBLESHOOTING:** If the Task List form does not display, double-click the Task List form in the Navigation Pane to open it.

h. Click the **Shutter Bar Open/Close button** to close the Navigation Pane, which enables you to see more table fields.

i. Enter the information for each field in the Task List form using the information displayed in Figure 37. In the Priority field, Status field, and Assigned To field, click the arrow and select the list of options. When typing the Start Date and Due Date, type the date and add **7 AM** after the date. Although the date does not show in the table, it is required.

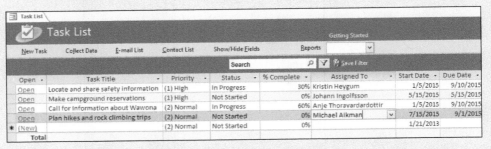

FIGURE 37 Task List Form

j. Close the Tasks table and click the **Shutter Bar Open/Close button** to open the Navigation Pane.

k. Double-click **Task Details** in the Forms category in the Navigation Pane.

l. Refer to Figure 38 to enter the information in the **Description box** and close the Task Details form.

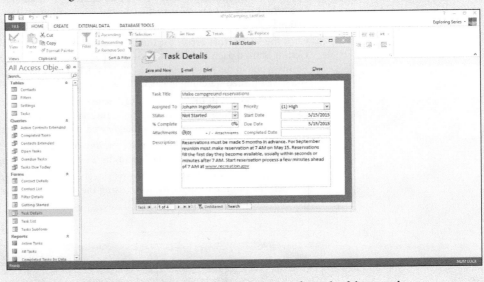

FIGURE 38 Description in Task Details Form

m. Refer to Figure 35 and continue entering the descriptions for each of the records.

n. Double-click **Task Details** in the Reports category in the Navigation Pane to view the report displaying the details about the tasks you have created. Scroll down to see all tasks.

o. Click the **FILE tab**, click **Print**, and then click **Print Preview**.

p. Click **Two Pages** in the Zoom group on the Print Preview tab. Note the report format groups the information by Task Title.

q. Click **Close Print Preview** in the Close Preview group. Close the report.

r. Click the **FILE tab** and click **Compact & Repair Database**.

s. Click the **FILE tab**, click **Save As**, and then double-click **Back Up Database**. Use the default backup file name.

t. Close Access. Submit based on your instructor's directions.

Practice Exercises

Mid-Level Exercises

1 Home Sales

FROM SCRATCH

You are the senior partner in a large, independent real estate firm that specializes in home sales. Most of your time is spent supervising the agents who work for your firm. The firm needs to create a database to hold all of the information on the properties it has listed. You will use the database to help find properties that match the goals of your customers. You will create the database, create two tables, add data to both tables, and create a relationship. Refer to Figure 39 as you complete this exercise.

FIGURE 39 Properties Table

a. Open Access and click **Blank desktop database**. Type **a01m1Homes_LastFirst** in the **File Name box**. Click **Browse** and navigate to the location where you are saving your files. Click **OK** to close the dialog box and click **Create** to create the new database.

b. Switch to Design view. Type **Properties** in the **Save As dialog box** and click **OK**.

c. Type **DateListed** under the ID field and press **Tab**. Select **Date/Time** as the Data Type.

d. Type the remainder of the fields and Data Types as shown:

Field Name	Data Type
DateSold	Date/Time
ListPrice	Currency
SalesPrice	Currency
SqFeet	Number
Beds	Number
Baths	Number
Address	Short Text
SubDivision	Number
AgentID	Number
Style	Short Text
Construction	Short Text
Garage	Short Text
YearBuilt	Number

e. Switch to Datasheet view. Type the first 10 records as shown in Figure 39.

f. Open the *a01m1Properties.xlsx* workbook file in Excel. Click **row 2**, press and hold the **left mouse button**, and then drag through **row 70** so that all the data rows are selected. Click **Copy** in the Clipboard group on the HOME tab. Click **Yes** to save the data to the Clipboard when prompted. Close the Excel file.

g. Return to Access and click on the **asterisk (*)** on the first new row of the Properties table. Click **Paste** in the Clipboard group to paste all 69 rows into the Properties table. Save and close the table.

DISCOVER

h. Click **Table** in the Tables group on the CREATE tab. Click **View** in the Views group on the TABLE TOOLS FIELDS tab to switch to Design view. Save the table as **Agents**. Change the primary key from ID to **AgentID**. Add the following fields and switch to Datasheet view. Save changes to the table design when prompted.

Field Name	Data Type
FirstName	Short Text
LastName	Short Text
Title	Short Text

i. Enter the following data in the Agents table and close the table.

AgentID	FirstName	LastName	Title
1	Kia	Hart	Broker
2	Keith	Martin	Agent
3	Kim	Yang	Agent
4	Steven	Dougherty	Agent in Training
5	Angela	Scott	Agent in Training
6	Juan	Resario	President

j. Click the **DATABASE TOOLS tab** and click **Relationships** in the Relationships group. Add both tables to the Relationships window and close the Show Table dialog box.

k. Drag the bottom border of the Properties table downward until all fields display. Drag the **AgentID field** from the Agents table and drop it onto the **AgentID field** in the Properties table. Click the **Enforce Referential Integrity check box** in the Edit Relationships dialog box to activate it. Click **Create** and close the Relationships window. Click **Yes** to save your changes.

l. Open the **Properties** table. Click **Advanced** in the Sort & Filter group and click **Filter By Form**. Set the criteria to identify properties with a list price less than $300,000 and with two bedrooms. (You will use the expression <300000 for the criteria of the list price.) Display the results and sort by ascending list price. Save and close the table.

m. Compact, repair, and back up the database.

n. Exit Access. Submit the database based on your instructor's directions.

2 National Conference

The Association of Higher Education will host its National Conference on your campus next year. To facilitate the conference, the information technology department has replaced last year's Excel spreadsheets with an Access database containing information on the rooms, speakers, and sessions. Your assignment is to create a room itinerary that will list all of the sessions, dates, and times for each room. The list will be posted on the door of each room for the duration of the conference. Refer to Figure 40 as you complete this exercise.

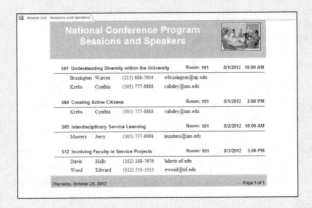

FIGURE 40 Sessions and Speakers Report—Room 101

a. Open the *a01m2NatConf* file and save the database as **a01m2NatConf_LastFirst**.

b. Open the Relationships window.

c. Review the objects in the database to see if any of the existing objects will provide the room itinerary information displayed in Figure 40.

DISCOVER

d. Open the SessionSpeaker table. Scroll to the first blank record at the bottom of the table and enter a new record using SpeakerID **99** and SessionID **09**. (Note: Speaker 99 does not exist.) How does Access respond? Close the dialog box, recognizing that you are not saving this record. Close the SessionSpeaker table. In the Relationships window, right-click the join line between the Speakers table and SessionSpeaker table and click **Delete**. Click **Yes** to permanently delete the selected relationship from the database. Close the Relationships window. Open the SessionSpeaker table and enter the same record again. How does Access respond this time? Close the SessionSpeaker table.

e. Open the Speakers table. Find and replace *YourName* with your name. Close the Speakers table.

f. Open the Speaker–Session Query and apply a filter to identify the sessions where you or Holly Davis are the speakers. Use *Filter by Form* and the Or tab. (Nine records should display.)

g. Sort the filtered results in ascending order by the RoomID field and save and close the query.

h. Open the Master List–Sessions and Speakers report. Right-click the **Master List–Sessions and Speakers tab** and select **Report View**.

i. Apply a filter that limits the report to sessions in Room 101 only.

j. Click the **FILE tab**, click **Print**, and then click **Print Preview**. Compare the report to Figure 40 and make any corrections necessary. Close Print Preview and close the report.

k. Compact and repair the database.

l. Back up the database. Use the default backup file name.

m. Exit Access. Submit based on your instructor's directions.

3 Used Cell Phones for Sale

COLLABORATION CASE

You and a few of your classmates decide to start a new business selling used cell phones, MP3 players, and accessories. You will use an Access database to track your inventory. To begin, one person in your group will locate the Access database for this exercise, complete steps b through f, and then post the database to a SkyDrive folder. The next person in your group will retrieve the revised database and also complete steps b through f (and so on until everyone has completed steps b through f). After everyone has completed steps b through f, you will retrieve the database again and complete step g. At the completion of this exercise, each person will submit his or her own Word document containing the answers to the questions below.

a. Open the *a01m3Phones* database and save it as **a01m3PhonesGroupX_LastFirst**. (Replace *X* with the number assigned to your group by your instructor.)

b. Open the Inventory table and review the records in the table. Take note of the data in the TypeOfDevice column. Close the table and open the DeviceOptions table. Review the data and close the table.

c. Open the Relationships window. What is the benefit of the relationship between the Inventory table and the DeviceOptions table? Create a Word document with both the question and your answer. After you complete this exercise, you will submit this Word document to your instructor using the file name **a01m3PhonesAnswers_LastFirst**. Close the Relationships window.

d. Open the Inventory Form and add the information about your cell phone to the table (or search the Internet for any model if you do not have a cell phone) in the first new blank record. Enter your name in the SellerName field. With your information showing in the form, take a screenshot of the form using the Snipping Tool. Paste the image into the Word document you created in step c. Close the form.

e. Open the Inventory Report by Manufacturer in Report view. Filter the records for only items that have not been sold. Take a screenshot using the Snipping Tool and paste the image into the Word document. Close the report, close the database, and then exit Access.

f. Create a folder on your SkyDrive account named **Exploring Access** and share the folder with other members in your group and the instructor. Upload the database to this new folder and notify another person in your group. The next person will complete steps b through f, and then the next person, until all group members have added their information.

g. After all the new phone records have been added, each person in the group should download the **a01m3PhonesGroupX** database again and use filters to answer the following questions. Add the questions and your answers to the Word document you created.

   1. How many phones are still for sale? _____
   2. How many phones are made by Apple or Samsung? _____
   3. How many phones were sold in the first half of 2013? _____ List the ID numbers _____
   4. Sort the phones from lowest to highest asking price. Which phone is the least expensive? _____ Most expensive? _____
   5. How many items are not phones? _____

h. Use e-mail or text messaging to communicate with the other members in your group if you have any questions.

i. Submit the Word document based on your instructor's directions.

Beyond the Classroom

Northwind Revenue Report

RESEARCH CASE

Open the *a01b2NWind* file and save the database as **a01b2NWind_LastFirst**. Open the Employees table and replace *YourName* with your first and last names. Before you can filter the Revenue report, you need to update the criterion in the underlying query to match the dates in the database. Right-click the **Revenue query** in the Navigation Pane and click **Design view** in the shortcut menu. Scroll to the right until you see *OrderDate*. Right-click in the **Criteria row** under *OrderDate* and click **Zoom**. Change the criterion to **Between#1/1/2015#And#3/31/2015#** and click **OK**. Click **Run** in the Results group on the Query Tools Design tab and save the query. Open the Revenue report. Use the tools that you have learned in this chapter to filter the report for only your sales of Confections. Close the report. Compact, repair, and back up your database and exit Access.

Lugo Computer Sales

DISASTER RECOVERY

You are having trouble with an Access 2013 database. One of the employees accidentally changed the CustomerID of Lugo Computer Sales. This change caused a problem in one of the relationships. Open the *a01b3Recover* file and save the database as **a01b3Recover_LastFirst**. Open the Customers and Orders tables and examine the data. Change the Lugo Computer Sales CustomerID in the Customers table back to the original number of 6. Reset the relationship between the Customers table and the Orders table and enforce referential integrity. Compact, repair, and back up your database and exit Access. Submit the database based on your instructor's directions.

Financial Literacy

SOFT SKILLS CASE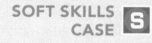

The Cambridge Resources Group stated that surveyed executives ranked the "toll on productivity caused by financial stress" as one of the "most critical unaddressed issues in the workplace today." Dr. E. Thomas Garman*, the president of Personal Finance Employee Education Foundation, stated that "60% of employees live paycheck to paycheck" and that research shows that "those with more financial distress report poor health; financially distressed workers (40–50%) report that their financial problems cause their health woes; and that positive changes in financial behaviors are related to improved health."

Tracking your income and your expenses enables you to see where your money is going. With this information you can create a budget that will help you reach your goals. To aid you with this process, Microsoft created a downloadable Personal Account Ledger template. This database includes a form that enables you to record transactions; reports to display transactions, expenses by category, and income by category; and a tax report. Open *a01b4Ledger*, a database based on the Microsoft Personal Account Ledger, and save it as **a01b4Ledger_LastFirst**. Use the Account Transaction List to enter your income and expenses for the previous month. Then view the Income by Category report and the Expenses by Category report. Compact, repair, and back up your database and exit Access. Submit the database based on your instructor's directions.

* Employee Financial Wellness slideshare presentation, http://www.slideshare.net/irwink/Employee-Financial-Wellness, by Dr. E. Thomas Garman, President, Personal Finance Employee Education Foundation.

Capstone Exercise

Your boss expressed concern about the accuracy of the inventory reports in the bookstore. He needs you to open the inventory database, make modifications to some records, and determine if the changes you make carry through to the other objects in the database. You will make changes to a form and verify those changes in a table, a query, and a report. When you have verified that the changes update automatically, you will compact and repair the database and make a backup of it.

Database File Setup

You will open an original database file and save the database with a new name, replace an existing author's name with your name, create a table, create table relationships, sort, and apply a filter by selection.

a. Open the *a01c1Books* file and save the database as **a01c1Books_LastFirst**.

b. Create a new table in Design view. Save the table as **Publishers**. Change the primary key from ID to **PubID** with a Data Type of **Short Text**. Add the following fields and switch to Datasheet view. Save changes to the table design when prompted.

Field Name	Data Type
PubName	Short Text
PubAddress	Short Text
PubCity	Short Text
PubState	Short Text
PubZIP	Short Text

c. Enter the following data in the Publishers table and close the table.

PubID	PubName	PubAddress	PubCity	PubState	PubZIP
BB	Bantam Books	1540 Broadway	New York	NY	10036
FS	Farrar, Straus and Giroux	12 Union Square West	New York	NY	10003
KN	Knopf	299 Park Avenue	New York	NY	10171
LB	Little, Brown and Company	1271 Avenue of the Americas	New York	NY	10020
PH	Pearson/ Prentice Hall	1 Lake Street	Upper Saddle	NJ	07458
SS	Simon & Schuster	100 Front Street	Riverside	NY	08075

d. Open the Maintain Authors form.

e. Navigate to Record 7 and replace *YourName* with your name.

f. Add a new Title: **Technology in Action**. The ISBN is **0-13-148905-4**, the PubID is **PH**, the PublDate is **2015**, the Price is $89.95 (just type **89.95**, no $), and StockAmt is **95** units. Move to any other record to save the new record. Close the form.

g. Open the Maintain Authors form again and navigate to Record 7. The changes are there because Access works from storage, not memory. Close the form again.

Sort a Query and Apply a Filter by Selection

You need to reorder a detail query so that the results are sorted alphabetically by the publisher name.

a. Open the Publishers, Books, and Authors Query.

b. Click in any record in the PubName column and sort the field in ascending order.

c. Check to make sure that four books list you as the author.

d. Click your name in the Author's Last Name field and filter the records to show only your books.

e. Close the query and save the changes.

View a Report

You need to examine the Publishers, Books, and Authors Report to determine if the changes you made in the Maintain Authors form appear in the report.

a. Open the Publishers, Books, and Authors Report.

b. Check to make sure that the report shows four books listing you as the author.

c. View the layout of the report in Print Preview.

d. Close the report.

Filter a Table

You need to examine the Books table to determine if the changes you made in the Maintain Authors form carried through to the related table. You also will filter the table to display books published after 2010 with fewer than 100 copies in inventory.

a. Open the Books table.

b. Use *Filter by Form* to create a filter that will identify all books published after 2010 with fewer than 100 items in stock.

c. Apply the filter and preview the filtered table.

d. Close the table and save the changes.

Compact and Repair a Database and Back Up a Database

Now that you are satisfied that any changes made to a form or query carry through to the table, you are ready to compact, repair, and back up your file.

a. Compact and repair your database.

b. Create a backup copy of your database, accept the default file name, and save it.

c. Exit Access. Submit based on your instructor's directions.

Glossary

Access   A database management system included in the Microsoft Office 2013 Professional suite.

Ascending   A sort that lists text data in alphabetical order or a numeric list in lowest to highest order.

AutoNumber   A number data type that is generated by Access and is incremented each time a record is added.

Back Up Database   An Access utility that creates a duplicate copy of the database.

Compact and Repair   An Access utility that reduces the size of the database and can repair a corrupt database.

Comparison operator   An operator used to evaluate the relationship between two quantities.

Criterion   A number, text phrase, or an expression used to select records.

Custom Web app   A database that can be built, used, and shared with others through the use of a host server (e.g., SharePoint or Office 365).

Database   A collection of data organized as meaningful information that can be accessed, managed, stored, queried, sorted, and reported.

Database management system (DBMS)   A software system that provides the tools needed to create, maintain, and use a database.

Datasheet view   A view that enables you to add, edit, and delete the records of a table.

Descending   A sort that lists text data in reverse alphabetical order or a numeric list in highest to lowest order.

Design view   A view that enables you to create tables, add and delete fields, and modify field properties; or to change advanced design settings not seen in Layout view, such as a background image.

Enforce referential integrity   A relationship option that ensures that data cannot be entered into a related table unless it first exists in a primary table.

Field   The smallest data element in a table, such as first name, last name, address, or phone number.

Field property   A characteristic of a field that determines how a field looks and behaves.

Field selector   The column heading of a datasheet used to select a column.

Filter   Displays a subset of records based on a specified criterion.

Filter by Form   A filtering method that displays records based on multiple criteria.

Filter by Selection   A filtering method that displays only records that match selected criteria.

Foreign key   A field in one table that is also a primary key of another table.

Form   A database object that is used to add, edit, or delete table data.

Join line   A line used to create a relationship between two tables using a common field.

Macro   A series of actions that can be programmed to automate tasks.

Module   An object that is written using Visual Basic for Applications (VBA) and adds functionality to a database.

Navigation bar   Bar located at the bottom of a table, query, or form that is used to move through records.

Navigation Pane   An interface element that organizes and lists database objects.

Normalization   The formal process of deciding which fields should be grouped together into which tables.

Object   A main component that is created and used to make a database function.

Primary key   The field (or combination of fields) that uniquely identifies each record in a table.

Query   Enables you to ask questions about the data stored in a database and then provides the answers to the questions by providing subsets or summaries of data.

Record   A group of related fields representing one entity, such as data for one person, place, event, or concept.

Record selector   A small box at the beginning of a row used to select a record.

Relational database management system (RDBMS)   A database management system that uses the relational model to manage groups of data (tables) and rules (relationships) between tables.

Relationship   A connection between two tables using a common field.

Report   An object that contains professional-looking formatted information from underlying tables or queries.

Sort   The process of listing records or text in a specific sequence, such as alphabetically by last name.

Table   An object used to store and organize data in a series of records (rows) with each record made up of a number of fields (columns) and is the foundation of every database.

Template   A predesigned file that incorporates formatting elements, such as theme and layouts, and may include content that can be modified.

Index